D0538931

1606

by the same author

1599: A YEAR IN THE LIFE OF WILLIAM SHAKESPEARE
CONTESTED WILL: WHO WROTE SHAKESPEARE?

1606
William Shakespeare and the Year of *Lear*

JAMES SHAPIRO

FABER & FABER

First published in 2015
By Faber & Faber Ltd
Bloomsbury House
74–77 Great Russell Street
London WC1B 3DA

Typeset by Faber & Faber Ltd
Printed and bound by CPI Group (UK) Ltd, Croydon CR0 4YY

All rights reserved
© James Shapiro, 2015

The right of James Shapiro to be identified as author
of this work has been asserted in accordance with Section 77
of the Copyright Designs and Patents Act 1988

A CIP record for this book
is available from the British Library

ISBN 978–0–571–23578–0

FSC
www.fsc.org
MIX
Paper from
responsible sources
FSC® C101712

2 4 6 8 10 9 7 5 3 1

For Mary and Luke

Contents

List of Illustrations

ILLUSTRATIONS IN THE TEXT

PLATE SECTION

A Note on Quoting the Plays

Quotations from Shakespeare's plays – with the exception of *King Lear* – are cited from David Bevington, ed., *The Complete Works of Shakespeare* (6th edn, New York, 2008). For *King Lear* I quote from Stanley Wells's edition, based on a text prepared by Gary Taylor (Oxford, 2000), that derives from the 1608 quarto and so is closer to what was staged in 1606 (and is divided into twenty-four scenes, rather than five acts). Like almost all recent editors, Bevington and Wells modernise Shakespeare's spelling and punctuation; I've done the same with the words of Shakespeare's contemporaries throughout the book.

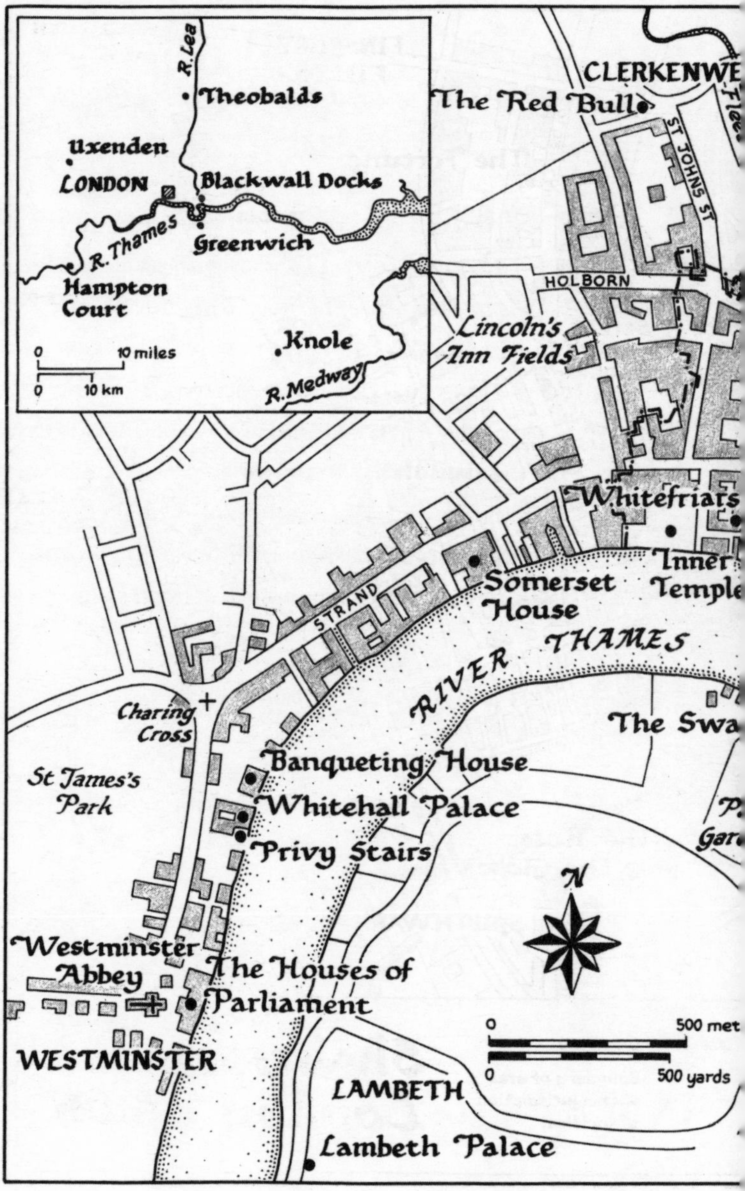
R. Lea
Theobalds
Uxenden
LONDON
Blackwall Docks
R. Thames
Greenwich
Hampton Court
Knole
R. Medway
0 10 miles
0 10 km
CLERKENWE
The Red Bull
ST JOHNS ST
HOLBORN
Lincoln's Inn Fields
Whitefriars
Inner Temple
Somerset House
STRAND
RIVER THAMES
The Swa
Charing Cross
St James's Park
Banqueting House
Whitehall Palace
Privy Stairs
N
Westminster Abbey
The Houses of Parliament
WESTMINSTER
LAMBETH
Lambeth Palace
0 500 met
0 500 yards

FINSBURY FIELDS
SHOREDITCH
GOLDEN LANE
The Fortune
The Curtain
HIGH ST
SPITALFIELDS
MOOR FIELDS
Silver Street
Shakespeare's lodgings)
Cripplegate
Moorgate
Aldersgate
Guildhall
Bishopsgate
St Paul's Cathedral
GRACE CHURCH
Boar's Head Inn
WEST CHEAP
CORNHILL
Blackfriars
EAST CHEAP
Aldgate
FENCHURCH
THAMES ST
Tower of London
Bull Ring
London Bridge
The Rose
The Globe
SOUTHWARK
City Wall
Boundary of area within jurisdiction of Guildhall
Shakespeare's London c.1606

Prologue : 5 January 1606

On the evening of 5 January 1606, the first Sunday of the new year, six hundred or so of the nation's elite made their way through London's dark streets to the Banqueting House at Whitehall Palace. The route westward from the City, leading past Charing Cross and skirting St James's Park, was for most of them a familiar one. Many had already visited Whitehall over a half-dozen times since Christmas, the third under King James, who had called for eighteen plays to be staged there this holiday season, ten of them by Shakespeare's company. They took their places according to their status in the seats arranged on stepped scaffolds along three sides of the large hall, while the Lord Chamberlain, white staff in hand, ensured that no gate-crashers were admitted nor anyone seated in an area above his or her proper station. King James himself sat centrally on a raised platform of state facing the stage, surrounded by his closest entourage, his every gesture scrutinised, rivalling the performers for the crowd's attention.

Shakespeare's portrait, by Martin Droeshout

This evening's entertainment was more eagerly anticipated than any play. They were gathered at the old Banqueting House to witness a dramatic form with which conventional tragedies and comedies now struggled to compete: a court masque. With their dazzling staging, elegant verse, gorgeous costumes, concert-quality music and choreographed dancing – overseen by some of the most talented artists in the land – masques under the new king were beyond extravagant, costing an unbelievable sum of £3,000 or more for a single performance. To put that in perspective, it would cost the crown little more than £100 to stage all ten of the plays Shakespeare's company performed at court this Christmas season.

The actors in this evening's masque, aside from a few professionals drawn from Shakespeare's company, were prominent lords – and ladies too. The entertainment thus offered the added frisson of watching women perform, for while they were forbidden to appear on London's public stages, where their parts were played by teenage boys, that restriction didn't apply to court masques. Those lucky enough to be admitted to the Banqueting House saw young noblewomen perform their parts in breathtaking outfits designed by Inigo Jones, bedecked in jewels (one onlooker reported that 'I think they hired and borrowed all the principal jewels and ropes of pearl both in court and city'). For many of these women, some of whom had commemorative paintings done of them wearing these costumes, this chance to perform in public would be one of the highlights of their highly constrained lives.

The building in which they performed was perhaps the only disappointment. Back in 1582, when the Duc d'Alençon had come courting, Queen Elizabeth had ordered that a temporary

Banqueting House be constructed in time for his reception. From a distance the large building, 'a long square, 332 foot in measure about', looked imposing, constructed of stone blocks with mortared joints. But as visitors approached they would have seen that *trompe l'œil* painting disguised what was actually a flimsy structure, built of great wooden masts forty feet high covered with painted canvas. As the years passed, Elizabeth saw no reason to waste money replacing it with something more permanent, and by the time that James succeeded her, the temporary frame that had stood for a quarter-century was in disrepair.

Shakespeare knew the old venue well and had played there fourteen months earlier on 1 November 1604, when his last Elizabethan tragedy, *Othello*, had had its court debut. Over the years he had performed often at Whitehall and would have recognised many of those in attendance. We can tell from the impact this masque had on his subsequent work that Shakespeare had secured for himself a place in the room that January evening. There probably wasn't a better vantage point for measuring the chasm between the self-congratulatory political fantasy enacted in the masque and the troubled national mood outside the grounds of James's palace. Insofar as most of his plays depict flawed rulers and their courts, he may have been as intent on observing the scene playing out before him as he was on viewing the masque itself.

The new king hated the old building; it was one more vestige of the Tudor past to be swept away. A few months after this masque was staged James commanded that it be pulled down and a more permanent, 'strong and stately' stone edifice, befitting a Stuart dynasty, be built on the site. In the short term, while there was little he could do about its rotting frame, James could at least replace Elizabeth's unfashionable painted ceiling. She favoured a floral and fruit design; he had it re-covered with a more stylish image of 'clouds in distemper'.

King James was no less committed to repairing some of the political rot his predecessor had left behind, and this evening's masque was part of that effort. Five years had passed since Queen Elizabeth had put to death her one-time favourite, the charismatic and rebellious Robert Devereux, second Earl of Essex. His execution still rankled with Essex's devoted followers and their further exclusion from power and patronage under James had left them bitter and alienated. Essex had left behind a young son, now fourteen, who bore his name and title, around whom they might rally. Essex's militant followers had to be neutralised in order to forestall division within the kingdom. But James couldn't simply restore them all to favour (as he had with the most prominent of them, the imprisoned Earl of Southampton), even if there were enough money, offices and lands to do so, for that would unsettle the balance of favourites and factions at court. And he couldn't imprison or purge them all either. That left one solution: binding enemies together through an arranged marriage. James would play the royal matchmaker, marrying off Essex's son, now a ward of the state, to Frances Howard, the striking fifteen-year-old daughter of the powerful Earl of Suffolk, who had served on the commission that had sentenced Essex to death. That evening's masque, intended to celebrate their union, doubled as an overt pitch for the political union of England and Scotland, a marriage of the two kingdoms that James eagerly sought and knew that a wary Parliament would be debating later that month.

Though he was now the most experienced dramatist in the land, Shakespeare had not written the masque and, had he been invited to do so, would have said no. It would have been a tempting offer. If he cared about visibility, prestige or money, the rewards were great; the writer responsible for the masque earned more than eight times what a dramatist was typically paid for a single play. And on the creative side, in addition to the almost unlimited budget and the potential for special effects, the masque offered the very thing he had seemingly wished for in the opening Chorus to *Henry the Fifth*: 'princes to act / And monarchs to behold the swelling scene' (1.0.3–4). That Shakespeare never accepted such a commission tells us as much about him as a writer as the plays he left behind. There was a price to be paid for writing masques, which were shamelessly sycophantic and propagandistic, compromises he didn't care to make. He must have also recognised that it was an elite and evanescent art form that didn't suit his interests or his talents. If this was a typical Jacobean masque, the evening's entertainment devolved into serious drinking and feasting after the closing dance. By then, I suspect, Shakespeare was already back at his lodgings, doing what he had been doing well into the night for over fifteen years: writing.

Or trying to. For the last few years, certainly since the beginning of the new regime, his playwriting wasn't going as well as it once had. The extraordinary productivity that had marked his Elizabethan years, when writing three or even four plays in a year was not unusual, now seemed a thing of the past. His sonnets and narrative poems were behind him. So too were twenty-eight comedies, histories and tragedies – though only five of these had been written since he had finished *Hamlet* at the turn of the century. Things had begun to look more promising with his first effort under the new king, *Measure for Measure*, finished by 1604, a darkly comic world of court, prison, convent and brothel, starring an intellectual ruler who, like the new monarch, enjoyed stage-managing how things worked out. But another fallow period followed. In the three years since King James had come to the throne Shakespeare had written only one other play, *Timon of Athens*. With *Timon* he went back to something that he hadn't tried since his earliest years in the theatre: working in tandem with another writer. He co-authored this tragedy of a misanthrope – a play about extravagance and its embittering consequences in which the hero, if you can call him that, withdraws from the world and dies cursing – with the up-and-coming Thomas Middleton. It was a smart choice. Middleton, sixteen years younger than Shakespeare, was already a master of those satiric citizen comedies to which sophisticated audiences were flocking. But if the version of that play published in the 1623 folio is any indication, their collaborative effort remained unpolished and perhaps unfinished. Young rivals may well have begun whispering that Shakespeare was all but spent, a holdover from an earlier era whose no longer fashionable plays continued to be recycled at the Globe Theatre and at court.

One of the challenges of writing about so pivotal a year in Shakespeare's creative life is that he kept such a low profile, preferring to remain in the shadows. Unlike most other leading dramatists at this time, he chose not to write civic or courtly entertainments in praise of the king. And unlike other authors, he even demurred when it came to writing a dedicatory poem (the equivalent of modern-day blurbing) in praise of a fellow writer's play. The only act of literary fellowship on Shakespeare's part that we know of during these Jacobean years occurred after hours at the famous Tabard Inn in Southwark, favoured by actors. There, Shakespeare had 'cut' or carved his name on the panelling, alongside those of Ben Jonson, his fellow actors Richard Burbage and Laurence Fletcher, and – according to the anonymous writer who recorded this in the 1640s – 'the rest of their roistering associates in King James's time'.

His published work was certainly less visible. In 1600, a theatregoer wishing to purchase some of his recently published plays could have chosen from the two parts of *Henry the Fourth*, *Richard the Second*, *Richard the Third*, *Romeo and Juliet*, *Henry the Fifth*, *Henry the Sixth Parts 2* and *3*, *Love's Labour's Lost*, *The Merchant of Venice*, *A Midsummer Night's Dream* and *Much Ado about Nothing*. His plays were everywhere. But a return visit to London's bookstalls six years later would have turned up only two other late Elizabethan works, *The Merry Wives of Windsor* and *Hamlet*. In 1606, for the first time since his writing began to be published in 1593, not even a poem or a reissue of an earlier play appeared in print. That could in part be explained by his diminished output, but it was also the result of a decision by Shakespeare or his playing company to hold back from publishing his more recent work – why, we don't know.

He was no longer so familiar a face on the Globe's stage either. Those long accustomed to watching Shakespeare act every day would not be seeing him so often. While records are scarce, there are none that identify him performing at the Globe after 1603 (the last time his name appears on a play's cast list) and the omission of his name from a 1607 fee list of 'players of interludes' that identifies the other leading members of his company further suggests that by 1606 he was no longer acting on a daily basis, though he would have been available to perform when needed and would have joined his company for performances at court.

There's no question, though, that his name was now a byword for literary accomplishment. A little-known letter which survives from this time, written by a young English gentleman, helps confirm this. John Poulett posted his letter from Paris in late 1605; in it the nineteen-year-old describes to his uncle what he has been up to in his foreign travels. Showing off a bit, the former Oxford student slips into the rhythms of blank verse: 'We for to pass the winter's bitter cold, so with a javelin chase the bristled boar, and sometimes, mounted on a foaming curtal, do rend the woods to hound the furious bull.' Poulett then explains that 'the danger in these sports makes them seem good; men seem in them as actors in a tragedy, and methinks I could play Shakespeare in relating'. It's a wonderfully revealing remark: a young man feels the drama of the hunt and in the act of describing it excitedly imagines that he could 'play Shakespeare', that is to say, reach the very heights of dramatic storytelling. But like many compliments this one was double-edged, for the style young Poulett emulates is that of early Elizabethan Shakespeare, the poet of *Venus and Adonis* rather than the grittier one of *Troilus and Cressida* or *Measure for Measure*.

The year 1606 would turn out to be a good one for Shakespeare and an awful one for England. That was no coincidence. Shakespeare, so gifted at understanding what preoccupied and troubled his audiences, was lucky to have begun his career during the increasingly fractured years of Elizabeth's decline. His early work had delved especially deeply into the political and religious cracks that were exposed as a century of Tudor rule neared its end. But it would take some time for him to speak with the same acuity about the cultural fault-lines emerging under the new and unfamiliar reign of the King of Scots. In the months leading up to that evening at the Banqueting House, their contours were already becoming more sharply defined for him, and his steadier grasp of the forces shaping this extraordinary time would result in one of his most inspired years.

Shakespeare turned forty-two in 1606. In an era in which people lived on average until their mid-forties, Shakespeare knew that he couldn't count on too many years left to write. In such plague-ridden times, who could? Though his parents had lived unusually long lives, only one of his four sisters survived childhood and only one of his three brothers made it to his forties. As a shareholder in a profitable playing company and part-owner of the Globe Theatre, Shakespeare had amassed a small fortune, most of it invested in real estate, including a leasehold interest in land on the outskirts of Stratford-upon-Avon that he had obtained for £440 the previous July, an outlay equal to what a Jacobean schoolmaster earned over twenty years. He had more than enough money to retire comfortably to Stratford, where his wife, Anne, who had recently turned fifty, lived with their two unmarried daughters, Susanna and Judith. A decade had passed since the death of their only son, Hamnet, and Anne was now beyond childbearing years. Shakespeare's fortune would have to be passed on to the husbands that his daughters might some day marry; his recently acquired status as a gentleman would die with him and the sword that went with that rank be given away.

But in 1606 Shakespeare wasn't ready to retire or rest on his past achievements; he still had more to say and hadn't yet tired of the gruelling writing regimen that had defined his life since his mid-twenties.

Not long after witnessing that masque, Shakespeare finished *King Lear*, which he had been working on through the autumn. Before the year was out he would also write two more plays, *Macbeth* and *Antony and Cleopatra*. He had his own ideas about union, both marital and political, and about much else that was ignored or suppressed in the glittering display at court that evening, ideas that would shape these three tragedies. This book is about what Shakespeare wrote in 1606 and what was taking place at that fraught time, for the two are so closely intertwined that it's difficult to grasp the meaning of one without the other.

Though it would have been impossible to tell from reading a contemporary account of that evening's masque, exactly two months earlier most of those who gathered to see it were almost killed in what we would now call a terrorist attack, one that had been prevented at the last moment. A group of disaffected Catholic gentry had plotted to blow up Parliament, kill the king and the country's entire political leadership, then roll back the Protestant Reformation begun under Henry VIII. Thousands of other Londoners would also have died in the explosion and ensuing fires. Remembered today as 'the Fifth of November', the Gunpowder Plot exposed in late 1605 reverberated powerfully through the ensuing winter and spring in which the captured plotters were tortured, tried and then publicly executed. It's less well known that after the plot was thwarted there was a short-lived armed uprising in Warwickshire. The plot and its aftermath in the Midlands touched close to home for Shakespeare; some of his neighbours were implicated, for his home town abutted the safe-houses where the plotters met, weapons for the intended uprising were stored and a supply of religious items for the hoped-for restoration of Catholicism was hidden.

Because nothing actually happened on that fateful day – only the plotters would suffer and die – the meaning of the Fifth of November turned on competing narratives, especially on how well the authorities could succeed in getting the nation to *imagine* the tragic death of a monarch. Shakespeare, who understood such plotting as well as anyone, had been inviting audiences to imagine the deaths of kings and queens for his entire career, and would do so again this year. He also grasped the dramatic potential of popular reaction to the plot, a maelstrom of fear, horror, a desire for revenge, an all too brief sense of national unity and a struggle to understand where such evil came from. This too profoundly shaped the tragedies he was now writing.

The fallout from the Gunpowder Plot led to a heightened anxiety over Jesuitical equivocation (a recent term, picked up by Shakespeare, that more than any other defined the hysteria of the moment), as well as to anti-Catholic legislation that included the scrutiny of everyone's mandatory church attendance. The old Elizabethan compromise in which the government agreed not to 'make windows into men's souls' was now a thing of the past. The search for 'recusants' – those who steadfastly maintained their Catholic faith and refused to participate in Protestant worship – extended to every shire in the land and by Easter would implicate the godparents of Shakespeare's twins as well as his elder daughter. A loyalty oath instituted this year in response to the perceived Catholic threat would create a stir that angered the Vatican and marked a fundamental realignment of political and religious authority. And in a year in which actors were jailed for seditious drama, Parliament enacted legislation against the players for using profanity on stage, a measure that would have an immediate impact on what Shakespeare would write, while requiring that every play he had already written be retroactively sanitised.

Even as the buried shards of religious division once again rose to the surface, so too did political ones when King James again pressed Parliament to secure a Union of Scotland and England. To James, this outcome had seemed inevitable: as the King of Scots who had inherited the English throne, he embodied in his own person the union of the kingdoms. But for his subjects on both sides of the border the increasingly bitter debate over Union raised troubling questions about what it really meant to be English or Scottish, or for that matter British, creating identity crises where none had been before. This too was grist for Shakespeare's mill. Under Elizabeth he had written English history plays; in 1606 under James he would shift his attention to British ones in both *King Lear* and *Macbeth.* It was also a year in which King James called for and oversaw a second Hampton Court Conference to resolve disagreements with his Scottish clergy over the absolute authority of kings.

Much more would take place during these hectic months. Nearly eclipsed in all this was a Star Chamber investigation of faked demonic possession. England also experienced the first state visit of a foreign monarch to its shores in living memory. And in a year that witnessed a growing disaffection with their Scottish king and an increasing nostalgia for the late Queen Bess,

Londoners would see their old queen dug up from her grave in Westminster Abbey, her bones dumped on top of those of her half-sister, Queen Mary, and a new monument raised over them. It was also the year in which the Union Jack was designed and first flown, as well as a signal one in the history of the British Empire, for in December 1606 ships sailed from London's docks to found the first permanent colony in America, at Jamestown. If all this were not enough, plague would return to London, the worst outbreak since the terrible devastation of 1603, arriving in late July and lasting until late autumn, striking especially close to home for Shakespeare himself.

At many points during 1606, English men and women must have felt overwhelmed. In an age in which there were as yet no newspapers (let alone radio, movies, television or an internet), the theatre was the one place where rich and poor could congregate and see enacted, through old or made-up stories, a refracted image of their own desires and anxieties. The stories Shakespeare told this year enabled his playing company to rise to this challenge. There's a paradox, then, at the heart of a book about so remarkable a year in Shakespeare's creative life: even as the playwright himself recedes from view, the ways in which his writing was able to give, in Hamlet's words, 'the very age and body of the time his form and pressure' (3.2.23–4) would never be greater, though it would test the resources of a dramatist as gifted as Shakespeare to make sense of a year like 1606.

Another challenge faced in writing about this time in Shakespeare's life is that we still tend to think of him as an 'Elizabethan' writer, even though the last decade of his career was spent as a King's Man under James. I'm as guilty as anyone of having done so. It's a difficult habit to break; try imagining a version of *Shakespeare in Love* that ends with a cameo appearance of the Scottish king rather than the Virgin Queen. His contemporaries certainly didn't think of him in this way. When Ben Jonson celebrated Shakespeare's achievements in 1623 he recalled how his plays had pleased both monarchs:

> Sweet swan of Avon! What a sight it were
> To see thee in our waters yet appear,
> And make those flights upon the banks of Thames,
> That so did take Eliza, and our James!
> (5.642)

It hasn't helped that modern historians, novelists and film-makers have so enthusiastically embraced the Tudors while mostly spurning King James, despite his reign's consequential legacy. Whether you admire James as Britain's most intellectual ruler or dismiss him (as Anthony Weldon did in 1650) as 'the wisest fool in Christendom', it's hard to understand what a Jacobean Shakespeare was writing without a deeper knowledge of what life was like during his reign. Compounding this problem, cradle-to-grave biographers have always tilted heavily towards the Elizabethan Shakespeare, given their interest in his formative experiences. Open any of their books to what Shakespeare was doing after James came to the throne in 1603 and there usually aren't many pages left to read. What the Jacobean Shakespeare was experiencing at one of the pinnacles of his writing career – which ought to matter hugely to those who study his life – is given short shrift, and biographers who have paused at

1606 often spend these pages fruitlessly speculating (based on gossip that circulated decades later) about whether Shakespeare carried on an illicit affair with a handsome innkeeper's wife in Oxford.

Having spent much of the past quarter-century researching and writing about Shakespeare's life I'm painfully aware that many of the things I'd like to know about him – what his political views and religious beliefs were, whom he loved, how good a father, husband and friend he was, what he did with his time when he wasn't writing or acting – cannot be recovered. The possibility of writing that sort of biography died by the late seventeenth century, when the last of those who knew Shakespeare personally took their stories and secrets with them to the grave. Modern biographers who nonetheless speculate on such matters, or in the absence of archival evidence read the plays and poems as transparently autobiographical, inevitably end up revealing more about themselves than they do about Shakespeare.

While Shakespeare's emotional life in 1606 may be lost to us, by looking at what he wrote in dialogue with these times we can begin to recover what he was thinking about and wrestling with while composing these three plays. We can also track his responses to what he was reading, whether it was an old play called *King Leir*, Samuel Harsnett's exposé of demonic possession or one of his recent favourites, Plutarch's *Life of Antony*. However much Shakespeare may have preferred to remain in the shadows, he can be glimpsed in the glare of what was going on around him. He can be spotted this year in his capacity as a King's Man who appeared with his fellow players before the king at Greenwich, Hampton Court and Whitehall, as well as in royal processions in his official role as a Groom of the Chamber – opportunities that offered him a privileged view of the court.

To that end, the pages that follow offer a slice of a writer's life, one that I hope will bring his world, and by extension his works, to life. The very richness of that cultural moment both impedes and enables this effort: to draw Shakespeare out of the shadows demands considerable effort and imaginative labour, for we need to travel back in time four centuries and immerse ourselves in the hopes and fears of that moment; but the rewards are no less great, for that richness, in turn, allows us to see afresh the tragedies he forged in this tumultuous year.

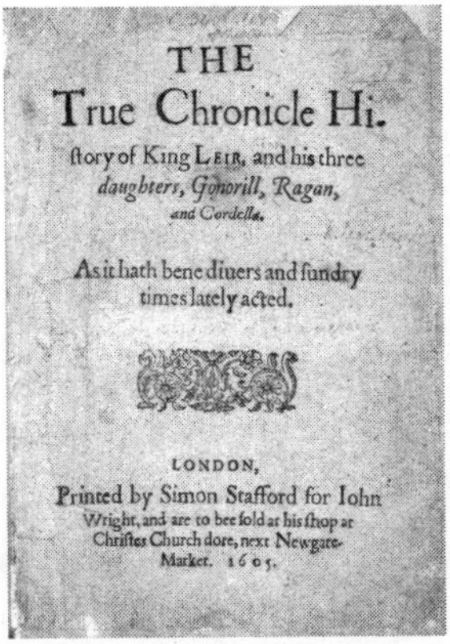

THE
True Chronicle Hi.
ſtory of King Leir, and his three
daughters, Gonorill, Ragan,
and Cordella.

As it hath bene diuers and ſundry
times lately acted.

LONDON,
Printed by Simon Stafford for Iohn
Wright, and are to bee ſold at his ſhop at
Chriſtes Church dore, next Newgate-
Market. 1605.

1 : The King's Man

In the summer of 1605 John Wright began selling copies of a newly printed play called *The True Chronicle History of King Leir*, which had first been staged around 1590. Not long after, William Shakespeare, who lived just a short stroll from Wright's bookshop, picked up a copy. A few years earlier Shakespeare had moved from his lodgings in Southwark, near the Globe Theatre, to quarters in a quieter and more upscale neighbourhood, on the corner of Silver Street and Muggle Street in Cripplegate. His landlords were Christopher and Marie Mountjoy, Huguenot artisans who made their living supplying fashionable headwear for court ladies. The walk from his new lodgings to Wright's bookshop took just a few minutes. Crossing Silver Street, Shakespeare would have passed his parish church, St Olave's, before heading south down Noble Street toward St Paul's Cathedral, passing Goldsmiths' Hall as Noble Street turned into Foster Lane, emerging onto the busy thoroughfare of Cheapside.

Title Page of the Quarto of *King Leir* (1605)

With Cheapside Cross to his left, and St Paul's and beyond it the Thames directly ahead, Shakespeare would have turned west, passing St Martin's Lane and then the Shambles, home to London's butchers. Christ Church was now in sight, and just beyond it Wright's shop, abutting Newgate market.

The advertisement on the title page of *King Leir* – 'As it hath been divers and sundry times lately acted' – made it sound like a recent play, an impression reinforced by the quiet omission of who wrote and performed it. But Shakespeare knew that it was an old Queen's Men's play and probably also knew (though we don't) who had written it. The Queen's Men were a hand-picked all-star troupe formed under royal patronage back in 1583. For the next decade they were England's premier company, touring widely, known for their politics (patriotic and Protestant), their didacticism and their star comedian, Richard Tarleton. If he wasn't busy acting that day in another playhouse, Shakespeare may have been part of the crowd that paid a total of thirty-eight shillings to see the Queen's Men stage *King Leir* at the Rose Theatre in Southwark on 6 April 1594 (in co-production with Lord Sussex's Men), or part of the smaller gathering two days later for a performance that earned twenty-six shillings – solid though not spectacular box office receipts.

Looking back, Shakespeare would have recognised that their appearance at the Rose marked the beginning of the end for the Queen's Men, who the following month sold off copies of some of their valuable playscripts to London's publishers, then took to the road, spending the next nine years touring the provinces until, upon the death of Queen Elizabeth, they disbanded. That year also marked the ascendancy of the company Shakespeare had recently joined as a founding shareholder, the Chamberlain's Men, who soon succeeded the Queen's Men as the leading players in the land, a position they had held ever since. *King Leir* had been among the plays the cash-poor Queen's Men had unloaded in 1594, and Edward White, who bought it, quickly entered his right to publish the play in the Stationers' Register. But for some reason, perhaps sensing that the play had little prospect of selling well, White never published it. Over a decade would pass before his former apprentice John Wright obtained the rights from him and the play finally appeared in print.

One of the many towns where the Queen's Men had performed in the late 1580s had been Stratford-upon-Avon. In the absence of any information about what Shakespeare was doing in his early twenties, biographers have speculated that he may have begun his theatrical career with this company, perhaps even filling in for one of the Queen's Men, William Knell, killed in a fight shortly before the troupe was to perform in Stratford in 1587. It's an appealing story – something, after all, must have brought him from Stratford to London – but there's no evidence to substantiate it, nor is there any that would confirm that Shakespeare briefly acted with or wrote for this veteran company. But what is certain from the evidence of his later work is that he was deeply familiar with their repertory.

Scholars can identify with confidence fewer than a dozen plays, mostly histories, performed by the Queen's Men during their twenty-year run. Several of their titles will sound familiar: *The True Tragedy of Richard the Third*, *The Troublesome Reign of King John* and *The Famous Victories of Henry the Fifth*. A defining feature of Shakespeare's art was his penchant for overhauling the plots of old plays rather than inventing his own, and no rival company provided more raw material for him than the Queen's Men. He absorbed and reworked their repertory in a series of history plays from the mid-to-late 1590s now familiar to us as *Richard the Third*, *King John*, the two parts of *Henry the Fourth*, and *Henry the Fifth*. Shakespeare's attitude to the Queen's Men was surely ambivalent. Their plays, which likely thrilled and inspired him in his formative years as playgoer, actor and then playwright, had stuck with him. Yet he would also have recognised that their jingoistic repertory had become increasingly out of step with the theatrical and political times.

Shakespeare was a sharp-eyed critic of other writers' plays and his take on the Queen's Men's repertory could be unforgiving, rendering these sturdy old plays hopelessly anachronistic. For a glimpse of this we need only recall his parody of an unforgettably bad couplet from their *True Tragedy of Richard the Third*: 'The screeking raven sits croaking for revenge / Whole herds of beasts come bellowing for revenge.' These lines from the old play, whose awfulness had clearly stuck with Shakespeare, resurface years later when Hamlet, interrupting the play-within-the-play and urging on the strolling players, deliberately mangles the couplet: 'Come, "the croaking raven doth bellow for revenge"' (3.2.251–2). At best this was a double-edged tribute, reminding playgoers of the kind of old-fashioned revenge drama they once enjoyed while showing how a naturalistic revenge play like *Hamlet* had supplanted the dated and over-the-top style of the Queen's Men.

Six years had passed since Shakespeare had last refashioned a Queen's Men's play in *Henry the Fifth*, a brilliant remake of their popular *The Famous Victories of Henry the Fifth*. If anything, the pace of change in those intervening years, especially the last three, had wildly accelerated. The Elizabethan world that had produced *King Leir* and in which the play had once thrived, like the playing company that had performed it, was no longer. But these years had enabled Shakespeare, as part-owner of his playhouse and shareholder in his acting company, to prosper financially. When Wright began selling copies of *King Leir* in July of 1605 (two months usually lapsed between the time a book was registered and sold, and he had registered it in May), it is likely that Shakespeare was away in Stratford-upon-Avon closing a large real-estate deal, so couldn't have picked up a copy until his return to London.

King Leir, like so many histories and tragedies of the 1590s, was fixated on royal succession. These plays spoke to a nation fearful of foreign rule or the outbreak of civil war after its childless queen's death. For a decade that stretched from *Titus Andronicus* and his *Henry the Sixth* trilogy through *Richard the Third*, *King John*, *Richard the Second*, the two parts of *Henry the Fourth*, *Henry the Fifth*, *Julius Caesar* and *Hamlet*, Shakespeare displayed time and again his mastery of this genre, exploring in play after play who had the cunning, wit, legitimacy and ambition to seize and hold power. Those concerns peaked in the opening years of the seventeenth century as the queen approached her end, but vanished after 1603, when King James VI of Scotland, who was married and had two sons and a daughter, succeeded peacefully to the throne of England. There would be no Spanish invasion and no return to the kind of civil strife that had torn the land apart in the late fifteenth century. In an unusually explicit allusion to the political moment, Shakespeare writes in Sonnet 107 shortly after James's accession that:

> The mortal moon hath her eclipse endured,
> And the sad augurs mock their own presage;
> Incertainties now crown themselves assured,
> And peace proclaims olives of endless age.
> (Sonnet 107, 5–8)

The language is elliptical but the meaning clear enough: all those anxious predictions that preceded the eclipse of Elizabeth – that 'mortal moon' – were misplaced; the crowning of the new king who promoted himself as a peacemaker had put an end to these 'incertainties'.

But other uncertainties remained. The period leading up to and following the change in regime appeared less smooth in retrospect than Sonnet 107 would on its surface suggest, for the nation and for Shakespeare professionally. The Chamberlain's Men, now established at the Globe, found themselves facing stiffer competition than ever. Back in 1594 there had been only three permanent outdoor playhouses in London: the Theatre and the Curtain in Shoreditch, and the Rose on Bankside. Since then, new theatres continued to sprout around the City, competing for the pennies and shillings of London's playgoers. Spectators were now flocking to watch the Admiral's Men at the Fortune Theatre (to the northwest, in the parish of St Giles without Cripplegate), as well as to see Worcester's Men perform at the Boar's Head Inn (in Whitechapel), and to playhouses at St Paul's and Blackfriars, smaller indoor sites where boy companies performed plays by

London's edgier young dramatists. Ageing public playhouses – the Curtain and the Swan in Southwark near Paris Garden Stairs – also peeled away customers.

Other and unexpected threats to the prosperity of Shakespeare and his fellow shareholders soon emerged. In early 1603, their influential patron, the Lord Chamberlain George Carey (second cousin to Queen Elizabeth), became seriously ill. More bad news followed. First came a Privy Council announcement on 19 March 1603 that because of concerns about civil unrest as Elizabeth lay dying, all public performances were cancelled 'till other direction be given'. News the following week of the queen's death and the declaration that the King of Scots was now King of England as well, while reassuring the English that regime change would not be bloody, also meant that during this mourning period the playhouses were unlikely to open any time soon. London's playing companies must have been rocked by the next piece of disturbing news, as they waited to see how supportive of the theatre King James would be. One of James's first royal proclamations, on 7 May 1603, was to ban performances on the Sabbath. It was a punishing decree that cut into theatrical profits, for Sunday was the only day of the week that most playgoers weren't labouring at work. Was this merely a sop to theatre-hating Puritans or was it a sign that the new king saw little value in public theatre?

The drumbeat of setbacks for Shakespeare and his company continued. King James didn't wait for the ailing George Carey to die before replacing him as Lord Chamberlain. This meant that Shakespeare was no longer a Chamberlain's Man, merely the servant of the disempowered Carey (who passed away in early September). The theatre companies were facing their own succession struggle, which would have to be resolved in the wake of the national one. At stake were royal patronage and the chance to be favoured at court. It could not have been reassuring that the Earl of Nottingham, patron of their long-time rivals the Admiral's Men, had secured a place in the new monarch's inner circle.

Other unexpected and nagging threats emerged as the change in government encouraged those who wanted a share of the lucrative business of staging plays. Richard Fiennes, an aristocrat badly in need of money, proposed that in exchange for an annual payment of £40 he be awarded a patent allowing him to collect a poll tax of 'a penny a head on all the playgoers in England'. Fiennes argued that since playgoing was a voluntary activity (much like what the king himself had deemed the 'vile custom of tobacco taking'), it could be regulated and taxed by the state, and he would be happy to pay for overseeing that activity in exchange for a hefty cut of box office receipts. Since admission to the public playhouses started at a penny, Fiennes's proposal was outrageously greedy. Luckily for London's actors nothing came of this, nor of another proposal not long after from the other end of the social ladder, by a disabled veteran of the Irish wars, Francis Clayton. Fiennes had hoped to obtain a royal patent to tax playgoers; Clayton appealed to Parliament to tax performances, seeking for himself a 'small allowance of two shillings out of every stage play that shall be acted . . . to be paid unto me or my assigns during my life by the owners and actors of those plays and shows'. It must have struck the players as absurd: anyone with a scheme and some political connections could submit a plan to cut into their hard-earned profits. Fiennes's and Clayton's proposals – although they went nowhere – were one more headache for Shakespeare and his fellows, vulnerable at this time of transition and of freewheeling and often unpredictable political largesse.

Then, suddenly, came news that profoundly altered the trajectory of Shakespeare's career: King James chose Shakespeare and his fellow players as his official company. After 19 May 1603 Shakespeare and eight others were to be known as the King's Men, authorised to perform not only at the court and the Globe but also throughout the realm, if they wished to tour. It was more than a symbolic title; Shakespeare was now a Groom of the Chamber, and he and the other shareholders were each issued four and a half yards of red cloth for royal livery to be worn on state occasions.

Exactly how and why Shakespeare's company was elevated to the position of King's Men has never been satisfyingly explained. Their talent and reputation surely played a part. So too did a little-known English actor named Laurence Fletcher. Fletcher had spent time acting in Scotland, where King James had come to know and like him. This relationship accounts for why Fletcher's name appears first, right before Shakespeare's, in the list of those designated as the King's Men, though he had never been affiliated with the company before this. Fletcher was merely a player; though a valuable go-between, he could not, by himself, have been responsible for Shakespeare's company's swift promotion. More powerful brokers were undoubtedly involved. One of them might have been the son of their dying patron, Sir Robert Carey, who had ridden posthaste from London to Edinburgh to bring James word of Elizabeth's death. Others might have included Shakespeare's former patron, the Earl of Southampton, newly released from the Tower, or perhaps the Earl of Pembroke, an admirer of Richard Burbage and a patron of poets and artists. Mystery will always surround how Shakespeare and his fellow players were chosen to be the King's Men. What matters is that it happened and that they had won their own succession struggle – and the plays that Shakespeare would subsequently write would be powerfully marked by this turn of events.

The King's Men did not have much of a chance to celebrate their good fortune, for London was soon struck by a devastating outbreak of plague. Even during years that were considered safe, Elizabethan London had rarely been entirely free of plague: there were forty-eight reported plague deaths in 1597, eighteen in 1598, sixteen in 1599 and four in 1600. The fresh outbreak apparently began in Lisbon in 1599 and spread to Spain and then elsewhere on the Continent. By February 1603 it had reached London. By May, plague deaths had risen to over twenty a week. Then, suddenly, the number of Londoners dying from the plague skyrocketed: by the end of July over a thousand were perishing every week. James had just arrived from Edinburgh for his coronation and massive precautions were taken to prevent the infected from getting near him. Travel near Westminster by road or river was barred to ordinary citizens and following the coronation James quickly withdrew to the relative safety of Hampton Court. The planned festivities and public celebration would have to wait.

King James wasn't the only one fleeing the plague-ridden city. Even those who were infected tried to. A court official reported that 'divers come out of the town and die under hedges in the fields, and divers places further off, whereof we have experience weekly here at Hampstead, and come in men's yards and outhouses if they be open, and die there'. Some of the plague-stricken hurled themselves out of windows or drowned themselves in the Thames. Others turned to drink or to religion, and special prayers were read in London's churches.

In late August, the height of the outbreak, desperate London's authorities were reporting over three thousand deaths a week, out of a population of roughly two hundred thousand. By the time that cold weather slowed the outbreak that winter nearly a third of the population had been struck: over thirty thousand Londoners had died, while another thirty thousand or so were infected but managed to survive the terrible visitation. Enough fatalities were still being reported that winter and spring for the playhouses to remain closed. They reopened briefly in April 1604 before the return of plague with the onset of warmer weather led to their closing again until September. The long outbreak of plague meant that the King's Men had to maintain themselves by touring through rural England's towns and visiting great houses (a royal handout of £30 also helped). Local records of their touring are spotty, but there are payments to them between 1603 and 1605 for performances at Bath, Shrewsbury, Coventry, Ipswich, Maldon, Oxford, Barnstaple and Saffron Walden.

It took an underemployed playwright turned pamphleteer, Thomas Dekker, in his mordantly titled *The Wonderful Year*, to capture the full horror of what it meant to be locked up by the authorities in an infested house:

> What an unmatchable torment were it for a man to be barred up every night in a vast silent charnel-house, hung (to make it more hideous) with lamps dimly and slowly burning in hollow and glimmering corners? Where all the pavement should, instead of green rushes, be strewed with blasted rosemary, withered hyacinths, fatal cypress, and yew, thickly mingled with heaps of dead men's bones. The bare ribs of a father that begat him, lying there; here the chapless hollow skull of a mother that bore him. Round about him a thousand corpses; some standing bolt upright in their knotted winding sheets; others half-moldered in rotten coffins, that should suddenly yawn wide open, filling his nostrils with noisome stench, and his eyes with the sight of nothing but crawling worms. And to keep such a poor wretch waking, he should hear no noise but of toads croaking, screech-owls howling, mandrakes shrieking. Were not this an infernal prison?

It's a challenge, four centuries later, to imagine the effects of this nightmare on those fortunate enough to survive.

While plague closures had suppressed the demand for new plays at the Globe, the royal family's desire for fresh entertainment was proving insatiable. Under Elizabeth, Shakespeare's company expected that two or three of its best plays each year would be selected for performance before the court between Christmas and Shrovetide. While King James may not have enjoyed watching plays as much as he enjoyed hunting, he nonetheless called for many more performances than his predecessor had and expected most of these from the company he patronised. The King's Men acted before James nine times in 1603–4, ten times during the expanded Christmas season of 1604–5, and yet another ten times during the similarly expanded winter holidays in 1605–6 – more court appearances in this brief span than they had made altogether before Elizabeth.

Frustratingly, the names of plays and those who wrote them are almost never listed in records of court performances. But a remarkable Revels Account of what was staged at court during the holiday season of 1604–5 gives us a snapshot of how central a role Shakespeare played. These records tell us that 'Shaxberd' was responsible for seven of the ten plays performed before king and court between Hallowmas Day in early November and Shrove Tuesday in late February: *Othello*, *The Merry Wives of Windsor*, *The Comedy of Errors*, *Measure for Measure*, *Love's Labour's Lost*, *Henry the Fifth* and *The Merchant of Venice* – the latter performed twice, that encore performance 'commanded by the king's majesty'. Along with the court debuts of *Othello* and *Measure for Measure*, Shakespeare's company served up revivals of some of their greatest Elizabethan hits, which the Scottish royal family had never had a chance to see. The King's Men also performed two of Ben Jonson's popular Elizabethan comedies, *Every Man in His Humour* and *Every Man out of His Humour*, along with the anonymous and now lost *The Spanish Maze*. If this holiday season was representative, it meant that over two-thirds of the plays staged at court by the company were Shakespeare's. And if we assume that a similar percentage of his Elizabethan plays were acted before the king in the nineteen command performances at the 1604–5 and 1605–6 holiday seasons, there's a good chance that by the beginning of 1606, of the close to thirty plays the King's Men had played before James, twenty or so had been by Shakespeare, leaving only a handful of his old plays as yet unstaged before the new court.

The pressure to provide new plays had, if anything, intensified. A letter survives from January 1605 to the Earl of Salisbury (the king's chief minister) from Sir William Cope, who had been tasked with finding fresh entertainment for the court, in which a frustrated Cope reports that 'I have sent and been all this morning hunting for players, jugglers, and such kind of creatures, but find them hard to find'. Having come up empty-handed, he left notes for the various entertainers to report to him. One of those summoned was Richard Burbage, star of the King's Men (or perhaps it was his brother Cuthbert, part-owner of the Globe), for Cope's letter continues: 'Burbage is come and says there is no new play that the queen has not seen; but they have revived an old one called *Love's Labour's Lost*, which for wit and mirth he says will please her exceedingly.' Burbage's enthusiastic pitch for Shakespeare's dated Elizabethan comedy notwithstanding, his admission that 'there is no new play' that Queen Anne 'has not seen' was not what the authorities wanted to hear. Demand was rapidly outstripping supply, even of old favourites. It was time to write another play, and not long after he came upon that copy of *King Leir*, Shakespeare had decided on its subject. He would turn another Queen's Men's play into a King's Men's play. It's not what one would have expected from a playwright struggling to connect with this Jacobean moment, especially a writer so identified with the drama of the 1590s. Yet however counter-intuitive it may have seemed, Shakespeare saw that the best way for him to grapple with the present was to engage with the past, refurbishing an old and unfashionable Elizabethan plot.

If the Queen's Men had been the all-star company of the 1580s, Shakespeare's company were the all-stars of their day, and had been for over a decade. When Shakespeare sat down to write *King Lear*, he knew that he would be writing the part for Richard

Burbage, the finest tragedian of the age. He had already created for him such career-defining roles as Richard III, Hamlet and Othello. Burbage was now in his late thirties, which also meant that Shakespeare could expand his imaginative horizons and write plays that starred more grizzled and world-weary protagonists. Before 1606 was over, he would challenge Burbage not only in the role of Lear, but also in another pair of older tragic roles, Macbeth and Antony (while this same year Ben Jonson wrote for Burbage the brilliant part of Volpone, who play-acts the role of an infirm old man). No actor may ever have faced more daunting newly written roles in so short a time-span. If Shakespeare was memorialised as the 'soul of the age', Burbage, some years later, and perhaps with a nod to that earlier tribute, was the acknowledged 'soul of the stage'.

Reflecting back on the special relationship between great playwrights and their star actors, Richard Flecknoe observed in the mid-seventeenth century that it 'was the happiness of the actors of those times to have such poets as these to . . . write for them', and those poets were no less fortunate 'to have such . . . excellent actors to act their plays as . . . Burbage', known for 'so wholly transforming himself into his part, and putting off himself with his clothes, as he never (not so much as in the tiring-house) assumed himself again until the play was done'. Flecknoe helpfully describes the naturalistic acting style in which Burbage excelled: audiences 'were never more delighted than when he spake, nor more sorry than when he held his peace; yet even then he was an excellent actor still, never falling in his part when he had done speaking, but with his looks and gestures maintaining it still unto the height'. Shakespeare knew that he could count on Burbage to convey not only Lear's words but also the telling gestures and great silences on which his part depends, something a reading experience of the play too often misses.

It wasn't only Burbage who had aged. Many of the talented and ambitious players who had come together in their twenties in 1594 to form the Chamberlain's Men were now approaching forty; Shakespeare, at forty-two, was the oldest in the company. Some of the founders were not in good health and others were no longer alive. Augustine Phillips was already dead and Will Sly and Laurence Fletcher would be buried before two years had passed. John Sinklo, a long-time 'hired man' for whom Shakespeare had been writing skinny-man parts for over a decade, was either dead or had left playing, for no more was heard of him after 1605. Their first star comedian, Will Kemp, had parted ways with them back in 1599, pursuing a solo career, a blow to the company, for audiences were drawn to the theatre for Kemp's clowning as much as they were for Burbage's tragic roles or Shakespeare's words. Kemp's replacement, Robert Armin, was a very different kind of comedian. While Armin could step into some of the roles Shakespeare had written for Kemp (such as Dogberry in *Much Ado*), Kemp's improvisational and physical style and commonsensical if at times dim-witted demeanour couldn't have been further from the sardonic, witty air of the diminutive Armin. It took a while for Shakespeare to figure out how best to write Armin into his plays. He had some early success with the parts of Touchstone in *As You Like It* and Feste in *Twelfth Night*, and with smaller roles as the Gravedigger in *Hamlet* and perhaps Thersites in *Troilus and Cressida*. But it wasn't until *King Lear* that Shakespeare created a truly defining role for Armin, Lear's Fool (and it was probably with this role in mind that, four years later, John Davies praised Armin as one who can 'wisely play the fool').

The Fool would be a role unlike any Shakespeare ever wrote before or after – witty, pathetic, lonely, angry and prophetic in turn, a part rich in quips and snippets of ballads and the kind of sharp exchanges for which Armin was famous. Armin's range was extraordinary and it's not surprising that this almost bewildering role was cut for much of *King Lear*'s stage history. It wasn't only Shakespeare's relationship with both Burbage and Armin that had matured, but also the relationship of the star comedian and tragedian with each other. In the past, Shakespeare had tended to keep clowns and kings apart; this time he would force them together, creating an unusually intimate and endearing bond, one that also depended on the personal familiarity and mutual understanding of his two lead actors. The poignancy of one of Lear's most heartbreaking lines, written for Burbage – 'And my poor fool is hanged' (24.300) – depends on it, reminding us not only of the manner of Cordelia's death but also of the loss of his beloved Fool, Armin, who disappears from the action midway through the play.

Genius may be a necessary precondition for creating a masterpiece but it's never a sufficient one. Shakespeare's Jacobean plays depended on the raw talent of his company. We don't know as much as we would like about who acted in them and must reconstruct this as best we can from a few surviving cast lists and from scattered anecdotes and records. The casts called for roughly a dozen men and two or three teenage boys, which meant that the ranks of the eight or so shareholders were fleshed out with experienced 'hired men' for the lesser adult roles and two or three boys for the women's parts. When he decided to rewrite the story of Lear and his three daughters Shakespeare knew that he had available at least two extraordinary teenage actors, their names now lost to us. They may even have been the same pair who had proven their mettle as early as Rosalind and Celia in *As You Like It* in 1599, and then Gertrude and Ophelia in *Hamlet* and Emilia and Desdemona in *Othello.* Shakespeare would challenge his young actors with more mature female roles this year: first Goneril and Regan in *Lear*, then Lady Macbeth and Lady Macduff, and finally Cleopatra and Octavia. John Heminges and Henry Condell, veterans of the company, had aged too, and were now better suited to such exceptional and older parts as Gloucester, Kent, Albany and Cornwall. Another veteran, Richard Cowley, for whom Shakespeare had written the sidekick role of Verges in *Much Ado*, could fill such roles as well. For younger male roles, the King's Men had recently added a pair of rising stars, still in their twenties, John Lowin and Alexander Cook, and it's likely that they stepped into such parts as Edgar and Edmund (if Cook, who had been apprenticed under Heminges, wasn't slated for leading female roles).

Despite its losses, the company was still deep in talent, and staging *King Lear* (which has eleven significant roles) without that depth, and without actors who know each other intimately from having worked together for so many years, is, as many modern companies have discovered, incredibly hard to do well. Shakespeare's division of the parts was unusually well balanced: Burbage, as Lear, spoke just under a quarter of the play's lines, while the roughly equal other major parts – the Fool, Edgar,

Kent, Gloucester and Edmund – accounted for half the play, and other roles the remaining quarter. While Shakespeare no doubt joined them on stage when needed, by 1606 it seems that either he or the company felt that his hours were better spent writing full-time than in the wearying business of rehearsing and acting in the mornings and afternoons, which had left only his evenings free for reading and writing. This meant that his days were free, for the first time since the early 1590s, to collaborate with other playwrights. That half of his last ten plays were co-authored is undoubtedly related to his withdrawal from full-time acting. Rehearsing and performing almost every day, year after year, was physically demanding; acting on the early modern stage was a young man's game. One need only look at the example of Burbage's great Elizabethan rival Edward Alleyn, who retired from the stage in his early thirties before making a brief comeback a few years later. There weren't many actors over forty performing in 1606. Condell would continue acting regularly into his forties, as would Heminges, who in his mid-forties was already and cruelly called 'old stuttering Heminges'. Burbage was probably exceptional in performing daily into his late forties or, at the very most, until his death at the age of fifty.

Shakespeare's days of touring rural town halls and great men's houses, especially during plague time, were probably over as well. That left him in an unusual position in 1606: while he had a first-hand knowledge of the strengths of each of his fellow players and could write plays that took advantage of their unrivalled depth and talent, he was no longer interacting with them every day. The impact of this was felt not only on the intimacy of his bond with his fellow players, but on his writing as well, which started to become, even by Jacobean standards, increasingly dense and knotty, as if he were liberated to write as much for himself as for others.

For confirmation of this, we need look no further than the reaction of his rival Ben Jonson, who reportedly singled out a work from this year as evidence of Shakespeare's turn toward writing that was deliberately opaque. Later in the seventeenth century the playwright (and Shakespeare admirer and adapter) John Dryden wrote that in 'reading some bombast speeches of *Macbeth*, which are not to be understood', Ben Jonson 'used to say that it was horror; and I am much afraid that this is so'. Jonson may well have had in mind passages like the soliloquy in which Macbeth wrestles with whether or not to kill King Duncan. That speech could not have begun more simply, as Macbeth cannot bring himself to name the horrific deed: 'If it were done when 'tis done, then 'twere well / It were done quickly.' But as the horror of the crime and his moral reservations about murdering his king sink in, Macbeth's speech becomes increasingly tortured. And as the long soliloquy nears its end and he has just about talked himself out of committing murder, Macbeth's palpable relief finds expression in a string of dense and paradoxical images that displace each other so rapidly that early playgoers at the Globe, including Jonson, must have struggled to follow his train of thought.

Yet few soliloquies have ever captured a feverish mind at work or traced an arc of a character's moral crisis more memorably. As Macbeth's imagination takes flight, he fears that Duncan's 'virtues' will 'plead like angels, trumpet-tongued, against / The deep damnation of his taking-off' (1.7.19–20). This powerful image in turn, leads him to think aloud in the kind of heightened language that so troubled Jonson:

> And Pity, like a naked newborn babe
> Striding the blast, or heaven's cherubim, horsed
> Upon the sightless couriers of the air,
> Shall blow the horrid deed in every eye,
> That tears shall drown the wind.
> (1.7.21–5)

To call such passages 'horror' is surely too strong, and 'bombast' unfair; both terms smack not only of jealousy but also of a failure to grasp what's gained, not just lost, when writing begins to verge on the impenetrable (though audiences have never needed to know precisely what Macbeth is *saying* in order to grasp what he is *feeling* at this moment). Lucidity as an end in itself can be overrated. This passage is, as critics have long noted, breathtaking – and few stretches in Shakespeare's work suffer more from crude glossing. Shakespeare's writing here is anything but imprecise and his passage's meaning is clear enough once its dense metaphorical network – which touches in condensed form on so much else that happens in the play – is unpacked. A reductive paraphrase that explains what Macbeth says also strips his remarkable lines of their mystery and resonance: he imagines here that a personified Pity, like an infant bestriding the winds, or soaring retributive angels riding the air, will spread word of his evil deed, eliciting so compassionate a response that the tears shed will be like a great rain that stops the wind. Jonson rightly recognised that Shakespeare's writing had taken a new turn, one far less accessible than Jonson's own efforts in neo-classical verse or colloquial prose. But if Shakespeare's actors and audiences now had to work harder, the rewards for doing so would prove greater too.

'The Unite' coin, minted in 1604

2 : *Division of the Kingdoms*

Back in 1599, still unsure whether he would ever attain the English throne, the forward-looking King of Scots wrote a political handbook, *Basilikon Doron*, for his eldest born, Prince Henry. In it, he warned his son about the dangers of dividing territory among children, especially if Henry were fortunate enough to inherit the kingdoms of England, Ireland, France and his native Scotland. James urged him to act as Abraham had with his first-born: 'in case it please God to provide you to all these three kingdoms, make your eldest son Isaac, leaving him all your kingdoms, and provide the rest with private possessions. Otherwise by dividing your kingdoms, ye shall leave the seed of division and discord among your posterity.' The royal treatise became a bestseller after James succeeded Queen Elizabeth in 1603, with fourteen thousand copies printed in London in that year alone. A few words were added to that sentence in these English editions that reminded readers of an earlier division of the kingdoms in British history, one that had led to centuries of bloodshed and strife: 'as befell to this isle, by the division and assignment thereof, to the three sons of Brutus, Locrine, Albanact and Camber'. This story of Brutus and his sons was pseudo-history, derived from Geoffrey of Monmouth's *History of Great Britain*, the source for King Lear's legendary reign as well. But it was a well-chosen example, for it was a precedent familiar to English audiences through the popular play *The Lamentable Tragedy of Locrine, the Eldest Son of King Brutus* (written around 1591 and later wrongly attributed to Shakespeare and even printed as his in the third folio of his plays in 1664). The flipside of the danger of division was ensuring union, and no domestic or foreign issue would more deeply preoccupy James and his subjects in the early years of his reign than the Union of Scotland and England.

Once crowned King of England, James was confident that a formal ratification of the Union of his kingdoms was imminent. After all, as both King James VI of Scotland and King James I of England, he personified that unification. As James saw it, Union was part of a larger divine plan: 'Hath not God first united these two kingdoms both in language, religion and similitude of manners?' One of his earliest proclamations upon arriving in England, published for the benefit of any 'who may stand in any doubt of the said Union', commanded 'all his highness's subjects to repute, hold and esteem both the two realms as presently united, and as one realm and kingdom, and the subjects of both the realms as one people, brethren and members of one body'.

While James understood that only Parliament could ratify the Union, he did all that he could to reinforce a sense of its inevitability, even issuing an accession medal in 1603 declaring himself to be 'emperor of the whole island of Britain'. While few of his subjects may have seen, much less owned, this celebratory medal, many more would handle the new £1 coin, minted in 1604 and called 'the Unite', on which James is identified as King of Great Britain. On its reverse was a Latin translation of Ezekiel 37:22 that lent scriptural authority to royal pronouncement: '*Faciam eos in gentem unam*' – 'I will make them one nation.'

The outbreak of plague of 1603 had postponed James's ceremonial entry into London and delayed as well the opening session of his first Parliament. Both finally took place almost a full year after Elizabeth's death. Union was at the top of James's agenda and figured largely in both pageantry and Parliament. But the long delay had hurt the Union cause, for James was unable to take full advantage of his initial enthusiastic welcome. As James paraded through London's packed streets on 15 March 1604, he passed various triumphal arches, constructed specially for the event nearly a year earlier and now brought out of storage. At the Fenchurch Street Arch, devised by Ben Jonson, James was welcomed to his 'empire's seat' (2.444). And further along, above the Conduit in Fleet Street, he encountered actors impersonating 'his majesty's four kingdoms' – England, Scotland, France and Ireland. To accompany this display, Thomas Middleton had been paid by the civic authorities to write a speech celebrating Union as something already accomplished, cleverly picking up on James's account of Brutus and the division of the kingdoms in *Basilikon Doron*:

> So rich an empire, whose fair breast
> Contains four kingdoms by your entrance blessed,
> By Brute divided, but by you alone
> All are again united and made one.

King James, who usually hated crowds, was thrilled by his reception. But not everything went quite as planned that day. Another playwright, Thomas Dekker, had arranged for James to encounter the patron saints of England and Scotland, St George and St Andrew, riding alongside each other on horseback and 'sworn unto a league of amity'. But Dekker hadn't counted on the huge crowds keeping the two riders apart and they didn't find each other in time to greet the king. It was a bad omen.

Four days later a confident king addressed his first English Parliament. In making his case for Union, James drew upon the same stories that Shakespeare had been telling in his series of plays about England's bloody Wars of the Roses, strife that was only resolved when Henry VII, the first of the Tudors, killed Richard III, the last of the Yorkist kings, at Bosworth Field. James argued that this union of 'these two princely roses of the two Houses of Lancaster and York, whereof that king of happy memory was the first uniter,' was 'nothing comparable to the union of two ancient and famous kingdoms' of Scotland and England. As his long speech wore on, members of Parliament were treated to an extended history lesson, as James schooled them not only in the benefits of unity but also in the dangers of division: 'Do we not yet remember, that this kingdom was divided into seven little kingdoms, besides Wales? And is it not now the stronger by their union?' And in language evocative of John of Gaunt's speech in *Richard the Second*, in which England is described as 'this little world, / This precious stone set in the silver sea' and as a 'fortress built by Nature for herself' (2.1.43–6), James urged that 'God has made us all in one island, compassed with one sea, and of itself by nature so indivisible' that a truly united kingdom of

Scotland and England 'is now become like a little world within itself, being entrenched and fortified round about with a natural and yet admirable strong pond or ditch, whereby all the former fears of this nation are now quite cut off'.

James stopped short of making specific demands on Parliament (and wasn't inclined to think of authority, which he saw ultimately grounded in his divinely chosen royal person, in legalistic terms). But he expected it to take two small but significant steps: formally declaring him head of Great Britain, then establishing a commission, made up of both Scottish and English representatives, to resolve any remaining obstacles to unification. The climax of his address to Parliament was a soaring and much-quoted passage in which he recast the political problem as a family one, not surprising coming from a ruler who had long seen kingship in deeply patriarchal and personal terms:

> What God hath conjoined then, let no man separate. I am the husband, and all the whole isle is my lawful wife. I am the head, and it is my body. I am the shepherd, and it is my flock. I hope therefore no man will be so unreasonable as to think that I that am a Christian king under the Gospel, should be a polygamist and husband to two wives.

In the abstract, who could disagree with this? While imagining political relations in marital or familial terms might work metaphorically, Parliament didn't deal in abstractions. The House of Commons dug in its heels and to James's frustration, little progress on Union was made. James next tried writing to Parliament to nudge the case along, explaining that 'his wish, above all things, was at his death to leave one worship to God; one kingdom, entirely governed; one uniformity of laws'.

The quest for Union, it soon became clear, could not be easily resolved, nor would it go away, since James was unwilling to relinquish it, forcing attention to concerns that until now had been largely glossed over. The widespread relief in 1603 that royal succession had been peaceful, and the further relief that the new monarch was not only a man but also one who was married with male heirs, had masked deeper problems about what it meant in practice for a King of Scots to govern England. In hindsight, that's understandable. The 1571 census of 4,500 aliens in London had located only forty Scots living in the city, which meant that most Elizabethans had little personal exposure to Scots and got their sense of Scottishness second-hand – from long-circulating stereotypes, from books like Raphael Holinshed's *Chronicles*, from memories of James's mother (the treacherous Mary, Queen of Scots), and from the stage (where Marlowe's *Edward the Second* recalled how the Scots humiliated the English at the Battle of Bannockburn, and Shakespeare's more recent *Henry the Fifth* casually alluded to their neighbours to the north as the 'weasel Scot' [1.2.170]). The arrival of many Scots in James's entourage in 1603 – along with rumours that they were lice-ridden and grasping – only stoked English xenophobia. It wasn't easy to forget that before 1560 England and Scotland had often been at war, and that Scotland was allied with England's sometime enemy, France. And it didn't help that the English considered themselves superior to their poorer and (to their minds) backward northern neighbours.

More delays followed. Parliament was scheduled to reconvene in February 1605 and resolve the legal issues raised by Union, since that much time was needed for English and Scottish commissioners to resolve their differences. Meanwhile, James issued a new proclamation on 20 October 1604, claiming by 'kingly power and prerogative' the 'name and style of King of Great Britain'. Despite James's eagerness to see the issue resolved, fresh setbacks meant that the next sitting of Parliament was postponed until early November 1605. The delay created a political vacuum, one that defenders and enemies of Union filled with a score of treatises. London's bookstalls were crammed with the latest arguments about Union, as the controversy attracted some of the finest English and Scottish legal and political minds, eager to ingratiate themselves with the king or, alternatively, warn their fellow subjects of new and unseen dangers.

One of the more fascinating tracts, published in 1605, was John Thornborough's *The Joyful and Blessed Reuniting the Two Mighty and Famous Kingdoms*. The pro-Union Thornborough found it useful to compare political union to a classical comedy of separation and reunion, Terence's *Adelphoe*. Terence's comedies were a staple of the grammar-school curriculum and Thornborough assumed that many of his readers would recall the old play and draw the right moral: 'How joyful it is for us to acknowledge one another Britains, as it was for the brethren in the comedy, which after so long time came to knowledge of one another, even as we now know one another to be Britains by all signs and tokens.' The Union of Scotland and England followed the formula of New Comedy: unfortunate separation and confusion, then at last mutual recognition, followed by reunion and joyous reconciliation. But when Thornborough concludes by asking 'Can any be English and not Scottish? Can any be Scottish and not English?', the answer, for too many sceptical readers on both sides of the border was surely 'yes'. When he asks why the English and Scots 'cannot but readily embrace each other, as the ancient Romans reconciled after long civil war', he could not help but remind readers of the historical enmity between Scotland and England, and of the brevity of that Roman amity.

With king and critics comparing the challenge of political union to working out family problems, it was not much of a stretch for dramatists to give plots that turned on royal domestic crises a political edge, especially when those stories were drawn from Britain's past. Even as Shakespeare was turning to *King Lear* in the autumn of 1605, the veteran playwright Anthony Munday was working on a new commission, a civic pageant called *The Triumphs of Reunited Britannia.* The pageant, held on 29 October 1605, was staged in honour of London's new Lord Mayor. The timing of its political message was crucial, as it was scheduled to be performed a week before Parliament reconvened at last to resolve issues standing in the way of Union. Lord Mayor's shows were among the highlights of London civic theatre and had the added attraction of being free and open to the public.

Munday didn't have to look far for his plot; he found it close at hand in the story of Brutus and his sons that James had alluded to in *Basilikon Doron*, and he relied heavily on Holinshed's account of Brutus's reign to flesh out his story. The content of Munday's pageant was no doubt cleared with his patrons, the company of Merchant Taylors, who spared no expense for this elaborate production – over £700, a huge sum that covered not just Munday's fee but also the elaborate sets, the costuming and feeding of the child actors who performed it, and the printed text that was soon published. Rather than simply retell the tragedy of a divided kingdom, Munday chose instead to transport Brute and his three children to the present time so that they could witness the undoing of their folly. The result is a happy ending, as Brute declares that 'Wales, England, Scotland, severed first by me' are by King James 'knit again in blessed unity' as 'these sister-kingdoms now shake hands'. British identity had never really disappeared, and in bringing Brutus and his offspring back from the dead to Jacobean London to applaud its restoration, Munday reinforced the argument that Union was no novelty and was better understood as a long-delayed reunion.

Unfortunately for the young actors performing in the pageant, London's weather on 29 October was awful, and 'great rain and foul weather' drenched the expensive sets. It's not even clear whether the show went on that day, but the Merchant Taylors made the best of the situation and had the pageant performed – either again or for the first time – three days later when the skies had cleared. In case anyone missed its pro-Union message, Munday underscored the point in a passage added to the printed text that soon circulated: 'King James' is 'our second Brute', by 'whose happy coming to the crown, England, Wales and Scotland, by the first Brute severed and divided, is in our second Brute reunited, and one happy Britannia again'.

For Jacobeans inundated by pageantry, polemic and gossip about the proposed Union, any play that turned to Britain's distant past to explore the consequences of a divided kingdom would have been seen as part of this conversation. And Shakespeare didn't wait long to locate *King Lear* within this ongoing debate. King James's warning about 'dividing your kingdoms' is closely echoed in the opening lines of *King Lear* in Gloucester's remark about the 'division of the kingdoms' (1.3–4). The contemporaneous feel of the beginning of Shakespeare's play is reinforced in Kent's first words: 'I thought the King had more affected the Duke of Albany than Cornwall' (1.1–2). Jacobean playgoers knew that King James's elder son, Henry, was the current Duke of Albany, and his younger one, Charles, the Duke of Cornwall – and, in fact, James did prefer Henry over his sickly younger brother. To speak of Albany was to speak of Scotland (James himself had previously been Duke of Albany, as had his father). It was, for Shakespeare, an uncharacteristically topical start – the opening gossipy exchange marking the play as distinctively Jacobean in its political concerns.

Shakespeare had spent much of his career writing about Englishness; indeed, a strong claim can be made that his nine Elizabethan English history plays did much to define English identity, if not English exceptionalism. That changed after he became a King's Man and his attention, and that of his Jacobean audiences, turned from Englishness to Britishness. The evidence for this is striking: the word 'England' had appeared 224 times in his Elizabethan plays. But in the decade after James became king, 'England' appeared only twenty-one more times in his works (most of them in his late and collaborative *Henry the Eighth*), and 'English', which he had used 132 times during the plays he wrote under Elizabeth, only appeared eighteen times in all of his Jacobean plays. Shakespeare had never found an occasion to use the word 'British' before James's accession; the first time that audiences heard it in one of his plays was in *King Lear*, where it occurs three times. Similarly, the word 'Britain', which had appeared only twice in Shakespeare's Elizabethan drama, occurs that many times in *King Lear* alone, and twenty-nine times in all in his Jacobean plays. In turning from Englishness to Britishness, Shakespeare was responding to questions that hadn't much interested his fellow countrymen before the arrival of King James. In pressing the case for Union, the Scottish monarch had foisted upon his subjects an identity crisis where none had existed before. What was proving unsettling for the culture at large proved to be a gift to a dramatist who had made a career out of exploring identity crises – be they political, familial, marital or religious. Union, in the terms set out by James, touched on all of them.

By the time that Shakespeare began writing *King Lear* it was clear that King James (and it seems almost everyone else on both sides of the border) had underestimated the extent to which Union would force both the English and the Scots to confront a hard set of questions about their identities. What was the difference between a Scot and an Englishman other than place of birth? Were the obvious commonalities between the two kingdoms – a shared monarch, a shared language (more or less), a shared island (which also included Wales), a shared religion (more or less), a shared view of law (more or less) and a shared system of government (more or less) – enough to overcome these differences? Francis Bacon, for one, wasn't sure; in a private treatise written for the king on the Union question, he warned that every one of these commonalities 'hath some scruple or rather grain of separation enwrapped and included in them'. It didn't take much to unwrap them.

What's in a name? Would officially changing James's title to 'King of Great Britain' unintentionally invalidate longstanding

English law and treaties (as some legal minds feared) and, as collateral damage, undermine hard-won constitutional authority? Along the same lines, James's plan to combine England's and Scotland's parliaments stoked fears that what really motivated the Union cause was an imperial monarch's desire to wrest power from the legislature – so he was quickly forced to drop that idea. Looking beyond metaphors of marriage and fraternity, what sort of Union was intended? Was it to be a Continental-style federation in which different local laws prevailed? Or alternatively, a so-called 'perfect Union', an incorporation closer to the English model, based on conquest, in which Wales had been all but swallowed up? James wasn't quite clear about this, and his views seem to have evolved over time based on what it was possible to achieve. The longer that Parliament delayed ratification the lengthier the list of theoretical and practical obstacles to Union grew. Other key terms whose meanings had long been taken for granted began to feel slippery as well. Did talk of a British 'empire' (a term both Ben Jonson and Thomas Middleton felt comfortable using) refer to its older meaning as simply an independent sovereign state, or did it mean, as the context of the pageantry suggests, something newer and to those at the margins more disturbing: a collection of territories that implied both a centre and a periphery to which less powerful kingdoms were relegated?

A decade earlier Shakespeare had looked deeply in *Richard the Second* into the question of the king's 'two bodies', a political theory that maintained that it was treasonous to distinguish between the physical and political bodies of kings (so that subjects couldn't swear allegiance to one and not the other). The proposed union of the crowns, by multiplying the number of bodies, created all sorts of difficulties for this theory (yet the failure to achieve Union, as far as James was concerned, would leave his body politic 'divided and monstrous'). King James continued to insist that his kingdoms were united under 'one imperial crown'. But if so, and if this was more than a metaphor, why didn't he melt down both his Scottish and English crowns and create out of them a single British one? Francis Bacon urged him to consider doing so, making literal what remained figurative, while acknowledging that this solution would probably introduce fresh problems. Would James then need to undergo a formal 'British' coronation? And shouldn't 'the frame' of this new British crown contain 'some reference to the crowns of Ireland and France'? When in the opening scene of his new play Shakespeare has King Lear insist on retaining 'the name and all the additions to a king' while at the same time formally relinquishing power, the plot turns on a version of this question, for Lear hands over to the Dukes of Albany and Cornwall a coronet and says, 'This coronet part betwixt you.' How exactly are the dukes to split a metal coronet in two? As with Union, each potential solution seemed to introduce a host of fresh difficulties.

Shakespeare returns to this unresolved issue of divided crowns and divided authority soon after the opening scene, when the Fool baits Lear, saying: 'Give me an egg, nuncle, and I'll give thee two crowns.' When Lear plays along and asks, 'What two crowns shall they be?' the Fool replies, punishingly: 'Why, after I have cut the egg in the middle and eat up the meat, the two crowns of the egg. When thou clovest thy crown i'th' middle and gavest away both parts, thou borest thy ass o'th' back o'er the dirt.

Thou hadst little wit in thy bald crown when thou gavest thy golden one away' (4.148–56). An egg (broken in half, with the jagged edges of the half-shells resembling two crowns) proved a lot easier to divide than what kings wore on their heads – and as difficult to put back together.

From its opening scene, when a map of Britain is brought on stage, *King Lear* wrestles with what Britishness means, especially in relationship to the longstanding national identities it superseded. Was it really possible to forget national origins, or do deeper loyalties and suppressed nationalism inevitably emerge? As with the question of the division of the crowns, to introduce such vexing issues was not to resolve them, or even necessarily to stake a position. The role in the play of the kingdom of France (one more of James's kingdoms, at least on paper) further complicated matters. Playgoers at the Globe should naturally have sympathised with the British forces in their efforts to defeat French invaders. But nationalistic sympathies become compromised when it turns out that the virtuous Cordelia, now married to the King of France, is on the wrong side (the whole French subplot, borrowed from *King Leir*, is never fully or adequately worked out, and Shakespeare doesn't quite solve the problem by having Cordelia rather than her husband lead the invading troops).

While Shakespeare first uses the word 'British' in *King Lear*, every time it appears it is troubling and a bit off. The first time we hear it is when Edgar, speaking as Poor Tom, uses it in a snatch of rhyme: 'Fie, fo, and fum; / I smell the blood of a British man' (11.166–7). But the final word we expect him to say here, from the old and familiar rhyme, is '*English*man'. Could this have been, as John Kerrigan has suggested, a joke on Shakespeare's part, a bit of Jacobean political correctness, with Edgar catching and correcting himself so that he doesn't make the mistake of saying 'Englishman'? The other two times the word appears are in ambiguous contexts as far as nationalism is concerned: first when a messenger warns that the 'British powers are marching hitherward' (reminding us that Cordelia is leading a French army against Britain), then later by Regan's servant, Oswald, who repeats that it is the 'British party' that is defending itself against a French invasion.

Even if the French are defeated and a British monarchy restored, who will lead it in the end, an Englishman or a Scot? The choice among the play's few survivors is limited: either the English Edgar, son of the Duke of Gloucester (whose namesake, the tenth-century King Edgar, was celebrated both for his peacefulness and for reuniting the kingdoms of England), or the ruler from the north, the Duke of Albany, the highest-ranking figure at the end of the play, and a character who held a title shared by the King of Scots. Much depends on who speaks last, for it was a convention in the drama of the time that the highest-ranking figure in historical drama has the last word.

The play famously turns on Lear's ill-fated decision to divide his kingdoms. Yet the consequences of this are not clear-cut. This may help explain why no other writer debating the Union question ever invoked Lear's reign as an example, even after Shakespeare's play was staged. Would it have been wiser for Lear to have left all to the wicked but eldest-born Goneril rather than divide it between his three daughters? Was Lear's mistake rather in reassigning Cordelia's share to her sisters – that is, in splitting his lands in two rather than three? Or was his more fundamental political error his failure to act on the principles of absolutism, and that the authority and not just the name of king should have remained with and in him alone while he was alive? Even if Lear had been restored to power at the end, wouldn't that, in the absence of a male heir, only have temporarily delayed inevitable civil strife? And on reflection, what political lessons, if any, should this legendary British history hold for the present, especially when that version of the past was derived from what contemporaries increasingly recognised as self-serving stories of origins found in Geoffrey of Monmouth, whose work was now understood to be more myth than fact?

The deck seems equally stacked by Shakespeare against both union and division. Those who try to identify a clear-cut position in *King Lear* are bound to be disappointed (though that hasn't stopped some critics from declaring it to be avowedly pro-Union and others to insist as assuredly that the play subverts and dismantles Union rhetoric). Further complicating this question, insofar as the Union debate evolved over time, the division of the kingdoms and ensuing issues of allegiance in the play registered quite differently with playgoers in February from how they would in December 1606. Challenged by James's rhetoric to imagine British political history in familial terms, Shakespeare does so with remarkable acuity, having discovered in and through this controversy deep cultural fissures, ones that shape this grimmest of tragedies, set in a universe in which every political alternative leads to devastating loss.

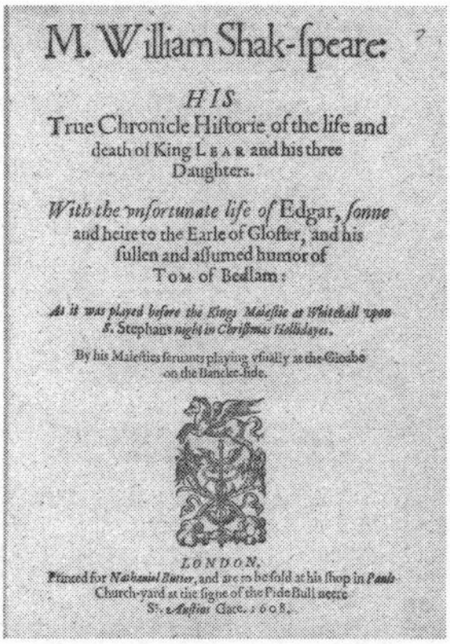
M. William Shak-speare:

HIS

True Chronicle Historie of the life and death of King LEAR and his three Daughters.

With the unfortunate life of Edgar, *sonne* and heire to the Earle of Gloster, and his sullen and assumed humor of TOM of Bedlam:

As it was played before the Kings Maiestie at Whitehall upon S. Stephans night in Christmas Hollidayes.

By his Maiesties seruants playing vsually at the Gloabe on the Bancke-side.

LONDON,
Printed for *Nathaniel Butter*, and are to be sold at his shop in *Pauls* Church-yard at the signe of the Pide Bull neere St. *Austins* Gate. 1608.

3 : From Leir to Lear

King Lear draws so extensively on *King Leir* that Shakespeare's indebtedness couldn't have come solely from what he recalled from acting in it or seeing it staged years earlier, however prodigious his memory. The profusion of echoes confirms that reading the recently printed edition proved to be the catalyst for the play now forming in his mind. *King Leir*'s survival in turn allows us a glimpse of Shakespeare as literary architect – performing a gut renovation of the old original, preserving the frame, salvaging bits and pieces, transposing outmoded features in innovative ways.

Demand for new work was as insatiable at the public theatres as it was at court. Because Elizabethan and Jacobean spectators expected to see a different play every day, playing companies had to acquire as many as twenty new plays a year while rounding out their repertory with at least that many older and reliably popular ones. Attendance would eventually drop when familiar plays

Title Page of the Quarto of *King Lear* (1608)

began to feel stale and the task of breathing fresh life into those staged at the Globe would almost certainly have fallen to Shakespeare. While we know that Shakespeare wrote or collaborated on as many as forty plays, we'll never know how many old ones he touched up. We do know (by comparing early and later versions) that he updated his earliest tragedy, *Titus Andronicus* (*c.*1590–2), adding a poignant new scene in which a maddened Titus tries to kill a fly with a knife. Some scholars believe he was also the author of the speeches added to that old chestnut, Thomas Kyd's *The Spanish Tragedy* (*c.*1587). For all we know, over the course of his career Shakespeare might have refreshed dozens of his company's plays in this way and was as practised as anyone at giving a cold hard look at an old favourite, recognising what now felt a bit off or what trick had been missed. His ability to pinpoint what was flawed in the works of others was one of his greatest gifts, though not one we know enough about nor celebrate today. It was a talent closely allied to his habit of relying on the plots others had devised rather than inventing his own.

Before he picked up a copy of the old *Leir*, Shakespeare was already familiar with several versions of this story. He may have first read about Lear's reign in his well-worn copy of Holinshed's *Chronicles of England, Scotland and Ireland*. He had also read Edmund Spenser's brief account of it in *The Faerie Queene* and had come across retellings of the tale in both *Mirror for Magistrates* and *Albion's England*. He might even have consulted Geoffrey of Monmouth's Latin version of Lear's story, from which all these other versions derive. Yet scholars who have painstakingly compared *King Lear* with each of these sources conclude that as voracious a reader as Shakespeare was, and as much as he might have drawn on these and other versions of the story for particular details, it was *King Leir* that he worked most closely from – and against.

That 'against' would have been obvious to anyone who compared the title page of *King Leir* with that of the first printed version of Shakespeare's play, a quarto that appeared in London's bookstalls in early 1608. Ordinarily, considerably more time passed before Shakespeare's playing company turned one of his plays over to a publisher; a delay of a couple of years was closer to the norm for his Elizabethan plays, and as yet not a single one of his Jacobean plays had been printed. So it's doubly surprising that Shakespeare's play was entered in the Stationers' Register in November 1607, less than a year after it was staged at court. The full title of the 1608 quarto of *Lear* feels like a riposte to the title page of the old play, which had read in full: 'The True Chronicle History of King Leir, and his three daughters, Gonorill, Ragan, and Cordella, As it hath been divers and sundry times lately acted'. This time, the publisher not only names the play's author but – and this was new – gives England's best-known playwright top billing in large font. The play is emphatically Shakespeare's: 'HIS' is in capital letters and even gets a separate line. The main title that follows is much the same as the old play's: a 'True Chronicle Historie of the life and death of King LEAR and his three Daughters'. It too claims to be the 'True Chronicle Historie' rather than distinguishing itself, say, as the 'True Tragedy of King Lear'. But the title page goes on to distinguish the new play from the old one by emphasising that it is about both the lives *and* the deaths of Lear and his three daughters. It also offers more than its predecessor: a secondary plot about 'the unfortunate life of Edgar, sonne and heire to the Earle of Gloster, and his sullen and assumed humor of Tom of Bedlam'. It would be the first and last time that Shakespeare ever included a parallel plot or subplot in one of his tragedies.

He needed it, because it was immediately clear that the story in *Leir* lacked counterpoint, a way to highlight Lear's figurative blindness by juxtaposing it with something more literal. It would also enable him to critique the very notions of authority and allegiance at the heart of the main plot. Shakespeare's genius was first in discovering the perfect foil to this story and then in almost seamlessly weaving it into the narrative of Lear and his daughters. He found it in a tale about a blinded father and his two sons, one virtuous, the other evil, that he had read years earlier in the most celebrated of Elizabethan prose romances, Sir Philip Sidney's *Arcadia*, published in 1590. Sidney's striking image of a blind and suicidal old man being led to the edge of a cliff by his good son, both of whom appeared 'weather-beaten' and in rags, had clearly stuck with Shakespeare. Sidney's words had also stuck with him, especially what the old man tells his son as he prepares to leap to his death: 'since I cannot persuade thee to lead me to that which should end my grief, and thy trouble, let me now entreat thee to leave me . . . Fear not the danger of my blind steps, I cannot fall worse than I am.' It took very few strokes for Shakespeare to make this scene central to his new play. In Sidney's story, the suicidal old man had been a king who was blinded and stripped of his kingdom by his bad son; it was easy enough for Shakespeare to turn him into an earl and a follower of King Lear, then have his evil son implicated in both his undoing and his blinding.

What seems inevitable in retrospect was anything but: merging plots from a play and a prose romance to form a double helix, firmly interlocked and mutually illuminating. Shakespeare also saw that Lear's elder daughters could vie for Edmund's affections while the good son, now named Edgar – in Sidney he eventually becomes king – could emerge as something of a hero. All this could replace the meandering and unsatisfying middle of *King Leir*, which Shakespeare would all but scrap. It also solved a major problem of the old play. The anonymous author of *Leir* had been content to build to a somewhat wooden reconciliation scene between father and daughter, one that failed to pack much emotional punch. Shakespeare's *Lear* would substitute for that not one but two powerful recognition scenes: the first between Lear and Cordelia, the second, soon after, where the two plots converge, between the mad Lear and the blind Gloucester. It's debatable which of the two is the most heartbreaking scene in the play.

As Lear's division of the kingdoms spills into a psychologically complex drama of two families, motives become more complicated and unsettled. Does Lear go mad because he has foolishly divided his kingdoms or because of his ruinous relationship with his daughters? It's impossible to tell, because in scene after scene the political, the familial and ultimately the cosmic are so deeply interfused. The fortunate survival of *Leir* enables us to see the sheer craftsmanship involved in all this. Yet it also needs to be acknowledged that Shakespeare didn't always get the parts to fit together quite so neatly. As keen as he was to work in that image of a suicidal man led by his son to the edge of a cliff, audiences have wondered ever since why Edgar, disguised at this point as Poor Tom, doesn't simply reveal himself to Gloucester (the excuse that Shakespeare gives Edgar, that he is trying to cure his father by putting him through all this, feels lame). And the French invasion of England, so central to *Leir*, sits uneasily in Shakespeare's version, a part of the old play that he did his best to integrate but that ends up feeling confused and confusing. He himself – or if not him, members of his company – would go back and tinker with the problematic invasion, though with only partial success.

Rather than rely entirely on his own considerable vocabulary, Shakespeare somewhat surprisingly recycled what he could from the language of the old play. He had a talent for recognising the untapped potential of resonant words, even the simplest ones. Take 'nothing'. The word appears often in *Leir*, even as part of a raunchy joke (Gonorill and Ragan laugh about women getting stuck with a man 'with nothing' – that is, one who is castrated, so has no 'thing' [2.3.22–3]). But it is never used with any particular emphasis in that old play, not even when the French king asks Cordella whether Leir has 'given nothing to your lovely self?' and she pointedly replies, 'He loved me not, and therefore gave me nothing' (2.4.71). Each Shakespeare play has its own distinctive music and, not unlike a symphony, its themes are established at the outset. At an early stage of recasting the old play, Shakespeare seems to have decided that 'nothing' would be the motif of *Lear*'s score. The first time we hear the word is after Lear demands of Cordelia what she 'can say to win a third more opulent' than her sisters, to which she replies: 'Nothing, my lord.' Lear, stunned by her response, hurls the word back at her: 'How? Nothing can come of nothing' (1.78–81). This first 'nothing' takes on a life of its own, reverberating with greater force from then on, punctuated by this pointed exchange between Lear and his Fool:

Lear. This is nothing, fool.

Fool. Then, like the breath of an unfee'd lawyer, you gave me nothing for't. Can you make no use of nothing, uncle?

Lear. Why no, boy. Nothing can be made out of nothing.
(4.122–6)

Shakespeare would also, and brilliantly, use 'nothing' to suture together the Lear and Gloucester plots. Even as Cordelia's initial response to her father is the words 'Nothing, my lord,' so too, in his first exchange with his father, Edmund, when asked by Gloucester about the contents of the letter he has hastily hidden, replies, chillingly, with the very same words: 'Nothing, my lord' (2.31).

In Shakespeare's hands 'nothing' becomes a touchstone – and the idea of nothingness and negation is philosophically central to the play from start to finish. Cruelly, by the play's end Lear turns out to be right: nothing does indeed come of nothing, only not in the way he first meant. Early on in imagining his version of Lear's journey, Shakespeare saw that what began with that first 'nothing' must end with Lear left with nothing, except, perhaps, the knowledge that his dead and beloved daughter will never return – 'never, never, never' (24.303). In the interim the words 'never' and 'nothing' recur over thirty times, 'no' over 120 times, and 'not' twice that often. The negativity is reinforced by the sixty or so times the prefix 'un-' occurs, as characters are 'unfriended', 'unprized', 'unfortunate', 'unmannerly', 'unnatural' and 'unmerciful'. Call it what you will – resistance, refusal, denial, rejection, repudiation – this insistent and almost apocalyptic negativity becomes a recurring drumbeat, the bassline of the play.

One other instance of how Shakespeare breathed new life into key words from the old play must suffice. Late in *Leir* Shakespeare came upon a scene in which the king admits to a follower that by dividing his kingdom he has diminished himself: 'Cease . . . to call me lord, / And think me but the shadow of myself' (4.2.16–17). Shakespeare lifts this potentially powerful image and has his furious Lear repeat these words – now turned into a question – as he stumbles towards a deeper awareness of what he has become:

> Doth any here know me? Why, this is not Lear.
> Doth Lear walk thus, speak thus? Where are his eyes?
> Either his notion weakens, or his discernings
> Are lethargied. Sleeping, or waking, ha?
> Sure, 'tis not so.
> Who is it that can tell me who I am?
> Lear's shadow?
> (4.217–23)

Someone, perhaps Shakespeare himself, would change that powerful line yet again, for in the subsequent folio text of 1623 the last two words – 'Lear's shadow' – are reassigned to the Fool: no longer Lear's rhetorical question, they are now his companion's sharp rejoinder.

As the example from the cliff scene lifted from Sidney's *Arcadia* suggests, Shakespeare was also comfortable borrowing and adopting a source's visual vocabulary. When in the old play Leir shows his daughter Ragan incriminating letters – 'Knowest thou these letters?' – the stage direction tells us that 'She snatches them and tears them'. Shakespeare thought well enough of this action to put it to better use in a later scene, where Albany confronts his wife with a letter that reveals her adulterous duplicity:

> Stop your mouth, dame,
> Or with this paper shall I stopple it.
> Thou worse than anything, read thine own evil.
> Nay, no tearing, lady . . .
> (24.150–3)

Having Albany hold that missive at arm's length while Goneril lunges to take it away and tear it to pieces was a better piece of stagecraft than simply, as in *Leir*, having Ragan snatch and shred the letter.

The central image of Lear struggling to his knees and begging forgiveness of Cordelia was also translated from the old play. Shakespeare must have admired the innovative idea, which hadn't appeared in any earlier versions of the story. Stage directions in the margin make the physical action explicit:

Cordella. But look, dear father! Look, behold and see:
Thy loving daughter speaketh unto thee! *she kneels*

Leir. Oh, stand thou up; it is my part to kneel,
And ask forgiveness for my former faults. *he kneels*

Cordella. Oh, if you wish I should enjoy my breath,
Dear father rise, or I receive my death. *he riseth*

Leir. Then I will rise to satisfy your mind,
But kneel again, till pardon be resigned. *he kneels*

Cordella. I pardon you? The word beseems not me,
But I do say so, for to ease your knee.

You gave me life; you were the cause that I
Am what I am, who else had never been.

While the stage image is riveting (though risks becoming comic when the old man creakily kneels, rises, then sinks and rises again), the accompanying duet in *King Leir* may have seemed as mawkish in 1605 as it does today. Shakespeare, looking past those clumsy rhymed couplets, grasped the potential power of what his predecessor had hit upon, and vastly simplifies and shortens the scene, at the same time transforming it into one that is also about self- and mutual recognition. Father and daughter each kneel once, and Cordella's unremarkable line – 'you were the cause that I / Am what I am' – is reworked into Cordelia's heartrending and succinct affirmation:

Cordelia. O look upon me, sir,
And hold your hands in benediction o'er me.
No, sir, you must not kneel.

Lear. Pray do not mock.
I am a very foolish, fond old man,
Fourscore and upward, and to deal plainly,
I fear I am not in my perfect mind.
Methinks I should know you, and know this man;
Yet I am doubtful, for I am mainly ignorant
What place this is; and all the skill I have
Remembers not these garments; nor I know not
Where I did lodge last night. Do not laugh at me,
For as I am a man, I think this lady
To be my child, Cordelia.

Cordelia. And so I am.
(21.55–67)

Even more than language and stage imagery, it was the frame of the old play that held Shakespeare's interest. The opening scenes of *King Leir* contained much that appealed to him, and much in it *almost* worked: a marriage plot about a father and his daughters, an absent mother, a love test and a division of a kingdom. But the old-fashioned play took far too long to develop. So Shakespeare went about compressing the first seven scenes into a single one that was half their length, beginning with Leir's overlong speech with which the play begins:

Thus, to our grief the obsequies performed
Of our too late deceased and dearest queen,
Whose soul, I hope, possessed of heavenly joys,
Doth ride in triumph 'mongst the cherubims,
Let us request your grave advice, my lords,
For the disposing of our princely daughters,
For whom our care is specially employed,
As nature bindeth, to advance their states
In royal marriage with some princely mates . . .
(1.1.1–9)

Stylistically, there wasn't much here worth keeping: the jingling rhyme and the heavily end-stopped lines were out of date, a throwback to the drama of an earlier age. Shakespeare had little interest in keeping any of the old play's Christian piety either. He saw that the less said about Leir's dead queen the better, and that marrying off three 'princely daughters' at once was two too many – better to pair off the older sisters before the action began and shift the axis of jealousy.

Beginnings mattered hugely to Shakespeare. Even when following in another writer's footsteps he searched patiently for the best point of entry and almost never started his story where a predecessor had. *King Lear* would prove an exception. Shakespeare's openings can feel casual and indirect, but as directors nowadays learn at their peril, they cannot easily be cut. Shakespeare almost never begins a play with his protagonist, as *King Leir*'s author does. We don't meet Romeo or Juliet, Shylock, Hamlet, Caesar or Othello until we have heard them described, allowing us to see them initially through the eyes of others (the notable exception is *Richard the Third*). He often introduces these minor characters already engaged in conversation. He would do so again in *King Lear*, squeezing in a compact thirty-six-line opening exchange between Kent, Gloucester and his bastard son, Edmund, that glances at the familial drama while establishing the play's central political concern: 'the division of the kingdoms'.

The conjunction of the love test and a divided kingdom undoubtedly drew Shakespeare to *King Leir*, and he saw how they could be fused more powerfully. In the old play, the love test is a trick, a deliberate and 'sudden stratagem' that Leir seizes on to resolve a succession problem: his youngest daughter's refusal to marry someone from Britain's ruling class ('if my policy may her beguile, / I will match her to some king within this isle'). Leir explains his plans at length:

I am resolved, and even now my mind
Doth meditate a sudden stratagem
To try which of my daughters loves me best,
Which, till I know, I cannot be in rest.
This granted, when they jointly shall contend
Each to exceed the other in their love,
Then at the vantage will I take Cordella,
Even as she doth protest she loves me best,
I'll say: 'Then, daughter, grant me one request
To show thou lovest me as thy sisters do,
Accept a husband, whom myself will woo.'
(1.1.75–85)

While his elder daughters are already committed to marrying British earls, Cordella stubbornly wants to marry for love rather than 'join in marriage with the Irish king' (1.2.94) as her father wishes. (The Irish angle is something that Shakespeare would no doubt have made much more of had he turned to *Lear* before the brutal Nine Years War with Ireland came to an end in 1603.) Exploring whether a daughter should marry for love or in accordance with her father's desires was not a stretch for Shakespeare. He had already handled the subject masterfully in plays like *A Midsummer Night's Dream* and *Romeo and Juliet*. But it held less appeal for him in *King Lear* – or rather, he saw beyond it to a much richer set of struggles between a dependent father and his daughters. Leir's stratagem and motives are reasonable enough and might well have worked were it not that Skalliger, a disloyal counsellor in whom he confides, rushes off to leak the plan to Gonorill and Ragan, Leir's two elder daughters. Informed in advance, they cheat on the love test (knowing that they face no penalty for lying or flattery) and leave Cordella isolated in her defiance.

Shakespeare's revision of *Leir*'s opening shows remarkable economy. Lear briskly announces that he will reveal his 'darker' purposes, calls for a map of Britain (no offstage lottery between sons-in-law here, as in *Leir*) and declares that he has already divided the kingdom:

> Meantime we will express our darker purposes.
> The map there. Know we have divided
> In three, our kingdom, and 'tis our first intent
> To shake all cares and business off our state.
> (1.36–9)

Lear's love test is no stratagem; rather, it is a pro forma confirmation of each daughter's worth, what each one merits in exchange for her share of his kingdom:

> Tell me, my daughters,
> Which of you shall we say doth love us most,
> That we our largest bounty may extend
> Where merit doth most challenge it?
> Goneril, our eldest born, speak first.
> (1.44–8)

Shakespeare gains a great deal by leaving intentions unspoken and uncertain. In the absence of clear-cut motives, playgoers are left struggling for answers. Why does Cordelia stubbornly refuse to humour her father? Does Lear even want her to marry? Is he already showing signs of mental decline? Shakespeare's Lear is enraged that his youngest daughter doesn't declare her unconditional love for him, not simply piqued, as Leir was, that his stratagem goes awry. And, at least at the outset, we have little inkling that Goneril and Regan (whose counterparts in *King Leir* signal their wickedness in advance of the love test) are so evil. Shakespeare also removes their motive for resenting their younger sister, whom they describe not inaccurately in *King Leir* as a sanctimonious and hypercompetitive 'proud pert peat' (1.2.2). Indeed, one of the most significant changes Shakespeare makes to the old play is all but silencing Cordelia, who in his version speaks fewer than a hundred lines – for in *King Leir* she consistently undercuts her appeal by going on at length and sounding holier than thou. Cordella's pious remark, 'I will to church and pray unto my Saviour, / That, e'er I die, I may obtain his favour' is typical (4.1.31–2). In *Leir*, the elder sisters' jealousy is directed against Cordella, who they fear will marry before them. Shakespeare, having married them off already, turns their petty jealousy into burning resentment directed first at their father, then at their husbands, and finally at each other.

Leir doesn't really do anything terribly wrong; Lear does. This difference is underscored through the king's blunt servant, Kent (a role derived from Leir's loyal follower, Perillus), who demands to know 'What wilt thou do, old man?' (1.137). Calling Lear 'old man' is insulting enough to modern ears, but Kent addressing his king as 'thou' would have struck contemporaries as even more extraordinary and foolhardy. In Jacobean England 'thou' and 'you' were used with precision and purpose. At the risk of oversimplifying usage that could be even more nuanced or ironic:

superiors (or members of the upper class speaking to each other) were addressed as 'you', inferiors as 'thou' – so that Cordelia shows great respect for her father when saying 'You have begot me, bred me, loved me' (1.87). Even addressing someone of equal rank as 'thou' could be taken as an insult (so that, for instance, audiences at the Globe understood exactly what Sir Toby Belch means in *Twelfth Night* when he eggs on Sir Andrew Aguecheek, urging him to address his adversary as 'thou' and to repeat the put-down: 'If thou "thou"-est him some thrice, it shall not be amiss' [3.2.43–4]). Shakespeare's opening scene becomes far more shocking for contemporary audiences once Kent – who moments earlier had respectfully called his monarch 'Royal Lear' – says to the king, 'I'll tell thee thou dost evil' (1.155). As these examples suggest, Shakespeare was alert to how the slightest and seemingly most insignificant of details defined a character or altered the mood of a scene. What other playwright would step back and invoke the simple stuff of daily life that humanises the action of this tragedy of state, whether it is the mad Lear speaking of 'toasted cheese' or of 'garden water-pots'? (20.89, 185).

It was not only playgoers who kept thinking of the old play in the course of experiencing the new one; Shakespeare himself did so. The 1608 quarto shows traces of the playwright absentmindedly naming his protagonist 'Leir' instead of 'Lear' in speech headings as well as the text – three times in the following exchange in the opening scene:

Leir. Go to, go to.
Better thou hadst not been born than not to have pleased me better.
Fran. Is it no more but this – a tardiness in nature,

That often leaves the history unspoke
That it intends to do? – My Lord of Burgundy,
What say you to the lady? Love is not love
When it is mingled with respects that stands
Aloof from the entire point. Will you have her?
She is herself a dower.

Burg. Royal *Leir*,
Give but that portion which yourself proposed,
And here I take Cordelia by the hand,
Duchess of Burgundy –

Leir. Nothing. I have sworn.
(1.223–35)

At this point Shakespeare catches himself and mistakenly writes 'Leir' only once more, not long after (it's far less likely that a compositor would make this change). It's the kind of slip cleaned up in modern editions, though a detail that tells us something about where Shakespeare's mind was as he began writing.

When in the eighteenth century the great critic and editor Samuel Johnson complained about what he found troubling in *King Lear*, he focused on the play's refusal to satisfy moral expectations:

A play in which the wicked prosper, and the virtuous miscarry, may doubtless be good, because it is a just representation of the common events of human life: but since all reasonable beings naturally love justice, I cannot easily be persuaded, that the observation of justice makes a play worse; or, that if other excellencies are equal, the audience will not always rise better pleased from the final triumph of persecuted virtue.

Given Johnson's view about the play's lack of justice, it's all the more surprising that *King Lear* is littered with sententious reminders that the world is ultimately a just place. The old play had been full of such moralising. Rather than eliminating these tiresome providentialist tags, Shakespeare keeps them. We hear, time and again, a version of 'The gods are just'. But the gods are not just; as the blinded Gloucester has learned, 'As flies to wanton boys are we to th' gods; / They kill us for their sport' (15.35–6). By preserving traces of the providentialism of the old play, and in juxtaposing this clear-cut sense of right and wrong with the brutality and amorality of the characters who inhabit his play, Shakespeare turned Elizabethan melodrama into the most searing of Jacobean tragedies. To Albany's reassuring words about Cordelia – 'The gods defend her!' (24.252) – Shakespeare's play has a silent and irrefutable response: Lear enters carrying the corpse of his murdered daughter.

Of all the changes that Shakespeare made to the old Queen's Men's play, none would prove more shocking than what he did to its ending, toying to the last with the frame he had retained from *King Leir*. For Shakespeare's revision depended on his playgoers' familiarity with the broad contours of the old story: the division of the kingdom, the banishment of the king's youngest daughter, and the civil war and ensuing invasion from France. Those in the audience who had seen *King Leir* or had read any of the other versions of Lear's reign in circulation already knew how the story ends. The warring forces do battle and the French army, joined by Cordella and Leir, emerges triumphant. Nobody dies in *King Leir* and all that is lost is restored. The gods defend Cordella, and Leir regains his throne, cheerfully thanking both God and his son-in-law for the victory. His final words, which bring the play to a close, offer a coda that confirms this restoration. All's well that ends well:

> Ah, my Cordella, now I call to mind
> The modest answer which I took unkind:
> But now I see I am no whit beguiled,
> Thou lov'dst me dearly, and as ought a child.
> . . . .
> Come, son and daughter, who did me advance,
> Repose with me awhile, and then for France.
> (5.11.29–44)

Audiences in 1606 would have expected Shakespeare's play to end in much the same way, with Lear restored to his throne and Cordelia spared. They might even have thought such a resolution was imminent in the scene in which Lear and Cordelia are at last reconciled, which takes place after close to three hours (or 2,800 lines), the typical length of one of Shakespeare's plays. But *King Lear*, which has another five hundred lines to go, doesn't end there, and when it does and they are both dead, we are confronted with a desolate scene that is all the more crushing, denying us not only what we wish for, but also what we expect, especially after the villainous Edmund has a change of heart and tries to save Cordelia's life. It helps explain why Samuel Johnson found the ending so unbearable: 'Shakespeare has suffered the virtue of Cordelia to perish in a just cause, contrary to the natural ideas of justice, to the hope of the reader, and, what is yet more strange, to the faith of the chronicles.' The result was the darkest tragedy that Shakespeare ever wrote – and for audiences in 1606, whose expectations would have been so upended, all the more wrenching and bewildering a theatrical experience.

4 : Possession

On 5 October 1605, in response to the persistence of plague, the Privy Council ordered that London's playhouses be closed once again and steps taken to keep those who were infected off the streets. The Florentine ambassador reported home the following week that 'various diligent things have been done by the aldermen, such as prohibiting plays, public bull- and bear-baiting, and above all keeping watch throughout the city for all kinds of dogs'. As grim as plague was for humans, it was worse for dogs; erroneously convinced that dogs spread plague, London's authorities had them rounded up and slaughtered.

The King's Men must have left the shuttered Globe shortly after this Privy Council decree, for only four days later they were performing in Oxford. Whether Shakespeare went with them is unknown, though if he were to tour anywhere with his company it's likely he would travel with them there, only a day's ride from his home in Stratford-upon-Avon. Not everyone left town. The

'Demonic Possession,' Pierre Boaistuau, *Histoires prodigieuses* (1598)

same evening that the King's Men were playing in Oxford, Ben Jonson was dining in London. He had been spotted having supper at the Irish Boy on the Strand, in the company of Catholic gentry unusually eager for King James to return to London and for Parliament to reconvene. Three of Jonson's companions – Robert Catesby, Francis Tresham and Thomas Winter – would soon be household names.

Jonson had received an important new commission on which he was probably already at work, for he was a notoriously slow writer. He had been the playwright hired to write the court masque which was to be staged in the first week of the new year. He was lucky to get the commission, for he had only recently been released from prison, narrowly escaping having his nose slit and ears cut for his part in a scandalous play, *Eastward Ho*, co-authored with George Chapman and John Marston. The playwrights had thought that they could get away with poking fun at Scots but had misjudged the shifting political winds. Satirical writing was now being taken far more seriously. King James himself was rattled this autumn by an anonymous satiric attack that he described as a 'cruelly villainous pasquil that railed upon me for the name of Britain'. That treasonous poem, now lost, went beyond mocking Union: it ominously 'prophesied' that 'something' would happen during harvest-time this year; that something, James feared, was his 'destruction'.

While plague continued to afflict London, James spent much of summer and early autumn outside the city. Six weeks before Shakespeare's company performed in Oxford, the king had paid the university town a visit, for which a series of academic plays had been commissioned. Unfortunately for James, who wasn't that keen a playgoer under the best of circumstances, these plays turned out to be excruciatingly dull. The king tried walking out of the first one 'before half the comedy had been ended', but was begged to stay. He nodded off at the next and when he awoke 'would have been gone', and was overheard saying in exasperation, 'I marvel well what they think me to be.' Taking no more chances, James refused to sit through a third play.

But he did enjoy a pair of surprise encounters the day he arrived in Oxford. As he rode into town on the afternoon of 27 August, accompanied by Queen Anne, Prince Henry and a retinue of noblemen, the king was greeted outside the gate of St John's College by three young men, dressed, as one bystander recorded, 'in habits and attire like nymphs'. Actually, the three were playing the parts of prophetic Sibyls, and they greeted the king and his entourage, first in Latin and then, for the sake of the queen, in English (though only the Latin version survives). The Sibyls then recounted the story of how, long ago, they had told Banquo that he would father a long line of Scottish kings who would possess empire without end. Now, in a similar manner, they prophesied the same future for Banquo's descendant, King James. At this point the first Sybil cried, '*Salve, cui Scotia servit*' ('Hail, whom Scotland serves,' probably translated into a more colloquial 'Hail, King of Scotland'). The next Sybil in turn greeted James with the words 'Hail, King of England,' followed by the third: 'Hail, King of Ireland.' This was followed by an additional pro-Union 'All-hail' for James, 'who divided Britain joins into one'. The king, an onlooker noted, 'did very much applaud' this 'conceit'.

The author of this historical pageant was Matthew Gwinne, a physician and academic playwright who lived in London and who had been brought to Oxford to help prepare for the royal visit. Gwinne, who proudly published the Latin version of this interlude, modelled his story on Holinshed's *Chronicles*. He probably drew on the 1587 edition in which 'the weird sisters, that is (as ye would say) the goddesses of destiny, or else some nymphs or fairies, endowed with knowledge of prophecy,' appear to Banquo and his friend Macbeth and say, first: 'All hail Macbeth, thane of Glammis'; 'Hail Macbeth, thane of Cawder'; and 'All hail Macbeth, that hereafter shalt be King of Scotland.' Only then do they turn to Banquo and add, in lines paraphrased by Gwinne: 'We promise greater benefits unto thee than unto him, for he shall reign in deed, but with an unlucky end. Neither shall he leave any issue behind him to succeed in his place, where contrarily thou indeed shalt not reign at all, but of thee those shall be born which shall govern the Scottish kingdom by long order of continual descent.' Because Gwinne's pageant so clearly anticipates the opening of the as yet unwritten *Macbeth*, some biographers like to place Shakespeare in the crowd that day in Oxford. It's more likely that Shakespeare heard about this royal entertainment from others, perhaps after his playing company toured there six weeks later and the king's recent visit was still the talk of the town.

Despite a schedule crammed with official welcomes and gift-giving, speeches, pageantry, prayers and academic disputations, King James found time that afternoon to mingle with his subjects, for we know that he met that day a troubled young woman whose case would soon preoccupy him. The best account of their meeting survives in a history, *Historia Rerum Britannicarum*, written in Latin by Robert Johnston, one of the

Scots who had followed the king down from Scotland. Here's a translation:

At the time when the king was staying at Oxford, a young girl of about eighteen years of age aroused the wonder of the people of Britain on account of her strange cleverness in deception, which imposed upon the astonished multitude. Whereupon James was seized with the wish to see someone so celebrated in popular report. Accordingly, she was at once brought to the king. To the great amazement of the bystanders she lacked all sense of pain when she was stuck with pins. The strangeness of this created great excitement. Not only was this wonderful in the eyes of those who were present, but she also cast out of her mouth and throat needles and pins in an extraordinary fashion. The king, wondering where the numerous pins she vomited so suddenly came from, questioned her repeatedly, but she remained obdurate, claiming that this happened to her miraculously, and that the sense of feeling taken away from her for the time being would soon, by divine providence, return to her.

The young woman's name was Anne Gunter and her story has been reconstructed by the historian James Sharpe (whose fascinating account, *The Bewitching of Anne Gunter*, I rely on here). She lived in the parish of North Moreton, twelve miles south of Oxford. Her father, Brian Gunter, was a gentleman with powerful connections in Oxford, including his son-in-law, rector of Exeter College. Anne Gunter was probably twenty-two years old the summer her father brought her to meet King James, not eighteen, as Robert Johnston had guessed.

Two years earlier she had mysteriously fallen ill. At first her parents thought she was suffering from epilepsy or perhaps 'the mother' (the Jacobean term for hysteria). Doctors were called in but couldn't find any natural cause for her malady, leading her parents to suspect that its origins must be supernatural. Her swooning, fits, foaming at the mouth, trances, vomiting and, soon, casting forth of pins from her mouth and nose confirmed the obvious: Anne Gunter was suffering from demonic possession, which could only happen if she had been bewitched. Who then had done this to her?

As was typical of reports of demonic possession at that time, neighbours gathered to see and validate the signs of the devil at work, visits encouraged by the family. A few weeks after first showing signs of possession, Anne identified three local women as her tormentors: Elizabeth Gregory, Agnes Pepwell and Agnes's daughter Mary. Anne was even able to describe the devilish spirits through which they afflicted her: 'Elizabeth Gregory's was like a black rat with a swine's face and boar's tusks. Agnes Pepwell's was like a mouse with a man's face and a long beard. Mary Pepwell's was like "a whitish toad and was called Visit."' The evidence was overwhelming and the villagers of North Moreton were convinced that Anne was possessed; so too were the physicians and clerics who visited from Oxford and closely observed her fits. Fearing punishment, Agnes Pepwell fled – she was already reputed locally to be a witch – but the other two women were brought to trial in nearby Abingdon, to be judged under the recently enacted Witchcraft Act of 1604, harsher than the Elizabethan law that it replaced. According to the new Act, anyone convicted of invoking or conjuring 'any evil and wicked spirit' or practising any 'witchcraft, enchantment, charm or sorcery, whereby any person shall be killed, destroyed, wasted, consumed, pined or lamed' shall 'suffer pains of death as a felon'.

Their trial took place on 1 March 1605, and the jurors heard evidence for eight hours. The trial's high point was the testimony provided by Anne herself, who was carried into the courtroom on a chair and promptly fell into a fit, beating her knuckles, rolling her eyes wildly, mumbling, then sprawling onto the floor in a trance. Brian Gunter demanded of the court that Elizabeth Gregory recite a spell, so that all could witness its effect – and she did so, but not to his satisfaction (he claimed she didn't say it right). Elizabeth Gregory and Mary Pepwell were acquitted. Though the trial was over, Anne Gunter continued to show signs of demonic possession. A furious Brian Gunter, denied the outcome he sought on behalf of his daughter, continued to pursue justice.

Two things would have confirmed in the minds of his English subjects King James's own unswerving belief in the dangers of witchcraft. The first was accounts of his role in persecuting as many as a hundred Scottish witches in the North Berwick trials fifteen years earlier. The condemned had been implicated in threatening the lives of James and his Danish wife, Anne, allegedly raising a storm while the newlywed royals were sailing back to Scotland from Denmark, as well as working their magic on a wax effigy of James. The second was James's book on witchcraft, *Demonology*, first published in Edinburgh in 1597 and twice reprinted in London the year that he became King of England. Those like Brian Gunter who were convinced of the malevolent power of witches must have been confident that so committed a demonologist as James would surely be an ally in so obvious a case of possession. Five months after failing to have his daughter's tormentors punished, Brian Gunter saw his chance and, relying on influential friends in Oxford, arranged for his daughter to meet the king. James became so fascinated by her case that he met with Anne Gunter again in September and twice more in early October. He had planned to see her yet again at the end of October, but an unanticipated crisis would prevent that.

King James's belief that witches were the devil's agents is confirmed in a letter Sir John Harington wrote not long after this, in which he recounted a recent, private audience with the king. In the course of their conversation, Harington writes, 'his majesty did much press for my opinion touching the power of Satan in matter of witchcraft, and asked me, with much gravity, "If I did truly understand why the devil did work more with ancient women than with others?"' Perhaps unsure whether James was merely testing him, or fearful of giving the wrong answer to so fraught a question, Harington tried dodging the matter by telling an off-colour, sexist joke. But that failed to derail James, who continued to speak with conviction of supernatural powers, and told Harington that the death of his mother, Mary, Queen of Scots, 'was visible in Scotland before it did really happen, being, as he said, "spoken of in secret by those whose power of sight presented to them a bloody head dancing in the air"'. Harington added that the king made much of this gift of second sight, and 'said he had sought out of certain books a sure way to attain knowledge of future chances'.

If we take Harington's reported conversation with the king at face value, James was someone who not only believed in witches, the devil and the supernatural, but was also deeply curious about how they worked. Their exchange also suggests something Macbeth-like about James's pursuit of this knowledge, especially his powerful desire to know what the future held. But James recognised that this pursuit, for those not capable of dealing with it, could drive them down a dangerous path to 'evil consultations' (precisely where Macbeth heads when he seeks out the Weird Sisters late in the play). It would have made good sense, then, for Brian Gunter to appeal to King James. But he failed to anticipate that whatever James thought about the demonic, he was also a ruler who prided himself on exposing fraudulent and secret plots. James may also have taken witches' activities that put his own life at risk more seriously than he did those that only threatened the well-being of his subjects.

The question of where natural explanations ended and supernatural ones began remained a vexing one, and we get a glimpse of James's views on this in a letter that he wrote that October to his chief minister, Salisbury. In it, the king would go on to tell him the latest about Anne Gunter, but before turning to her case James joked about the superstitious reactions many people had to a recent and unusual pair of heavenly events: an eclipse of the sun on 17 September followed by one of the moon on 4 October. James offered a witty parody of doom-and-gloom prognosticators who read these natural signs as divine warnings, playfully imagining the impact of these eclipses on the marital habits of courtiers. At this point, his letter turns to instances of prognostications about the supernatural as far-fetched as those made about the eclipses: 'First, a great dreaming divine hath closed his prophetical mouth and taken up the clyster spoon again. And now very lately a strangely possessed maid, whose breast was nothing but a pillow for pins.' That 'great dreaming divine' was Richard Haydock, a Puritan doctor celebrated for being able to preach sermons while sound asleep. King James had Haydock brought to Whitehall and stayed up late to hear him perform; while others were convinced, James soon enough exposed him as a fraud (and after extracting a written confession, graciously forgave him). And that 'strangely possessed maid' was none other than Anne Gunter.

Shakespeare probes this cultural fault-line between natural and supernatural explanations early on in *King Lear* in a passage spoken by Gloucester, likely written at much the same time as James's letter, in the wake of the same striking heavenly signs, the successive eclipses of the sun and moon this autumn:

> These late eclipses in the sun and moon portend no good to us. Though the wisdom of nature can reason thus and thus, yet nature finds itself scourged by the sequent effects. Love cools, friendship falls off, brothers divide; in cities mutinies, in countries discords, palaces treason, the bond cracked between son and father. (2.101–7)

Gloucester's interpretation of these heavenly signs sounds like just the sort of thing that James had mocked in his letter to Salisbury. Similar examples were soon in wider circulation, such as the interpretation of those eclipses that appeared in print a few months later in a pamphlet called *Strange Fearful and True News* that prophesied nothing short of 'traitorous designments, catching at kingdoms, translation of empire, downfall of men in authority, emulations, ambition, innovations, factious sects, schisms, and much disturbance, troubles in religion and matters of the Church'.

Shakespeare, having reproduced this sort of political prophecy in Gloucester's speech, then allows the bastard Edmund to puncture it, in much the same debunking spirit as we find in James's letter:

> This is the excellent foppery of the world: that when we are sick in fortune – often the surfeit of our own behaviour – we make guilty of our disasters the sun, the moon and the stars, as if we were villains by necessity, fools by heavenly compulsion . . . and all that we are evil in, by a divine thrusting on. An admirable evasion of whoremaster man, to lay his goatish disposition to the charge of stars! (2.110–19)

King James, while not as radically sceptical as Edmund, believed that the fake could be distinguished from the real. To that end, after first meeting Anne Gunter in Oxford, he arranged for her to be put under the care of the Archbishop of Canterbury. He in turn had her observed by one of his chaplains, Samuel Harsnett, as expert as anyone in England about fraudulent claims of demonic possession. Under Harsnett's close scrutiny, it didn't take long for Anne Gunter to confess that her symptoms had been faked. She had been acting. King James, who obviously relished his Solomonic role in the case, reported the outcome to a curious Salisbury:

> For your better satisfaction touching Anne Gunter . . . whereas not long since she was a creature in outward show most weak and impotent, yet she did yesterday in our own view dance with that strength and comeliness, and leap with such agility and dexterity of body that we, marvelling thereat to see the full and great change, spent some time this day in the examination of her concerning the same. And we find by her confession that she holdeth herself perfectly cured . . . [She] was never possessed with any devil nor bewitched; that the practice of the pins grew at the

> first from a pin she put into her mouth, affirmed by her father to be cast therein by the devil; and afterwards that and some other such pin-pranks which she used, together with the swelling of her belly occasioned by the disease called 'the mother', wherewith she was oftentimes vehemently afflicted, she did of long time by daily use and practice make show to be matters of truth to the beholders thereof.

We know a great deal about the circumstances of her case because even after the exposure of the deception, James and his Privy Council remained deeply interested in its particulars. A court of Star Chamber was even called in February 1606, at which England's privy councillors, despite having to attend to far more pressing national concerns, were required to evaluate the testimony of over sixty witnesses brought there to reveal what they knew about Anne's case. It emerged from their depositions that Brian Gunter had consulted a number of books about recent accounts of possession (some had even been presented to him as gifts by concerned onlookers). Anne recalled that among these volumes was 'the book of the witches of Warboys' – that is, *The Most Strange and Admirable Discovery of the Three Witches of Warboys Arraigned.* And her father admitted to the privy councillors that in addition to a copy of the Warboys tract he also owned a book written by John Darrell 'concerning some that were bewitched', as well as 'a book of certain persons said to be possessed with wicked spirits at Denham'.

This last volume, *A Declaration of Egregious Popish Impostures* (about the fraudulent exorcisms that had been conducted by Catholic priests at Denham in Buckinghamshire in 1586), proved vital to the success of their deception. It had been written by Samuel Harsnett, the very man appointed to oversee Anne Gunter. Harsnett was an experienced and equal-opportunity derider of fraudulent exorcisms. He had established his reputation exposing the Protestant fraud John Darrell, who had professed to freeing a young boy, William Sommers, from demonic possession. Harsnett had sat on the commission that condemned Darrell, then published *A Discovery of the Fraudulent Practices of John Darrell* in 1599.

In what may be thought of as his anti-Catholic companion volume, *A Declaration of Egregious Popish Impostures*, first published in 1603, Harsnett builds on the testimony of those who had years earlier confessed to having faked possession, including a sixteen-year-old girl, Friswood Williams, who had fooled many observers. Her Catholic handlers managed this, she reported, by having her

> drink above a pint of sack and sallet oil, being hallowed, and mingled with some kind of spices; when she took this drink, which they termed a holy potion, it did so much dislike her, that she could drink but a little of it at once, her stomach greatly loathing it, and then the priest said: 'all that comes from the devil, who hateth nothing worse, than that holy drink': so as she was held, and by very force caused to drink it up at divers draughts. Hereupon she grew to be very sick, and giddy in her head, and began to fall into a cold sweat: verily, then believing, that (as the priest said) it was a wicked spirit that caused her to be in such a case.

She acknowledged that the potion did 'so intoxicate and benumb her senses' that when 'two needles [were] thrust into her leg by one of the priests' she didn't even feel them. In her deposition before the Star Chamber in February 1606, Anne Gunter admitted that her father had forced her to down a similar horrible drink so that she too might display the telltale symptoms of the possessed. Brian Gunter had also subjected his daughter to another trick described by Harsnett: holding the victim's face over burning brimstone. Where Harsnett wrote his book to expose impostures, Brian Gunter, in collaboration with his daughter, had reverse-engineered the *Declaration of Egregious Popish Impostures*, turning it into a how-to manual.

They were not alone in doing so. Even as Brian and Anne Gunter were consulting Harsnett's *Declaration* as a guide for faking demonic possession, so was Shakespeare. Crucial to *Lear*'s subplot is Edgar's disguise when fleeing his father's home (after Edmund has persuaded Gloucester that Edgar had sought his life). A hunted man, Edgar decides to save himself – and this is Shakespeare's innovation, not found in Sidney's original – by taking 'the basest and most poorest shape' imaginable, that of a mad and possessed beggar, the kind who is haunted by devils and who pricks himself with pins and nails:

> The country gives me proof and precedent
> Of Bedlam beggars who with roaring voices
> Strike in their numbed and mortified bare arms
> Pins, wooden pricks, nails, sprigs of rosemary,
> And with this horrible object from low farms,
> Poor pelting villages, sheep-cotes and mills
> Sometime with lunatic bans, sometime with prayers
> Enforce their charity. 'Poor Turlygod, poor Tom!'
> That's something yet. Edgar I nothing am.
> (7.178–86)

Various possession stories in the *Declaration* are the likely source for these authentic touches. Harsnett describes one counterfeiter acting as though he is 'rent with a thousand nails' while another complains of feeling 'so many fiery needles in his skin at once'. Soon enough, Edgar expands his repertory, ventriloquising one who is possessed, crying out against that 'black angel' Hoppedance, that 'foul fiend' within him: 'The foul fiend haunts Poor Tom in the voice of a nightingale. Hoppedance cries in Tom's belly for two white herring. Croak not, black angel: I have no food for thee' (13.25–8). The demon's odd name, like many others Edgar invokes, is also lifted from Harsnett's book. In seeking to create the distinctive language and mannerisms of a character seemingly possessed, Shakespeare found in Harsnett's *Declaration* an invaluable guide.

Shakespeare had dealt with possession in a few earlier plays and the contrast with *King Lear* is striking. The first time, in his early work *The Comedy of Errors*, Antipholus of Ephesus and his servant Dromio are subjected to a sort of exorcism by 'Dr Pinch', who declares that 'both man and master is possessed; / I know it by their pale and deadly looks' (4.4.92–3). The scene is funny because playgoers know that the pair are sane, the exorcist a self-righteous fool and the exorcism itself absurd and fruitless. That was slapstick. The exorcism Shakespeare wrote into *Twelfth Night* is uglier and more sustained. As part of a practical joke, Malvolio is cruelly mocked as a man possessed. His tormenters revenge themselves on this puritanical killjoy, with Feste conducting a mock exorcism to cure Malvolio, in which he employs the familiar and predictable language of the exorcists: 'Out hyperbolical fiend! How vexest thou this man!' – and demands to know, 'do you but counterfeit?' (4.2.26, 115). In both comedies the emphasis is on the exorcism rather than on the experience of possession, and though Antipholus and Malvolio find the experience maddening, in both cases there are no supernatural forces at work and no deeper exploration of the demonic. In both plays Shakespeare taps into the casual brutality of the exorcism rites, which both darkens the comedy and stirs compassion for otherwise unsympathetic characters. But by steering well clear of the possibility of actual possession, these plays stop short of confronting anything darker or more disturbing than human maliciousness.

For Shakespeare, one of Harsnett's attractions was his habit of describing those who feigned possession in theatrical language. His book is littered with hundreds of allusions to acting, players, counterfeiting, feigning, tragedians, comedians, playing one's part well, and the like. When reaching for handy analogies Harsnett turns to strolling players, the Vice figure of the old morality plays or the experience of watching bear-baiting at Paris Gardens. He even compares the exposure of fraudulent exorcists to various dramatic genres, and concludes that this 'devil fiction' is neither pure comedy nor tragedy but a tragicomic hybrid of the two. Shakespeare may well have agreed with this, insofar as depicting the suffering of those possessed (faked or real) cannot help but generate sympathy. Harsnett's theatrical vocabulary was no accident. As chaplain to Richard Bancroft, the Bishop of London, one of Harsnett's duties was reading and approving of stage plays prepared for print (including one that was staged by Shakespeare's company, Ben Jonson's *Every Man out of His Humour*). Harsnett understood the extraordinary power of theatre and was disturbed by the extent to which fake exorcisms appropriated that power. But it would be a mistake to turn him into a caricature of a theatre-hating Puritan or to conclude that his rage was ever directed against London's players and their fictions.

In addition to providing a ready vocabulary for rendering a character feigning possession, Harsnett wrote in a lively style to which Shakespeare clearly responded:

> If they want devils in Italy to exorcise and ask oracles of, let them come but over into London in England, and we have ready for them Darrell's wife, Moor's minion, Sharpe, Skelton, Evans, Swan, and Lewis, the devil-finders and devil-puffers, or devil-prayers; and they shall start them a devil in a lane as soon as any hare in Waltham Forest, that shall nick it with answers as dead as Weston's and Dibdale's devils did. And we shall as easily find them a route, rabble and swarm of giddy, lunatic, illuminate holy spectators of both sexes, but especially a sisternity of mimps, mops and idle holy women that shall grace Modu the devil with their idle holy presence.

'Dibdale's devils' would have caught Shakespeare's attention, for the Jesuit priest and exorcist Robert Dibdale was a native of Stratford-upon-Avon, eight years older than Shakespeare. It wasn't the only Stratford connection in the book: Harsnett also attacked the memory of Jesuit martyr Thomas Cottam, brother of Stratford's schoolmaster at the time Shakespeare was fifteen. And his interest may have also been piqued when Harsnett recalled Edward Arden of Park Hall, who was executed on treason charges in 1583. Just a few years earlier, when they obtained the rank of gentlemen, Shakespeare and his father had appealed to the heralds to link their coat of arms to that distinguished branch of his mother's family, though we don't know whether they were indeed distant cousins or this was wishful thinking.

Shakespeare was a shrewd enough student of his culture to understand that the authorities' recent and obsessive interest in demonic possession touched on a deeper set of concerns. These are visible in the transcripts of confessions that serve as an extended appendix to the *Declaration* and read, unintentionally, as a counter-narrative in which Protestant authorities are seen as extracting from the same victims of the Catholic exorcists yet another forced confession. The government, uneasy with the charismatic nature of public exorcisms, whether performed before crowds by Jesuits or Puritans, was nonetheless eager to assert exclusive authority over how to combat the forces of evil. This was understandable enough, and made sense in a culture in which it was believed that a divinely anointed monarch could lay hands upon subjects and cure them of disease. In 1604 English canon law was therefore revised. From now on it was forbidden for anyone without a special licence from a bishop to 'attempt upon any pretence whatsoever, either of possession or obsession, by fasting and prayer to cast out any devil or devils, under pain of the imputation of imposture, or cozenage, and deposition from the ministry'.

But to deny the right to practise exorcism without official permission was not to deny the existence of evil or demonic 'possession or obsession', or, for that matter, the belief in witches and the devil on which they were premised. As one defender of John Darrell, following through the dangerous implications of such scepticism, defiantly put it, 'No devils, no God.' Even as explanations for why the devil would possess (mostly) young men and women fell short, so did legitimate cures or remedies, leaving mainstream Protestant Jacobean culture somewhat helpless in the face of the demonic, especially when compared to Catholic exorcists, who could enlist the help of 'holy water, holy oil, the holy candle, hallowed brimstone' and the like.

The campaign against unauthorised exorcism refused to confront the pressing and unspoken question at the heart of this controversy, one that would have mattered deeply to anyone who had brooded over characters like Richard III, Claudius and Iago: Where does evil come from? It's exactly the sort of question Shakespeare raises at the end of *Othello*, when, striking but failing to kill Iago, Othello says, 'I look down towards his feet; but that's a fable. / If that thou be'st a devil, I cannot kill thee' (5.2.294–5). Devils should have cloven feet, but this one doesn't, and Othello has no explanation for why this 'demi-devil' Iago 'hath thus ensnared [his] soul and body' (5.2.309–10).

The question raised at the end of *Othello* is taken up again in Shakespeare's next solo-authored tragedy, *King Lear*. Were people literally possessed with evil? Was evildoing rather the product of the circumstances of birth or culture? Or was it innate? These are questions that frustrate and eventually madden Lear: 'let them anatomise Regan, see what breeds about her heart. Is there any cause in nature that makes this hardness?' (13.70–2). Edmund himself weighs in on this early in the play, opting for nature over nurture. According to him, some people are simply born bad: 'I should have been that I am, had the maidenliest star of the firmament twinkled on my bastardy' (2.122–4). And yet, even in the one Shakespeare play in which complex characters fall almost embarrassingly into the familiar binaries of 'good' and 'evil' – with

Cordelia and Kent and Edgar lined up on one side and Goneril, Regan, Oswald and Edmund on the other – Shakespeare doesn't turn his story into a morality play and refuses to explain causality in reductive ways.

While Shakespeare may have initially turned to the *Declaration* to lend authenticity to Edgar's disguise, his engagement with Harsnett's protagonists led him in two fresh directions: toward a reflection on some of the social ills that fractured Jacobean society, and then toward the more general and related exploration of what possesses men and women to do evil things. In Harsnett's account there is plenty of evildoing to go around, the kind that few other books in London's bookstalls described so vividly, almost offhandedly. It's not even clear that Harsnett saw the social contexts of what he portrays as especially immoral; he seems as insensitive to the suffering of others as the drugged Friswood Williams was to the needles jabbed into her leg. While ostensibly an indictment of fraudulent Catholic exorcisms, the *Declaration* is also, unwittingly, a portrait of the many ills besetting mainstream English culture in the early seventeenth century: a world of callous and self-righteous male authorities, of casual violence and wilful deception, a brutal world in which young people are abandoned and mistreated, the physically or psychologically ill are abused, and those who give the 'wrong' answers are punished – a disturbing social universe not all that far from the one imagined in *King Lear*.

Scholars have identified over eighty passages in *King Lear* that are indebted to Harsnett's *Declaration*. So deep an immersion in a source's distinctive language was a departure for Shakespeare. Though he would follow other sources more closely, Shakespeare would never borrow so many distinctive words and compounds from a single book as he did from the *Declaration* – words that he had never used before nor would again, including 'meiny', 'propinquity', 'auricular', 'carp', 'gaster', 'yoke-fellow', 'asquint', '*Hysterica passio*' and 'vaunt-courier'. Sometimes more than just the odd word is borrowed, such as when Harsnett writes, 'All these sensible accidents should be made pendulous in the air like Archimedes' dome.' Shakespeare's Lear recalls both word and visual image when he speaks of 'all the plagues that in the pendulous air / Hang fated o'er men's faults' (11.60–1). At other points, Harsnett's book works like a palimpsest; beneath the disguised Edgar's description of himself as a 'hog in sloth, fox in stealth, wolf in greediness, dog in madness, lion in prey' (11.83–4) are Harsnett's words: 'the spirit of sloth in the likeness of an ass; the spirit of envy in the similitude of a dog; the spirit of gluttony in the form of a wolf'. Most of the time, though, borrowed words and images appear in markedly different contexts from those in Harsnett. They just seem to have lodged in Shakespeare's memory and rushed to the surface in the act of writing *King Lear*. The unrelentingly vicious, scabrous and manipulative world of the *Declaration* – a world in which what people do to each other is more cruel than anything thought up by devils – acts like a varnish that seeps into and stains the dark play.

Shakespeare discovered a treasure trove in the devils' names that appear in the *Declaration*. Many of these are conveniently gathered by Harsnett in a chapter 'touching the strange names of their devils'. Shakespeare would do much, for example, with Harsnett's account of how priests claimed to have cast out of Sara Williams a score of spirits: 'Lusty Dick, Killico, Hob,

Cornercap, Puffe, Purre, Fraterretto, Flibertigibet, Haberdicut, Cocobatto, Maho, Kellicocam, Wilkin, Smolkin, Nur, Lusty Jolly Jenkin, Portericho, Pudding of Thame, Pourdieu, Bonjour, Motubizanto, Bernon, Delicate . . .' Many of these names are directly transferred to *King Lear* – Puff, Pure, Frateretto, Flibbertigibbet, Mahu, Smulkin and Obidicut – and deployed in a pair of key scenes, the first in the hovel, the other on the road to Dover. The effect is incantatory and haunting: 'Five fiends have been in Poor Tom at once, as of lust Obidicut, Hobbididence prince of dumbness, Mahu of stealing, Modo of murder, Flibbertigibbet of mocking and mowing, who since possesses chambermaids and waiting-women' (15.56–60). This last allusion to the devilish spirit 'who *since* possesses chambermaids' is an especially nice touch, connecting through these timeless and malevolent spirits the ancient Britain in which the play is set to the present-day Jacobean world, where the same devils continue their destructive ways.

King Lear is often considered anomalous among Shakespeare's great tragedies because it lacks a supernatural element, like the ghosts of Caesar and Old Hamlet in *Julius Caesar* and *Hamlet*, the magic in the web of Desdemona's handkerchief in *Othello*, or the Weird Sisters in *Macbeth*. Yet demonic possession, though only feigned by Edgar, serves a similar function in *King Lear*. Invocations of the 'devil' and the 'fiend', sliding uneasily between the literal and figurative, appear throughout the play ('fiend' alone recurs twenty-one times). When, for example, Albany tells Goneril, 'See thyself, devil. / Proper deformity shows not in the fiend / So horrid as in woman' (16.58–60), it feels more than metaphorical. Similarly, as Lear leaves the heartless Goneril for the equally cruel Regan, he sees 'Darkness and devils!' (4.243). In Lear's increasingly maddened and diseased imagination, women and their sexual organs are reimagined as a site of the demonic, a kind of hell that fills him with revulsion:

> But to the girdle do the gods inherit;
> Beneath is all the fiend's. There's hell, there's darkness,
> There's the sulphury pit, burning, scalding,
> Stench, consummation. Fie, fie, fie; pah; pah!
> (20.121–4)

Tellingly, most of the echoes of Harsnett are divided between the speeches of Lear and Edgar, and most of these are concentrated in that stretch of Act 3 where the two cross paths, most notably in the so-called 'mock trial', a six-hundred-word scene saturated with the language of possession. The scene does little to advance the plot and can easily be cut in performance; in a play that is already grim it takes us to an especially disturbing place. Edgar, as Poor Tom, sets the tone when he cries out, 'Frateretto calls me, and tells me Nero is an angler in the lake of darkness,' and we hear Lear for the first time truly experiencing hellish visions when he replies in words that make him sound genuinely possessed: 'A king, a king! To have a thousand / With red burning spits come hissing in upon them!' (13.11–12).

What follows is an extraordinary exchange, one deeply coloured by Harsnett's language, as the mad and now seemingly possessed Lear interrogates what he imagines to be his cruel daughters Goneril and Regan. In its shifts in and out of lucidity, from prose to blank verse to snatches of song, the scene captures the ways in which sanity yields to overpowering and terrifying visions. And in collapsing the distance between the possessed and the truly mad, it is unlike anything else Shakespeare would ever write – closer to Samuel Beckett than to Jacobean drama, and worth quoting at length:

Edgar. The foul fiend bites my back.

Fool. He's mad, that trusts in the tameness of a wolf, a horse's health, a boy's love, or a whore's oath.

Lear. It shall be done, I will arraign them straight.
Come, sit thou here, most learned justicer.
Thou sapient sir, sit here. – No, you she-foxes –

Edgar. Look where he stands and glares. Want'st thou eyes, at troll-madam?
Come o'er the burn Bessy to me.

Fool. Her boat hath a leak,
And she must not speak,
Why she dares not come over to thee.

Edgar. The foul fiend haunts Poor Tom in the voice of a nightingale. Hoppedance cries in Tom's belly for two white herring. Croak not, black angel: I have no food for thee.

Kent. How do you, sir? Stand you not so amazed.
Will you lie down and rest upon the cushions?

Lear. I'll see their trial first.
(13.13–31)

The highly experimental passage, which continues in this vein for another forty lines, may have proved too much for playgoers and perhaps even Shakespeare's fellow players, for by the time the play was republished in the 1623 folio it was cut.

In the scenes that follow, in a play that otherwise lacks the supernatural, Lear experiences something like the torments of hell, climaxing in the scene in which he is reunited at last with Cordelia, and thinks her a heavenly spirit:

> You do me wrong to take me out o'th' grave,
> Thou art a soul in bliss, but I am bound
> Upon a wheel of fire, that mine own tears
> Do scald like molten lead.
> (21.43–6)

It is hard not to hear the echoes of Harsnett's devil in hell crying out, 'Oh, oh, oh, I burn, I burn, I scald, I broil, I am tormented.' Lear may feel that he is in hell, but we know that he is not possessed, only made mad, however much the two experiences seem to converge in the course of the play. His experience recalls that of Richard Mainy, one of those subjected to brutal exorcism rites at Denham: 'When they had made me in effect mad, no marvel though I spake and fared like a mad man.' Harsnett had mocked those who act 'so cunningly' and 'feign the passions and agonies of the devil, that the whole company of spectators shall by his false illusions be brought into such commiseration, and compassion, as they shall all weep, cry, and exclaim, as loud as the counterfeit devil'. His description anticipates Lear's encounter with Poor Tom, by which point Lear has begun at last to feel compassion for the suffering of his subjects and confesses,

I have ta'en
Too little care of this. Take physic, pomp,
Expose thyself to feel what wretches feel.
(11.29–31)

Surely the most unbearable scene to watch in this agonising play is the one in which Cornwall gouges out Gloucester's eyes. Here, too, the influence of Harsnett's book, whose pages are rife with violence and casual cruelty, is felt. Shakespeare is explicit about how the scene is to be staged: Cornwall, before setting his boot in Gloucester's eyes, first orders his attendants to 'bind fast his corky arms' and then 'to this chair bind him' (14.26, 31). Harsnett had written that one of the central techniques of the exorcists was to bind their subject in a 'holy chair'. The binding of Anne Smith, for example, was especially cruel: 'They did bind her so fast . . . in a chair, as they almost lamed her arms, and so bruised all the parts of her body with holding, tying, and turmoiling of her.' Cornwall commands his servants to bind Gloucester, then repeats the order, 'Bind him, I say,' and Regan urges them to do so even more violently: 'Hard, hard' (14.29). Gloucester's terror and confusion as he is being bound to the chair – 'What means your graces? Good my friends consider / You are my guests. Do me no foul play, friends' (14.27–8) – recalls the account of one of the maids in the *Declaration*, Fidd Williams, who was placed in a chair before 'they began to bind her with towels, whereat she greatly marvelled, and was therewith cast into a great fear, as not knowing what they meant to do to her'. Gloucester's arms are described as 'corky', an unusual adjective, one that had only recently entered the language; it's the only time Shakespeare uses the word. Predictably, one of the first places it had appeared in print was in the *Declaration*, where Harsnett writes of teaching 'an old corky woman to writhe, tumble, curvet, and fetch her morris gambols'.

One of the great ironies of Shakespeare's play is that the blind and suicidal Gloucester is cured of his despair by Edgar, who manages to persuade him that it was indeed a 'fiend' that led him to the cliff at Dover, from which Gloucester believes he has hurled himself and yet providentially survived the fall. Edgar describes to his sightless father in great detail what the fiend that led him looked like:

> methoughts his eyes
> Were two full moons. A had a thousand noses,
> Horns whelked and waved like the enridged sea,
> It was some fiend. Therefore, thou happy father,
> Think that the clearest gods, who made their honours
> Of men's impossibilities, have preserved thee.
> (20.69–74)

What Edgar does to his father is not an exorcism, though it has a similar result. Gloucester admits that he was mistaken in his companion: 'That thing you speak of, / I took it for a man. Often would it say / "The fiend, the fiend"' (20.77–9). No longer suicidal, Gloucester agrees to 'bear / Affliction till it do cry out itself / "Enough, enough" and die' (20.75–7). The scene is a puzzle: it would have been much more plausible for Edgar to reveal himself to his father on the road to Dover, but the play's cruel logic won't allow it.

Shakespeare's engagement with Harsnett's book deepens over the course of *King Lear*. The abuse of authority, so transparent in page after page of the *Declaration*, is a kind of nightmare that Lear at last comes to recognise. For Lear – and for playgoers – at the play's end, authority is shown to be arbitrary, its 'great image' a beggar running from a barking dog (20.149–53). In what is arguably the most explicit piece of social criticism in all of his work, Shakespeare has Lear conclude that violence, deception and hypocrisy in the kingdom are endemic:

> Thou rascal beadle, hold thy bloody hand.
> Why dost thou lash that whore? Strip thine own back.
> Thy blood as hotly lusts to use her in that kind
> For which thou whip'st her. The usurer hangs the cozener.
> Through tattered robes small vices do appear;
> Robes and furred gowns hide all.
> (20.154–9)

There is the evil that stems from the abuse of authority and there is another kind that cannot be so easily explained by self-interest and the human propensity for cruelty. In *King Lear*, Shakespeare wrestles with the nature of this kind of evil as well, something that Harsnett, in a book about the demonic, takes as a given but never confronts. Historical events would soon ensure that this question would take on even greater relevance as Shakespeare was finishing *King Lear* that winter. And he wasn't done with Harsnett quite yet, or with questions of possession, bewitching or where evil originates.

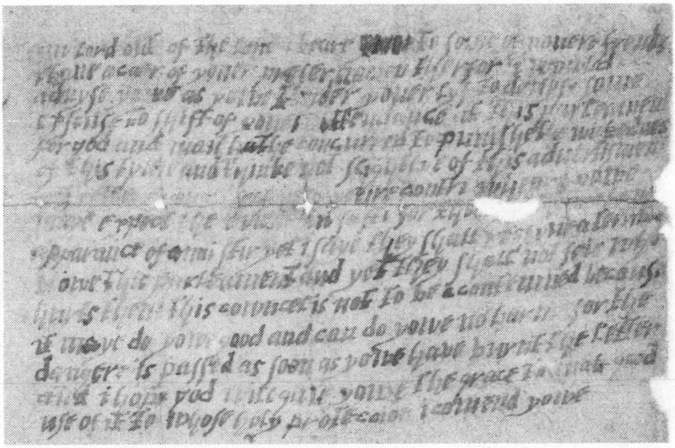

The Monteagle Letter (1605)

5 : *The Letter*

By the end of October 1605 and the arrival of cooler weather, plague deaths had dropped to a level where England's nobility and gentry could safely return to town and the oft-delayed Parliament at last convene. London's acting companies must have expected the ban on playing announced earlier that month to be lifted any day, enabling them to capitalise on the increased traffic. By now, Shakespeare was likely well past the opening scenes of *King Lear*, including the one in which Gloucester enters, sees Edmund hurriedly putting away a letter and demands that it be handed over. When Edmund reluctantly does so, Gloucester reads it aloud:

'This policy of age makes the world bitter to the best of our times, keeps our fortunes from us till our oldness cannot relish them. I begin to find an idle and fond bondage in the oppression of aged tyranny, who sways not as it hath power but as it is suffered. Come to me, that of this I may

speak more. If our father would sleep till I waked him, you should enjoy half his revenue for ever, and live the beloved of your brother,
Edgar.'
(2.45–52)

Gloucester mulls over its veiled message, rereading and repeating to himself key phrases – 'Slept till I waked him', 'you should enjoy half his revenue' – before demanding of Edmund, 'When came this to you, who brought it?' (2.54–7). Edmund, having shrewdly allowed Gloucester to decipher the letter for himself, does his best to keep its source a mystery: 'It was not brought me, my lord, there's the cunning of it. I found it thrown in at the casement of my closet' (2.58–68). Convinced that the letter has brought to light a plot to kill him, Gloucester demands to know where its instigator may be found, at which point Edmund urges him to proceed cautiously: 'I do not well know, my lord. If it shall please you to suspend your indignation against my brother, till you can derive from him better testimony of this intent . . . If your honour judge it meet, I will place you where you shall hear us confer of this.' Gloucester likes the plan and encourages Edmund to 'Find out this villain' (2. 78–107). This use of a forged, opaque letter is found nowhere in his sources and was something Shakespeare had never tried before.

Not long after Shakespeare wrote this scene, a similar one played out in the evening of 26 October at Whitehall, where members of the Privy Council were conducting state business while the king was off hunting at Royston. They were interrupted by the arrival of Lord Monteagle, who had come at this late hour from his house a mile or so away in Shoreditch. Monteagle, who was about to be seated among England's peers at the upcoming Parliament, was well known to them. Four years earlier he had been among the participants in the Earl of Essex's ill-fated rising. Salisbury would no doubt have remembered their exchanges at that time, when Monteagle had written to him from the Tower of London begging for mercy. His life was spared, though he was fined. Monteagle's rebelliousness hadn't ended there, for he was soon involved in a Spanish plot against Queen Elizabeth in the waning months of her reign, but he again escaped punishment. With the coming of the new monarch, Monteagle, by now in his late twenties, professed to be 'done with all former plots'. He publicly renounced his Catholicism and even served as one of the English commissioners responsible for meeting with their Scottish counterparts to remove the remaining obstacles to Union. Yet Salisbury and his fellow councillors may have heard rumours that Monteagle was still 'exhorting the Jesuits to arm against the king'. They must have wondered which Monteagle had come knocking.

Monteagle had brought a letter that he thought the councillors should know about. The letter read as follows:

My lord, out of the love I bear to some of your friends, I have a care of your preservation. Therefore I would advise you, as you tender your life, to devise some excuse to shift your attendance at this Parliament. For God and man hath concurred to punish the wickedness of this time, and think not slightly of this advertisement, but retire yourself into your country, where you may expect the event in safety. For though there be no appearance of any stir, yet I say they shall receive a terrible blow this Parliament and yet they shall not see who hurts them. This counsel is not to be contemned because it may do you good and can do you no harm for the danger is passed as soon as you have burnt the letter. And I hope God will give you the grace to make good use of it to whose holy protection I commend you.

Like Edmund's letter, its origins were cloaked in mystery. When asked how it fell into his hands, Monteagle told them how at dusk earlier that day a 'reasonable tall' stranger had stopped one of his footmen, handed him the letter, charged him to deliver it to his master, then disappeared. 'Perplexed what construction to make of it,' and deciding that it was best to ignore the warning to burn the letter, Monteagle, though it was late and dark, thought it wise to rush over immediately to Whitehall and turn it over to the privy councillors.

Salisbury read the letter then handed it to the Earl of Suffolk. The two agreed that it was similar to what they had heard from French sources of recusant plans to stir up rebellion. They then shared it with the Earls of Worcester, Nottingham and Northampton. Monteagle was thanked for bringing to their attention 'a matter of such a nature, whatever the consequences might prove'. For his part, to clear himself from any suspicion in a manner that recalls Edmund's protestations, Monteagle said 'that whatsoever the event hereof might prove, it should not be imputed to him', and that he handed over the letter as a 'demonstration of his ready devotion'.

Five days later, on 31 October, James returned to London. Salisbury didn't show him the letter until the following afternoon. Fresh from his recent exposure of the chicanery of Anne Gunter and Richard Haydock, James would have found in the mysterious letter yet another opportunity to demonstrate his detective skills. In an account published a month later that James reprinted in his collected *Works*, he recalls how he 'read the letter' and 'after a little pause' reread it, pausing at two key lines: 'for the danger is past as soon as you have burnt the letter', and 'they should receive a terrible blow at this Parliament and you should not see who hurt them'. These were all the clues he needed, for James intuited – even though it meant construing the meaning 'against all ordinary sense of construction of grammar' – that there 'should be some sudden danger by blowing up of powder, for no other insurrection, rebellion, or whatsoever other private or desperate attempt could be committed or attempted in time of Parliament, and the authors thereof unseen, except only it were by a blowing up of powder'.

Salisbury made sure that credit for this interpretation of the cryptic letter, and therefore for the discovery of the conspiracy, belonged to the king alone. We know, though, from a letter he wrote not long after this, that he and Suffolk had figured things out for themselves pretty quickly: 'we both conceived', he wrote, that the 'blow' could 'not be more proper than the time of Parliament, nor by any another way like to be attempted than with powder, when the king was sitting in that assembly'. And Suffolk, familiar with the layout of the building, guessed that the attack was likely to come from 'a great vault under the said chamber, which was never used for any thing but for some wood or coal'.

The next day it was determined, at the king's behest, to search the Parliament houses, 'both above and below'. But not quite yet. Delaying until the day before Parliament convened would stay 'idle rumours' while at the same time allowing the plotters to expose themselves, 'the nearer things were in readiness'. At last, on 4 November, a search was made of the 'great vault' underneath Parliament. They found it filled with 'piles of billets and faggots heaped up'. When they asked who had rented the property, they were told it was Thomas Percy. Percy was a Gentleman Pensioner, that is, part of the royal bodyguard, placed in that office by his cousin, the powerful and Catholic privy councillor the Earl of Northumberland. Percy had even served as a trusted and secret messenger between the earl and King James before Queen Elizabeth's death, when Northumberland was seeking assurances from the Scottish king that he would be more tolerant to Catholics than Elizabeth had been. The mention of Percy's name further roused suspicions: Why would a member of the king's bodyguard rent a vault beneath Parliament?

The search party decided at this point to investigate no further and reported back to the king and councillors about the piles of wood and the 'very tall and desperate fellow' they had encountered there. When told this, James ordered that the search be resumed late that night. They returned to the vault and found 'Thomas Percy's alleged man standing without the doors', booted and spurred. He was immediately apprehended and the vault examined once again. During this painstaking search 'some of the billets and coals' were overturned, underneath which barrels of gunpowder were spotted. Further searching led to the discovery of thirty-six barrels in all. Percy's man was then frisked and 'three matches and all other instruments fit for blowing up the powder' were found on him. Had the search party failed in its mission that night, the damage done the following day when Parliament was in session would have been catastrophic, almost unimaginable:

the entire leadership of England, from King James, Queen Anne and Princes Henry and Charles, to the nobility and political representatives and heads of the Church gathered there from every corner of the land would have been wiped out in a single blow.

Percy's man was hauled off to Whitehall to be interrogated in the early hours of 5 November. He told the authorities that his name was John Johnson and that he was a Yorkshireman from Netherdale, and a Catholic. His interrogators reported that he appeared to them 'so constant and settled upon his grounds as we all thought we had found some new Mutius Scaevola born in England' – recalling here the famous Roman assassin who, when threatened with torture, put his hand in the fire and held it there until the flames consumed it. Johnson refused to reveal the names of his confederates, other than Percy, though he freely admitted that 'if he had not been apprehended this last night, he had blown up the upper house, when the king, lords, bishops and other had been there'. When asked who would have ruled after the death of King James, he said that 'Percy never entered into that consultation' and that 'the people of themselves should decide'. He did provide a motive: 'When this act had been done they meant to have satisfied the Catholics that it was done for restitution of religion.' He hoped that others would have supported their action on political grounds, for it was also 'done to prevent the Union that was sought to be published at this parliament'. And Johnson brazenly told the Scottish courtiers gathered in the king's bedchamber where he was being interrogated that he hoped the explosion would 'have blown them back again into Scotland'.

The government was unsure how deep the conspiracy ran and impatient to discover who was behind it. King James personally drew up a detailed list of questions he wanted put to Johnson (and added, ominously, 'If he will not confess, the gentler tortures are to be first used unto him, *et sic per gradus ad ima tenditur*' – that is, 'and step by step until the ultimate is reached'). A manhunt was set in motion to locate the only other named suspect, Thomas Percy, and all English ports were closed. The Venetian ambassador reported home that a hundred men had been despatched to prevent Percy from fleeing to the Continent. It was vital to learn whether Percy was trying to leave the country or on his way to join up with other conspirators in a co-ordinated rebellion. A royal proclamation was rushed into print – a 'Wanted' poster – notifying one and all 'to make all diligent search for the said Percy, and him to apprehend by all possible means, especially to keep him alive, to the end the rest of the conspirators may be discovered' (shades here of how, in the manhunt for Edgar in *King Lear*, 'his picture' is sent 'far and near, that all the kingdom may have note of him' [6.81–3]). Percy, 'privy to one of the most horrible treasons that ever was contrived', is described as 'a tall man, with a great broad beard, a good face, the color of his beard and head mingled with white hairs, but the head more white than the beard, he stoopeth somewhat in the shoulders, well-colored in the face, long footed, small legged'.

As they awoke on the morning of 5 November to news of the thwarted plot, Londoners were in a state of alarm. The chronicler Edmund Howes recalled that 'the Privy Council, not knowing how far this treason might extend, nor what degrees of persons were in this conspiracy, yet well perceived to be commenced, and practised by some discontented Papists, gave order to the Lord Mayor of London and the City of Westminster to set a civil watch at their gates'. Bonfires were lit that evening 'in the principal streets', by order of the Lord Mayor, serving a double purpose: signifying relief at being spared, while at the same time keeping the jittery city lit at night, as it had been when threatened with invasion in the past. John Chamberlain, one of the great letter-writers of the age and an invaluable source, wrote that there was 'great ringing and as great store of bonfires as ever I think was seen'.

Though devastation had been prevented on 5 November it wasn't clear that bloodletting could now be averted. Nicolo Molino, the Venetian ambassador, vividly describes the fear that gripped London: 'the city is in great uncertainty; Catholics fear heretics, and vice versa; both are armed. Foreigners live in terror of their houses being sacked by the mob that is convinced that some, if not all, foreign princes are at the bottom of the plot.' As 'a precaution against a tumult', trained bands were posted on the city's streets. 'All', as another observer put it, 'was in a buzz.' Molino was grateful that the authorities had 'thought it advisable to quiet the popular feeling by issuing a proclamation, in which they declare that no foreign sovereign had any part in the conspiracy. God grant this be sufficient, but as it is everyone has his own share of alarm.' Salisbury was warned that the people 'do so murmur and exclaim against the Spaniards' that precautions needed to be taken. The Lord Lieutenant of the Tower, preparing for as yet unknown threats, reported to the council his military preparedness: 'because I hear all the gates of London are kept, I have brought all the warders into the Tower and set a watch at the postern, and the gate of S. Katherine's, and at the landing stage. The night-watches are the severest in any fort in Christendom.'

No one as yet knew how deep the conspiracy ran. Rumours circulated that the attack on Parliament was part of an orchestrated international campaign of murder and anarchy. According to Howes, 'many factious persons' were 'reporting that against the aforementioned Tuesday, the French king and the King of Denmark should have been murdered, and that the Duke of Saxony . . . should be offered like violence'. London's foreign embassies took their own measures to calm the anger in the streets. The Spanish ambassador lit celebratory bonfires and 'threw money amongst the people', and 'the like gladness was showed by the ambassador of the Archduke, and by those of the French and Dutch Church'. The latter were Protestant Huguenots; having been subject to anti-alien violence in the past in London, discretion was clearly called for. One can only wonder what the mood was like on the corner of Silver Street and Muggle Street, where Shakespeare lodged in a French Huguenot household.

Edmund Howes recalled how in the immediate aftermath the 'common people muttered and imagined many things, and nobles knew not what to say nor whom to clear or suspect, and for certain days a general jealousy possessed them all'. What they muttered or imagined, and the nature of this collective atmosphere of 'general jealousy', crucial to understanding the national mood, is largely lost to us. And muttering too loudly could be dangerous, as a man named Beard, who lived on Fetter Lane, learned that day. He asked a servant to a shoemaker in Holborn, who had come to measure him for a new pair of boots, about the 'watching and warding' going on in London's streets, then commented that 'it had been brave sport if it had gone forward'. And he didn't say this 'in any laughing or jesting manner'. Beard quickly caught himself and 'spoke against the [plot] very much', but it was too late and he was reported. Even as there were those who spoke their minds a little too freely that day, there were others eager to ingratiate themselves with the authorities by assisting in the hunt for potential conspirators or their supporters. We know about Beard's case because Francis Bacon, undertaking a bit of freelance investigating, had gone to the Inns of Court to learn what he could that might interest the Privy Council.

The problem at this moment was that, in Molino's words, 'as yet it is very difficult to arrive at the truth'. A plot masterminded by a disgruntled court servant (and his man, Johnson) made no sense. There had to be someone ambitious or powerful behind it, as yet unknown: 'People say that this plot must have its roots high up,' Molino adds, 'for it is not to be supposed that Percy, if guilty, embarked on this affair alone and without an object; for it was not a question of simply killing the king, but his sons and all the nobility as well . . . The first suspicion then falls on the disaffected nobility, among the chief is the Earl of Northumberland.' The government had already been keeping a close eye on prominent Catholics and potential troublemakers, and on 5 November began interrogating some of them. A day after the discovery of the Gunpowder Plot, Salisbury already had in hand a list of suspects, all disaffected Catholic gentry. The list turned out to be surprisingly accurate, especially since none of these men, as yet, had been implicated: 'There is pregnant suspicion to be had of . . . Robert Catesby, Ambrose Rookwood, one Keyes, Thomas Winter, John Wright and Christopher Wright and some suspicion of one Grant.' Most of them had had brushes with the authorities in the past and several had been locked up, as a precautionary measure, in the politically fraught days following the death of Queen Elizabeth, before James's peaceful succession was assured. That list was presumably cross-checked against others, including the list of those who had been spied dining together a month earlier at the Irish Boy on the Strand, including Robert Catesby, Thomas Winter, Lord Mordaunt, Francis Tresham and the Earl of Northumberland's brother, Sir Jocelyn Percy. Ben Jonson, a known recusant, had been spotted dining with this group. Jonson was probably unaware that he had been seen in their company or even that some of them were now suspects in the plot. But in the close-knit recusant community, everyone risked guilt by association. So it must have been unnerving for Jonson to receive – a day after a list of suspects sent by the Lord Chief Justice, Sir John Popham, arrived on Salisbury's desk – a warrant from the Privy Council instructing him to use his Catholic contacts to find an unnamed priest and escort him to them. Quite possibly, the priest was needed to persuade John Johnson that it was both necessary and permissible for him to reveal the names of his co-conspirators.

Ben Jonson seems to have done as he was told, or at least said that he did, explaining in a fawning letter on 8 November that he had immediately approached Molino's chaplain to assist him – for both agreed that 'no man of conscience or any indifferent love to his country would deny to do it'. But he failed in his efforts – if in fact he tried at all – to find the priest, who, Jonson assumed, must have fled town. Was Jonson, who at this very moment was writing a court masque, secretly working for the government, reluctantly or in exchange for patronage? Even if he were, was he nonetheless a confidant of the Gunpowder conspirators? Four centuries later, it is impossible to know. But however deeply he was implicated, and whichever side he might have been playing against the other, how terrified he must have been – and others like him – to have been caught up in this expanding manhunt for those who had tried to destroy the state. A week later Molino reported that 'not a day passes but what some one is arrested or some baron confined to his own house, or placed in the custody of others. This is merely a precautionary measure, because they are leading Catholics, and they arrest them till full light can be thrown on the whole affair.' Though he put on a good public face, King James himself was shaken by this threat to his life. Molino reported back to Venice that his sources tell him that the 'king is in terror; he does not appear nor does he take his meals in public as usual. He lives in the innermost rooms, with only Scots about him.'

A massive explosion caused by thirty-six barrels of gunpowder would have carried considerably further than the House of Lords, under which the barrels had been positioned. King James privately told Molino that 'had the scheme been carried out thirty thousand persons would have perished at a stroke, the city would have been sacked, and the rich would have suffered more than the poor; in short, the world would have seen a spectacle so terrible and terrifying that its like has never been heard of'. While thirty thousand dead sounds exaggerated, contemporaries with knowledge of explosives agreed that the devastation would have been massive and widespread. The repositories of English law and history, along with London's greatest architectural landmarks – 'the Hall of Judgement, the Court of Records, the Collegiate Church, the City of Westminster, yea, Whitehall' – would also have been casualties of the explosion and ensuing flames.

In the absence of any physical damage, this terrible outcome had to be imagined. Other than that ambiguous and unsigned letter, as yet the only concrete proof of the intended blow was the unexploded barrels of gunpowder and the mysterious servant prepared to detonate them. Nor was there any knowledge of who was ultimately behind it. Yet a compelling narrative had to be circulated quickly to shape popular perception before competing versions took hold. The government immediately turned its energies to crafting a convincing story, one that dwelled less on the unknown perpetrators or their motives and more on the sheer evil and destructiveness of the intended plot. But in encouraging the nation to reflect upon the reach of the destructiveness of the Gunpowder Plot, extending to the king himself, the authorities were caught in a bind. In 1351 statutes had been established in England which were still in force, declaring it treason to 'compass or imagine the death of the king' (and in the coming months, when he confronted the Gunpowder plotters, Attorney General Sir Edward Coke recalled this statute, reminding them that it 'is treason to imagine or intend the death of the king, queen or prince'). If this were the law, then the government was now in the awkward position of urging the nation to engage in just such an act – one of the things that made it so nervous about those histories and tragedies in London's public theatres that invited playgoers to imagine such outcomes.

On the Sunday following the failed attack, Bishop William Barlow stood in the pulpit at Paul's Cross before a large outdoor crowd of anxious citizens who until now had had to subsist on gossip and rumour, as reports, sometimes wild ones, circulated in the city. What was needed was one powerful and unifying message. Barlow was the right man to deliver it, having proved himself in similar challenging circumstances from this very pulpit in the tumultuous aftermath of the Earl of Essex's abortive uprising just a few years earlier. He began his sermon by reminding his fellow Londoners that the destruction would not have stopped with the deaths of so many leaders and citizens in the initial explosion. Terrible aftershocks would have shredded the fabric of the nation and in the ensuing chaos the social contract itself would have disintegrated. It would only have been a matter of time before a defenceless England was conquered and laid waste. Those killed in the initial conflagration, Barlow suggested, would have been the lucky ones: 'what rapes, what rapines, what riflings, what slaughters had ensued? A thing more miserable to the survivors than to them which were slain?' The time would have been ripe for 'a foreigner to invade' or a 'domestical usurper to intrude'. After conjuring this apocalyptic vision, Barlow read to the crowd the letter that Monteagle had delivered to the Privy Council a fortnight earlier, which had providentially delivered in turn the king and kingdom. It's understandable why the authorities felt that the incriminating letter had to be shared with the public: much had irrevocably changed in England the previous week, yet nothing visibly.

The government didn't feel that it could wait five days before getting out its version of what might have happened. The day before Barlow preached to the throng gathered at Paul's Cross, King James himself addressed the nation's political and religious leaders about 'this great and horrible attempt, whereof the like was never either heard or read', in the very building where they had all come so close to dying. It was more sermon than anything else, with James at the outset of his speech comparing recent events to nothing less than the Apocalypse. While reminding them that assassination threats had been the recurring story of his life, James also acknowledged that this most recent plot had threatened 'a destruction prepared not for me alone, but for you all that are here present, and wherein no rank, age nor sex should have been spared'. The king's speech contained a drumbeat of key words, singly and in pairs, that offered a much-needed working vocabulary for a plot and a sense of evil the enormity of which contemporaries were struggling to put into words: 'cruel and unmerciful', 'horrible and fearful', 'raging and merciless'. While acknowledging that he had 'spoken more like a divine' than a king, James could not resist circling back to his Union agenda, reminding those gathered that day that if not for the delivery of the Articles of Union, 'which was thought most convenient to be done in my presence', his appearance in Parliament on 5 November 'had not otherwise been requisite'. Having risked life and limb in support of the Union of England and Scotland, James wanted Parliament to ratify it when they reconvened on 21 January.

It is a testament to the brilliance of the government's story that its version of what happened remains largely intact four hundred years later. To reinforce this message, James's speech to Parliament was hurried into print that month. It was widely read and reprinted with fresh material added to it, and was known simply as 'The King's Book'. In the nineteenth century the government's account of what happened was further codified in 'The Gunpowder Plot Book', a compilation of surviving primary documents of which the crown jewel is the Monteagle letter. Further cementing this providentialist narrative, in January 1606 a new section was added to the Prayer Book, a thanksgiving service condemning 'Popish treachery' and commemorating for all time how the English nation was spared that day.

Counter-narratives, dismissive of this selective official account, argue that a great deal of evidence was suppressed or destroyed, and maintain that these gaps in the record indicate that the authorities knew about the plot well before 5 November but allowed it to go forward in order to advance the ends of the state, especially the suppression of England's Catholics. In an extreme version of this view, the plot is thought to have been the brain-child of a Catholic-hating Salisbury, the plotters his manipulated and doomed puppets, who until the moment of their execution believed that they would be spared. But such claims have never gained much traction, in large part because the Jacobean regime, which had a near monopoly on evidence, told its version of the story so effectively by ignoring *why* and emphasising instead *what might have been*. It is easy to forget that what sets the Gunpowder Plot apart from subsequent infamous terrorist plots (especially those also significant enough to be remembered by their date) is that in this case *nothing happened*. Which meant that, like one of those great Jacobean dramas, its impact and aftermath didn't depend on actual violence but rather on making people imagine an unforgettable tragedy, the kind that feels as real as *Lear* or *Macbeth*. The catharsis would have to await the capture, torture and spectacular public execution of those responsible.

England's dramatists, forbidden from writing about current events except obliquely, must have looked on in grudging admiration. The shrewdest of them must also have recognised that even if nothing had been physically destroyed, something had inescapably changed in their world. The plot was itself decisive evidence that things had been bubbling up – pressures, resentments, fantasies – that even a government with a network of spies had missed. It was not an intelligence lapse so much as a failure of imagination, an inability to grasp what, thirty months into James's reign, had for some of his subjects become intolerable. And despite the lip-service paid to the work of the devil, it was also a failure to imagine the possibility that anyone, possessed or not, was evil enough to commit such an indiscriminate atrocity. In the ensuing year it would fall to England's writers to probe more deeply and search for what was ultimately at stake in this unfolding story.

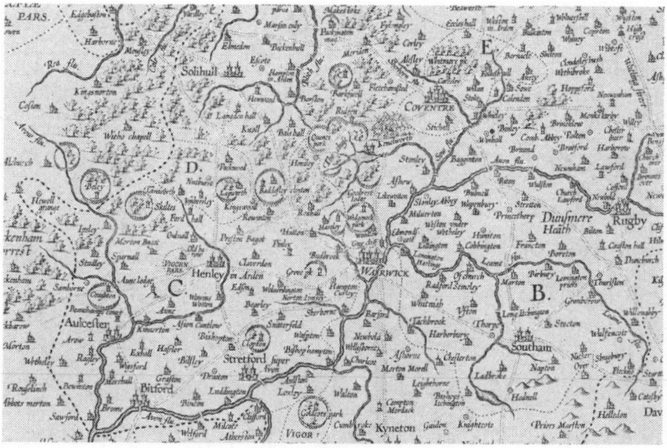

Detail from Map of Warwickshire, by John Speed (*c.*1610)

6 : *Massing Relics*

A report reached court the day after the Gunpowder Plot was discovered, before news of that near disaster had reached much of the country, describing the theft of ten horses from a stable in Warwick in the early hours of 6 November. Though eighty miles away, the seemingly unrelated incident caught the attention of the authorities, for these were no ordinary horses, such as the geldings usually employed for travel on England's roads, but rather war horses each 'worth some threescore pound'. The location of the theft was also troubling. Thirteen miles away in Coombe Abbey, King James and Queen Anne's nine-year-old daughter, Princess Elizabeth, was being raised in the household of Lord Harington (for royal children did not live with their parents). The man in charge of the Warwick stables, Mr Benock, aware of the potential threat, wrote immediately to Harington, informing him that 'this night all my great horses are taken out of my stable' and that 'it cannot be but some great rebellion is at hand'.

Benock had recognised one of the horse-thieves, a gentleman named John Grant, known locally as a recusant, and described the others as 'Papists' as well. Grant lived just four miles away at his manor in Norbrook, halfway to Stratford-upon-Avon.

Shakespeare would have known Grant; their families had done business together. Grant was one of the best educated men as well as one of the most defiant recusants in the community, and countryfolk alert to the comings and goings of strangers might well have spotted some of the priests, travelling on foot or by horse, who held Mass at Norbrook almost every week. Grant too had been caught up in the Earl of Essex's failed rising four years earlier. It didn't take long for the authorities to track him and his companions to Norbrook after the break-in at Warwick. Though they had already fled, the manor was searched and then 'beset with a great watch and guarded'. Grant's servants told the authorities that sixty or so riders had stopped there at three in the morning in order to 'refresh themselves with drink and fire' before arming themselves with 'swords and daggers, pistols and petronels'. The servants reported that the rebels, who left in haste, had also taken with them fifty muskets and calivers – infantry weapons. These arms, along with barrels of gunpowder and suits of armour, had been hidden there the previous midsummer. The arms depot for the Midlands rising, and perhaps the base of operations for the planned abduction of Princess Elizabeth, had been located just a few miles north of Stratford-upon-Avon.

Lord Harington forwarded Benock's letter to court that same morning and asked for Salisbury's 'opinion and the king's pleasure touching the king's daughter'. But when fresh reports of incidents in the area reached him he had second thoughts. The possibility that Princess Elizabeth might be kidnapped or killed on his poorly defended estate drove him to seize the initiative, and he quickly removed her to the safety of nearby Coventry and wrote again to the council in London. A messenger riding posthaste and changing horses every two hours could cover the eighty miles to London in under eight hours, though Harington's letters may have been slowed by muddy roads caused by recent heavy rains. What, if anything, the theft of war horses had to do with the discovery of the Gunpowder Plot a day earlier in London remained unclear.

The following day, 7 November, as messengers raced across the English countryside and frantic reports reached court linking events in Warwickshire to the foiled plot in London, the government hastily drafted a royal proclamation accusing Percy and unnamed confederates of stealing the war horses in Warwick, thereby 'seeking to raise some rebellion in our realm'. It would have been Shakespeare's first inkling of how close he was to both epicentres of what was now emerging as a two-pronged attack, beginning with the planned explosion in London and continuing with a Catholic uprising centred near his home in Warwickshire. The king and Privy Council, convinced that a revolt was underway in the Midlands, decided to send an army to crush it. According to Oswald Tesimond, a Jesuit who subsequently joined the rebels, the number of those who planned to join the insurrection 'was soon said to be more than a thousand. Indeed, it was feared that many more might join them. For this reason the king gave order to enlist soldiers.' The army was to be led by the Earl of Devonshire, the Elizabethan war hero who in 1603 had brutally subdued the Irish uprising, ending the Nine Years

War and defeating the Earl of Tyrone, the Irish leader who had humiliated the Earl of Essex.

It was surely wishful thinking on the part of Tesimond, yet he was confident that if the rebels 'had succeeded at any time in putting the sheriff of Warwick to rout, it is believed certain that many others would have joined the conspirators. These would have had ample time to organise themselves at their leisure before the royal forces arrived on the scene.' The authorities in London feared as much. According to the Venetian ambassador, the Earl of Devonshire 'was soon at the head of one thousand two hundred gentlemen, partly English, partly Scottish'. These gentlemen volunteers would lead a larger force of conscripts, as England had no standing army. The number seems exaggerated but the estimate speaks to an immediate and widespread enthusiasm to enlist. Salisbury's report to England's ambassadors stationed abroad provides a few more details about the hastily ordered campaign: 'it is also fit that some martial men should presently repair' to 'where the Robin Hoods are assembled, to encourage the good and to terrify the bad. In which service the Earl of Devonshire is used, and commission going forth for him as general, although I am easily persuaded, that this faggot will be burnt to ashes before he shall be twenty miles on his way.' In joking about the Midlands rebels as 'Robin Hoods', Salisbury may be half-remembering the description in *As You Like It* of a ragged band of romantic outlaws in the Forest of Arden, who 'live like the old Robin Hood of England' (1.1.111–12).

The politics of this rapidly assembled force, the first Anglo-Scots military expedition in Britain since Malcolm relied on English troops to defeat Macbeth, seems to have been fraught, and its composition altered almost immediately in response to King James's continued fear for his personal safety: it 'was much noticed that all the Scots who had offered to follow the Earl presently withdrew' after the 'king had let it be known that he wished to have the Scots about his person'. Shakespeare had read and heard enough about military campaigns to know what armies did on the march. What his thoughts were as he contemplated an armed force riding through the Midlands can only be imagined. Few in England would have known the roads, towns and terrain as well as he, both as a strolling player and a native of Warwickshire.

The rumours, military preparations and sheer confusion in London on 6 and 7 November were mirrored in many parts of England, nowhere more so than in the towns around Stratford-upon-Avon. Old Sir Fulke Greville – father of the poet of the same name – was deputy lieutenant of Warwickshire and one of only a handful of experienced men in the area not off in London for the opening of Parliament. He quickly secured 'the munition and armour of all gentlemen about him, either absent from their houses or in doubtful guard', actions that would earn the praise of the king himself. On the very day of the Warwick break-in Greville was already interrogating servants who had either slipped away from the treasonous war party or couldn't keep up with it and were captured. One prisoner, a labourer, told Greville that while he didn't know where the rebels were heading, 'he heard Mr John Grant's boy say their purpose was to go suddenly into Wales'. A day later, Greville's son-in-law Sheriff Richard Verney and his associates William Combe and John Ferrer forwarded to Salisbury what Greville had learned about the rebels and also reported, no doubt to the consternation of the councillors, that their 'number do increase and are thought to be about two hundred'. Shakespeare knew Greville well, though the extent of their connection or even of Greville's patronage remains uncertain. Verney, Combe and Ferrer were well known to him too; at this social and economic level Warwickshire was a small world.

It's hard to imagine what it must have felt like to be in the thick of things in and around Stratford-upon-Avon at this moment, with reports filtering in of the Warwick raid, war horses heard thundering across the country roads, rebels arming at Norbrook and rumours circulating of the threatened abduction of Princess Elizabeth. The time had come to place chains across all bridges and prepare civil defences, though local defenders resembled nothing so much as the hapless band of English conscripts Shakespeare had portrayed so devastatingly in his *Henry the Fourth, Part 2*. Stratford-upon-Avon's schoolmaster, Alexander Aspinall, played a leading role in his town's preparations. He had been teaching in the town since the early 1580s, when the teenage Shakespeare was still living there, and had moved in 1594 to Chapel Quad (Shakespeare's current home at New Place, purchased three years later, was just a stone's throw away). In late 1605 Aspinall was serving as an alderman as well as Stratford's chamberlain, responsible for payments made for local defence. His accounts for early November convey the scramble to put the sleepy town's defences on a war footing. Basic military supplies were needed and on 6 November gunpowder was purchased from Richard Dewes and Mrs Quiney. What a plumber and the keeper of a tavern were doing with a supply of gunpowder is unclear. Mrs Quiney's husband, Richard (author of the only surviving letter to Shakespeare), had died three years earlier; she was also the future mother-in-law of Shakespeare's daughter Judith. Weapons were gathered for defending the town (though most were broken or too rusty to fire) along with a handful of raw recruits to use them.

The following day, Bartholomew Hales came by to inspect the town's military preparedness. Hales's connection to Shakespeare's family went back many years. Shakespeare's uncle Henry had lived on the Hales manor in Snitterfield. After Hales's inspection revealed that many of the weapons were useless, a local cutler was paid to get them in working order. By 9 November Verney could confirm that we 'have assembled all our trained soldiers and sent for the horse to be in readiness'. Other areas across the Midlands were ready too; a labourer from Lillington recalled how 'during the rebellion, being commanded by the constable, he watched five nights at Shefford Bridge, which was chained up'.

These preparations came none too soon, for that very night local forces were on high alert 'when it was said that Sir Fulke Greville's house was besieged'. It made good sense for the rebels to attack Greville's house at Beauchamp Court eight miles away, and if successful, the besiegers could have eliminated a key foe in the region and made off with a sizeable cache of arms and horses. The Stratford guard, though alerted to the reported siege, remained safely in town, spending the night burning candles and drinking Mrs Quiney's wine, perhaps to bolster their courage. The report of the attack on Beauchamp Court, like many others that circulated widely in those fraught days, proved to be yet one more unfounded rumour. Stratford's guard improved their battle-readiness over the coming days and weeks, purchasing more ammunition and adding a few swords and daggers to their collection of arms. As late as 21 December they kept up their preparations, cleaning their swords and daggers and purchasing 'a new scabbard for the old sword'. It all seems a bit comical in retrospect and it is hard to imagine what these citizens might have done against a band of accomplished and desperate swordsmen on war horses. But their preparation underscores the extent to which tensions in and around Stratford-upon-Avon ran high – and stayed that way – until Christmas.

One of the strips of land that Shakespeare had leased the previous July abutted Clopton House, an estate belonging to Lady and Lord Carew. Carew, who had served in Ireland and had helped crush the revolt there, had subsequently been appointed to the council of Queen Anne. He and his wife were now living near the court at the Savoy in London. Knowing that the Carews were likely to be out of town for some time, Ambrose Rookwood had visited Clopton House on the Saturday before Michaelmas 1605, accompanied by two friends, John Grant and Robert Winter of nearby Huddington. The three approached Carew's tenant, Robert Wilson, and Rookwood breezily informed him that he planned to lease the house for the next four years. Wilson replied that there was no way he would permit that without first having the consent of his master. Rookwood insisted that he was 'a gentleman well known to the Lord Carew and would easily obtain his consent'. Whereupon, according to Wilson's subsequent testimony, 'without more ado', and while Wilson was absent from the house, Rookwood brazenly 'brought in his stuff', reassuring Wilson's wife, who was there, that 'he had fully agreed with her husband'. Once he had moved in, Rookwood invited many guests to Clopton, including Winter and Grant, Grant's brother-in-law Mr Bosse, Edward Bushell, and Robert Catesby and his servant Thomas Bates. Wilson recalled in particular a 'great dinner and many strangers' at Clopton 'upon the Sunday after Michaelmas Day' and additional 'strangers' arriving by 'coach' on 4 November (to come by coach was highly unusual, since these vehicles had only recently been introduced, and mostly in London). Wilson's choice of the word 'strangers' is unusual; that term, like 'aliens', was usually reserved for what we today would call foreigners. His report suggests that the locals kept a sharp and suspicious eye out for people who weren't from around those parts. In this instance, Wilson had good cause to do so, for Clopton House had become a nerve centre of the Gunpowder Plot.

According to the wonderfully named servant Thomas Tempest, who wrote to the Carews in London about the goings-on at their estate, Sheriff Verney arrived at Clopton 'with a great company' on 9 November to search the house. Tempest also informed the Carews that a large 'cloakbag' had been confiscated, 'full of copes, vestments, crosses, crucifixes, chalices and other massing relics'. Where these goods had come from and precisely how and where they were seized remains a bit hazy. According to Tempest they had come from Norbrook and were to be 'delivered to one George Badger there', and Badger, caught red-handed, was then jailed. It was a brave if dangerous thing to do, but could not have come as a surprise to his neighbours, for Badger had long been known in town as a committed Catholic and had been willing to lose his place as an alderman because of his faith. Badger was also Shakespeare's long-time next-door neighbour, and still owned the house adjoining the one on Henley Street in which Shakespeare grew up and where his mother still lived. Besides serving as a safe-house for planning the uprising, Clopton House also appears to have been the site where a trove of long-hidden and precious objects used in Catholic worship was stored in anticipation of the restoration of Catholicism to England. It would have been a cunning move to warehouse these 'massing relics' there rather than at nearby Norbrook, a notorious recusant's house.

On 26 February 1606 a jury of twenty-four leading citizens met in Stratford-upon-Avon's town hall 'to view and value' the goods Badger had been caught trying to hide. Among the jurors were friends and acquaintances of Shakespeare, including July Shaw (who lived two doors down from New Place and a decade later was one of the friends that Shakespeare asked to sign his will). Their responsibility that day was to affix a cash value on each of these twenty or so objects, now forfeited to the crown, since they had belonged to a traitor. Forty-seven years had passed since the death of the Catholic Queen Mary, the last time these objects would have been used in public. As the men gazed upon these goods, they saw England's vanished past before them in objects that had been hidden away and carefully preserved for nearly a half-century. Only the older jurors would have remembered from their childhood what it was like to see priests in these garments, finger these rosary beads, page through these prayer books or gaze upon the painted image of Christ on a crucifix. Some of the older men must also have remembered that their town had held on to its costly velvet and damask vestments for well over a decade after Elizabeth had come to the throne and Catholic worship was banned, just in case the old faith would be restored.

It's impossible to know whether these objects now stirred feelings of nostalgia or revulsion; that depended on the juror's religious convictions. While neighbours probably had a pretty good idea of how devout those they lived and worked and prayed with every Sunday were, Queen Elizabeth's decision not to pry too deeply into anyone's religious convictions had ensured that a quiet if uneasy coexistence had settled on England. What people did in the privacy of their hearts or homes was, most of the time, nobody else's business. While church attendance was mandatory, Stratford had not been the kind of town where neighbours turned in Church Papists who refused to take Communion. But as the jurors gathered at Stratford's town hall that day must have recognised, the now Protestant nation's Catholic past had never really disappeared. With the threat of a bloody Catholic uprising all too real, who of those still clinging to the old faith could now be trusted?

The jurors probably passed around these objects before determining their value. The first to circulate were 'a chalice with a cover of silver and gilt' valued at twenty-six shillings and eight pence, 'a little silver bell' worth twenty shillings and a 'silver and gilt crucifix' worth three shillings and four pence. The jurors next turned their attention to items used in the Mass: 'two white surplices', a 'vestment of white stuff like tissue with a pall and armlets belonging to the same, and a piece of red sarsnet to wrap up the same', another 'vestment of crimson satin with a pall and armlets belonging to the same and a piece of red sarsnet to wrap up the same', and then 'a black vestment of damask with a pall and armlets belonging to the same'. These, taken together, were valued at sixty shillings.

The men would have continued handing around curious objects that many had until now probably never seen, only heard described. In a town that had its share of recusants but whose leadership leaned towards Puritanism – so much so that they banned performances by strolling players, including the King's Men – the sight of these 'massing relics' may well have been loathsome. Yet even those most disturbed by these objects also knew that for the grandparents of everyone in the room, and most likely for their parents as well, these objects had been sacred. The jurors next examined 'a bracelet of ten amber beads' and 'a pair of praying beads of bone'. They decided that these weren't worth more than a few pence each, nor were the five Latin books they examined, including a service book and a small lay Psalter.

While several copies survive of the extensive list of items – probably one of the larger hoards of Catholic objects discovered in Jacobean England – there is no record of what happened to these goods. In all likelihood, the books were burned, the rich vestments sold off, perhaps to travelling players in search of costumes for their Italian or Spanish tragedies, and the valuable silver and gilt crucifixes melted down. Prompted by such cases, and impatient with local officials who allowed confiscated Catholic objects to recirculate among the faithful, a few months later Parliament passed an Act 'to prevent and avoid dangers which grow by Popish recusants', one of several legislative measures enacted in the wake of the Gunpowder Plot intended to curb or punish those who still clung to the old faith. Henceforth, 'if any altar, pax, beads, pictures, or such like Popish relics, or any Popish book or books, shall be found' they shall presently be 'defaced and burnt . . . and if it be a crucifix, or other relic of any price, the same [is] to be defaced'.

One of the more melancholy sights at this time, whatever one's religious persuasion, must surely have been the parade of prisoners, many of them neighbours and a surprising number of them women, led to London for further interrogation. Sheriff Verney wrote to the Privy Council on 12 November that he had turned over a number of prisoners, including the wives (most of them now widows) of 'the principal offenders in this late insurrection', and reassured the councillors that he would take care of their children until he received further instruction. Verney must have been relieved to be free of his prisoners' care, because, as he wrote, the jail and many houses in which they were being held were full. There seems to have been some local resistance to his efforts, for his house was set fire to twice while Verney was holding these prisoners. Inevitably, as he also acknowledged, many of those snared in the dragnet were 'detained too long by mistake', for locals were turning in anyone who seemed suspicious, including travellers passing through the wrong place at the wrong time. In forwarding the prisoners, Verney warned the Council that the danger in Warwickshire was far from over: 'This country is full of recusants and many coming out of far remote countries, most of them well furnished with horses and armour.'

A day later Verney wrote again, informing them that Bartholomew Hales would be escorting Mrs Grant to London, since she had been 'sent for by your warrant'. As eager as Verney was to punish the rebels, it seems that he did so reluctantly in the case of this neighbour, for he added that he had 'never received shifting or untrue answers to any demand propounded to her. That makes me hope she was as much tormented with her husband's practices as she is now become miserable by his fault.' Three days later another group of twenty-five prisoners – all men this time, masters, servants and quite a few suspected priests – was led south. The Warwickshire prisoners, totalling roughly fifty, may well have passed from their overcrowded and makeshift jails in Alcester over Stratford-upon-Avon's Clopton Bridge on their grim journey south to the capital, toward incarceration and interrogation there. One can only wonder what effect the sight of these prisoners might have had on neighbours with whom until so recently they had lived together in peace. Were they jeered and cursed or viewed with pity and in silence? Either way, who knew how deep the insurrection ran, how long this had been plotted, and who now was to be fully trusted? For the near future, life in what had so recently been a peaceful and quiet backwater was unlikely to be quite the same.

It's tempting to imagine Shakespeare, riding northward, passing this group of prisoners who included townsfolk that he had grown up with. But it's unlikely that he would have been travelling to Stratford-upon-Avon in November, with the Christmas season fast approaching at court. John Aubrey recorded in the mid-seventeenth century that Shakespeare went home once a year; if so, the likeliest time was during the annual break from playing that lasted from Shrove Tuesday until Easter. Had he gone home during Lent, he would have arrived in the immediate aftermath of the inquisition of the Catholic objects his neighbour George Badger had been trying to hide. He may have heard versions of the story from both sides – Badger's family as well as July Shaw and others who had evaluated those relics. There's little doubt that Shakespeare would have returned to a deeply unsettled town. Religious difference, long a private matter, was now everyone's business. When he arrived at New Place his friends and family were no doubt as eager to learn what it had been like in London, including details of the trial and executions of the plotters, as he was to hear their accounts of what had happened to those involved in Stratford. It would have been a novel experience for a writer who had spent much of his adult life reading and writing about epochal moments in history to realise that he was living through one himself. It also offered Shakespeare the opportunity to observe how recent events were being refashioned by others, and to reflect on the as yet unanswerable questions of what they were ultimately about and how they might alter his world.

It would be hard to find many individuals in Jacobean England more intricately linked than he was to those whose lives were touched by the Gunpowder Plot. In the close-knit world of the Midlands gentry, it was rare to find many degrees of separation. When in the late 1590s Shakespeare and his father successfully applied for a coat of arms and the rank of gentlemen, their application made much of their connection to Edward Arden of Park Hall. Shakespeare may well have regretted that decision now, for Edward Arden happened to be uncle to two of the leading conspirators, Catesby and Tresham, and, through his extended and claimed Arden relations, Shakespeare would also have been the distant relative of two other plotters, Robert and Thomas Winter. He was connected through business ventures as well. 'Mr Bushell', mentioned as surety for a requested loan in the only surviving letter addressed to Shakespeare, was most likely Thomas Bushell, a local gentleman related through marriage to many of the plotters. The dense network reached into the next generation: Shakespeare's daughter Judith's brother-in-law Adrian Quiney would later marry Eleanor Bushell, whose aunt Elizabeth Winter was also the aunt of Thomas and Robert Winter.

When in 1613 Shakespeare purchased a London residence, the Blackfriars Gatehouse, he was acquiring what had been a well-known Catholic safe-house, where the conspirators had tried to meet and where one of the hunted priests, after the exposure of the plot, had sought refuge. The friend whom Shakespeare asked to serve as a trustee for the purchase, William Johnson, ran a London tavern that had hosted the plotters. If anything, Shakespeare was even more intimately connected to those in or near his home town who were swept up in this traumatic event, not only those at Norbrook and Clopton House, but also, more familiarly, George Badger, Mrs Quiney, Alexander Aspinall, old Fulke Greville, Bartholomew Hales, and neighbours on the jury who handled the confiscated 'massing relics'. And as the events set in motion on the Fifth of November continued to reverberate in Stratford-upon-Avon as Easter approached, those even closer to him – Judith and Hamnet Sadler, godparents of his twins, and even his daughter, Susanna – would experience its aftershocks as well.

7 : *Remember, Remember*

By the time that the inquisition of the 'massing relics' took place in Stratford-upon-Avon in late February, Ambrose Rookwood was dead. So too were his friends John Grant and Robert Winter, as well as many others who had plotted with them at Clopton House.

After several rounds of interrogation and debilitating torture, the defiant John Johnson was finally broken. When he supplied the authorities with a full confession on 9 November he was so weak he could barely sign it. But he did so with his real name, Guido Fawkes. Guy Fawkes – as he was universally called – and his fellow conspirators had plotted 'to blow up the king with all the nobility about him in Parliament', then 'to surprise the Princess Elizabeth' and 'make her queen', and had 'prepared, in her name, a proclamation against the Union of the kingdoms'. The plan, according to another conspirator, Sir Everard Digby, was for Catesby to proclaim her heir apparent at Charing Cross before riding north to abduct

'The Gunpowder Plotters', by Crispijn de Passe the Elder (1606)

the princess. As idealistic as they were, the plotters were pragmatic enough to reach out to non-Catholics. Fawkes confessed that they had intended to make 'use of all the discontented people in England'; the appeal, Digby writes, would have been broad, including a call for abolishing 'wardships and monopolies'.

The originators of the conspiracy had been Robert Catesby, his cousin Thomas Wright and Thomas Winter. The charismatic Catesby, who came up with the plan to blow up James and Parliament, had approached the other two in early 1604. They then recruited Thomas Percy and Fawkes (whose military experience in the Low Countries and training as a mining engineer were major assets). The five soon realised that more manpower and money were needed and over the course of the next year or so hand-picked eight others to join them. Percy rented a building next to the old Palace of Westminster, and they planned to tunnel from there to a spot under the House of Lords where they could set off the explosion. Three new recruits, John Grant, Christopher Wright and Catesby's trusted retainer Thomas Bates, helped with the digging. It was gruelling manual labour for gentlemen unused to it, and noisy enough to attract attention, so there was considerable relief when a lease for a spacious ground-floor storeroom directly beneath the first floor of the House of Lords became available in March 1605. Percy secured the lease, enabling the plotters to hide nearly a ton of gunpowder, then cover it with stones, wood and iron bars, to disguise the explosives and increase their destructive force.

Because the plot had grown more expensive, two others, Sir Everard Digby and Ambrose Rookwood, were invited to join and provide much-needed funds. Expanding the group one final time was its undoing; the well-to-do Francis Tresham, recruited just three weeks before the plot was discovered, was probably the author of the letter delivered to his brother-in-law Monteagle. When first told the details of the plot Tresham was so horrified that he offered to pay the others to flee to the Continent rather than go through with it, fearing that if it failed 'the whole kingdom' would turn its 'fury upon such as were taken for Catholics'. Quite a few others – besides their Jesuit confessors and English Catholic contacts on the Continent, who were in on the secret – must have suspected or known that a plot was in the works, though their identities are now lost to us. The conspirators had much in common. Many were bound by ties of blood or marriage and had roots in the Midlands. Most of them were gentlemen in their thirties, young enough to be daring but old enough to have had some experience of failure. All were recusants who chafed at the mistreatment of Catholics in England and, three years into the new reign, held out little hope that things would change.

Word of Fawkes's arrest reached them in the early hours of 5 November. With fresh horses waiting, they raced north on an eighty-mile dash to Warwickshire, to their appointed rendezvous that evening with Digby's hunting party at an inn at Dunchurch – a cover for the planned abduction of Princess Elizabeth – stopping only to arm themselves at Percy's home at Ashby St Ledgers. When they met up with Digby's party, Catesby flat-out lied about what had happened in London, still hoping to keep the floundering rebellion alive, telling Digby that 'there was such a pudder bred in the state by the death of the king and the Earl of Salisbury as the Catholics would now stir'. There was talk as well of joining forces with an army of a thousand supporters at

Stephen Littleton's estate at Holbeach, in Staffordshire. But it was impossible to conceal the truth for very long and most of Digby's friends, rather than join them, quietly slipped away into the night. The conspirators were left at this point with 'not above fifty horse', but they remained hopeful that they could attract followers and their uprising succeed. They failed to see that while England's Catholics were suffering under punitive recusancy laws and might grumble about their limited toleration, they weren't about to commit treason and risk all to right those wrongs. Yet in truth, nobody at this moment had sounded the depth of Catholic resentment. The government certainly took the possibility of a Catholic rising seriously. The attempted rebellion would put the loyalties of English Catholics to the test. Digby was especially crushed by their failure to find popular support: 'Not one man came to take our part,' he lamented, 'though we expected so many.' Their own servants abandoned them and guards soon had to be stationed to prevent further desertions.

The next forty-eight hours passed in a nightmarish haze. The rebels covered fifteen miles to Warwick to steal Benock's horses, then another twenty-six or so after their brief stop at Norbrook on their way toward Huddington (while, whatever rumours local officials had heard, their numbers continued to dwindle). Thomas Bates peeled off from the group as they passed Alcester, riding a few miles north to Coughton Court, an estate that had been rented by Digby. His mission was to deliver a letter to Henry Garnet, England's senior Jesuit, who was hiding there and knew of their plans, urging him to join them. Garnet refused, but another Jesuit, Oswald Tesimond, rode back with Bates, and the two caught up with the conspirators still riding hard to Huddington, where they slept on the night of the 6th. Early the next morning the troop, now shadowed by a local posse, made a short detour to find more arms (but once again disappointingly few recruits), raiding Lord Windsor's home at Hewell Grange. If any doubts remained about the reluctance of the people to join them, they were put to rest here. When Catesby cried out to the villagers, 'Will you come with us?' one of them said in response, 'It may be, if we know what you mean to do.' Catesby's reply – 'We are for God and the country' – failed to win any of them over. One of the villagers coolly answered: 'We are for King James as well as for God and the country, and we will not go against his will.'

The tired troop, their numbers still shrinking and travelling more slowly now through muddy roads while towing a cart full of weapons, veered north rather than heading westward towards the imagined safety of Wales, perhaps having heard that roads and bridges ahead were manned. They arrived at Holbeach House, Stephen Littleton's home, on the evening of 7 November. They would ride no further. They had left London less than three days earlier and had covered over 150 miles. That evening, while they were drying out gunpowder dampened by the rain, disaster struck. The gunpowder accidentally exploded, badly wounding some of the core group, including Rookwood, Catesby and Grant, whose 'face was much disfigured and his eyes almost burnt out'. The irony was not lost on any of them. A shaken John Wright grabbed hold of the injured Catesby and said, 'Woe worth the time that we have seen this day,' before calling for the rest of the gunpowder, so that 'they might all together be blown up'. A despondent Catesby 'began to think he had offended God in this action, seeing so bad effects follow from the same'.

The conspirators and their handful of supporters determined to make their final stand there and die fighting. By morning, Holbeach was surrounded. When some of the leading rebels charged out, local forces fired on them, hitting both Percy and Catesby. Other plotters were soon shot or fatally stabbed. Several were captured, including those too badly injured to fight on. A few managed to flee in the confusion but didn't get far. Robert Keyes was caught the next day. Robert Winter and Stephen Littleton evaded the authorities for two months before they were betrayed and arrested. Winter later told Fawkes (their conversation overheard by a spy in the Tower of London) that while on the run he was haunted by nightmares in which he saw 'steeples stand awry and within those churches strange and unknown faces', before realising to his horror that 'the faces of his associates so scorched resembled those which he had seen in his dream'. Only Tesimond, a long-hunted Jesuit experienced at making his way unnoticed through England, eluded his pursuers and found safety on the Continent.

The Midlands rising was over, though not even members of the posse at Holbeach, now fighting over spurs, stockings and all the other booty they could lay their hands on, knew it. Local forces throughout the Midlands remained on alert and England's ports remained closed. Devonshire's army was still attracting volunteers – including, brazenly, Francis Tresham, the sole conspirator remaining free in London. When King James addressed Parliament the following day, 9 November, he focused on what had happened in London. News of the shoot-out at Holbeach reached the court that same day, and the bedraggled remnants of the conspiracy arrived in London three days later, exactly a week after they had left, knowing full well the punishment that awaited them. James's 'King's Book' would describe their entry into the city itself. The passage, attributed to the king and deemed significant enough to be reprinted in his collected works in 1616, recalls how they were 'met with a huge confluence of people of all sorts, desirous to see them, as the rarest sort of monsters; fools to laugh at them, women and children to wonder, all the common people to gaze, the wiser sort to satisfy their curiosity, in seeing the outward cases of so unheard of a villainy'. It must have been an extraordinary scene, regardless of whether onlookers felt fury, pity or a mixture of both. The phrasing of the official and royal account of crowds gazing on these 'rarest sort of monsters' stuck with Shakespeare, for the words are closely echoed in his next play in Macduff's challenge to that archfiend Macbeth:

> yield thee coward,
> And live to be a show and gaze o'th' time!
> We'll have thee, as our rarer monsters are,
> Painted upon a pole.
> (5.8.23–6)

Hearing James's description of the 'rarest sort of monsters' who tried to kill him repeated in this way (in words spoken to a man who had in fact killed a Scottish king) must have come as a jolt to crowds at the Globe in 1606, one of those moments in Shakespeare's work – akin to the Chorus's words in *Henry the Fifth* about Londoners welcoming home the Earl of Essex – that neatly elides past and present and sharpens the topicality of the play.

The government might easily have held their trial that week or the next, while outrage was still fresh. Their treason, after all, was manifest. But their trial and execution were put off until late January. One reason for the delay was that nobody in authority really believed that a group of gentry could have done this without the assistance of a foreign enemy or an as yet unidentified English nobleman. The king shared this view: Molino writes that James 'was amazed that so vast and so audacious a scheme should have been hatched in the mind of a man of such low and abject estate'. So the surviving conspirators – along with anyone with knowledge of the plot – were repeatedly interrogated and their stories checked against each other in the hope of discovering who was really behind it.

Sir Thomas Edmondes, the English ambassador in Brussels, reported in mid-November how hard he was finding it to persuade others of 'the truth of the said conspiracy'. Those he spoke with on the Continent were convinced that if not a devious Puritan plot, or a Dutch-inspired anti-monarchical one, it could only have been the work of a Protestant-leaning devil, eager to rid England of her Catholic subjects. No friend to the Catholics himself, Edmondes added that he hoped that his government 'may make that use of it, as we have just cause to do'. His words point to the two great challenges facing the authorities. The first was to craft a version of the story that would displace competing ones already circulating. The official report, first published as *A True and Perfect Relation of the Proceedings at the Several Arraignments of the Late Most Barbarous Traitors* in the winter of 1606, was written in part to combat the 'diverse uncertain, untrue and incoherent reports' that 'do pass from hand to hand'. The second challenge was to discover what advantages could be gained, an early modern version of the political adage that 'no crisis should go to waste'. But King James was only interested in punishing extremists. At a time when his primary political goal was Union and he felt as threatened by radical Puritans as he did by seditious Catholics, it wouldn't help to create fresh divisions within his kingdoms.

Still, the story had to be told, whatever the uses to which it might be put. And that task fell to Salisbury, whose hand is visible behind both James's speech to Parliament and Barlow's sermon at Paul's Cross. Over the course of the next two months Salisbury played a role familiar to London's playwrights, as he pored over his sources and chose key plot lines and characters. Survivors of the skirmish at Holbeach, along with plotters seized in London, were forced to provide long and detailed accounts of their involvement. Salisbury then took their various confessions and wove them into a narrative that suited the government's interests. He knew that he had to strike the right balance between a main plot (in London) and the subplot (those 'Robin Hoods' in Warwickshire), as well as between heroes and villains. King James, in uncovering the conspiracy, had to play a starring role, and Monteagle was cast as best supporting actor. There were several candidates for the leading villain. Should this be, as initially scripted, Percy's plot? Or should Catesby, whose plan it was, be the arch-traitor? Though not fully satisfied with the choice, Salisbury decided to cast one of the lesser players, the one who most captured the popular imagination and acted as a lightning rod for their feelings: that mysterious and foreign-sounding 'Guido' Fawkes, the 'villain in a vault', the 'Machiavellian with a match'.

Though only the plotters themselves would be destroyed in this high drama, emphasis had to be placed on the king and kingdom as the tragic victims. Barlow was correct, then, to draw attention in his early sermon at Paul's Cross to the plot as 'a devilish brutishness, and an hyperbolical, yea an hyperdiabolical devilishness'. But he overreached in then speaking of it as 'this late tragic-comical treason'; 'comical' would have to be suppressed. So too would the plotters' accusatory words that cast the king and his plans for Union in an unfavourable light. The plotters' hit list, mentioned by Molino, of 'all the houses inhabited by Scots, so that after the explosion they could be massacred' was also quietly omitted from all governmental accounts of the plot.

Visuals, too, were needed. The Privy Council was disappointed to learn that the authorities in Staffordshire had thoughtlessly buried the bodies of the conspirators they had killed and stripped at Holbeach. So they ordered that their corpses 'be taken out of their graves and bowelled and their quarters to be set up in some principal towns where they most led their lives, and the heads of Percy and Catesby to be sent up hither purposely'. Their heads, soon displayed on iron poles at Parliament, had the intended effect on onlookers. One sixteen-year-old student at Westminster was so struck by the frightening sight that he wrote a poem, 'Trayterous Percyes & Catesbyes Prosopopeia', in which he imagines seeing, as if in a dream, the pair of severed heads conversing. It's a terrifying vision:

> Two monsters' skulls, which never plotted good,
> Grim, ghastly, pale, shagged-hair, sulphurous eyes,
> Piercing the air with howlings, yells, and cries.

On both sides, then, if we consider Winter's dream of his friends' scorched faces and this teenager's dream of talking heads, the Gunpowder Plot was producing nightmares, tapping deep into Jacobean political and religious anxieties.

On 27 January the eight surviving plotters – Guy Fawkes, Thomas Winter, Robert Winter, Robert Keyes, John Grant, Thomas Bates, Ambrose Rookwood and Sir Everard Digby – were brought from the Tower to stand trial at Westminster Hall. King James was present, though hidden, as were Queen Anne, three months pregnant, and Prince Henry. As in the public theatres, you had to pay more for a decent view. One member of Parliament felt cheated when he and 'diverse others' paid ten shillings for standing room in a space reserved for members, only to discover that many of the 'baser sort' were squeezed into their crammed section for as little as three or four pence each. The crush for this once-in-a-lifetime event, and the price, too, were far greater than at any sold-out performance at the public playhouses.

The judges, a special commission made up of the leading officials in the kingdom, were also part of the show. It wasn't a trial in the modern sense: the accused weren't permitted to defend themselves and had no counsel. From the perspective of the state, there was no need. It must have caused a stir when, 'contrary to the general expectation', with the exception of Digby they all pleaded not guilty. Digby chose to plead guilty with an explanation: he had acted because the government's 'promises were broken with the Catholics'. The punctilious Attorney General, Sir Edward Coke, got in the last word before the verdict was read. He reminded those present how lucky these traitors were that the king hadn't devised any 'new torment or torture' for them.

He then provided a plot summary of the spectacle that would soon follow. Everyone already knew what was coming, but Coke understood that they needed to hear once more the horrific punishment facing the conspirators. After being 'drawn to the place of execution', each traitor was to be hanged, then cut down before he could strangle to death. While still alive, he was then 'to have his privy parts cut off and burned before his face' and his bowels 'taken out and burned', before his head would be 'cut off'. Lastly, his body was to 'be quartered, and the quarters set up in some high and eminent place, to the view and detestation of men and to become a prey for the fowls of the air'.

The show trial was almost over. After the guilty verdicts were delivered Digby asked for forgiveness, Robert Winter pleaded for mercy and his younger brother Thomas gallantly if fruitlessly begged that he 'be hanged both for his brother and himself'. The blinded Grant 'was a good while mute' before admitting that he was guilty of 'conspiracy intended but never executed', and Fawkes, aggressive to the last, sought to exonerate the Jesuit priests who were implicated in the plot, insisting that 'we never opened the matter to them'. Rookwood begged for mercy, not because he feared death, but because 'so shameful a death should leave so perpetual a blemish and blot unto all ages upon his name and blood'.

On 30 January, Digby, Robert Winter, Grant and Bates were bound and drawn on wicker sleds to St Paul's to be hanged, castrated, eviscerated, then cut to pieces. Having plotted 'not only to make our kingdom headless but memberless', as the preacher Samuel Garey put it, they would now suffer that very fate themselves. London itself was the stage and there was room for everyone keen on viewing part of the spectacle. The procession to the gallows had its own drama as family members hoped to greet the condemned for the last time. Martha Bates managed to slip past the armed guards and throw herself on the bound body of her husband Thomas as he was dragged to St Paul's. The executions took place at the western end of St Paul's churchyard and offered a combination of sanctity and savagery in equal measure. Digby was the first to mount the scaffold, followed by Winter, Grant and then Bates. According to John Aubrey, Digby was eloquent to the end. After asking forgiveness he prayed quietly for a quarter of an hour, 'often bowing his head to the ground', before ascending the scaffold. He was only hanged for a very short while before being cut down and butchered. It was said that when the executioner plucked out his heart and exclaimed to the crowd, 'Here is the heart of a traitor,' Digby in his dying breath cried out, 'Thou liest!' True or not, it was reported that common folk gathered there 'marvelled at his fortitude' and talked 'almost of nothing else'.

It was not the wisest time to criticise how the government chose to stage these executions, but Sir Arthur Gorges took that chance, complaining to Salisbury about the choice of site, not finding St Paul's 'a fit place' to 'make a butchery in the churchyard, and almost under the eaves of the most famous church of our kingdom'. Gorges added that it might generate invidious comparisons between King James and Queen Elizabeth: 'I well remember that that was the place of happy memory . . . where our late dread and dear sovereign offered up in all humility upon her knees her thanksgiving to God for the great victory upon the Spaniards and therefore too worthy to be now polluted with gibbets, hangmen, or the blood of traitors.' Salisbury saw that

Gorges was right, and the cumbersome set was dismantled and hastily moved to a new site, the Old Palace Yard at Westminster, so that on the following day Londoners could witness a repeat performance. On this day Thomas Winter went first, followed by Rookwood, Keyes and last of all the star attraction, Guy Fawkes. His body broken by torture, Fawkes was 'scarce able to go up the ladder'. But his end was luckier than that of the others, for his neck snapped when he was hanged, killing him before he had to endure the horrors then visited upon his body. When the carnage ended, 'their quarters were placed over London gates' and their heads overlooking London Bridge.

While we will never know in what ways the Gunpowder Plot and its aftermath affected Shakespeare personally, it's nonetheless possible to recover some of the traces it left on his work. Its most obvious impact would be on the next play he would write, *Macbeth*, which begins and ends with the killing of a Scottish king. In its use of squibs in the opening scene – small fireworks made of brimstone and saltpetre that made a slight but noisy explosion – it must have even smelled like a Gunpowder play. The plot also left its mark on *King Lear* before that play had even been staged. How uncanny was it to have imagined before the Fifth of November a story that turned on a mysterious and forged letter, in a play that took an old tragicomedy and reworked it into a tragedy that ended apocalyptically, with the destruction of the entire British royal family? Kent's grim question at the end of the play – 'Is this the promised end?' – and Edgar's rejoinder: 'Or image of that horror?' (24.59–60) foreshadowed the language of 'The King's Book' and Barlow's Gunpowder sermon. In Lear's words on the heath, confronting the terrible elements, decrying ingratitude and calling down destruction on his head, Shakespeare had written one of his most powerful speeches:

> Blow, wind, and crack your cheeks! Rage! blow!
> You cataracts and hurricanoes, spout
> Till you have drenched our steeples, drowned the cocks!
> You sulphurous and thought-executing fires,
> Vaunt-couriers to oak-cleaving thunderbolts,
> Singe my white head; and thou all-shaking thunder,
> Smite flat the thick rotundity o' the world,
> Crack nature's mould, all germens spill at once,
> That make ingrateful man.
> (9.1–9)

The effect of this speech would be intensified in the wake of the trial of the traitors, with the words of Sir Edward Coke still fresh in Londoners' minds, linking this description of elemental violence with the forces that would have been unleashed on the Fifth of November: 'Lord, what a wind, what a fire, what a motion and commotion of earth and air there would have been!' Lines in the play such as the Fool's jibe about monopolies (4.146), the kind of oblique political criticism that only a few months earlier would have slipped by the censor, now had to be cut, once the king's abuse of monopolies had been invoked by the Gunpowder plotters to justify regicide. And in its handling of the consequences of the division of the kingdoms, the politics of *King Lear* had become more fraught, if more timely, for the expected resolution of the Union question by Parliament in early November had been delayed once more. There would be other effects on as yet unwritten plays. After the Fifth of November, with the exception of the late and collaborative *Henry the Eighth* Shakespeare would never again delve into what had been a recurrent interest in his work, most famously in *Hamlet* with its ghost come from purgatory: nostalgia for the residual pull of Catholicism in a world in which the old religion continued to make its presence felt. It was not that Shakespeare had stopped thinking about these matters. Who could, at a time when neighbours of opposing faiths were eyeing each other more warily than before? But it had become too volatile to engage as comfortably or as directly as he once had.

Along with Shakespeare's late plays and the King James Bible, the story commemorated every Fifth of November is the only cultural artefact created during the first decade of King James's reign that still matters four hundred years later. Why these three? The Authorised Version of the Bible is perhaps the easiest to explain. The teams of scholars and churchmen that James commanded at the Hampton Court Conference to produce a new translation were phenomenally knowledgeable and talented, and the English language, as the many celebrated poets and playwrights of the day recognised, was at a particularly rich moment in its evolution. The result, rare in anything done by committee, was a sonorous translation that made the divine word more accessible and urgent. And it has probably helped that, in sharing that moment's linguistic heritage, it sounds so 'Shakespearean'.

The longevity of the Fifth of November is more surprising. A ruler can't simply declare that a day is a holiday and assume that it will last forever. If that were so, every August the Scots and English would still be lighting bonfires in celebration of Gowrie Day. What's all the more strange is that the Fifth of November recalls a collective experience, a day of communal deliverance, on which nothing actually happened. Nobody has fully explained the deep hold that 'Remember, Remember the Fifth of November' continues to have on the British psyche (though its grip seems to be slackening and the image of Guy Fawkes may soon be associated more with the visage on the masks worn by Anonymous protesters). The holiday clearly touched upon religious and political issues not so easily identified or named, and, like Shakespeare's plays, managed to evolve over time as political and religious circumstances and anxieties changed. Perhaps, too, much like the public theatres, the holiday filled the vacuum left in the late sixteenth century by the elimination of Catholic pageantry and communal celebration, as saints' days were suppressed and removed from the public calendar. The King James Bible, Shakespeare's plays and the Fifth of November all managed to preserve the past, sacred and secular, for present-day needs. The plotters had tried to do the opposite, obliterating the history of post-Reformation England, for the intended blast would have eliminated England's rulers along with the archives of her parliamentary and ecclesiastical history. Had their attempt succeeded, they would have effectively turned the clock back sixty years.

It's not widely known that John Milton, born in 1608, too late to have lived through the Gunpowder Plot itself, was obsessed as a teenager with it and wrote five short Latin poems, school exercises, on the subject. He then returned to it in a more substantial Latin poem on the twentieth anniversary of the threatened attack, titled simply '*In Quintum Novembris*' ('On the Fifth of November'). In this poem Satan flies to Rome and urges the Pope to destroy Britain's leaders 'and scatter their bodies through the air, burning them to ashes, by exploding gunpowder under the room where they will assemble'. But God intervenes and 'thwarts the daring Papists' outrages'. The evildoers are punished, God thanked, bonfires lit and a promise made that henceforth 'throughout the whole year there shall be no day more celebrated than the Fifth of November'. The poem, in touching on temptation, the nature of evil and providential intervention, anticipates much of what, decades later, Milton explores so incisively in *Paradise Lost* (not least Book 6, where Satan invents gunpowder as a weapon to challenge God's powers). Yet what makes this Fifth of November poem so unreadable today is that for the young Milton the Gunpowder Plot was about answers, not questions. He knows where evil originates. Good and bad, fair and foul, are always legible. They aren't in *Paradise Lost* (even if Milton thought they were) and they certainly aren't in Shakespeare.

Though he had finished writing *King Lear*, Shakespeare would continue to brood over Harsnett's stories of possession, deception and the human propensity for evil. The Fifth of November, that 'confection of all villainy', gave those issues fresh relevance, for it prompted not only Shakespeare but everyone else in the land to confront questions they had never been forced to grapple with so deeply or desperately: how can ordinary people attempt such horrible and unthinkable crimes? In doing so, what kind of lies or stories must they tell themselves and others? Does this evil come from satanic forces or from within us? What binds us together – be it a family or a marriage or a country – and what can destroy these bonds? Recognising the hunger for a play that probed the very questions now haunting his world, Shakespeare began to read and think about Macbeth.

8 : *Hymenaei*

The seasonal festivities at the outset of 1606 were no holiday for either the king or the King's Men. King James had slipped out of London in early December, returning to Whitehall Palace just three days before Christmas. Molino, the Venetian ambassador, reported home that the day after his return James 'appeared very subdued and melancholy' both 'at chapel and afterwards at dinner', where, uncharacteristically, he ate in silence. The king's dark mood was understandable. Though he was strengthened politically in the aftermath of the failed attempt on his life, it was unclear how long that good will would last. The path ahead was fraught for a king who saw himself as a peacemaker both at home and abroad. An increasingly headstrong Parliament would convene at last in less than a month to debate the future of the Union. Its members would also decide whether to subsidise their profligate and financially overstretched monarch. If James cracked down too hard on England's Catholics it might provoke

'Le Combat à la barrière', by Jacques Callot (1627)

fresh attempts on his life; if he were too lenient it might lead to the same end while alienating a House of Commons keen on passing harsh anti-recusancy laws. Complicating matters further, his own wife, Queen Anne, raised as a Lutheran, had converted to Catholicism, but for the sake of appearances was now attending Protestant services. Domestic challenges were exacerbated by threats from abroad, as Pope Paul V, worried about the fate of English Catholics, warned of countermeasures.

After his sullen dinner that Sunday before Christmas, James 'broke out with great violence', his melancholy silence giving way to explosive rage. In his report home Molino tried to capture the king's rant word for word (though this was so sensitive he sent it in code). His quotation of James's tirade offers the rarest of glimpses into the king's state of mind at this time:

> 'I have despatches from Rome informing me that the Pope intends to excommunicate me; the Catholics threaten to dethrone me and to take my life unless I grant them liberty of conscience. I shall most certainly be obliged to stain my hands with their blood, though sorely against my will. But they shall not think they can frighten me, for they shall taste of the agony first . . . I do not know upon what they found this perfidious and cursed doctrine of Rome that they are permitted to plot against the lives of princes and to deprive them of their crown and sceptre.'

King James continued in this vein for an hour. His attendants obligingly 'praised and approved' everything he said, urging him 'to adopt severe measures against the Catholics'. Molino, sensitive to the plight of his fellow Catholics, also reported that 'nothing is occupying more attention than the arrest of priests;

and though most of them are in hiding they cannot feel safe against the wiles adopted by the officials. Many are already prisoners, and it is thought they will be put to death, while in the coming Parliament severe measures will be enacted against the Catholics.'

If negotiating all this were not challenging enough, James planned to use the New Year's festivities to heal an old and still festering Elizabethan wound by marrying off the late Earl of Essex's son to Frances Howard. It would be a Jacobean rewrite of *Romeo and Juliet*, the sacrificial union of teenage lovers binding hostile families. The political motives behind this coupling were transparent to all. Molino, an astute and gossipy observer, writes that 'there is no doubt but that, when the Earl of Essex is a little older, suggestions and persuasions to revenge will not be wanting. Lord Salisbury hopes by creating ties of relationship to cancel the memory of these ancient enmities; many, however, are of opinion that this is too feeble a medicine for so great an ill.' Salisbury and the Howard faction probably feared as much, so sought to cinch the rival clans more tightly together through a secondary pair of marriages to Frances Howard's older sisters. Two days before Christmas her nineteen-year-old sister Elizabeth was married to Sir William Knollys, uncle to the late Earl of Essex. Knollys's first wife, Dorothy, a widow twenty years his senior, had conveniently died two months earlier. Knollys, now sixty years old and eager for an heir, was happy to take a teenager for his bride, six decades younger than the wife he had just buried. The third Howard sister, Catherine, would marry Salisbury's only son, William (he would be seventeen and she twenty at the time of their wedding). The marriage of Essex and

Frances Howard would be the centrepiece of the festivities at court ushering in 1606, the occasion marked by a masque on 5 January and a staged combat, or 'barriers', between the rival factions the following evening, Twelfth Night.

The Jacobean masque was a genre in its infancy. While there had been perhaps a half-dozen masque-like entertainments in the first years of the new reign, two early productions had defined the form: Samuel Daniel's *Vision of the Twelve Goddesses*, sponsored by Queen Anne and performed at Hampton Court in January 1604, and Ben Jonson's *The Masque of Blackness*, also under the queen's sponsorship, performed at the old Banqueting House a year later. Daniel's masque reassembled the remains of an Elizabethan political rhetoric into a new Jacobean one. Even the masque's costumes signalled a reworking of the past: the former queen's clothing was recycled, some of the thousands of pieces of her now unwearable wardrobe cut up and refashioned into new garments. Daniel had no pretensions about the artistic merit of masques, speaking of them as no more than 'dreams and shows', whatever those 'deeply learned in all mysteries' might think. Jonson would have none of that. His ambitions were greater and he was finding his way towards a more complicated form, discovering in the masque's 'more removed mysteries' an art that he believed transcended its brief moment of performance and its inescapably sycophantic nature. It was Jonson, despite his rocky relationship with the authorities, rather than Daniel, who was asked to create the masque in 1606. It would be called *Hymenaei* ('marriage rites') and would celebrate union, conjugal and political.

Hymenaei was one of the most expensive entertainments ever staged in England. It was a collaborative effort, with Jonson responsible for the script and overall concept. The staging would fall to Britain's leading architect and designer, Inigo Jones. The dance-master Thomas Giles handled the choreography and the composer Alfonso Ferrabosco the music. Eight young ladies at court and eight courtiers with whom they danced would be the stars of *Hymenaei*'s cast, and on the second day, when the barriers would be staged, thirty-four noblemen would be part of the elaborate and carefully scripted show. The logistics of bringing all this talent together – and preparing for the sole performance with four dozen lords and ladies unused to the rigours of rehearsal and to being ordered about – must have been nearly overwhelming. While the lavishly attired aristocrats were at the heart of the masque and barriers, a supporting cast of court musicians and professional actors was still needed – at least five adult players and perhaps as many boy actors, including a pair impersonating the bride and groom. These, almost surely, were drawn from the ranks of the King's Men, who are named as the performers hired to act in later Jonsonian masques.

Rehearsing and then performing in *Hymenaei* and the barriers on 5 and 6 January was only a small part of unprecedented demands facing Shakespeare's company. News of the lifting of the two-month ban on performances at the commercial theatres on 16 December must have come as a mixed blessing with all that was going on. Given the pent-up demand, the Globe and rival playhouses would have been packed this Christmas season. With the sun rising at 8 a.m. and setting at 4 p.m., the players may well have begun rehearsing that day's play shortly after dawn and moved up their regular playing time, 2 p.m., so that their outdoor performances ended before dark. And, of course, members of the company involved in the court masque would have had to find time to learn their parts and rehearse that complicated and tightly choreographed production at the Banqueting House as well.

In Queen Elizabeth's day, the argument that the vagabond players were tolerated because they were rehearsing and preparing year-round for a handful of court performances was largely a fiction. Under James, especially during the winter months, it must have felt like a painful reality for the King's Men. They knew exactly what Dudley Carleton meant when he wrote to John Chamberlain in early 1605, regarding the endless revels at court, that 'it seems we shall have Christmas all the year'. Because of the trial and expected execution of the Gunpowder traitors, court performances in late January and early February were almost surely ruled out, and with the Prince's Men already booked for Shrovetide performances on 3 and 4 March at Whitehall, Shakespeare and his fellows had to shoehorn their performances into a surprisingly narrow period, beginning the day after Christmas and probably ending by mid-January. With likely court performances on 26, 28, 29 and 31 December and then on 2 and 3 January, as well as on the 5th and 6th in Jonson's masque, followed by four more performances in the next fortnight, it was a wearying schedule, made even more exhausting if they played what were essentially matinees at the Globe in the afternoon when they were expected to perform the same evening at court.

One other (and little-known) feature of court performance made this demanding schedule that much more taxing. Edmund Tilney, Master of the Revels under Queen Elizabeth as well as

King James, was responsible for vetting every play staged at court, and his livelihood depended on neither the king nor his courtiers taking offence at anything staged before them. Tilney selected plays, old and recent, that had already been publicly staged (and whose scripts, for a small fee, he had previously approved for performance). But to ensure that there was no potentially dangerous matter, and to exclude any old play that might take on a disturbing topicality in light of recent events, Tilney then required that the companies come to the Revels office in the former Priory of St John in Clerkenwell for a pre-performance run-through. It was at Tilney's office, recalled the veteran playwright Thomas Heywood, 'where our court plays have been in late days yearly rehearsed, perfected and corrected before they come to the public view of the prince and the nobility'. Tilney saw his responsibilities in much the same way: when submitting his expenses for reimbursement for the 1606 season he specified that the amount included the cost of overseeing the 'rehearsal and making choice of plays and comedies and reforming them'.

The key words in these accounts are the 'perfecting', 'correction' and 'reforming' of plays. Censorship may be too loaded a term; Tilney, himself an author, probably thought of his role as more editorial and collaborative than that. Regardless, it meant that changes would necessarily be made to the scripts that the actors had already memorised for public performances. Tilney did not have to explain to the King's Men that this was as tense a political moment as any of them could recall. Prisoners in the Tower were being tortured, priests hunted and Gunpowder plotters still on the loose. Jonson, Chapman and Marston had all recently fallen foul of the authorities for mocking Scots in

Eastward Ho, and seemingly benign scenes in old plays could easily be charged with unexpected meaning. It would fall to Shakespeare to act on Tilney's instructions on how best to reform and correct ten of his company's plays – those that he had written as well as others purchased by the company now chosen to be performed at court.

Ben Jonson, whose occasional poetry dutifully promoted James's vision of Union as the marriage of two kingdoms, had been all but auditioning for such a lucrative writing commission since James's arrival in London. The masque scheduled for 5 January offered a perfect opportunity to celebrate the binding of court factions while at the same time promoting the Union of Scotland and England. While marriage was a powerful political metaphor, staging a wedding was taboo: the Act of Uniformity prohibited any but Anglican clergy to perform sacramental rites (which explains why Shakespeare's comedies end with betrothals, never wedding ceremonies). In *Hymenaei*, Jonson found a way around this by celebrating the marriage of the Jacobean teenagers not as a Christian but as a classical Roman wedding ceremony. He even consulted authoritative sources on wedding rituals in ancient Rome. It was a canny move, one that allowed him to show off his considerable erudition while at the same time pleasing a king who fancied himself a modern-day Augustus Caesar.

This celebration of marriage and its blessings also served as a quiet rebuke to those who were beginning to look back fondly to the days of the Virgin Queen, reminding them of how perilous England's future had been under a childless Elizabeth. *Hymenaei*'s opening lines, directed at James and his pregnant queen, encapsulate the masque's multi-layered arguments for political union, for marriage as sacrifice, and against the cult of virginity. The message was simple: if you don't believe in union, leave now:

> Bid all profane away;
> None here may stay
> To view our mysteries,
> But, who themselves have been,
> Or will, in time, be seen
> The self-same sacrifice.
> For Union, mistress of these rites,
> Will be observed with eyes,
> As simple as her nights.

Jonson was familiar enough with older, static court entertainments to understand that some form of conflict or threat was needed if the masque was to rise above mere pageantry. He provided this through the dramatic appearance of the eight courtiers, cast as the 'four Humours and four Affections'. The men had remained hidden from view within an enormous silver and gilt globe that seemed to float in the air, one of the technological wonders that Inigo Jones had created for the occasion, perhaps a sidelong glance at that other Globe in Southwark. We learn from an eyewitness that Jonson inserted himself as the controlling genius at this point in the masque, personally turning the giant globe as the eight masquers exited from it two by two. The professional actor who played Hymen provided a running commentary as these eight lords emerged, swords drawn, to the sound of 'contentious music': 'save the virgins! . . . The four untemp'red humours are broke out, / And, with their wild affections, go about / To ravish all religion.' At this moment of danger, another professional actor cast as Reason steps in, demands submission and ends the threat. Admonished by her, the noblemen 'sheathed their swords and retired amazed to the sides of the stage' (2.671–2).

Their departure cleared the way for the arrival of Juno and her powers (her very name, 'IUNI', Jonson notes, anagrammatically signifying 'Union'). Their entrance is breathtaking, calling on all of Inigo Jones's skill in stagecraft. In his printed text of *Hymenaei* Jonson describes in vivid detail how Juno appeared 'sitting in a throne supported by two beautiful peacocks'. Beneath her, he adds, was another mythological figure, Iris, symbolising the rainbow, and eight court ladies, all 'richly attired' (2.669, 675–6). These eight now joined the eight men – a surprising first for the Jacobean masque, which had previously been staged with either men or women but had never mixed the two – and what ensued was probably the most captivating moment of the production for those privileged enough to witness it, as the elaborate dance culminated in their spelling out the names of the young married couple in choreographed steps. In the masque's magical climax the fantastic play-world merged with the world of the court as the dancers then stepped forward and chose as new partners the queen, Prince Henry, the bride and groom, ambassadors and other leading lords and ladies.

Jonson saw how pleasing his masque was and understood how seamlessly its language, action and message fitted together. He was proud enough of what he had accomplished to publish it in quarto in 1606, in which he was almost at a loss for words to describe its effects: 'Such was the exquisite performance, as (beside the pomp, splendour, or what we may call apparelling of such presentments) that alone (had all else been absent) was of power to surprise with delight, and steal away the spectators from themselves' (2.686). In this printed text Jonson added a declaration of his artistic principles, a powerful defence of masques and their lasting value. They were not, as Francis Bacon would claim in his *Essays*, merely expensive 'toys'. To accept that, Jonson argues, is to confuse things that appeal to our senses with those that penetrate more deeply to our intellect.

As Twelfth Night approached, and the court slept off a long night of feasting and drinking, labourers dismantled Inigo Jones's elaborate sets. In their place, in the centre of the long room, they erected a wooden barrier designed to separate armed combatants. They also put up a wire screen to shield the king and queen from the fighting. The young Earl of Essex and Frances Howard had not spent the night consummating their marriage, despite Jonson's leering encouragement to the bride to 'Shrink not, soft virgin, you will love / Anon what you so fear to prove' (2:683). Their wedding had been no more than political theatre. Contrary to what is widely believed about marriage in Shakespeare's day, teenagers rarely married and sexual relations between those who did were highly discouraged (it was considered dangerous for their still developing bodies and made childbirth, always risky, especially so for a young girl). The average age of marriage at the time in England was roughly twenty-five, for both men and women, even if a handful of wealthy aristocrats, concerned about cementing alliances and ensuring male heirs, chose to marry off much younger children. The legal age of consent was fourteen for men and twelve for women; so as Arthur Wilson later wrote, Essex and Frances Howard were 'too young to consider, but old enough to consent'. Their physical union would be postponed: young Essex was packed off for an extended Continental tour, while his bride was sent home to her family, both having successfully played the roles in which they were cast.

King James himself may have regretted this. The previous Christmas season he had married off the twenty-year-old Philip Herbert to Susan De Vere, the seventeen-year-old daughter of the Earl of Oxford. Herbert, one of James's favourites, flirted brazenly with the king, who was clearly attracted to him. On New Year's Day in 1604 he had appeared before James bearing a ceremonial shield on which was painted a stallion in a green field. When James asked him what it meant, the young man teasingly replied that 'none could mount him but one as great as Alexander'. The king got the hint and, Dudley Carleton reported, 'made himself merry with threatening to send this colt to the stable'. James had also joked with the bride that 'if he were not married he would not give her but keep her himself'. Masques celebrating marital chastity were one thing, royal desires something else entirely. The morning after their wedding masque was celebrated at court, King James, dressed 'in his shirt and his nightgown', visited the newlyweds while they were still in bed. Dudley Carleton notes in his account of this *ménage à trois* that James 'spent a good hour with them in the bed or upon', adding, 'Choose which you will believe best.' Essex and Frances Howard were at least spared an unannounced royal visit.

For those at court, especially the participants, the symbolic combat offered in the barriers on Twelfth Night must have been eagerly anticipated and promised a different sort of drama from the previous evening's spectacle. Thirty-two knights were enlisted as combatants, sixteen against sixteen. The opposing sides were not chosen at random. On one side were arrayed mostly Essex's followers, wearing his familiar colours, 'carnation and white'. Opposing them were the Howard faction and their followers, dressed in light blue and white. They faced each other across an ideological barrier as well. Those identified with Essex's cause were seen as opponents of peace with Spain and of Union with Scotland, aggressively Protestant, proponents of territorial expansion and believers in alternative and ancient sources of political rights, positions for which King James had little patience.

The barriers began excitingly with 'a battle being sounded under the stage' and the appearance of two actors, each claiming to be Truth. They looked like twins and 'could by no note be distinguished' (2.690). Since only one of them could be Truth, the other was an imposter, Opinion. At a time when some of those at court were still suspected of complicity in the Gunpowder Plot, the challenge of distinguishing truth from falsehood, fair from foul, remained a pressing one, especially when so many of the Gunpowder plotters had previously been involved in the Essex uprising. At the barriers, at least, a solution was at hand: combat would decide the matter, though for the spectators the answer was never in doubt, since the 'Truth' the Essex fighters defended was a fierce advocate of virginity and described marriage as little more than subjection, while the opposing 'Truth' (for whom their opponents fought) celebrated union and disparaged virginity as 'a strange and stubborn thing'. From the outset, then, the deck was stacked against the Essex camp.

Though the outcome was predetermined, it must have been thrilling and unnerving in equal measure for those gathered at

Whitehall Palace that evening – the very site that five years earlier the Essex faction had hoped to seize – to watch the two sides square off with pikes and swords. For many of the combatants, this was personal. Two of the Howard fighters, Lord Effingham and Sir Robert Mansell, had personally led the siege of Essex House that crushed the revolt, and Mansell had afterwards played a leading role in rounding up Essex's followers. Sir John Grey, who fought alongside them, had been responsible for custody of some of the Essex rebels and would have recognised among those opposing him both the Earl of Sussex and Sir Carey Reynolds, close supporters of Essex who had been imprisoned for their role in the rebellion, as well as Sir William Constable and Sir Oliver Cromwell (great-uncle of the future Lord Protector), who were imprisoned and stood in danger of execution in 1601. Many of those who wore the Essex colours had been knighted by the earl on military campaigns in Cadiz or Ireland and remained fiercely loyal to him. Some of those opposing them may well have had mixed feelings, having themselves been knighted by Essex (though they had refused to follow him into rebellion). The oddest man out was surely Monteagle, who had been a key supporter of Essex's rebellion but who had to be shifted to the winning side, given how bad it would look to have the man who had so recently helped save the nation fighting against Truth. The thirty-two combatants thrust with their pikes and slashed with their dulled swords for hours, first in solo combat, then three against three. Which follower of Essex sought out which opponent is unknown, but Jonson records that both sides fought in earnest.

The battle of the final group of six fighters had 'scarcely ended' when there was a sudden and brilliant flash of light in the hall and a new actor appeared, 'an Angel or messenger of glory', who announced that Truth was about to arrive. She made a spectacular entry, riding a chariot, in a true Roman triumph, in which her captured foes were paraded and humiliated:

> On her coach wheels Hypocrisy lies racked,
> And squint-eyed Slander, with Vainglory backed,
> Her bright eyes burn to dust, in which shines Fate.
> An angel ushers her triumphant gait,
> Whilst with her fingers fans of stars she twists,
> And with them beats back Error, clad in mists.
> (2.698)

As Truth descended from her chariot she announced that her rival had been exposed as a counterfeit, Opinion. She consoled Essex's followers but firmly insisted that they must yield: 'It is a conquest to submit to right.' Truth herself then submitted to an even greater authority, the king, since even Truth must bend to his will. Her action reiterated the message of submission that defined the two-day entertainment: of virgins to marriage, wives to husbands and subjects to rulers. As the 'reconciled' enemies were led forth, Jonson brought the barriers to an end with the briefest of allusions to the recent plot, until now unspoken but still much on everyone's mind: 'Lastly, this heart, with which all hearts be true; / And Truth in him make treason ever rue' (2.699). Inside the old Banqueting House, at least, violence and division had been suppressed, and for the duration of the entertainment, the kingdom rid of treasonous threats.

Jonson wasn't wrong in believing that *Hymenaei* would leave a lasting impression on English literature; it did, just not in the way he expected. Among those in attendance was Shakespeare, who was challenged on many levels by what he saw. One early response to what he witnessed was his decision later that year to stage for the first time, in *Antony and Cleopatra*, a full-blown Roman triumph. In visualising such a spectacle (which both Antony and Cleopatra dread will be their fate in defeat) the scene serves a crucial function in that play, though nowadays it is invariably cut; its rich associations lost, modern directors don't quite know what to do with a Roman captain entering in a chariot, 'as it were in triumph' over his enemies (3.1.0 stage direction).

Shakespeare's experience of Jonson's masque stuck with him and he almost surely picked up a printed copy of *Hymenaei*. We don't typically think of Shakespeare as envious, but if he did feel that way after seeing *Hymenaei* it would be easy to understand why. Just a few years earlier, under Queen Elizabeth, his plays were – and had been for the better part of a decade – the centrepiece of the holiday season at court. But that was when the two or three new plays he wrote each year roughly corresponded to the number of plays his company was asked to perform before the queen. His new work not only risked being swamped by the volume of plays now staged over the season, but also paled in comparison with the splendour of the court masque. How, in a few short years, had his work gone from main event to opening act? Even Samuel Daniel, for all his reservations, conceded that masques were 'that which most entertain the world'. It was difficult to compete with such glamour and special effects when the members of your company wore second-hand clothing, had modest musical skills, and their stagecraft, intended for an uncluttered scaffold with at most a few familiar props, was even more constrained. While Shakespeare's comedies might end in a formal dance rather than the bawdy jigs of rival companies, they still could not approach the extraordinary choreography, let alone the celebrity factor, provided by members of the court and royal family dancing in public.

While Shakespeare never wrote Jacobean court masques, he was clearly fascinated by them, none more so than *Hymenaei.* One way of measuring its effect on him is to compare the two wedding masques that appear in his plays, one written before and the other after he saw *Hymenaei*. Six years earlier, at the end of *As You Like It*, the god Hymen had entered to musical accompaniment and sung a brief, formal hymn in praise of marriage:

> Wedding is great Juno's crown,
> O blessed bond of board and bed!
> 'Tis Hymen peoples every town;
> High wedlock then be honoured:
> Honour, high honour and renown,
> To Hymen, god of every town!
> (5.4.140–5)

Yet the god's unexpected entry fails so completely at transcendence that for over two hundred years Shakespeare critics have been insisting that Hymen couldn't really have been intended as an actual divinity; Rosalind must have fitted up Corin or one of the other foresters to impersonate the god of marriage. Much depends, of course, on who played Hymen, how magnificently he was costumed and how grandly he entered – none of which is specified in the text. It could well have been an early and experimental attempt on Shakespeare's part to appropriate masque-like elements, an effort to move beyond the naturalism that until this moment had defined his play. But at this late Elizabethan moment, neither the crucial special effects nor the fully-fledged notion of what a masque could be, both formally and ideologically, was as yet available to Shakespeare or his contemporaries.

Five years after seeing *Hymenaei*, Shakespeare wrote another play in which he embedded a masque: *The Tempest*. Written to be performed both at the Globe and in his company's new indoor Blackfriars Theatre, *The Tempest* was also staged at Whitehall Palace, very likely in the new Banqueting House itself, on 1 November 1611. The nuptial masque in Act 4 is designed by Prospero, the exiled Duke of Milan, who calls it 'some vanity of mine art'. Performed by Ariel and other spirits at Prospero's command, the masque celebrates the betrothal of Prospero's daughter Miranda to Ferdinand, son of the King of Naples. As was the case with *Hymenaei*, this is also a marriage between young and inexperienced lovers designed to heal old political rifts, and whose consummation is delayed.

The debt to *Hymenaei* is considerable. Iris, goddess of the rainbow, once again plays a starring role. So too does Juno, who had appeared in Jonson's masque 'sitting in a throne supported by two beautiful peacocks', unusual props that reappear in Shakespeare's text, where Iris specifies that Juno's 'peacocks fly amain' (4.1.74) – perhaps played by costumed actors who serve as her entourage. The stage machinery installed at the Globe and Blackfriars theatres – windlasses that slowly lowered actors from a trapdoor in the ceiling of the stage – allowed Shakespeare to approximate Juno's spectacular appearance. One of the most masque-like features of this scene in *The Tempest*, though one that playgoers never see, is the descriptiveness of its stage directions, which provide far more information than Shakespeare typically offers. Some scholars refuse to believe that Shakespeare, usually so laconic in his guidance to the actors, was responsible for such over-elaborate stage directions as: 'He vanishes in thunder; then, to soft music, enter the shapes again, and dance, with mocks and mows, and carrying out the table' (3.3.82 stage direction). Working closely from the elaborate printed edition of *Hymenaei*, Shakespeare seems to slip into his rival's florid style when writing these stage directions, including an unusual and quite specific one (also lifted from *Hymenaei*), describing how Prospero appears 'on the top' of the stage observing his handiwork (3.3.18 stage direction). Shakespeare carefully keeps him in our sightlines, reproducing the effect at the Banqueting House of seeing the masque-maker as an integral part of his own show.

Shakespeare even reproduces a version of *Hymenaei*'s memorable scene in which for the first time men and women danced together in a masque. At Iris's command, a group of rustic Reapers enter and join with an equal number of Nymphs in 'a graceful dance' (4.1.138 stage direction). Prospero's art perfectly renders the idealising spirit of the Jonsonian masque: the formal dance of the Reapers and Nymphs reinforces the image of concord symbolised by Ceres and Juno, as heaven and earth are bound together by a rainbow, Iris. Yet in the very act of demonstrating that even with limited resources he was fully capable of creating a Jacobean masque and understood its ideological terms and structural elements perfectly well, Shakespeare, shockingly, punctures the entire enterprise by bringing the masque to a sudden halt, for it is interrupted by a 'strange and confused noise' and the dancers scatter. Prospero, who has been absorbed in his artistic creation, terminates the masque after realising that he has been so distracted that he 'forgot that foul conspiracy / Of the beast Caliban and his confederates / Against my life. The minute of their plot / Is almost come' (4.1.139–42). The last time that Prospero was so 'transported / And rapt in secret studies' he lost his kingdom of Naples (1.2.76–7). Real-world plots expose the masque's propensity for self-absorption and self-celebration.

What follows is one of Shakespeare's most hauntingly beautiful speeches, as a chastened Prospero explains to the young lovers and future rulers what he already knows: masques are evanescent. These words have long been interpreted autobiographically, the poet's summation of his career and his view of his art as he is about to retire to Stratford (before scholars conceded that Shakespeare would write at least three more plays after this, and may have contemplated yet more). On closer examination, its visual details seem to hark back less to the special effects of the masque we have just witnessed than to the elaborate ones that Shakespeare had seen staged, great globe and all, before King James at the Banqueting House years earlier:

> Our revels now are ended. These our actors,
> As I foretold you, were all spirits and
> Are melted into air, into thin air;

And, like the baseless fabric of this vision,
The cloud-capped towers, the gorgeous palaces,
The solemn temples, the great globe itself,
Yea, all which it inherit, shall dissolve,
And, like this insubstantial pageant faded,
Leave not a rack behind.
(4.1.148–56)

Why go to the trouble of so painstakingly recalling the earlier masque only to sabotage it? In wrestling with the challenge of *Hymenaei*, Shakespeare responded on both political and artistic levels to what he saw as the court masque's intrinsic limitations when compared to the art of the public stage. By situating Prospero's show within the larger contours of his own play, Shakespeare invites spectators to see how masques, however captivating, are inescapably implicated in political self-interest. In doing so, he poses the sorts of question left unasked by court masques. Is Prospero's allusion to 'the baseless fabric of this vision' a concession that this 'insubstantial pageant' rests on unstable foundations? Is his benevolent art meant to distract us from Prospero's absolutist exercise of authority over his subjects? Unlike masques, the kind of plays that Shakespeare had been writing for the past two decades challenged audiences to reckon with such questions – which goes a long way towards explaining why his play continued to be staged long after the masque it recalled and critiqued was all but forgotten.

When *The Tempest* was performed at Whitehall in 1611 many of those in the audience knew that the premature marriage of the third Earl of Essex to Frances Howard was in tatters. The ironies of recalling at this moment *Hymenaei*'s celebration of their union were great. When the young earl returned to her after three years of foreign travel the two made each other miserable. She would subsequently claim that he was impotent, and he would insist that he never had this problem with other women. Their marriage disintegrated and the fallout would lead to the greatest scandal of James's reign. Around the time that *The Tempest* was performed at court, Frances Howard became romantically involved with one of the king's handsome favourites, Robert Carr. Not long after, thanks to the king's personal intercession, she had her marriage annulled so that she could marry Carr. But she had been so worried about Carr's friend Sir Thomas Overbury blocking their union that she conspired to have Overbury poisoned, a crime to which she eventually confessed. Both Howard and Carr were then imprisoned in the Tower. So much for what Jonson had called 'the binding force of unity'. When the time came to reprint the quarto of *Hymenaei* in his 1616 collected works, Jonson quietly omitted the names of all the noble participants in the masque, so as not to embarrass or implicate them further in a scandal that had tarnished the reputation of the king himself.

If the plays that Shakespeare would turn to next are any indication, what he saw at the Banqueting House in early January 1606 only sharpened his sense of the rifts that the masque and barriers failed to paper over. The problems posed by – and faced by – England's Catholics remained. If anything, nostalgia for the days of Queen Elizabeth was growing. And the ongoing debate about Union was exposing deeper fissures in national identity. What the masque suppressed and the barriers failed to contain were the very forces that Shakespeare was grappling with in his own drama. If he had not already begun writing *Macbeth*, he would do so shortly. Those who believe that this play was written to flatter King James fail to see that if Shakespeare wished to fawn over his monarch, there were easier and more remunerative ways to do so.

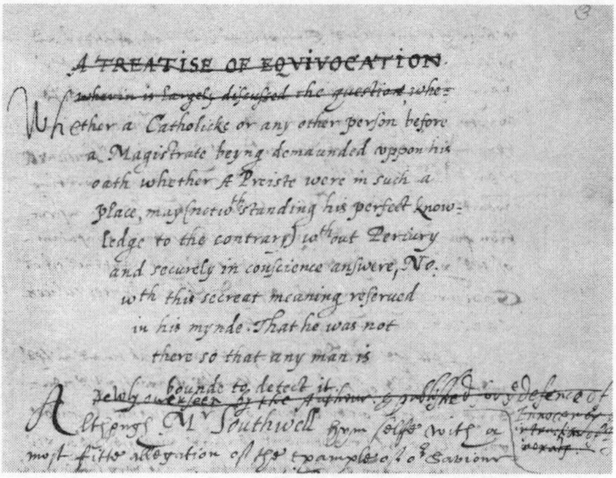
A TREATISE OF EQUIVOCATION
wherein is largely discussed the question whe-
Whether a Catholicke or any other person before
a Magistrate beyng demaunded uppon his
oath whether A Preiste were in such a
place, may (notwithstanding his perfect knowledge to the contrary) without Perjury
and securely in conscience answere, No.
with this secreat meaning reserued
in his mynde. That he was not
there so that any man is
bounde to detect it.

9 : *Equivocation*

Before *Macbeth*, the word 'equivocation' appeared only once in Shakespeare's plays, around the turn of the century, when Hamlet, after yet another of the witty Gravedigger's maddening replies, tells Horatio: 'How absolute the knave is! We must speak by the card, or equivocation will undo us' (5.1.137–8). A 'card' was a sailor's compass-card on which the points of the compass were marked, so Hamlet is saying that in navigating their way through this conversation they must choose their words carefully to prevent being steered off course. Equivocation was a rare and scholarly term, one that had appeared in only a few dozen books in sixteenth-century England, mostly religious polemics, and never in a printed play, poem or story. With the exception of a few theologians in whose work equivocation had begun to take on pejorative and fiercely anti-Catholic associations, English writers who knew the word thought it another way of saying that an expression was ambiguous. As late as the autumn of

Title Page of 'A Treatise of Equivocation', by Henry Garnet (*c.*1598)

1605, that's how Francis Bacon defined it in his *Advancement of Learning*.

By 1606, when Shakespeare next used the word, familiarity with it was nearly universal. Almost overnight, 'equivocation' had become a byword that transfixed the nation and suffused the play he was writing. No longer neutral, it was now taken to mean concealing the truth by saying one thing while deceptively thinking another. Shakespeare counts on playgoers understanding that this is what Macbeth means when he says, 'I pull in resolution, and begin / To doubt th' equivocation of the fiend / That lies like truth' (5.5.42–4). It's unusual, almost unprecedented, for the primary definition of an established word to change so quickly. And even stranger is what accounted for this sudden shift: the discovery of a manuscript, one whose dangerous argument would never have been committed to paper had it not been for the sexual assault and turning of a Catholic prisoner years earlier.

After the initial discovery of the Gunpowder Plot the government methodically extended its investigation. Francis Tresham, the lone conspirator who had remained in London undetected, was eventually summoned by the Privy Council from his lodgings at the Inner Temple and committed to the Tower on 12 November, where he would die, officially of illness, a month later. Before his death he was questioned, along with his brothers and their friend George Vavasour, by Sir Edward Coke. Brilliant, vain and relentless, Coke (as Sir Edward Conway put it) 'would die if he could not help ruin a great man at least once every seven years'. In the past few years he had helped bring low both the Earl of Essex and Sir Walter Ralegh.

Prosecuting the Gunpowder plotters would be another feather in his cap. The Treshams and Vavasour were well known to Coke, not only because they were the sons and ally of the recently deceased and prominent recusant Sir Thomas Tresham, but also because all were residents of the Inner Temple, London's training ground and residence for aspiring young men seeking careers in law and government. It was Coke's alma mater; his association with the Inner Temple went back over thirty years, and he had served as treasurer, its highest elected officer.

Due diligence required that the men's lodgings at the Inner Temple be searched and Coke himself joined in. It was there, on 5 December, that he made a staggering discovery, one almost as astonishing as catching Guy Fawkes red-handed. The searchers stumbled upon what the authorities believed would never be committed to paper: a treatise on equivocation, essentially a manual for teaching Catholics how to lie under oath. So that he could take credit for the find (or perhaps ensure that it was properly entered as evidence), Coke carefully inscribed on its flyleaf what he had found and where he had found it: 'This book, containing 61 pages, I found in a chamber in the Inner Temple, wherein Sir Thomas Tresham used to lie, and which he obtained for his two younger sons. This 5th of December, 1605. Edward Coke.' Coke's search party had discovered it not in a priest's hiding hole in some recusant's Warwickshire estate but here, in one of the legal bastions of England, his own Inner Temple. Its original title, now crossed out, had been *A Treatise of Equivocation*. This had been replaced with another on the previous page: *A Treatise of Lying and Fraudulent Equivocation*. But that too had been changed: the word 'of' was crossed out and replaced with its seeming opposite, 'against', so that it now read: *A Treatise against Lying and Fraudulent Equivocation*.

Francis Tresham's brothers were re-examined, as was George Vavasour. Coke learned that four or five years earlier Vavasour, at Francis Tresham's request, had made another copy of the manuscript. It was one thing to confirm that Jesuits encouraged equivocation; it was another to discover a how-to guide to the practice, with the fingerprints of their English Superior all over it, and then be told that one of the Gunpowder plotters had ordered it copied. Coke studied the manuscript closely, appending notes to it, determined to make it an incriminating piece of evidence at the upcoming state trial of the conspirators, where he, as Attorney General, would prosecute the case.

He learned from the treatise that Jesuits distinguished between four ways of equivocating. The first and simplest was by deliberately choosing ambiguous words. You could deny that you were harbouring a priest by saying that the priest 'lyeth not in my house', since he wasn't telling lies there. The second way was to omit a crucial piece of information, telling the authorities, for example, that you were visiting a friend's house for dinner (but leaving unmentioned that you were also going there to attend a Catholic Mass). It was just this sort of equivocation, the treatise maintained, that Abraham practised in Genesis 12 when he told the Egyptians (who would otherwise have killed him and taken her) that his wife, Sarah, was his 'sister'. The third way depended on the interplay of word and gesture. If asked where someone the authorities were hunting could be found, you could reply, 'He came not this way,' while secretly pointing in your sleeve in another direction. As infuriating to the authorities as these three techniques might be, it was only the fourth that was truly beyond the pale, the kind involving what English writers this year began to call 'mental reservation', when your words and thoughts were at odds, though the person with whom you were speaking could have no idea that this was the case. This sort of equivocation meant saying, for example, 'I didn't see Father Gerard . . .' while finishing the sentence in your head with the words '. . . hide himself in a well-concealed priest-hole.' It wasn't a lie, exactly, if you believed that God knew your thoughts, even if the person questioning you could not. Yet if this wasn't a lie, what was? A few years later, when the full implications of mental reservation had sunk in, a court succinctly described how this tempting doctrine, once widespread, would lead to chaos: 'The commonwealth cannot possibly stand if this wicked doctrine be not beaten down and suppressed, for if it once take root in the hearts of people, in a short time there will be no faith, no troth, no trust . . . and all civil societies will break and be dissolved.' It's difficult to read this sort of despairing Jacobean vision and not think of Scotland under an equivocating Macbeth, a nightmare world where words belie intentions and honest exchange is no longer possible; Malcolm admits as much to Macduff, a fellow Scot he would like to trust but dare not: 'That which you are my thoughts cannot transpose' (4.3.22). In such a world, Macduff, equally suspicious, feels he has no choice but to respond by equivocating.

Coke publicised this dangerous doctrine at the state trial held on 27 January, brandishing the recently discovered manuscript before the eight surviving Gunpowder plotters. It's unclear whether any of them had ever seen it or even knew of its existence, but that mattered little. For Coke, and for those who packed the room to observe the trial, including King James, it was Exhibit A, the means whereby the traitors were able to conceal their plans with the blessing of their Jesuit handlers. Coke spoke of 'their perfidious and perjurious equivocating abetted, allowed and justified by the Jesuits, not only simply to conceal or deny an open truth, but religiously to aver, to protest upon salvation, to swear that which themselves know to be most false'. He explained how 'mental reservation' was at the heart of this Jesuitical doctrine, 'reserving a secret and private sense inwardly to themselves, whereby they are, by their ghostly fathers, persuaded, that they may safely and lawfully elude any questions, whatsoever'. A lawyer who believed that words spoken under oath were the bedrock of an orderly society, Coke was at pains to convey how deeply destructive equivocation was, an 'art of cozening' that could tear apart the social fabric no less than barrels of gunpowder could destroy bodies and buildings.

The trial underscored how the government's account of the Gunpowder Plot had evolved since early November. What had begun as the vilification of Guy Fawkes, then turned into the story of the villainous ringleaders Percy and Catesby, was undergoing further revision. It was now less about a handful of discontented Catholic gentry who plotted the death of their king and more about the pernicious ideas that enabled their plan. Traitors could be eviscerated, decapitated and quartered, but it was proving more difficult to eradicate treasonous ways of thinking and speaking.

Back in the spring of 1586, the Superior General of the Jesuits had despatched two young recruits to England. Given the fate of those who had previously been sent, it was likely to be a suicide mission, with the expectation of eventual capture, torture and public execution. Twenty-eight years had passed since the Protestant Queen Elizabeth had succeeded her Catholic half-sister Mary, and sixteen years since Pope Pius V had excommunicated Elizabeth. The previous year, with fears of a Spanish invasion looming, Elizabeth had passed an Act that considered as traitors and condemned to death 'professed Jesuits' or 'seminary priests' despatched from Rome 'not only to withdraw her highness's subjects from their due obedience to her majesty, but also to stir up and move sedition'. The Act also declared it a felony to harbour them. During the last quarter-century of Elizabeth's reign, five hundred or so seminary-trained priests secretly tended to roughly forty thousand recusants. But there were never more than a handful of Jesuits to oversee their work. By the time that the decision to send the pair into England had been reached, the Jesuit foothold there had been almost entirely eliminated: at the time of their arrival, only a single Jesuit, William Weston, had managed to evade spy networks and tireless English pursuivants (officers authorised to execute warrants).

Robert Southwell and Henry Garnet were chosen for this mission. In May 1586 the two left Rome together, bound for their native land. They landed undetected, had some close calls but evaded capture, met up in London with Weston (who would soon be caught and imprisoned), then, for safety's sake, went their separate ways, seeking shelter among Catholic gentry. Their orders were to meet but twice a year. It was a lonely and often harrowing existence in which Southwell and Garnet had to balance the demands of their calling with an instinct for self-preservation, since, with spies and informants everywhere, each stay at a

Catholic household might end in betrayal and death. Southwell found solace in writing, including a poem called 'The Burning Babe' that Ben Jonson so admired he said he would have been content to destroy many of his own poems to have written it.

The threat of arrest loomed larger once the authorities learned what Southwell looked like from a captured English priest who had met him in Rome: thirty years old, clean-shaven, auburn-haired and of medium build. It was just enough to go by, and Richard Topcliffe, the most sadistic of England's pursuivants, redoubled his efforts to hunt him down. Torture, when authorised in England, had previously been restricted to the rack, and the only one of those contraptions was in the Tower of London. Topcliffe, though, had secured permission to set up his own shop, a private torture chamber in his house next to the Gatehouse prison in Westminster. Topcliffe didn't need a rack to extract information. He had devised an inexpensive technique that was equally effective: hanging his chained victims against a wall (which took just enough of the body's weight), their wrists pressed with tight manacles. A Jesuit priest who was subjected to it described its effect: 'All the blood in my body seemed to rush up into my arms and hands and I thought that blood was oozing out from the ends of my fingers . . . The pain was so intense that I thought I could not possibly endure it.' As far as the authorities were concerned, Topcliffe's method for extracting information didn't rise to the level of torture, since it didn't visibly maim or threaten the life of the victim. As Topcliffe himself cheerfully put it in a letter to Elizabeth: 'if your highness's pleasure be to know anything' in a prisoner's 'heart', he will arrange for his victim 'to stand against the wall, his feet standing upon the ground, and his hands but as high as he can reach against the wall,' which 'will enforce him to tell all'.

On 26 January 1592 a Catholic woman was arrested as an 'obstinate recusant' by order of the Bishop of London, and imprisoned in the Gatehouse. Her name was Anne Bellamy. She was twenty-nine and the unmarried daughter of Richard and Mary Bellamy. The Bellamys were a celebrated recusant family. Six years earlier they had even sheltered some of those involved in the Babington Plot to free the Catholic Queen of Scots, for which Anne's kinsman Jeremy Bellamy had been executed and other family members imprisoned. Topcliffe and other priest-hunters were sure that Anne's parents had, in his words, 'received, relieved and harboured in their house fifteen or sixteen Jesuits and seminary priests'. The Bellamys had hosted them in their home in Uxenden, a twelve-mile ride from the walled City of London (currently where the Metropolitan Line intersects with the Bakerloo Line, but in Shakespeare's day wooded country). Their house was well equipped with cleverly disguised hiding places, confounding searchers even when they had been tipped off by informants or simply raided the house in the hope of turning up a stray priest. No priest had ever been captured there. An ingenious plan was needed to land so wary a prey as Southwell.

Not long after her imprisonment in the Gatehouse in late January 1592, Anne Bellamy was handed over to Topcliffe. As for what happened next, historians have had to rely on Topcliffe's correspondence as well as a pair of independent and corroborative accounts, one by Anne's brother Thomas, the other by a family friend, Robert Barnes, who later fell foul of Topcliffe. According to Barnes, Anne Bellamy wasn't imprisoned six weeks before she was 'found in most dishonest order'. It's unclear what he meant by that, but by late March she was pregnant. Topcliffe was almost surely the father. What led to that outcome is unknown, though for the sixty-year-old Topcliffe, who had no previous record of sexual assault, it was likely less about sex than about control, the most effective way to break and turn a prisoner. Anne Bellamy was isolated, no doubt terrified, and under the thumb of one of the most violent men of the age. Whether (as some Jesuit writers subsequently insinuated) she might have consented seems irrelevant; she was his prisoner. Having impregnated her, Topcliffe then managed to flip her, using her to trap Southwell. That, clearly, had been his plan all along.

At this point Topcliffe, confident enough of his control over Anne Bellamy, allowed her to go free on bail, though not to return home or travel a mile outside London. She took lodgings in Holborn. When her brother Thomas visited town on Midsummer's Day she sent word to Southwell to meet him near Fleet Street and the two men agreed to travel to Uxenden together. Anne shared the information with Topcliffe and provided him with instructions 'directing him right unto a secret place within the house' where Southwell would likely be hidden. Topcliffe agreed to Anne's one condition: that her family would be spared. When news that Southwell was bound for Uxenden reached him at Greenwich, Topcliffe and his armed men raced there to intercept him, waiting until midnight to burst in. Topcliffe then showed the family the detailed instructions he had been given about Southwell's whereabouts. As Henry Garnet later wrote to their handlers in Rome, Southwell 'judged for a certainty that the game was up and presented himself before Topcliffe there and then'. Bound hand and foot, he was dragged off to Topcliffe's private torture chamber. The brutal interrogations were soon moved to the Gatehouse, where members of the Privy Council joined in questioning Southwell, including the future Earl of Salisbury, who discussed with him, among other things, the Jesuitical doctrine that permitted Catholics, under oath, to say one thing while secretly thinking another.

After Southwell's capture, Topcliffe ordered Anne to return to the Gatehouse prison. From there, perhaps fearing that her pregnancy would be discovered, he sent her first to his sister's house, and then to his own in Lincolnshire, where in late December she gave birth. He had taken the added precaution over the summer of marrying her off – without her family's knowledge – to his 'boy', Nicholas Jones, the son of a weaver, who assisted him at the Gatehouse. Topcliffe then wrote to Anne's family, demanding that they provide the couple with a handsome dowry. When her outraged father refused, Topcliffe had him arrested on the charge of harbouring priests. Her mother too was arrested and imprisoned, as were their friends and relatives.

Though repeatedly tortured by Topcliffe, Southwell revealed little and was left to rot in prison. The government, unwilling to turn him into a martyr, saw little advantage in a trial and public execution. What, after all, had Southwell done other than defy the law by returning to his native land? Eventually Southwell, broken physically, begged to be put on trial, though he knew well enough what the outcome would be. In February 1595 his wish was granted. Southwell's trial by jury was held at the King's Bench in Westminster. Arrayed against him were Sir John Popham, Richard Topcliffe and Sir Edward Coke. The government's carefully scripted prosecution broke down, though, when Southwell spoke gamely in his own defence. The verbal sparring led to an unseemly shouting match, with Southwell accusing Topcliffe of torture and a flustered Topcliffe countering, 'I did but set him against a wall.' The case for the prosecution didn't regain its stride until Coke called a surprise witness, the only one asked to testify: Anne Bellamy. It was through her that Coke was able to incriminate Southwell. She told the court that Southwell 'had told her that if upon her oath she were asked whether she had seen a priest or not, she might lawfully say no, though she had seen one, keeping this meaning in her mind that she did not see any with intent to bewray him'. It sounded as if the Jesuit had told her there was nothing wrong with her lying under oath to save his life. Southwell was blindsided. He did his best to justify having encouraged Anne to engage in mental reservation, insisting that its lawfulness 'was not his opinion only, but the opinion of the Doctors and Fathers of the Church'. But it came across as a weak defence and the prosecution repeatedly interrupted him, charging that this was a 'barbarous doctrine', designed to teach people that 'it was lawful to commit wilful perjury'.

Southwell then played his last card, challenging Coke that 'you must admit my doctrine, or else I will prove you no good subject or friend of the queen'. Coke, his curiosity getting the better of him, agreed to hear him out. Southwell then asked him to imagine that the French had invaded England and Queen Elizabeth had sought safety in a private house. Only Coke knew that she was hiding there. If Coke was then questioned but was unwilling to swear that he didn't know where she could be found, the queen's enemies would surely know that she was hiding in that house.

His refusal to swear and lie in such a situation, Southwell concluded, proved that Coke was 'neither her majesty's good subject nor friend'. Stymied, Coke feebly replied that 'the case was not like', though it clearly was. It was Popham who finally responded to Southwell, the implications of saying one thing and meaning another having sunk in: 'If this doctrine should be allowed, it would supplant all justice, for we are men and not gods, and can judge but according to men's outward actions and speeches, and not according to their secret and inward intentions.'

This, Southwell must have recognised, was the real problem with the doctrine he was advocating. It was too easy to caricature, to reduce it, as Popham just had, to something that sounded flagrantly at odds with the ways in which honest people spoke. What could he say in response? That St Augustine had been wrong in concluding that all lying is sinful? That in an age of illegitimate persecution and torture, mental reservation was justified? That language is by its very nature slippery? It was hopeless. It wasn't easy walking a jury through these philosophical arguments and biblical precedents, certainly not when one's memory was impaired by torture and solitary confinement. It didn't help that Southwell was repeatedly interrupted by Coke, who kept mocking him as 'boy-priest'. Order in the court was restored, Southwell's defence cut off and the jurors dismissed by Coke. It took only fifteen minutes for them to arrive at a guilty verdict. Anne Bellamy's testimony about this troubling doctrine – never named in the court proceedings – had, as Coke expected, clinched the government's case. Southwell was led to Tyburn the following day, where he was hanged, then butchered.

Three years later, in April 1598, Henry Garnet wrote to a friend in Rome that he had composed 'a treatise of equivocation'. His tract reads like the point-by-point defence that Southwell had been prevented from making at his trial (and Garnet mentions that Southwell had 'long since' written of this matter though his observations on it could not be found). Garnet has some harsh words for those he mockingly calls 'our new divines of the King's Bench' – presumably Coke and Popham. He even circles back to Anne Bellamy's testimony and promises to show how it was perfectly lawful for her to swear and lie about whether Southwell was 'at her father's house' in order to save a priest's life. Garnet wrote the tract out of loyalty to his friend as well as out of the need to defend what he saw as a legitimate doctrine, though one that was increasingly at risk of being misrepresented by the authorities and used as a weapon against Jesuits and those who harboured them. The doctrine now had a name: equivocation. Garnet had no way of knowing it at the time, but his defence of it would cost him his life, even as it had cost Southwell his.

*

Jacobean playgoers didn't often hear lines from old plays echoed in Paul's Cross sermons, but they did on 1 June 1606, when John Dove preached there. Describing the origins and history of equivocation, Dove recalled the first time he encountered an example of it, probably in his grammar-school days: '*Aio te, Acacida, Romanos vincere posse*'. This ambiguous Latin phrase could either be construed as a promise that the questioner 'shall conquer the Romans', or its opposite, that 'the Romans shall conquer' him. Retelling the classical story in Christian terms, Dove told the crowd gathered that day outside St Paul's Cathedral that this was the 'doubtful answer' that the oracle of Apollo gave Pyrrhus when he went there 'to ask counsel of the devil' before challenging the Romans in battle. Fatally, Pyrrhus failed to grasp that it could be read two ways, naively assuming that it meant he would emerge victorious, though it 'was understood by the devil in the worser sense, and so it proved by the event, because, contrary to his own construction, he was conquered'. In Dove's retelling, it wasn't simply that the line was ambiguous; rather, the devil, knowing how hopeful Pyrrhus was, cunningly took advantage of his susceptibility. The contemporary application of this story for Dove was clear: equivocation was diabolical and now prevalent thanks to the Pope, who 'hath made that which was the device of Satan to be the practice of Christians'.

Some of those in the crowd may well have had a flash of recognition when Dove told this story, for they had heard or read the identical Latin words, no doubt familiar to many from their own grammar-school education, in an old and popular Shakespeare play, now known as *Henry the Sixth, Part 2*, reprinted in 1600 and likely still in repertory fifteen years after it was first staged around 1590. Early in that play we encounter a precursor to Lady Macbeth: Eleanor, wife of Humphrey, Duke of Gloucester. So great are her 'ambitious thoughts' that Eleanor encourages her more cautious husband to seize the crown from the pious and unsuspecting King Henry VI: 'We'll both together lift our heads to heaven,' she urges him, 'And never more abase our sights so low / As to vouchsafe one glance unto the ground' (1.2.14–16). Eleanor enlists the aid of Margery Jourdain, 'a cunning witch', and 'Roger Bolingbroke the conjurer', who promise to raise a spirit 'from depth of underground / That shall make answer to such questions / As by Your Grace shall be propounded him' (1.2.79–81). The Latin formula for raising spirits is recited, and, as in *Macbeth*, a spectacular conjuring scene follows, accompanied by thunder and lightning. A spirit slowly rises from the trapdoor and speaks as commanded of the fate of King Henry VI, then of various others who stand between Eleanor and Humphrey and the crown. Bolingbroke writes down each of the 'false fiend's' prophecies in turn, all of them, predictably, as in *Macbeth*, equivocal.

At this moment the Duke of York, who has been warned of these treasonous plans, bursts in with an armed guard, who arrest the conjurers and the witch. York then reads aloud the equivocal prophecies that Bolingbroke has just transcribed: 'Now, pray, my lord, let's see the devil's writ' (1.4.58). The ambiguous prophecy anticipates the familiar Latin tag that appears in Dove's sermon, and York quotes it here in a dismissive aside; the words stand as a kind of shorthand, mocking the responses that the hellish spirit delivered. As in *Macbeth*, Shakespeare is at pains to underscore the equivocal nature of these 'hardly understood' oracles:

> 'The duke yet lives, that Henry shall depose;
> But him outlive, and die a violent death.'
> Why, this is just '*Aio te, Acacida,*
> *Romanos vincere posse.*'
> (1.4.60–3)

York then reads of Suffolk's fate – 'By water shall he die' – then Somerset's: 'Let him shun castles.' The verbal tricks press equivocation to the limit, for Suffolk will be killed by a man named

Walter Whitmore, while Suffolk meets his end under the sign of an alehouse called the Castle (1.4.64–9). The brief scene reads like an early and compact version of *Macbeth*, its defining features all here, if less skilfully interwoven at this early stage of Shakespeare's career, as if he were feeling his way towards something more profound but not fully visible: the ambitious wife, the ambivalent husband, the attempted regicide, the witches, thunder, conjuration, spirits, and the equivocal and devilish prophecies.

Though popular in its own day, *Henry the Sixth, Part 2* is no longer much taught or performed, so this intriguing passage, in which Shakespeare first explores what he and others would later call equivocation, is largely unfamiliar. Those hunting for the sources of Shakespeare's plays tend to overlook the extent to which he returned to his earlier work, discovering, as he did here, something hinted at or only tentatively mapped out and later rethought. It's also striking how sharply Shakespeare diverged from his historical sources when he wrote this conjuring scene. His ultimate source, the English chronicle of Edward Hall, describes how Eleanor plotted 'by sorcery and enchantment . . . to destroy the king' and 'advance and promote her husband to the crown'. But when it comes to how she plotted, Hall tells a very different story, one in which Eleanor, conspiring with Roger Bolingbroke and Margery Jourdain, 'devised an image of wax, representing the king, which by their sorcery by little and little consumed, intending thereby in conclusion, to waste and destroy the king's person'. Playgoers familiar with the chronicle might well have expected this scene to include wax figures, an easy enough prop to bring on stage or take on tour. But Shakespeare's imagination led him elsewhere, towards a large-scale conjuration scene, one that turned on witches, spirits and the equivocal language that nowhere figures in his sources.

It's impossible to tell what steered him in this direction. Perhaps in the background were recent reports reaching London from Scotland of dozens of suspected witches who had treasonously conspired against King James in the 1580s. Another and stronger possibility points to something that Shakespeare almost certainly read: the most important guide to poetry and poetics to appear in his lifetime, which had just come out, George Puttenham's *The Art of English Poesy*. It's easy enough to imagine an aspiring writer devouring a book that rehearses every imaginable verbal trick and offers telling examples of each. One of the devices that Shakespeare encountered there is the odd-sounding 'Amphibologia', which, Puttenham explains, occurs when 'we speak or write doubtfully and that the sense may be taken two ways'. Puttenham himself never speaks of the equivocal. Where for Dove, some years later, the origins of this device were diabolical, for Puttenham they were political and clerical: 'These doubtful speeches were used much in the old times by their false prophets, as appeareth by the oracles of *Delphos* and of the *Sybil's* prophecies devised by the religious persons of those days to abuse the superstitious people, and to encumber their busy brains with vain hope or vain fear.'

Puttenham was especially struck by the role such ambiguous oracles had played in shaping British history. They had stirred up 'many insurrections and rebellions' in the land, he writes, including Jack Cade's. Given such dangerous associations with rebellion and treason, Puttenham warns that it is best to 'avoid all such ambiguous speeches' unless a writer has a particular objective in mind. Shakespeare is likely to have paid close attention at this point, since Jack Cade's rebellion figures prominently in *Henry the Sixth, Part 2*. It may well be that it didn't take more than this hint from Puttenham (though, notably, Shakespeare found in Eleanor's devilish plotting a better fit for equivocation than the play's Jack Cade scenes).

Shakespeare was clearly fascinated by the various ways in which one could equivocate and had been employing this device in his plays and poems long before he or his culture had settled on a name for it. For better or worse, it was simply part of how people communicated (a view perfectly encapsulated in the deeply equivocal Sonnet 138, which begins: 'When my love swears that she is made of truth, / I do believe her though I know she lies'). What, after all, did actors do for a living other than convincingly recite words they didn't actually mean while at the same time suppressing their own thoughts? And what did playwrights do, in an age of theatrical censorship, but encourage actors to say one thing while slyly pointing at another? Though the scene in *Henry the Sixth, Part 2* was the first time Shakespeare so explicitly employed what would come to be called equivocation, it would be far from the only instance of this verbal trick to appear in his plays. One of the great pleasures afforded by his works is watching his many lovers, rivals, servants, avengers and villains equivocate, sometimes playfully, sometimes in the most cunning and destructive ways imaginable. He would have understood efforts to reduce equivocation to the diabolical, to something that could somehow be rooted out and eliminated, as hopelessly if not dangerously naive.

*

On 15 January 1606 the government circulated a proclamation for the apprehension of Henry Garnet, along with two other Jesuit priests. It described Garnet as fat and grizzled (and rumours that a Falstaffian Garnet drank sack to excess and was an 'old fornicator' soon circulated, part of the government's campaign to sully his reputation). The nation was told to be on the lookout for a man 'between fifty and threescore' who was 'of a middling stature, full faced, fat of body'. It's unclear why the authorities had waited so long to act. Perhaps they had thought, as did the surviving conspirators, that any Jesuit implicated in the Gunpowder Plot would have already fled the country. More likely, it reflected evolving policy. Prosecuting the Jesuit leadership while assuring loyal English Catholics that they were blameless could create a rift between those who pledged allegiance to Rome and those whose first loyalty was to the king. The proclamation charged that Garnet and the other Jesuits 'did maliciously, falsely and traitorously move and persuade Catesby and the other conspirators' that 'it was lawful and meritorious to kill . . . the king and all other heretics within the realm of England'.

For a week or perhaps two, back in early November, after Catesby's man Thomas Bates had been despatched to Coughton Court in an unsuccessful effort to persuade him to join their ill-fated Warwickshire uprising, Garnet had sat tight. But after news of the debacle at Holbeach reached him, he thought it best to find a safer hiding place. He relocated sixteen miles west to Hindlip House, just outside Worcester, home to the recusant Thomas Habington. Hindlip had been custom-built to shelter priests, with intricately disguised hiding places – secret stairs, trapdoors and chimneys with double flues – some designed by Nicholas

Owen, a skilled carpenter who, as it happens, was now travelling with Garnet. After arriving there Garnet chose for his quarters a well-disguised if cramped chamber below the dining room.

Fearing that the plotters now undergoing torture in the Tower would eventually implicate him, Garnet wrote to the Privy Council, conceding that he had administered the Holy Sacrament to the conspirators before their attempt to blow up Parliament, but denying 'being any accessory thereto' and insisting that Catesby and the others had never 'sought his consent'. It was an equivocal declaration, since as early as June 1605 Catesby had sounded out Garnet, asking him whether it was legitimate to kill innocents in a lawful attack on an enemy's city. A month after that conversation, Oswald Tesimond, who was by now fully informed of the plot, tried to discuss the matter with Garnet, who insisted on hearing of it under the seal of the sacrament of Holy Confession, which meant that he could not then speak or act in good conscience upon hearing of what he already suspected, his commitment to the tenets of his faith trumping any loyalty to the king.

At dawn on 20 January, five days after the proclamation was issued, Sheriff Henry Bromley and a troop of a hundred armed men descended on Hindlip and broke down the gates, leaving those seeking refuge there little time to scatter. Edward Oldcorne, a fellow Jesuit who had long ministered at Hindlip, joined Garnet in his tight quarters, where they had enough food to last a couple of months but not enough room to stand or even stretch out their legs. Worse still, there was no way to dispose of their excrement and the stench soon grew unbearable. Elsewhere in the house, Nicholas Owen and Ralph Ashley, a fellow lay brother, were also hidden, with only an apple to share between them. On the fourth day of the search, the famished Owen and Ashley tried to escape but were caught. Though priest-hunts that went on this long were rare, the authorities continued their efforts and on 26 January received assurances that at least one of the Jesuits was still hiding there. That tip had come from the recusant Humphrey Littleton, who had heard that Oldcorne was now at Hindlip. Littleton had recently been caught harbouring his fugitive nephew Stephen Littleton as well as Robert Winter, the last of the Gunpowder plotters to be apprehended. All three men were captured and the desperate Humphrey Littleton, who was now being interrogated in nearby Worcester, decided to barter away the lives of those hiding at Hindlip in the deluded hope of saving his own. The following day, 27 January – the day of the trial of the eight surviving plotters in London – Garnet and Oldcorne, unable to bear the stench any longer, finally surrendered; even their captors were appalled by the conditions of their hiding hole.

Garnet was transported to London, where he was imprisoned. On 13 February he was brought to the Star Chamber at Westminster – two days after the privy councillors had questioned Brian Gunter in that very room about his daughter Anne's faked possession. To the councillors, the dangers to social order posed by fake demonic possession and Jesuitical equivocation were not that far apart. Though over sixty witnesses would be called before the Star Chamber in investigating fake possession – most of them while the Gunpowder Plot was still being prosecuted – it was Garnet and the Jesuitical doctrine that would prove for the government the more useful story, and supplant the demonic possession case that had so captivated King James.

If Garnet expected to be harshly interrogated about his whereabouts on 5 November or what he knew about the plot, he was mistaken. The councillors gathered there to question him could not have been more cordial. Garnet wrote to a friend that when he kneeled they bid him stand, and when addressing him they would ceremoniously remove their hats. He was at pains to reassure them that when Bates had found him at Coughton and asked him to join the conspirators he had told him that 'they should not enter into so wicked actions'. The interrogation lasted for another three hours, but that seems to have been the last time that anyone mentioned the plot. Salisbury steered the conversation instead to matters of doctrine. The copy of the manuscript that Coke had recently discovered was handed to him and Garnet was asked to say what he knew of it and what he thought of equivocation. No doubt relieved to discuss a less incriminating topic, Garnet obliged and admitted that he had corrected it and was responsible for changing its title, though he had discouraged its publication. Garnet had walked into a trap. He could not have known that Salisbury had just published a book – the only one he would ever publish – in which he had savaged 'that most strange and gross doctrine of equivocation' which would 'tear in sunder all the bonds of human conversation'. Salisbury would soon call the *Treatise of Equivocation* nothing less than 'the visible anatomy of Popish doctrine'. Along with Coke's words at the state trial a fortnight earlier, these were the first of many co-ordinated attacks on how 'the Papists now maintain it lawful to deny all truth under a mental reservation'. Salisbury's book – *An Answer to Certain Scandalous Papers* – was already being 'read greedily' and Prince Henry himself was among its early admirers.

A full account of all that Garnet said in defence of equivocation does not survive. We know that discussions of this subject continued, relentlessly, up to and even after Garnet's trial in late March. King James himself passed along a set of questions to be put to Garnet, including the request that the Jesuit explain 'what he thinketh of the doctrine in the "Book of Equivocations"'. Garnet must have realised that in the course of the earlier sessions he had said more than was wise, for before his trial he sent the authorities a panicky follow-up letter on the subject, in which he is at pains to qualify his earlier remarks: 'Concerning equivocation, which I seemed to condemn in moral things, my meaning was in moral, common conversation in which the virtue of verity is required among friends. For otherwise it were injurious to all humanity.' But these belated justifications came across as double-speak, the kind of statements on which the damning case against him would be built.

Worse still, Garnet was caught practising what he preached. While imprisoned in the Tower he was deliberately lodged near his fellow priest, Oldcorne, and led to believe that their jailer was sympathetic enough to let the two meet and secretly communicate. But a pair of government spies had been hidden nearby to record what passed between them. The priests, after shriving each other, were eager to get their stories straight, though they said little that was incriminating. The problem was that Garnet, when challenged, denied 'upon his soul' that they had even spoken. When shown Oldcorne's statement admitting as much, Garnet conceded that 'he had offended, if equivocation did not help him'. Retroactively invoking equivocation to excuse trivial acts of deception infuriated his captors, and unfortunately for

Garnet a letter he had written was intercepted and revealed the truth. It reached the point where one of his interrogators had to ask Garnet to add to his written statement that it was made 'without equivocation', for what that was worth.

On 28 March Henry Garnet was brought by coach to Guildhall to stand trial. The venue was chosen to underscore the severity of the crime. Lady Jane Grey had been tried and condemned to death here, as had other high-profile traitors under the Tudors, including the Earl of Surrey, Archbishop Cranmer and Dr Lopez. The large hall was packed and the audience included the king himself, hidden from sight behind a wicker screen. It took Coke six hours to establish his case (which wasn't easy, since the plot hadn't been Garnet's idea and had clearly caused him great anguish, as he understood the price English Catholics would pay if it failed). Coke chose to portray Garnet as a kind of playwright, the author of the plot, relegating those who carried it out to mere actors, and described his trial as the final 'act of that heavy and woeful tragedy which is commonly called the Powder Treason'.

With a flair for alliteration, Coke called Garnet – who had worked under the aliases of Darcy, Roberts, Philips, Wally and Farmer – the 'doctor of five Ds': 'dissimulation, deposing of princes, disposing of kingdoms, daunting and deterring of subjects, and destruction'. His dissimulation was grounded in equivocation, which predictably became the centrepiece of the trial, given the paucity of other evidence, as the means by which Garnet 'taught not only simple lying, but fearful and damnable blasphemy'. Garnet's doctrine was described as a form of infidelity, a divorce of the heart and tongue: 'This equivocating and lying is a kind of unchastity against which they vow and promise.' To prove his point, Coke asked Garnet why Francis Tresham, before his death in the Tower, had protested 'upon his salvation' that he hadn't spoken with Garnet in sixteen years – even though Garnet himself, unaware of what Tresham had said, had freely admitted that the two had been in regular contact. The only explanation Garnet could offer Coke was lame and incriminating: 'It may be, my lord, he meant to equivocate.'

Garnet was forced to defend the doctrine with which he had become identified; as Southwell had discovered before him, that wouldn't be easy. Despite his powerful command of the subject and his telling examples out of Scripture, he undermined his own case when insisting that 'our equivocation is not to maintain lying, but to defend the use of certain propositions', and, in what may well have inadvertently come across as comic, saying that 'no man may equivocate when he ought to tell the truth, otherwise he may'. Coke, well prepared, crushed this line of defence. Though Garnet was accused of having had a hand in every treasonous act going back a quarter-century and of having failed to reveal what he knew of the impending attack on Parliament, it was as an equivocator that he was effectively prosecuted and convicted. The jury deliberated for only fifteen minutes before rendering a guilty verdict.

Garnet's punishment was delayed for five weeks. When word circulated that plans for a May Day execution had been pushed back another two days, Dudley Carleton wrote to his friend John Chamberlain that 'Garnet should have come a-maying to the gallows which was set up for him in Paul's Churchyard on Wednesday, but upon better advice his execution is put off till tomorrow for fear of disorder amongst prentices and others in a day of such misrule.' Carleton could not resist adding a joke, indicative, one suspects, of others circulating at the time: 'It is looked he will equivocate at the gallows; but he will be hanged without equivocation.' An eyewitness reported that 'multitudes of people' gathered to watch Garnet die: 'All windows were full, yea, the tops of the houses were full of people, so that it is not known the like hath been at any execution.' Asked to confess his treason at last, Garnet admitted only to having concealed his knowledge of the plot under constraint of confession. When challenged at the scaffold – 'You do but equivocate' – he wearily replied, no doubt exhausted by the ceaseless harping on this subject, 'It is no time now to equivocate; how it is lawful and when, I have shown my mind elsewhere; but I do not now equivocate, and more than I have confessed I do not know.' Sympathisers in the crowd pulled on Garnet's feet as he was hanging so that he didn't have to face evisceration while still alive. His head was cut off and displayed on a pole on London Bridge. Within a few days a London printmaker brought out a ballad that broadcast the official storyline: Garnet 'was acquainted with the plot of late, / Though by equivocation, he denied, / The Pope allows them to equivocate, /The root of their abhorred intents to hide'.

A month later, on 1 June, Londoners returned to the site of the execution to hear John Dove preach on the subject of equivocation. Dove's text was the same one cited in Garnet's infamous treatise, Genesis 12, where Abraham equivocated to save his own life. Dove would have none of it, condemning the patriarch for his equivocations: 'He told a lie and could no way be excused' – and he reminded those gathered there that Protestant martyrs had never resorted to such measures to save themselves. The government was clearly not yet done with the case against the insidiousness of equivocation: 'He that lyeth', Dove preached, 'doth deprive himself of all credit among men (for they will also suspect him to be a liar), so that he that once deceiveth his neighbour by equivocation, shall always be suspected to equivocate.' The doctrine's effects were legally and economically destructive too: 'If deceit by equivocation be used, then all covenants and contracts between man and man must cease, and have an end, because all men will be suspicious of one another . . . So, no commonwealth can stand, no civil society can be maintained.' In the end, for Dove, it was God's fixed word and piety on the one side, and the devil, the Jesuits and the dangerous flexibility of language on the other. There was no room for ambiguity and he roundly condemned those who would 'have one lie to be malicious, whose end is to do harm, another sportful, whose end is to delight'.

Though Garnet was dead, the doctrine closely identified with him remained a threat. The drumbeat of condemnation lasted through August before gradually abating. Coke made much of it when addressing the Norwich Assizes on 4 August, in a speech considered significant enough to merit publication. Unlike many of those who trained at the Inns of Court, Coke seems to have shown little interest in playgoing (and that very day at Norwich he had encouraged local authorities to crack down on 'stage players, wherewith I find the country much troubled'). But five years earlier he had closely read *Richard the Second*. He had done so in the aftermath of Essex's uprising, on the eve of which the Chamberlain's Men had been paid forty shillings by some of Essex's supporters for a command performance of that old play. Essex's followers were eager to wrest Shakespeare's words to their own political ends and hoped that playgoers would recognise the obvious parallels between Richard II and their own childless monarch, surrounded by flatterers, burdened with an Irish war, who needed to be deposed for the nation's good. In the course of investigating the failed uprising, Coke questioned one of Shakespeare's fellow shareholders, read the offending play and determined that the Chamberlain's Men were not to be prosecuted. One of *Richard the Second*'s great speeches had stuck with him: John of Gaunt's prophecy about the dangers besetting the English nation. Gaunt had memorably described the wonders of the land –

> This royal throne of kings, this sceptred isle,
> This earth of majesty, this seat of Mars,
> This other Eden, demi-paradise,
> This fortress built by Nature for herself
> Against infection and the hand of war,
> This happy breed of men, this little world,
> This precious stone set in the silver sea . . .
> (2.1.40–6)

– before warning that all this was now threatened. In the aftermath of the Gunpowder Plot, Gaunt's vision of the endangered kingdom had taken on new meaning for Coke, who here threads the speech into a fresh political reading. Coke spoke of how this 'sea-environed island' had faced grave danger during 'the last horrid treason, by inhuman savages complotted':

> I know not what to speak, because I want words, to describe the traitorous, detestable, tyrannical, bloody, murderous villainy of so vile an action.

Only this had their horrible attempt taken place. This sea-environed island, the beauty and wonder of the world. This so famous and far-renowned Great Britain's monarchy, had at one blow endured a recoverless ruin, being overwhelmed in a sea of blood, all those evils should have at one instant happened, which would have made this happiest kingdom of all kingdoms, the most unhappy. Our conquering nation conquered in her self: her fair and fertile bosom, being by her own native (though foul unnatural children) come in pieces, should have been made a scorn to all the nations of the earth. This so well planted, pleasant, fruitful, world's-accounted Eden's Paradise, should have been by this time, made a place disconsolate, a vast and desert wilderness.

Shakespeare's words continued to redefine the ways in which the English made sense of their world. What had changed was the source of danger to the nation: for Gaunt, in Shakespeare's original, it was a feckless King Richard; for Essex's followers, it was a queen manipulated by flatterers; for Coke, it was the Jesuits' 'hellish sophistry, equivocating'. Coke described how the plotters 'had practised a most hellish attempt, wherein their devilishness brought itself nearest to the nature of the devil, making fire and brimstone the instruments of our destruction. And though the principal actors of that evil have thereby themselves destroyed, yet the former experience of their continual attempting may give us warning.' The destructive plot may have been foiled, but the diabolic threat posed by the doctrine of equivocation remained.

10 : *Another Hell above the Ground*

Not long after these traumatic events, Francis Bacon gently admonished an imprisoned friend, Tobie Matthew, who had chosen this dangerous year of 1606 to convert to Catholicism, for which he would soon be exiled. Bacon urged him to consider how 'this last Powder Treason' was 'fit to be tabled and pictured in the chambers of meditation, as another hell above the ground'. Bacon was prescient, for it would be memorably pictured, not just in the imagination but also, and vividly, in a print called 'The Powder Treason', executed by Michael Droeshout (father of the artist responsible for Shakespeare's portrait in the 1623 folio). The large sheet is crammed with words and images, including a central panel of King James seated before Parliament, the scene of the crime, its intended victims going about their business unaware of the forces of good and evil arrayed around them. Above, angels hover protectively beneath the watchful eye of God, while below, Guy Fawkes is paired with the barrels of gunpowder in the vault

Detail from 'The Powder Treason' (*c.*1620)

beneath the House of Lords. On the lower left a priest swears to secrecy those planning the explosion; on the lower right we see the plotters' grisly executions. Between these two scenes is the print's most arresting image: Garnet and a dozen of his accomplices are depicted as spectators who witness their own terrifying fate – arriving at hell's mouth, where devils await their traitorous souls. Illustrative lines, lifted from the broadside *Princeps Proditorum*, confirm the message: 'their lives heathenish, practice devilish, the deeds damnable, their ends miserable'. The print invites us to reflect on that which is never actually represented but is described at the very top of the page: the treasonous killing of the king, an action 'propounded by Satan' and 'founded in hell'.

When audiences first saw Shakespeare's *Macbeth* in the spring of 1606, they may have been surprised that they didn't get to witness the play's central action, on which everything turns, the murder of King Duncan. Locating the killing offstage is an unusual decision, given what audiences craved and what Shakespeare had offered them in all of his previous tragedies. Over the years, playgoers had watched Titus kill Tamora, Romeo stab Tybalt, the conspirators butcher Julius Caesar, Hamlet stab and then poison Claudius, Othello smother Desdemona and then stab himself, and Edgar fight and mortally wound the bastard Edmund. Because Duncan was a Scottish monarch, it may simply have proved impolitic to stage the scene, especially at this fraught moment (though if so, the entire plot, which also ends with the killing of a King of Scots, again – surprisingly – offstage, invited censorship). For Shakespeare to write a tragedy so fixated on a regicide and its repercussions yet not let playgoers see the act itself suggests instead that it was for him a deed – like the detonation that would have killed King James and devastated Britain – more powerfully 'tabled and pictured in the chambers of meditation'. But where Shakespeare's play differs from Droeshout's propagandistic print is in its cosmology, its refusal to portray hell as subterranean. The nightmarish tragedy that Shakespeare creates in *Macbeth* is all the more terrifying for taking place, to borrow Bacon's words, in 'another hell above the ground'.

In the immediate aftermath of Duncan's offstage murder we are offered by way of compensation one of the most incongruous scenes in all of Shakespeare, so atypical that Samuel Taylor Coleridge and other early critics suspected that it was 'written for the mob by some other hand'. A hungover and garrulous Porter, whose job is to admit visitors, slowly responds to repeated knocking at the castle's gate. The role was probably first made famous by Robert Armin, the company's witty comic star for whom Shakespeare had most recently written the Fool's part in *King Lear*. The knocking begins before his entrance. It's Macbeth who first hears it – 'Whence is that knocking? / How is't with me, when every noise appals me?' (2.2.61–2) – at the very moment that Lady Macbeth is offstage smearing Duncan's blood on the sleeping grooms. Re-entering, Lady Macbeth hears it too and tells her husband: 'I hear a knocking / At the south entry. Retire we to our chamber' (2.2.69–70). The persistent knocking is heard yet again, at which point they hurriedly exit.

A few years after Coleridge questioned Shakespeare's authorship of the ensuing scene, Thomas De Quincey defended it in an inspired essay, 'On the Knocking at the Gate in Macbeth': 'Another world has stepped in; and the murderers are taken out of the region of human things, human purposes, human desires.

I KING JAMES King of Scotland since infancy, James succeeded Elizabeth to the English throne in 1603. He turned forty in 1606, a year in which he struggled, unsuccessfully, to persuade Parliament to ratify the Union of England and Scotland. In this portrait, executed not long after he became King of England, James wears a fabulously expensive hat jewel – the Mirror of Great Britain – its diamonds, drawn from his various kingdoms, symbolising the much desired Union.

2 A VIEW OF LONDON FROM SOUTHWARK Painted around 1630 and indebted to earlier drawings, this panorama shows many of the familiar sites of Shakespeare's London, including (from left to right) Whitehall, St Paul's Cathedral, and the Tower. Outdoor playhouses, including the Globe Theatre, appear in the foreground. The severed heads of convicted traitors, mounted on spikes, can be spotted near the south end of London Bridge.

3 KING CHRISTIAN OF DENMARK
King Christian was twenty-nine years old and had ruled Denmark for a decade when he arrived in England in the summer of 1606 to visit his sister Anne and brother-in-law King James. The martial Christian sailed to England on his flagship, the *Tre kroner*, at the head of an impressive Danish fleet. The hard-drinking Danish king was a patron of the arts and employed English and Scottish architects, musicians, and shipbuilders.

4 ANNE OF DENMARK Born and raised in Denmark, and daughter, sister, and wife of a king, Anne had married King James in 1589. Anne was a major patron of English arts, including the theatre, masques, music and architecture. She was privately a Catholic, though she attended Protestant sermons and services. In June 1606 she gave birth to a daughter, Sophia, who died shortly after – the last child that King James and she would have.

5 THE EXECUTION OF THE CONSPIRATORS IN THE GUNPOWDER PLOT
This contemporary Continental print shows London's streets in late January 1606 packed with spectators viewing the punishment of the plotters – four of whom are seen drawn on wicker sleds to their place of execution adjoining St Paul's Cathedral.

6 THE EXECUTION OF THE CONSPIRATORS IN THE GUNPOWDER PLOT
Visscher's print depicts Londoners gazing from rooftops and windows as four plotters are drawn to their execution. The image shows the various stages of the execution rites, as the plotters are hanged, eviscerated, then beheaded.

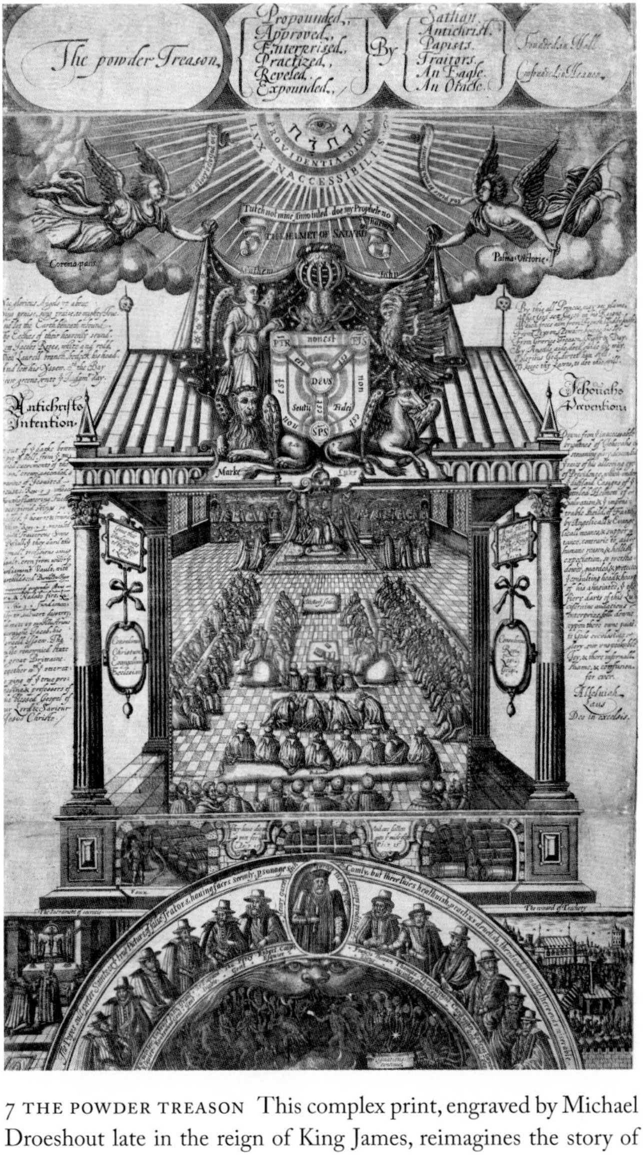

7 THE POWDER TREASON This complex print, engraved by Michael Droeshout late in the reign of King James, reimagines the story of the Gunpowder Plot vertically, from the divine protection in the heavens above to the subterranean and hellish forces below. At the centre of the print is King James addressing Parliament. Cutaways depict Guy Fawkes and the barrels of gunpowder; the plotters sworn to secrecy by a priest; their execution; thirteen of the conspirators with Henry Garnet at the centre; and hellmouth, where terrifying devils await the traitors.

8 WILLIAM SHAKESPEARE The iconic and celebrated Chandos portrait, traditionally attributed to John Taylor. It likely dates from 1605–10, so close to what Shakespeare might have looked like in 1606.

9 BEN JONSON In 1606 Jonson wrote some of his greatest work, including *Volpone* as well as the court masque *Hymenaei*. He was also charged with recusancy (and had been spotted dining with several of the Gunpowder plotters).

10 LANCELOT ANDREWES In 1606 Andrewes, the finest preacher of his day, delivered sermons before the King and court on many important occasions, including Gowrie Day, the anniversary of the Gunpowder Plot, and Christmas.

11 RICHARD BURBAGE Jacobean England's star tragedian, in 1606 he played Lear, Macbeth, and Antony and most likely Vindice and Volpone as well, if so, the greatest five roles first performed by any actor in one year.

12 ROBERT CECIL, EARL OF SALISBURY King James affectionately called his secretary of state his 'little beagle'. In 1606 Salisbury hosted James and Christian at his fabulous estate at Theobalds.

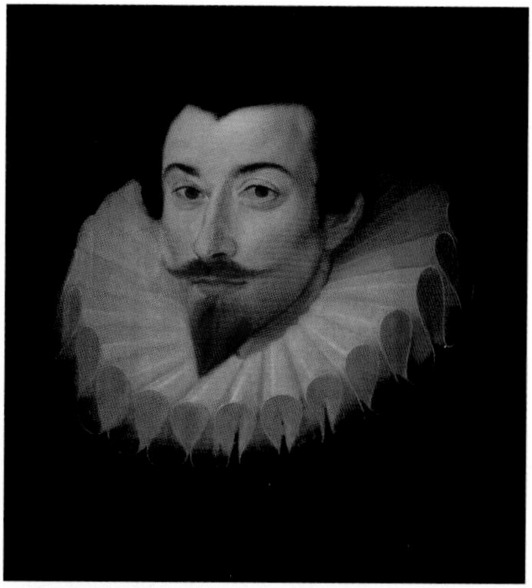

13 SIR JOHN HARINGTON Courtier, author, translator, and one of the shrewdest observers of his times, Harington's letters provide us with some of the most vivid and trenchant critiques of the age.

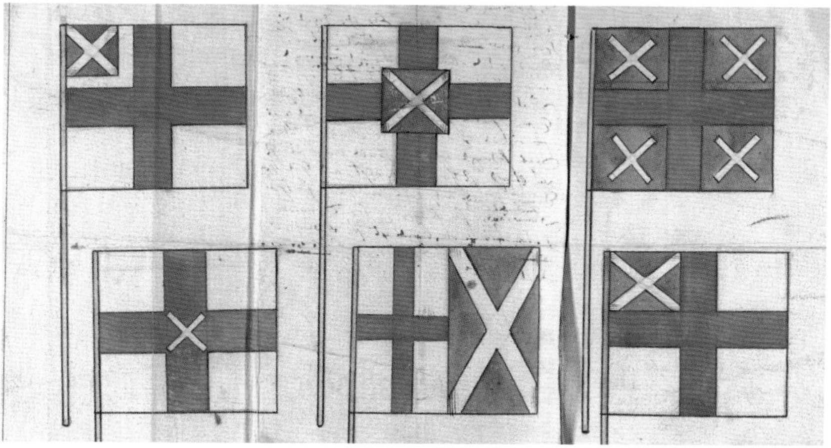

14 DESIGNS FOR THE FIRST UNION FLAG It proved easier in 1606 for King James to order that a Union flag be flown by all English and Scottish ships than it was to design such a flag. These early and unsuccessful sketches from that year – commissioned by the Lord Admiral, the Earl of Nottingham – underscore the difficulties faced in combining the Scottish and English flags, given the power relations necessitated by heraldic conventions. After the design for the Union flag was finally chosen, the Scots made clear their resentment that the Cross of St George had been imposed over that of St Andrew.

15 LUCY HARINGTON, COUNTESS OF BEDFORD Born in 1581 and married at the age of thirteen, the Countess of Bedford was a close companion to Queen Anne. She appears in this full-length commemorative painting, at the age of twenty-five, as one of performers in Ben Jonson's masque *Hymenaei*, her striking and elaborate costume designed by Inigo Jones. Already a major patron of the arts, she supported many of the leading poets, playwrights, musicians, and translators of the day.

16 EFFIGY OF CATHERINE OF VALOIS When medieval and early modern English kings and queens died, life-like effigies were employed in their funeral processions. A number of these mannequins, with moveable limbs and constructed out of wood, plaster, fabric, straw, and wax, were subsequently preserved in Westminster Abbey. In 1606, in anticipation of the visit of King Christian of Denmark, King James ordered that seven of the effigies of these royal predecessors, including this one of Henry V's French queen, be 'newly beautified, amended, and adorned with royal vestures', and then displayed.

They are transfigured: Lady Macbeth is "unsexed"; Macbeth has forgot that he was born of woman; both are conformed to the image of devils; and the world of devils is suddenly revealed.' Even as Shakespeare refuses reductive explanations of the diabolic, he allows us to reflect on the living hell that the Macbeths will henceforth experience – and impose on Scotland. He does so by having the Porter imagine that he's a 'porter of hell gate' (2.3.2) in the tradition of the devil porters who had been a fixture of medieval England's now barely remembered mystery plays. Through this conceit Shakespeare offers us, in the most down-to-earth scene in the play, the closest thing to an evocation of hell itself. As he had in *Lear*, Shakespeare invokes the supernatural while steering clear of the moral certitude that staging the demonic typically invites.

More knocking follows, and more complaining, as the Porter invokes hell's chief devil and wonders what lost and self-justifying soul has now come knocking: 'Knock, knock, knock! Who's there, i'th' name of Beelzebub? Here's a farmer, that hanged himself on th' expectation of plenty. Come in time! Have napkins enough about you; here you'll sweat for't' (2.3.2–6). While 'farmer' is a common enough word, it's one that Shakespeare almost never used. But he may have heard about Garnet passing under the alias of Farmer, one of the several pseudonyms mentioned at his trial. While that is the only time that this alias appears in the public record or in surviving English correspondence, it was what Garnet was called within his close-knit circle, as we know from the letters of Luisa de Carvajal y Mendoza, a confidante of the English Jesuits who was living at the time in the Spanish ambassador's residence in London. She writes home to a friend in Spain less familiar with the English Jesuits that 'Mister Farmer . . . is Father Garnet.' It may simply be a coincidence that the Porter uses this word or else Garnet's alias may have been more widely known at the time than surviving evidence suggests.

The Porter next imagines greeting another arrival in hell, an unnamed equivocator: 'Knock, knock! Who's there, in th' other devil's name? Faith, here's an equivocator, that could swear in both the scales against either scale, who committed treason enough for God's sake, yet could not equivocate to heaven. Oh, come in, equivocator' (2.3.7–11). It's as if Shakespeare had heard the joke making the rounds that spring – that the treasonous Garnet 'will equivocate at the gallows' – and taken it a step further, inviting us to imagine the Jesuit arriving at his next and final destination, hell itself, having failed to equivocate his way to heaven.

It's no one-off topical allusion, for the Porter is not yet done with equivocation, explaining to Macduff, who finally enters, why it took him so long to respond to his knocking: 'Faith, sir, we were carousing till the second cock: and drink, sir, is a great provoker of three things' (2.3.23–4). When Macduff rises to the bait and asks, 'What three things does drink especially provoke?' the Porter answers:

> Marry, sir, nose-painting, sleep and urine. Lechery, sir, it provokes and unprovokes: it provokes the desire but it takes away the performance. Therefore, much drink may be said to be an equivocator with lechery: it makes him and it mars him; it sets him on and it takes him off; it persuades him and disheartens him, makes him stand to and not stand to; in conclusion, equivocates him in a sleep, and, giving him the lie, leaves him. (2.3.27–35)

His joking about lechery, drink and equivocation likely doubles as another dig, linking the Jesuit equivocator's excessive drinking to his reputed philandering (even Salisbury couldn't resist teasing Garnet about this).

Yet the Porter's lines about equivocation are themselves equivocal. As much as they seem to repeat contemporary gossip about Garnet, they can also be read as sympathetic to the infamous equivocator. While many no doubt accepted official claims that he was implicated in the plot, for others he was a devout figure who 'committed treason enough *for God's sake*' rather than for any personal gain, and deserved clemency. Though he might have equivocated under duress and perhaps even torture, he 'could not equivocate *to heaven*', for God himself knew what was in his heart when he practised mental reservation under such trying conditions. Context matters too. How seriously are we to take the word of a drunken porter who imagines himself an agent of the devil? And the imagined equivocator who had been knocking turns out to be Macduff, hardly a man we think of as a traitor who swears and lies.

The most consequential act of equivocation in the play occurs when Macbeth and Banquo first encounter the Sisters (we never hear them referred to as 'witches', only as Weird or Weyard Sisters). The first hails Macbeth as Thane of Glamis, the second as Thane of Cawdor, and the third promises him he 'shalt be king hereafter'; they then tell Banquo, 'Thou shalt get kings, though thou be none' (1.3.50, 67). All true, but equivocal, insofar as they withhold vital information (they don't tell Macbeth that he'll have to kill to do it, or Banquo that he won't be alive to see it). Equivocation makes following *Macbeth*'s dialogue a mentally exhausting experience, for playgoers – much like those conversing with equivocators – must decide whether a claim should be accepted at face value, and if not, must struggle to reconstruct what may be suppressed though mental reservation. But with equivocators, one never knows what, if anything, is left unspoken. The meaning of the seemingly paradoxical phrase 'Fair is foul . . .' (1.1.11) becomes clear only when we learn to finish the thought: '. . . once we look past false exteriors'.

Equivocation permeates the play. When Macbeth writes to his wife he withholds from her the prophecy that Banquo's heirs will be kings. He equivocates again when justifying why he killed Duncan's guards: 'who could refrain, / That had a heart to love, and in that heart / Courage to make's love known?' (2.3.118–20). Mental reservation becomes second nature to him. He chooses not to tell the pair of murderers he despatches to kill Banquo and Fleance that a third will join them. And when Lady Macbeth then asks him, 'What's to be done?' he demurs: 'Be innocent of the knowledge' (3.2.48). It's ironic that the doomed Banquo offers the best description of the pretence at the heart of mental reservation, insisting that God can read the minds of men and see through their treasons:

> In the great hand of God I stand, and thence
> Against the undivulged pretence I fight
> Of treasonous malice.
> (2.3.132–4)

The more that equivocating becomes habitual for Macbeth the more reassurance he demands from the Sisters, who in turn play upon his hopes and further equivocate, summoning apparitions who urge him to 'Be bloody, bold and resolute,' since 'none of woman born / Shall harm Macbeth,' while assuring him that he shall never be vanquished until 'Great Birnam Wood' shall come to Dunsinane (4.1.79–81, 93). By the play's end, when he watches in disbelief as the branches cut from Birnam Wood are carried by an approaching army to Dunsinane, a shattered Macbeth fully grasps the destructive consequences of the 'equivocation of the fiend / That lies like truth' (5.5.43–4). At the last, after learning that Macduff is not of woman born (that is, he had a Caesarean birth so was from his mother 'untimely ripped' [5.8.16]), Macbeth reflects a final time on how equivocation has destroyed him:

> be these juggling fiends no more believed
> That palter with us in a double sense,
> That keep the word of promise to our ear
> And break it to our hope.
> (5.8.19–22)

We follow Macbeth's descent into a despairing world, a hell on earth: 'I 'gin to be aweary of the sun,' he says, 'And wish th' estate o'th' world were now undone' (5.5.49–50). Unlike most other tragic heroes in Shakespeare, Macbeth is denied a dying, self-revealing speech; the last we hear from him by way of reflection are these hard-earned insights into the workings of equivocation.

Equivocating breaks Lady Macbeth as well. In her efforts to deflect attention from her own complicity, and that of her husband, in the murder of Duncan, she becomes adept at it, especially during the banquet where Macbeth is so shaken by the sight of Banquo's ghost. She effortlessly equivocates, reassuring their guests:

> my lord is often thus,
> And hath been from his youth. Pray you, keep seat;
> The fit is momentary; upon a thought
> He will again be well.
> (3.4.53–6)

That equivocal 'well' will echo a couple of dozen times through the rest of the play. Perfectly exemplifying the division between that which is spoken and that which is suppressed in the act of equivocating, the maddened and sleepwalking Lady Macbeth is compelled to write down then compulsively reread the 'undivulged pretence' that cannot openly be spoken: 'I have seen her rise from her bed,' her gentlewoman reports, 'throw her night-gown upon her, unlock her closet, take forth paper, fold it, write upon't, read it, afterwards seal it, and again return to bed; yet all this while in a most fast sleep' (5.1.4–7).

Because Shakespeare had drawn on Harsnett's *Declaration of Egregious Popish Impostures* when writing the scenes in which Edgar plays the part of a possessed madman, that work is universally cited as an important source for *King Lear*. Yet this work is rarely discussed as a source for *Macbeth*, though it's obvious that in writing this play Shakespeare found himself reflecting even more deeply on Harsnett's exploration of the ways in which the human capacity for evil was falsely, if at times convincingly, located in the diabolic. His indebtedness is most visible when he draws upon Harsnett's account of Friswood Williams, a serving girl who as a teenager was persuaded by Catholic priests that she was possessed by the devil. She had tripped while working in the kitchen and hurt her hip; the persistent pain she afterwards suffered, the priests assured her, was from demonic possession rather than from the fall itself. To 'cure' her, the priests subjected her to exorcisms, making her drink potions that dazed her, sticking pins in her legs and forcing her to swallow nails – which they then pulled from her mouth, dazzling witnesses unaware of their tricks. They even placed in her mouth relics of martyrs, including, she recalled, Edmund Campion's 'thumb or finger', all in the service of banishing the devil that possessed her. It wasn't long before the cruelly abused Williams came to believe that she was indeed possessed – and whenever she raised doubts they responded that it wasn't she who was sceptical but rather the devil speaking through her.

On one occasion she was led into a gallery by a priest, where she spotted 'a new halter and two blades of knives'. When she asked the priest what the blades were doing there he replied that 'he saw them not, though he looked fully upon them'. Fearing that they were merely a figment of her imagination, Williams reached out and began 'pointing to them with her finger, where they lay within a yard of them, where they stood both together'. But the priest still denied seeing what she saw before her, whereupon she finally picked them up and said: 'Look you here.' At this point the priest admitted, 'Now I see them indeed,' though he continued to insist that 'before I could not see them'. She was later assured that 'the devil laid them in the gallery, that some of these that were possessed might either hang themselves with the halter or kill themselves with the blades'.

Shakespeare recalled this powerful account, in which what is truly diabolical turns out to be the nasty handiwork of equivocating priests, when he came to write the scene in which Macbeth, on his way to kill Duncan at that time of night when 'witchcraft celebrates / Pale Hecate's offerings', sees a 'fatal vision' of a blade floating in the air before him (2.1.52–3). As in Harsnett, it is initially unclear whether the dagger is real, the product of his fevered imagination, or the devil's work, set before Macbeth to lead him to damnation:

> Is this a dagger which I see before me,
> The handle toward my hand? Come, let me clutch thee.
> I have thee not, and yet I see thee still.
> Art thou not, fatal vision, sensible
> To feeling as to sight? or art thou but
> A dagger of the mind, a false creation,
> Proceeding from the heat-oppressed brain?
> (2.1.34–40)

The suggestion of possession proves no less crucial to what we make of Lady Macbeth, whose kinship with the forces of evil is so central to the terrifying speech in which she calls on demonic forces to possess her:

> Come you spirits
> That tend on mortal thoughts, unsex me here
> And fill me from the crown to the toe top-full
> Of direst cruelty! Make thick my blood;
> Stop up th' access and passage to remorse,
> That no compunctious visitings of nature

Shake my fell purpose, nor keep peace between
Th' effect and it! Come to my woman's breasts
And take my milk for gall, you murd'ring ministers,
Wherever, in your sightless substances,
You wait on nature's mischief!
(1.5.40–50)

She can call great spirits from the vasty deep, but what possesses her and destroys her, and her husband, ultimately comes from within.

In refusing easy explanations for what possesses people to do evil things, Shakespeare wrote a play well suited to its times. In the aftermath of the Gunpowder Plot, contemporaries found themselves searching for the ultimate source of such a hellish crime. For most of those writing about the roots of evil actions in the years preceding the plot, the role of the devil had been important but secondary. So, for example, five years earlier, John Deacon and John Walker in their *Answer to . . . Master Darrell His Books* describe the process that begins with human corruptibility and ends with those who have turned evil, persuaded that they are 'essentially possessed' by satanic forces: the devil first seeks out some 'lewd disposed person as is naturally inclined to all manner of knaveries', and then 'worketh so cunningly upon the corruption of that lewd person's nature, as the party himself is easily brought to believe, and to bear others also in hand, that he is (in deed and in truth) essentially possessed of Satan'. This ongoing interplay between human susceptibility and satanic seduction was close to King James's view in 1597, when he concluded in his book on *Demonology* that the 'old and crafty serpent being a spirit, he easily spies our affections, and so conforms himself thereto to deceive us to our wrack'. It's a view that is shared in the play by Banquo, who warns Macbeth:

> oftentimes to win us to our harm
> The instruments of darkness tell us truths,
> Win us with honest trifles, to betray's
> In deepest consequence.
> (1.3.123–6)

But after November 1605, that dynamic shifted. Perhaps it was the sheer magnitude of the threatened destruction from the vault below Parliament that led to the demonisation of the plot. In the first official sermon after Guy Fawkes was caught, William Barlow had spoken of a 'fiery massacre . . . kindled and sent from the infernal pit'. A year later, when Lancelot Andrewes delivered the first of many annual Gunpowder sermons, that explanation was no longer metaphorical. Andrewes rejected claims that such evil could have originated in the minds of men. It was pointless looking for earthly explanations: 'We must not look to pattern it upon earth, we must to hell; thence it was certainly, even from the devil.' The print of the 'Powder Treason' likewise concluded that while the act was 'practised' by the traitors, it had been 'propounded by Satan'. The pronounced shift in blame is no less visible in the sermon at St Paul's that John Dove delivered on equivocation as the invention of the devil less than a month after Garnet was punished there. This perspective would harden over ensuing decades; by the time we get to young John Milton's poems on the Gunpowder Plot, human responsibility hardly figures, the focus now almost exclusively on evil's satanic origins. The increasing weight given to diabolic forces suggests that the executions at St Paul's and Westminster that stretched from late January into early May of 1606 served, in part, as a kind of public exorcism meant to rid the kingdom of that devilish evil – a rite recalled and symbolically re-enacted every Fifth of November.

The fear of ever-present if unseen forces threatening king and kingdom was not simply propaganda preached from London's pulpits; at least for some English subjects at this time the danger was real. A recent and remarkable archaeological discovery that can be dated precisely to the immediate aftermath of the Gunpowder Plot confirms this. In early 1606 the Lord Treasurer, Thomas Sackville, was hastily remodelling his recently acquired home at Knole in Kent, twenty-five miles southeast of London, including a renovation of a royal suite in the King's Tower, in anticipation of a visit from King James. In 2013–14, archaeologists from the Museum of London, at the behest of the National Trust, examined the site and in the course of their investigation came upon a seventeen-foot-long tie beam, long hidden from view, under the floorboards in that royal suite. On it, Jacobean carpenters had carved or burned more than a dozen unusual markings, including demon-trap mesh designs, interlocking Vs and scorch marks.

These apotropaic symbols (the adjective derives from the Greek, 'to turn away') were intended to prevent devils, witches and other malevolent spirits from entering and potentially threatening the room's occupants. The markings were restricted to the side of the oak beam that faced the room's fireplace, and so presumably served as a barrier between that fireplace and a sleeping king. The scorch marks, made with a candle or a taper, were a way of fighting hellfire with fire; the mesh designs, a kind of debased pentagram, were designed to trap invading demons; and the interlocking Vs, a holdover from a long-Catholic England, invoked the protection of the Virgin Mary. Other apotropaic symbols were also found carved into the stone jamb of the fire surround in the same room (as fireplaces and chimneys were thought to be rapid transit systems favoured by hellish spirits).

While it is unusual to date old timber with such precision, dendrochronological analysis revealed that the oak tree from which this beam was cut had been felled in late 1605. The beam, while still green and malleable, had then been prepared by carpenters before it was placed in the King's Tower in the spring or early summer of 1606. The archaeologists also determined that the scorching and carvings could not have been done after the beam was put in place; Matthew Banks, the master carpenter overseeing the renovations, either in consultation with Sackville or on his own initiative, ensured that these protective markings were made in advance of the beam's installation in the royal suite.

The hidden symbols at Knole, and the complex and now largely lost beliefs that they speak to, serve as a correlative to the story forming in Shakespeare's mind at much the same time, a play that begins with threatening witches, a royal visit to a trusted retainer, and the murder of that vulnerable and sleeping king. Shakespeare's *Macbeth* was written not for posterity but for contemporaries like Matthew Banks and his fellow carpenters, playgoers drawn to a post-Gunpowder Plot tragedy that in its exploration of the source of unfathomable evil – be it human or diabolic – touches on, and to a surprising degree exploits, deep cultural anxieties that had now risen to the surface.

So far as we know, no playgoer who witnessed *Macbeth* in 1606 wrote down his or her reactions to it. The earliest recorded response dates from five years after it was first staged, when the astrologer and physician Simon Forman, a regular playgoer, jotted down notes after seeing it performed at the Globe in April 1611. Forman described the Sisters as simply 'three women fairies or nymphs'. While recognising that the play was full of prophecies and visions, Forman places the blame for the murder squarely on the Macbeths themselves: 'Macbeth contrived to kill Duncan and through the persuasion of his wife did that night murder the king in his own castle, being his guest.' Forman never mentions Hecate, raising the possibility that the two scenes in which she appears were added later. The current scholarly consensus is that Thomas Middleton, who had already collaborated with Shakespeare and subsequently revised several of his Jacobean plays for the King's Men, was responsible for adding some and perhaps all of the Hecate material, especially a pair of songs – the first, in Act 3, scene 5, 'Come away, come away', the second, in Act 4, scene 1, 'Black Spirits' – sung by Hecate, accompanied by witches and spirits. Both of the additional songs subsequently appeared in Middleton's supernatural play *The Witch*, written after Shakespeare's death. It may be that Middleton, revisiting Shakespeare's play a decade or so after it was first staged, felt that *Macbeth* wanted to be a devil play, or playgoers wanted it to be one. It didn't take much to fix that. When the time came to print *Macbeth* in the 1623 folio, Shakespeare's company handed over to the publishers a transcript of a promptbook that contained

Middleton's minor changes. No record survives of what was actually staged in 1606. While only the titles of Middleton's songs appear in that 1623 edition of Shakespeare's plays, some modern editions and productions now include their complete lyrics, lifted from *The Witch.* There's no question that the inclusion of Middleton's songs and of the Hecate material tilt what Shakespeare probably first wrote in the direction of a play in which the supernatural holds sway.

This early impulse to exaggerate the power of devilish forces has been reinforced by a theatrical tradition which maintains that *Macbeth*, alone among all of Shakespeare's works, carries with it a curse: disaster will strike anyone who carelessly names '*Macbeth*' in a theatre; actors who forget to call it 'The Scottish Play' or another safe title must say a charm to remove that curse. Despite strenuous efforts to trace this curse back to the play's early performances, it goes back no further than the late nineteenth century, when the humorist Max Beerbohm reviewed a production for the *Saturday Review* and fabricated a story – falsely attributing it to the seventeenth-century biographer John Aubrey – that Hal Berridge, the youth who was to have acted the part of Lady Macbeth, 'fell sudden sicke of a pleurisie, wherefor Master Shakespeare himself did enacte in his stead'. What Beerbohm had invented – and his period spelling lent it a touch of authenticity – quickly became accepted as fact. Actors soon adduced additional examples of disasters that befell performers injured while staging *Macbeth* (not all that surprising in a play in which sword-fighting and slippery blood-splattered knives figure heavily), and in our internet age this Victorian myth is now impossible to dislodge.

The perception of *Macbeth* as a play defined by the supernatural – behind Middleton's early revisions and reinforced by the actors' myth of a curse – has shaped much of the play's modern stage history as well. Directors have made the Sisters and Hecate omnipresent, lurking in the wings, doubling in the roles of minor characters, handing Macbeth the dagger, and reappearing at the end of the play to tempt again. While this interpretation works theatrically, it says more about the reception of the play and the cultural moment of these revivals than it reveals about what Shakespeare wrote in 1606. *Macbeth*'s stage history suggests that it has proved easier for actors and directors to tip the play toward the diabolic than to give equal weight to the living hell above ground that Shakespeare first imagined. Far less often there has been a counter-effort to strip the play of a supernatural stranglehold, placing responsibility for the evildoing entirely upon the ambitious couple, seeing it as compensatory for some personal loss or trauma (their childlessness figures largely in such productions). While no less theatrically powerful – for the play has proven elastic enough to succeed as domestic tragedy no less than *Lear* has – it underscores how hard it has been to sustain the careful balance Shakespeare wrote into the play. Indeed, as Middleton's likely revisions show, that balancing act didn't survive a decade.

One of the hardest things to measure in the unsettled aftermath of the Gunpowder Plot is the extent to which contemporaries questioned the government's ever-changing version of events and its surprisingly harsh treatment of those implicated in the failed plot. Traces of dissent are visible in Arthur Gorges's request that the site of the plotters' bloody executions not desecrate St Paul's Cathedral. They are visible, too, in the reluctance of the authorities to execute Garnet on May Day, fearing mayhem. Another hint of such criticism appears in the work of a government apologist, Oliver Ormerod. Ormerod had just finished writing an attack on English recusants – *The Picture of a Papist* – when the Gunpowder Plot was foiled. He added fresh material in part to blunt increasingly vocal criticism of the government's response to the plot, or as he bluntly puts it, 'to stop the mouths of those that complain of rigour, and scandalise the state of cruelty, in their just severity'. In his unrelenting assault on those who dared criticise the government's overreaction he unwittingly gives voice, otherwise lost, to what was being murmured at the time. He does so through invented dialogue that pits a minister (like himself) against a strawman recusant. So, for example, when the recusant asks the minister what punishment was meted out to the Gunpowder plotters, the minister describes in gory detail how their hearts were torn out and their heads cut off. The recusant, disgusted, responds, 'I pray you sir, what warrant have you for these bloody ceremonies, which you used at their execution?' A modern reader might mistakenly conclude that Ormerod sympathises with the recusant's horror. When the minister then luridly describes how their bodies were drawn and quartered, the recusant demands to know what justifies such brutality, and the minister triumphantly replies, 'Our warrant is the word of God,' adding: 'I see no reason why you should complain of rigour, and accuse his majesty of more than Scythian cruelty. Nay, you should commend his clemency.'

Similar resistance was expressed by another – and not imaginary – recusant at this time, Ben Jonson, who had been hauled before the courts for his religious convictions in early January

1606 and then wrote a play, *Volpone*, that would also touch upon the fallout of the Gunpowder Plot. Jonson claimed to be a notoriously slow writer but he wrote the play in a white heat, in less than five weeks. Begun in early January, it was finished, then hurriedly copied, rehearsed, and probably staged by Shakespeare's company at the Globe by late February, before the public theatres were closed for a month or so for Lent on 5 March. *Volpone*, true to its moment of creation, is rife with plots and counter-plots. It tells the story of a pair of greedy schemers – Volpone and his sidekick Mosca, their names denoting a crafty old fox and a parasitic fly – who in the end are exposed, tried and condemned to unduly harsh punishment. Its sharp critique is masked as a beast fable, but there is no mistaking the allusions to contemporary events. A partial list would include a casual suggestion that those being harshly interrogated be subject to the *strappado*, a joke about 'tinder-boxes' that can be carried into an arsenal (3.133), a passing reference to 'liberty of conscience' (3.139) and the reported searching of a foolish minor character's study for incriminating papers, after a spy overhears that he has professed 'to sell the state' (3.135). There's even a barely veiled allusion to an imprisoned Garnet's reputedly gluttonous ways – 'I have heard / The rack had cured the gout' (3.150) – yet the joke is sardonic in its view of a government that resorted to torture, worse than the ill it sought to cure, in interrogating the Jesuit. Collectively, these and other hints at current events would have been hard for Jacobean playgoers to miss.

For Jonson, no less than for Shakespeare, the source of evil was to be found in men and women, not in the imaginary devils who possess them. To this end, he makes clever use in *Volpone* of the recent Anne Gunter case to show the ways in which, like equivocation, claims of demonic possession allowed one to swear and lie. Toward the end of the play, during a hectic trial scene, Volpone persuades the avaricious lawyer Voltore to fall down and feign that he is possessed in order to convince the court that everything he has previously sworn is false – though not perjury, for it was spoken by the devil through him. Volpone even coaches Voltore on how to act the part of one possessed, imitating some of the tricks Anne Gunter had been taught: 'Stop your wind hard, and swell,' Volpone tells Voltore, before turning to the court and urging everyone to 'See, see, see, see! / He vomits crooked pins!' They respond, predictably: 'Ay, the devil!' In what feels like a parodic version of what is being enacted on a large scale in London itself, Jonson stages a mock exorcism before the devil is at last banished and Voltore 'comes t' himself'. A seemingly dazed Voltore play-acts brilliantly – 'Where am I?' – before Volpone reassures him and the court, 'Take good heart; the worst is past, sir. / You are dispossessed' (3.181). By the end of the play almost every character – except those caricatures of goodness, Celia and Bonario – is seen to plot and counter-plot out of self-interest, willing to swear and lie. Trials are merely good theatre. Though no less a Gunpowder play than *Macbeth*, Volpone's connections to its moment of creation have largely been lost as well.

Shakespeare's *Macbeth* – likely in repertory with *Volpone* at the Globe shortly after the resumption of playing after Easter – managed to do something more profound, registering deeper tectonic shifts taking place in Jacobean England. The world in which Hamlet could still speak of equivocation in a neutral way was over. By early 1606, the fear was all too real that once equivocation took root, 'in a short time there will be no faith, no troth, no trust'. One of Shakespeare's most powerful insights in *Macbeth* is that in so infected a climate – be it medieval Scotland or Jacobean London – the good, along with the evil, embrace equivocation. The culture of suspicion in London as well as in his native Stratford-upon-Avon stirred up in the aftermath of the plot would be difficult, perhaps impossible, to reverse. By the end of *Macbeth* even the most admirable characters swear and lie, muddying the moral landscape. Take, for example, the seemingly noble Macduff, who flees Scotland, leaving his family behind. What are we to make of the exchange in which his wife tells their son that Macduff is a 'traitor' who 'swears and lies'?

Son. Was my father a traitor, mother?

Lady Macduff. Ay, that he was.

Son. What is a traitor?

Lady Macduff. Why, one that swears and lies.

Son. And be all traitors that do so?

Lady Macduff. Every one that does so is a traitor,
And must be hanged.

Son. And must they all be hanged that swear and lie?

Lady Macduff. Every one.
(4.2.46–54)

Either Lady Macduff equivocates or Macduff, who has abandoned his family, does indeed swear and lie. Perhaps both have been forced to become equivocators. Moments after this exchange, murderers sent by Macbeth burst in, declare that Macduff is 'a traitor' and put to Lady Macduff the very question asked of those harbouring reputed traitors, one so central to the defences offered in *A Treatise of Equivocation*: 'Where is your husband?' To which she can only reply equivocally – 'I hope in no place so unsanctified / Where such as thou mayst find him' (4.3.78–80) – after which she and her children are summarily butchered.

Macduff himself is soon the victim of equivocation, however well-meaning, as a reluctant Ross equivocates with the meaning of that resonant word 'well' when forced to report the murder of Macduff's wife and children. It's understandable, but textbook equivocating nonetheless:

Macduff. How does my wife?

Ross. Why, well.

Macduff. And all my children?

Ross. Well too.

Macduff. The tyrant has not battered at their peace?

Ross. No; they were well at peace when I did leave 'em.
(4.3.177–80)

When Ross eventually breaks the terrible news to Macduff that his entire family has been killed, Malcolm, who has heard their exchange, offers what he imagines are uplifting words: 'Be comforted. / Let's make us med'cines of our great revenge / To cure this deadly grief.' Macduff's response – 'He has no children' – is one of the most harrowing lines in all of Shakespeare (4.3.214–17). It is also equivocal. Is Macduff saying that it will be impossible to exact adequate vengeance upon the childless Macbeth? Or is he speaking to and about himself, in the third person, taking in for the first time the emptiness of his own now childless state? Or, disgusted by Malcolm's attempt to spur his revenge, is he speaking in an aside, reflecting on how only someone like Malcolm who never had children could say something as heartless and as ignorant as that by way of comfort?

In the long and unsettling scene that follows, yet another seemingly virtuous character, Malcolm, swears and lies to Macduff, telling him that his rapacious and violent nature renders him unfit to rule in Scotland, before suddenly reversing course. He then blames a devilish Macbeth for having driven him to equivocate, and declares that he will 'unspeak mine own detraction'. We share Macduff's bewilderment, for what constitutes honesty in a world in which noble characters can speak and unspeak at will?

Though no destructive attack took place on the Fifth of November, something had changed irrevocably in the culture, a change registered in *Macbeth*. Its moment of creation may partly explain why *Macbeth*'s ending feels so unsatisfying, its hasty restoration of order so flimsy and inadequate. Small wonder that almost every modern director, on stage and in film, feels compelled to tinker with that ending. That desire for clarity and closure, for sealing off the equivocal, for locating the source of evil in the diabolical, recalls the hopes of demonisers like Coke and Dove. Macduff's final entrance holding aloft Macbeth's severed head – once again the killing of a Scottish king must occur off stage, something to be imagined but not seen – distracts us from many unanswered questions. Is evil defeated once the head of a traitorous equivocator is displayed on a pole? Is it enough to vilify 'this dead butcher and his fiendlike queen'? (5.8.70). If Banquo, through Fleance, is to be the father of kings, why does *Macbeth* conclude with Malcolm in power? What further blood must be spilled or devilish forces intervene before Banquo's heirs, culminating in King James himself, do what Macbeth failed to do and supplant Duncan's line?

The political resolution of a stage play can easily be reworked in performance; in the real world, what's done cannot be undone. Social historians tend to fix 1615 as the moment when the great hopes for King James's reign ended, in the wake of the Overbury scandal in which he was implicated. Economic historians tend to date it a bit earlier, with the failure of the Great Contract to resolve the nation's fiscal problems in 1610. Literary historians would probably locate the end of high hopes for James's regime as early as the spring of 1606, and Londoners who saw *Macbeth* and passed below the severed heads of Garnet and his fellow traitors on their way home from the Globe would likely have agreed.

11 : *The King's Evil*

The first reports of the assassination of King James reached London as dawn broke on Saturday 22 March. According to the Venetian ambassador, as word spread 'the uproar was amazing' and once again, much like the previous November, 'everyone flew to arms'. Catholics and strangers feared mob violence as 'cries began to be heard against Papists, foreigners and Spaniards'. The chronicler Edmund Howes records that upon hearing the 'certain news that the king was slain' twenty-five miles southwest of London at Woking, the government acted quickly. The Lord Mayor gave orders 'to levy trained soldiers' in every ward and placed armed guards at each of the City's gates, while the Lieutenant of the Tower raised his drawbridge, secured all of his prisoners and loaded his cannons to fend off any organised assault. The privy councillors joined the pregnant queen and Prince Henry at Whitehall Palace, where double guards were posted. Where the king was slain was known, but how was as yet unclear, with

'Henry IV of France Touching for Scrofula', by Pierre Firens (*c.*1610)

fresh and conflicting reports claiming that he had been stabbed, smothered in his bed or 'shot with a pistol as he was riding'.

According to Howes, members of Parliament meeting that morning debated what to do. Some wanted to flee, fearful that the building would be targeted again, but others, concerned that 'their sudden rising should add more terror . . . to court, city, and country', persuaded them to 'sit still in their accustomed peaceable manner'. Updated reports reaching town provided fresh details, including word that some of the Scots closest to the king had been killed fighting in his defence. While 'most reports agreed that the king was stabbed with an envenomed knife', the identity of the assassins was as yet unknown; some said that the treasonous act 'was performed by English Jesuits, some by Scots in women's apparel, and others said by Spaniards and Frenchmen'. Howes writes that Londoners were at once 'exceedingly amazed', 'sore frighted' and 'full of sorrow', for the 'bitter news was more grievous unto all sorts of people than can well be here expressed, great weeping and lamentation both in old and young, rich and poor, maids and wives'.

It was as if the gamut of the emotions collectively experienced at a Shakespearean tragedy had spilled out of the playhouse and into London's streets. The drama took an unexpected turn by mid-morning, when word reached town that the king was alive! The false report had spread after King James had travelled through a village where a man was being arrested for some small offence. The offender then escaped on horseback, with sword drawn, and the local constables had pursued him, shouting 'Traitor, traitor.' Bystanders thought 'that he must have attacked the king, who had passed through a while before', and some then raced to London to report that 'the king was dead'. The normally staid councillors gave a great shout for joy when they heard that the king hadn't been killed, news that was quickly confirmed by fresh messengers. But it wasn't until the privy councillors, eager 'to quiet the people's distracted minds', read a proclamation at Cheapside Cross condemning the 'seditious rumour' and declaring that the king was safe that 'London's universal fear and grief' began to abate. The councillors ordered the jittery citizens to disarm and not gather in assemblies until the 'tumultuous spirits' behind the uproar were found.

King James, who at first had known nothing of the hue and cry, initially sent messengers to town confirming that he was alive, then had second thoughts and returned in person, where he 'was welcomed as one risen from the dead'. What had begun as tragedy had turned into romance. Prince Henry, the privy councillors and thousands of citizens raced to meet him at Knightsbridge, and when his subjects saw him alive, 'they fell on their knees, breathless with running and speechless with tears and joy'. Bells rang out in the city and there were 'fireworks and fetes'. It took longer for the rest of the country to be so reassured. John Chamberlain wrote to a friend that once the rumour had spread 'far and near' it took three or four days to persuade those in the countryside that it was a false alarm.

Chamberlain added that the king 'took these demonstrations more kindly than if they had won a battle for him', and told his people 'that a better king they might have, but a more loving and careful for their good they could not'. Ben Jonson wasted no time in ingratiating himself with his monarch, dashing off 'To King James, Upon the Happy False Rumour of His Death, the Two and Twentieth Day of March', an epilogue to the day's drama:

> That we thy loss might know, and thou our love,
> Great heaven did well to give ill fame free wing,
> Which, though it did but panic terror prove,
> And far beneath least pause of such a king;
> Yet give thy jealous subjects leave to doubt,
> Who this thy 'scape from rumour gratulate,
> No less than if from peril; and devout,
> Do beg thy care unto thy after-state.
> For we, that have our eyes still in our ears,
> Look not upon thy dangers, but our fears.
> (5.137)

The poem's opening couplet was especially canny, attributing the rumour to God rather than, as many suspected, seditious Catholics hoping to unsettle the state. The king, gratified by his warm welcome, was reassured that 'reports that were spread abroad . . . of mislikes and distastes between him and his people' were clearly unfounded.

Arthur Wilson was only ten years old that day yet remembered it well when he wrote a history of James's reign decades later, recalling how Londoners spent that morning 'mustering up their old fears, every man standing at gaze, as if some new prodigy had seized them'. For Wilson, the hysteria was inseparable from the Fifth of November, a kind of aftershock: 'Such a terror had this late monstrous intended mischief imprinted in the spirits of people that they took fire from every little train of rumour, and were ready to grapple with their own destruction before it came.' The chaos of this 'agony' was so unsettling, he adds, that the king had to issue a proclamation 'to re-establish the people'. Modern-day historians ignore this episode, though few events can rival it for what it reveals about this volatile moment.

Successful dramatists know that their plays best please when rooted in what audiences long for or dread; people tend to weep at tragedies because they are mourning their own real or imagined losses. Jonson had said as much at the end of his poem: we look 'not upon thy dangers, but our fears'. That day London playgoers wrote their own script, imagining and with every fresh rumour revising 'their own destruction'. In doing so they turned to what they had seen in the playhouses. Reports that James had been smothered in his bed – Desdemona's fate – may have seemed too passive a royal end and gave way to a more fitting death for a king: like Hamlet, stabbed by an envenomed blade. The imagined perpetrators had to be familiar stage villains and foreigners – this despite the homegrown nature of the most recent and terrible assassination plot. The only real oddity was the bizarre report that the king had been attacked by Scots in women's clothing, cross-dressed figures who uncannily resemble the ambiguously gendered Weird Sisters ('You should be women,' Banquo says when he first sees them, 'And yet your beards forbid me to interpret / That you are so' [1.3.45–7]).

Some that morning misjudged the mood in the street. When Parliament resumed its deliberations later that afternoon, Sir Edwin Sandys proposed banishing 'all Papists from London and twenty miles compass'. The motion was first 'entertained with applause', but as the xenophobic fervour receded there was 'nothing done nor farther spoken in it'. King James failed to recognise that the joyous outpouring was more about his subjects' concern with the stability of their own lives and less, or only secondarily, about their love for him. Reports of how James 'cheerfully returned all princely thanks and acknowledgement of their singular love and loyalty' uncomfortably resemble King Duncan's misprision of the loyalty and love of his subjects; few lines are as painful in *Macbeth* as Duncan's greeting to Lady Macbeth, who wishes him dead, when he arrives at her home: 'The love that follows us sometime is our trouble, / Which still we thank as love' (1.6.11–12). Certainly, Macduff's cry upon discovering that the King of Scots had been assassinated would have resonated powerfully with Jacobean audiences seeing *Macbeth*, probably first staged a month or so later: 'Awake, awake! / Ring the alarum bell. Murder and treason!' (2.3.74–5).

James's misreading was understandable, since the episode reproduced what he saw as the defining story of his life. While this time around it was only a rumour, it fitted the pattern of previous failed attempts to murder him, confirmation that as God's anointed he had been providentially spared. Fifteen months earlier, in December 1604, Shakespeare and his fellow players had tried to capitalise on the most famous of these assassination attempts in *The Tragedy of Gowrie*. We don't know who wrote it or whether Shakespeare acted in it (though one of the very few anecdotes that survives about his playing career says that he acted the parts of kings). But it was an immediate hit. John Chamberlain reported that its first two performances attracted 'exceeding concourse of all sorts of people'. Other than word of mouth, there was only a single source available to the playwright responsible for this tragedy: the anonymous and propagandistic *The Earl of Gowrie's Conspiracy against the King's Majesty*, a bestseller twice published in London in the immediate aftermath of the episode in 1600, then reprinted four times in 1603 after James was crowned King of England. Any play on the subject would have relied on this twenty-page pamphlet, which, happily, was rich in dialogue and action.

According to this official version, James, then King of Scotland, went hunting at Falkland with his entourage on Tuesday 5 August 1600. He was lured from there to the Earl of Gowrie's house in Perth by the earl's younger brother, the dashing Alexander Ruthven, who told him about the discovery of a huge treasure of foreign gold. Once in Gowrie's house, James left his followers and was led upstairs by Ruthven through a series of chambers to a small turret closet. At this point Ruthven turned and accused James of having killed his father. When Ruthven tried to bind the king's hands James fought him off, saying that he 'was born a free king, and should die a free king'. Ruthven tried to draw his sword but James, fighting for his life, managed to seize Ruthven's fist and sword hilt with his own right hand. Both men then throttled each other with their free hands, with Ruthven managing to stick a few fingers in James's mouth to keep him from crying out for help. 'In this manner of wrestling', the pamphlet continued, the two men struggled across the room towards an open window. At that very moment the king's train was passing by below in the company of the Earl of Gowrie. Thrusting his head out the casement, James cried out that 'they were murdering him there'. The fierce struggle would have made for a breathtaking scene at the Globe.

The denouement was swift: the king was quickly rescued and both Ruthven and the Earl of Gowrie were immediately slain by the king's loyal supporters. The earl's pockets were searched in vain for any letters that might cast light on the conspiracy; only 'a little close parchment bag, full of magical characters and words of enchantment' was discovered, suggesting to onlookers that he put his faith in witchcraft. James was the sole surviving witness to what had happened in the turret closet. Even in the sanitised printed version obvious inconsistencies hadn't been ironed out. Was it a botched kidnapping? Otherwise, why would Ruthven bother binding the king if he intended to kill him? And why would the ordinarily wary king go alone with Ruthven to a private chamber to see a pot of gold? Those who knew of James's attraction to handsome young men might have thought it likelier that this was a flirtatious pass or assignation gone wrong. Or was the cover story cleverly concocted by James himself, who used the visit to kill off rivals to whom, as many in Scotland knew, he owed a great deal of money? It certainly looked suspicious that the alleged perpetrators had been killed and not taken prisoner and interrogated. The Scottish clergy had an especially hard time swallowing this incredible story. James, furious, gave them an ultimatum: support and preach his story or risk banishment, for to refuse to promote the royal version of events was to impute that he himself was a liar and a murderer. In the end, most, though not all, fell in line.

We'll never know how closely the King's Men's version of the story stuck to the royal script, for despite its initial popularity the play was quickly banned and never printed. It may well be that even a faithful re-enactment of the king's story raised too many unanswered questions. Chamberlain, our only source of information about the lost play, wasn't able to learn why it was censored: 'Whether the matter or manner be not well handled, or that it be thought unfit that princes should be put on the stage in their life time, I hear that some great councillors are much displeased with it.' There were a few unspoken rules in Shakespeare's day. One was that you never portrayed a living monarch on stage (the risk of seeming to mock James's gait or Scottish accent was far too great). Another was that public holidays should commemorate the dead, not the living (these were, after all, holy days, with a divine warrant). In staging *The Tragedy of Gowrie*, Shakespeare's company broke the first rule; in insisting that his subjects celebrate 5 August as a public holiday, James broke the second. Shortly after his accession in 1603 the royal printer published *A Form of Prayer with Thanksgiving, to be Used by All the King's Majesty's Loving Subjects Every Year the Fifth of August Being the Day of his Highness's Happy Deliverance from the Traitorous and Bloody Attempt of the Earl of Gowrie and His Brother.* James also commanded that a special sermon annually be preached at court as part of the holiday celebration. He put great stock in having been spared on a Tuesday – and the fact that Guy Fawkes was also caught on that day of the week confirmed God's grace, so much so that throughout his reign he would hear special sermons every Tuesday.

While the Privy Council grudgingly acceded to James's demand for a new holiday, some English clergymen initially balked, including one of the most loyal, Lancelot Andrewes, who reportedly 'fell down upon his knees before King James and besought his majesty to spare his customary pains upon that day, that he might not mock God unless the thing were true'. To which James, hypersensitive to criticism on this subject, replied: 'Those people were too much to blame who would never believe a treason unless their prince were actually murdered.' He then assured Andrewes, 'in the faith of a Christian, and upon the word of a king, their treasonable attempt against him was too true'.

Though they could no longer perform this play, the King's Men knew how popular, if controversial, its subject matter was. Shakespeare took note of two things in the aftermath of the suppression of *The Tragedy of Gowrie*, a play that had failed to recoup the company's investment: audiences had flocked to see the story of the plotted assassination of a Scottish king; and the King's Men had to be careful about sailing too close to the political winds.

If the King's Men could not revive the Gowrie story, Shakespeare could help them do the next best thing: to stage a more guarded and historically distant story of a plot against a different King of Scots, a play in which King James would make only a fleeting cameo appearance. James – or rather his reflected image, along with those of his royal line, as seen in a magical mirror – appears late in Shakespeare's play, after Macbeth revisits the Sisters, desperate to know whether 'Banquo's issue' shall 'ever / Reign in this kingdom' (4.1.102–3). Though the Sisters warn him to 'Seek to know no more', Macbeth insists, and they summon a 'show of eight kings' (4.1.112 stage direction). In this dumb-show each of Banquo's royal heirs appears. The eighth one carries a magical mirror that shows Macbeth many more of Banquo's descendants, including some who bear 'twofold balls and treble sceptres' (4.1.121). This show of kings culminates in James himself, the eighth Stuart King of Scotland (his mother, Mary, Queen of Scots, executed on Queen Elizabeth's order in 1587, is skipped over, as far too sensitive a political issue to raise, so the count is off by one).

The use of a magical mirror in which Macbeth sees a figure easily recognised as King James avoids the delicate issue of impersonating a living prince on stage, and James himself may have been flattered by it. But it also raises questions. Might this be one more equivocal distortion on the part of these supernatural apparitions? Should we doubt what Macbeth imagines he sees? There is no way of knowing for sure. There happened to be a similar sort of mirror – it was a major tourist attraction – in the royal palace at Richmond. Now cracked and not in working order since the days of Henry VII, the 'round mirror', a visitor in 1610 records, enabled the king 'to see everything, and it was almost believed he had a *spiritum familiarem* sitting in it'. These familiar spirits prove easy to believe in but hard to trust.

The allusion to the 'twofold balls' (the double orbs or mounds that surmount the Scottish and English crowns) and 'treble sceptres' (signifying the union of Britain, France and Ireland) is a clear nod to the anticipated Union of the kingdoms and seemingly supportive of the royal position. And Malcolm's decision in the final scene of the play to honour his Scottish thanes by making them earls, 'the first that ever Scotland / In such an honour named' (5.8.64–5), is another seeming piece of flattery, for James had been busy doing much the same thing in his first three years on the English throne. Yet in drawing attention to James's own practice of rewarding Scots with English titles (which, by 1606, many in England felt had gone too far, and for mocking which in

Eastward Ho Ben Jonson had ended up in prison), Shakespeare may well have been offering a backhanded compliment. As is so often the case, his intentions remain inscrutable and open to competing interpretations.

The allusions in *Macbeth* to James and Union are no less slippery than another that has received less critical attention: the overlong digression at the English court on 'the Evil'. The scene in which this subject is introduced does nothing to advance the plot. In fact it slows things down to a point where even so short a play begins to drag. It is typically cut in modern productions, partly because it feels so digressive and partly because the cultural context that motivated Shakespeare to write it is now lost. But for Jacobean playgoers the exchange at the English court about 'the Evil' would have been seen as central to what is contested in the play.

As Malcolm and Macduff's long and equivocal exchange comes to an end, a doctor enters and is asked whether the English king – never named but clearly Edward the Confessor – comes forth. The doctor, whose only role in the play is to speak these few lines, replies:

> Ay, sir. There are a crew of wretched souls
> That stay his cure. Their malady convinces
> The great assay of art; but at his touch –
> Such sanctity hath heaven given his hand –
> They presently amend.
> (4.3.142–5)

Macduff, new to the English court, asks Malcolm what disease the king hopes to cure through the royal touch, to which

Malcolm replies: ''Tis called the Evil' (4.3.147), and then explains this English custom, unfamiliar to the Scots:

> A most miraculous work in this good king,
> Which often, since my here-remain in England,
> I have seen him do. How he solicits heaven
> Himself best knows: but strangely-visited people,
> All swoll'n and ulcerous, pitiful to the eye,
> The mere despair of surgery, he cures,
> Hanging a golden stamp about their necks,
> Put on with holy prayers: and 'tis spoken,
> To the succeeding royalty he leaves
> The healing benediction.
> (4.3.148–57)

The strangely named disease – 'the Evil' or 'King's Evil' – is wonderfully appropriate for a play that turns on the need to rid the land of an evil king. It was the early modern term for scrofula, a tubercular affliction typically affecting the lymph nodes on the neck and face, resulting in lumpy, bluish swellings (symptoms that sometimes went into remission). In a tradition that continued into the eighteenth century, diseased subjects would be brought before English monarchs, who, as prayers were recited, would either touch or pass their hands over the ulcerous sores before placing around the neck of the sufferer a gold coin or 'stamp' hung on a ribbon, aptly called an 'angel'.

At stake – for James, for Jacobean playgoers and for the play itself – is the doctor's breezy assurance that the cure, while effected by the king's touch, is ultimately enabled by God: 'Such sanctity hath heaven given his hand'. Malcolm is not so sure, and his qualified response – how the king 'solicits heaven / Himself best knows' – cuts to the heart of the problem: how exactly is God involved? Accept the premise that a king can heal the Evil through his touch because once anointed he is divinely endowed with that supernatural power, and you implicitly accept the divine right of kings. Though Malcolm hopes, like his father before him, one day to rule Scotland, he first has to depose an anointed king, Macbeth. Understandably for him, the Evil is a sticking point.

James had never practised touching for Evil during his many years of ruling Scotland; his fiercely reformed ministers would never have stood for what it would imply about his powers. Given his squeamishness about mingling with his lowly and diseased subjects, as well as his own intellectual and theological reservations, that probably suited him. But when he arrived in England in 1603, though he believed that the age of miracles had passed, James no longer had much choice, for it was an established tradition, one that had been regularly practised by his Tudor predecessors. By 1606 he had overcome his scruples and often engaged in the practice (including during Holy Week, shortly before Garnet's execution). Arthur Wilson, a close observer of the king, writes that James knew full well that the practice of 'curing the King's Evil' was merely a 'device to aggrandise the virtue of kings when miracles were in fashion'. Nonetheless, James was comfortable equivocating and played along: he 'smiled at it', Wilson writes, thinking 'the imagination a more powerful agent in the cure than the plasters his surgeons prescribed for the sore'. All that he had to do was play his part convincingly enough.

A copy of the service James followed in 1606 doesn't survive, though it probably resembled one from around 1618 reproduced in a broadside (and this in turn corresponds to the ceremony first recorded in the *Book of Common Prayer* in 1634). As James touched each sufferer in turn, a passage from the Gospel of Mark would be recited: 'In my name they shall cast out devils, they shall speak with new tongues, they shall drive away serpents . . . They shall lay their hands on the sick, and they shall recover.' The conviction that kings were divinely ordained hinges here on the belief that demonic possession is real. James famously remarked at the Hampton Court Conference in 1604, 'No bishop, no king'; he might have added, 'No devil, no divine right.'

Life imitated art in late 1606, as a King of England once again cured the Evil before Scottish visitors to his court. The first Hampton Court Conference of 1604 is well known in large part because it was there that the King James Bible was first proposed and royally authorised. The main purpose of that conference had been to resolve outstanding religious differences in the land, and to that end James had invited moderate Puritans as well as Anglicans to make their case and dispute theology with him. Almost unknown today, but no less important for the king, was a second Hampton Court Conference in September 1606, at which James once again matched wits with theologians. Invited to attend were eight representatives of the Scottish Kirk, including the headstrong Andrew Melville and his nephew James Melville, said to be the man most hated by King James in all of Scotland for staunchly rejecting royal claims to religious authority. Reports of their defiance were soon the stuff of popular gossip in London; writing to a friend in Spain in early April, Luisa de Carvajal y

Mendoza describes how 'six or seven ministers from Scotland, among others, have been condemned as traitors for an attempted rebellion there. In this country it is part of everyday conversation to talk about treason.'

James had summoned them to London to bring them to heel. They had recently defied his will by holding a general assembly at Aberdeen. It was obvious to many, including the new Venetian ambassador, Zorzi Giustinian, that James also hoped to make the Scottish ministers, who had 'great weight in civil matters, more amenable to his will, so as to approach the subject of Union with better chances of success in the coming Parliament'. They received their instructions to head south in May and arrived at court in August. When they reached London, James's Dean of the Chapel tried talking sense to James Melville; the two men agreed that the Pope lacked religious authority in the land, but when Melville argued that 'the presbytery hath it', he was told that it was treason in England to say so, 'for the prince has it by our laws'. When Melville pointed out that according to Scottish law this wasn't so, he was warned: 'But you must have it so.'

We tend to think of plays as the main site for exploring sensitive issues of authority in Shakespeare's day. But for King James, sermons – both those for public consumption at Paul's Cross and those delivered before him at court – better served that purpose, and for every play he saw James may have heard a half-dozen sermons. In advance of the arrival of the Scottish delegation, James called upon four of his finest preachers – William Barlow, John Buckeridge, John King and Lancelot Andrewes – to write interlinking sermons that the Presbyterians would hear over a two-week period in late September. These preachers were king's men too; they just engaged in a different sort of writing and public performance, and they too turned to the distant past to explain the present. In ways now lost to us, these two popular literary forms, both of which explored the divisive issues of the day, were in conversation with each other. James also ordered that the four sermons be published – this was unusual – to allow wider circulation of what were essentially position papers setting out his views on royal and religious authority.

John Buckeridge was assigned the second one, a Tuesday sermon delivered on 23 September in the King's Chapel at Hampton Court 'about the magistrate's authority in matters ecclesiastical'. The Scots were given front-row seats. Buckeridge's message was clear: Presbyterians were really no different from Papists insofar as both were 'enemies to the king's supremacy'. His task was to reject the Scots' position that they were merely acting as the earliest Christians had done (and implicitly positioning James as a tyrant who persecuted them). 'Tyrant', a word that coincidentally appears fifteen times in *Macbeth* – more often than in any other Shakespeare play – was an especially loaded term at this moment of governmental crackdown; even a hint of an accusation had to be fiercely resisted. To that end, Buckeridge argued that the Scottish ministers had misread ancient history: 'Although the church was governed for the first three hundred years before any emperor or king became a public professed Christian . . . yet the times were different then and all things have their time.' That was then, this is now. One of the incredulous Scots who had to sit quietly through the long sermon was unsure whether Buckeridge spoke out of 'ignorance or malice'. The royal message, so far, hadn't got through.

If James couldn't bend them to his will he could at least provoke them. One such provocation was forcing the Scottish delegation to watch the king and queen receive Communion at an altar on which sat two basins with two candlesticks. For the Calvinist Scots, who despised such rituals, this hint of traditional Catholic practice was outrageous; James might as well have been attending a Mass. Andrew Melville was foolhardy enough to write and circulate a Latin pasquil on the subject, translated into English as:

> Why stands there on the royal altar by,
> Two closed books, blind lights, two basins dry?
> Doth England hold God's mind and worship close,
> Blind of her sight, and buried in her dross?
> With Romish rites King's Chapel doth thee dress,
> Religious she the Red Whore doth express!

When challenged about his poem, Melville lost his temper; he grabbed the Archbishop of Canterbury's robes and shouted: 'Romish rags, and a part of the Beast's mark!' For his seditious literary efforts he earned a stay in the Tower, then exile.

If the English Communion weren't provocation enough, there would be one last show of royal supremacy. After Buckeridge's sermon the Scots were led to 'the king's closet'. There they witnessed something they had never seen before, the king engaging in the royal ceremony of curing the Evil, touching diseased children brought there for this special performance. This bit of royal theatre confirmed what Buckeridge had said at length and the king's other three preachers reiterated: James's authority extended beyond the political sphere, for God worked miracles through him. The idea of bringing children to the royal palace to be cured was an especially nice touch on James's part, for the Scots, who would lose this fight, were like wilful children who had to be brought to the English court and cured of what afflicted them.

The best outcome of the assassination scare for King James was that a relieved Parliament, which held the purse-strings, finally agreed to provide him with the revenue he so badly needed. Back in February the king's representatives had pleaded his case before Parliament: Elizabeth had left the crown £400,000 in debt, largely because of her wars in Ireland and the Low Countries. The expense of burying her, then the cost of James's coronation, coupled with the annual outlay for maintaining multiple royal households, had left the crown with debts of over £700,000. Having dragged its heels for months, and still worried at how costly James's reign was turning out to be compared to that of his frugal (and unmarried) predecessor, Parliament finally came around and authorised the subsidy. But there wasn't enough political will in either house of Parliament to confront the ongoing matter of Union, which James fully expected to be resolved in this parliamentary session. It would have to be postponed one more time, until Parliament reconvened in mid-November 1606. Given the exploration of Union in both *Lear* and *Macbeth*, continued debate over the division of the kingdoms would have made those plays, now in repertory, even more timely.

Two other parliamentary measures this spring would have a more direct impact on Shakespeare. The first was an Act 'to Restrain Abuses of Players' that had been taken up in the House of Commons back on 17 February and made law on 27 May. It was the only parliamentary directive against players enacted during Shakespeare's professional career and would remain the only one until Parliament closed the theatres in 1642. London's theatre community was well aware of what had precipitated this legislation: John Day's *The Isle of Gulls*, staged in February at the Blackfriars Theatre by the Children of the Queen's Revels. According to Sir Edward Hoby, offence was taken over its handling of the Union question. The scandalous play was discussed in Parliament on either 15 or 16 February, a day or two before the Act was taken up. Hoby also reports that those involved in staging it were committed to Bridewell prison. The playing company was quickly stripped of royal patronage. It was one thing for parliamentarians to express misgivings about the Union; it was quite another for players to express what many of the English really thought about their northern neighbours. There already existed mechanisms for the political censorship of staged plays (overseen by the Master of the Revels) as well as printed ones (authorised by the Bishop of London and the Archbishop of Canterbury). The problem, clearly, was not in the language of the text, which was soon printed and seemed innocuous, but in how it was performed. It would have been easy for the boy actors to mock Scottish accents or parody in dress or mannerisms specific court figures (Hoby seems to hint as much when he writes how the children had acted all men's parts, 'from the highest to the lowest'). Outraged members of the House of Commons seized on this episode to censor what they could control: profanity.

From now on, any actor who jestingly or profanely invoked the name of God, Christ, the Holy Ghost or the Trinity would be fined a hefty £10 (roughly half a year's wages). Shakespeare's plays would henceforth be God-less. To encourage enforcement, the Act specified that while half of the penalty went to the king's coffers, the other half went into the pockets of those who reported the offence. The Act would affect not only the plays Shakespeare would write but also those he had already written. The constraints went further than simply not having characters swear 'by God', 'by the Lord' or 'by my troth'. All those earthy common oaths – swearing by God's wounds (''swounds' or 'zounds') or his blood (''sblood') or his foot (''sfut' or 'fut'), familiar Christian exclamations that helped define such great roles as Mercutio, Hamlet, Richard III, Falstaff, Edmund and Iago, were now prohibited from being spoken on stage. The Porter's words about the equivocator 'who committed treason enough for *God's sake*' (2.3.10) and Dogberry's hilarious line 'Write down that they hope they serve *God*; and write *God* first, for *God* defend but *God* should go before such villains' (*Much Ado*, 4.2.19–21) – would never be heard by playgoers at the Globe again, early casualties of the rising tide of Puritanism that would lead to the tearing down of the playhouses four decades later.

In practical terms, every theatre company now had to search carefully through the promptbook of every old play and eliminate each instance of blasphemy in order to avoid steep fines. We know, from comparing texts of older plays prepared either before or after 1606, that Hamlet's taunting of Laertes at Ophelia's graveside, ''Swounds, show me what thou'lt do' (5.1.277) was changed in the folio to the disappointingly bland, 'Come, show me what thou'lt do.' And Iago's explosive and disarming oath, the first word he speaks in *Othello* – ''Sblood, but you will not hear me' – had to be cut, leaving the folio line all too plaintive: 'But you'll not hear me' (1.1.4). The cumulative loss was great. Though justly celebrated, the First Folio of Shakespeare's works, when compared to the more profane early quartos, is a bowdlerised edition.

Though the plays Shakespeare wrote in 1606 have much in common, the parliamentary Act serves as a dividing line between his practice in *King Lear* and *Macbeth* on the one side, and *Antony and Cleopatra* on the other. Insofar as many of his most vivid characters had also been great swearers, the Act would not only cramp how he created characters in future plays but also influence their physical settings. Given the new constraints on how characters could express themselves, it was much easier to locate plays in classical or pagan lands than in Christian ones, and this is likely to have influenced the choice of the plays that followed, most immediately *Antony and Cleopatra* and soon *Coriolanus* and *Pericles* as well. As challenging as this was for Shakespeare, it could not have been much easier for the experienced actors in his company who had long committed parts to memory verbatim, for it meant catching themselves before falling into familiar, and now profane, language. There's no record of the Act to Restrain the Abuses of Players leading to a single fine; it didn't have to. Along with the imprisonment of those behind *The Isle of Gulls* and that company's loss of royal patronage, it sent a clear message.

If that piece of legislation influenced Shakespeare at work, a final legislative act struck closer to home. The near disaster of the Fifth of November put significant pressure on the government to act against English recusants. Those who cried loudest for a crackdown believed that if forced to choose, Catholics would follow directives from Rome and rise in revolt when instructed to do so. More moderate voices called for selective legislation, arguing that there were essentially two sorts of Catholics: a loyal majority still committed devotionally to the old faith, and a potentially treasonous minority who placed their obedience to the Pope above their allegiance to the king. Immediately after the plotters were tried and executed in late January, Parliament began drafting a 'Bill of Recusants' and debating various solutions to England's Catholic problem, with the more rabid in the House of Commons proposing that children of recusants be taken from their parents and marriage barred between recusants and members of the Church of England. The pervasive fear that English Catholics were now experiencing is conveyed in a letter to a friend in Spain sent by Luisa de Carvajal y Mendoza:

> They fear that the present hostility and threats will end in death or exile for them all, or that the laws like those put forward in the Parliament will leave no man standing . . . In any case, the Catholics have got to the point that, even in the bravest and most pious hearts, fear has effectively prevailed over the confidence that was once felt in the preservation of the faith.

After months of negotiation, a less draconian and multi-pronged legislative response was agreed upon, 'An Act for the Better Discovering and Repressing of Popish Recusants'. The easiest way to discover recusants was by identifying those who refused to receive Communion. Though weekly church attendance was technically mandatory, parishioners were required to receive Communion only three times a year, including Easter. From now on, those who refused to do so – and the presumption was that only a practising Catholic would choose not to – would be identified by churchwardens and fined incrementally, the first year £20, the next year £40, and after that £60 annually. For all but the wealthiest recusants this meant eventual impoverishment.

Once it was clearer to the authorities who were recusants, a test was still needed to determine which ones could then be trusted. This was the second and more cunning part of the new legislation. Those who refused to take Communion and agreed to pay the fine were required, upon pain of imprisonment, to swear not only that James was their rightful king, but also that the Pope had no authority to depose him, to discharge recusants from their allegiance to him or to encourage them to take up arms against England's government. Wary of Jesuitical deception, the authorities insisted that recusants had to swear to all this 'without any equivocation or mental evasion or secret reservation whatsoever'.

What came to be called the Oath of Allegiance was a brilliantly worded document; it's not clear, in retrospect, if those who wrote it were fully aware of its powerful implications. It was hotly contested in England and abroad, with both King James and the Pope weighing in, and continues to be debated in our own day. Some modern historians see it as little more than a benign test of loyalty to the state. Others see in its razor-sharp distinction between religious and secular obligations one of the signal moments in the emergence of the modern political state. The more cynical consider the Oath of Allegiance a barely veiled effort to fracture English Catholicism. For recusant men and women in 1606 the legislation culminating in the Oath was less a theoretical matter than a practical choice they were now forced to make. Though the legislation was not officially made law by King James until early July, it was clear to local authorities and parishioners as early as February that this Easter would effectively divide English communities into loyal subjects and potential traitors. Allegiance was a new buzzword. Though *King Lear* was completed and first staged before this spring, its conflicts over divided allegiance would carry unusual resonance in light of the controversy over the Oath of Allegiance, including Lear's sharp words to Kent in the opening scene: 'Hear me; on thy allegiance hear me!' (1.156). Divided or multiple allegiances are rife in *Lear* (in which a French army joins Cordelia in invading England) even as they are in *Macbeth* (in which an English army helps invade Scotland). The doomed Banquo's words to Macbeth about keeping his 'bosom franchised and allegiance clear' (2.1.29) would likewise have resonated powerfully, as would Enobarbus's self-lacerating words on his own failure of allegiance in *Antony and Cleopatra*: 'To follow with allegiance a fall'n lord / Does conquer him that did his master conquer' (3.13.44–5).

Come Easter Sunday 1606, refusing to participate in Communion was no longer personal, it was political. This was certainly so in Stratford-upon-Avon, a town near the heart of the failed Midlands uprising, where the potential for violence between neighbours had been real and where there could no longer be so quiet an accommodation between those who still had strong ties to the old faith and those whose beliefs were reformed. The Catholic past of the entire community, once visible to all in the vivid paintings of hell's mouth in Stratford's chapel, had been whitewashed over in living memory, and could be restored once again. And as George Badger's sack of Catholic prayer books and relics had revealed, there were those committed to just such a restoration. Some recusant neighbours directly or indirectly implicated in the Gunpowder Plot were dead; others were still in prison; still others, who had been led in chains to London, were now trickling back to town. The recent if false reports that the king had been assassinated in late March would have done little to allay concerns. So particular care was taken by local authorities this Easter to identify who in the community of perhaps two thousand souls would dare risk being labelled disloyal by refusing to appear in church and take Communion.

Historically, recusants had never been subject to much surveillance or retribution in Stratford-upon-Avon. While records from Shakespeare's day are spotty, it appears that fewer than one per cent of townspeople were ever charged with not attending church. Setting aside the year 1606, in the quarter-century between 1590 and 1616 only three townspeople were ever accused of not receiving Communion. One of them was Shakespeare's father, John, back in 1592 (and scholars disagree over whether he avoided church because of his Catholicism or because, as the evidence strongly suggests, he was dodging creditors). Of course, he might have been in debt and a devoted Catholic; we just don't know, any more than we know what his son William believed or professed. These figures should not be taken to mean that the town was largely Catholic-free; it suggests rather that a tolerant Stratford had long turned a blind eye to Church Papists.

It must have been shocking when on 20 April 1606, Easter Sunday, when Communion was mandatory, an unprecedented twenty-one parishioners refused to appear at Stratford's Holy Trinity Church. At least a third of them were deeply committed Catholics, the kind who harboured Jesuits or whose sons became priests. Shakespeare was acquainted with several of the twenty-one, including the godparents of his twins, Hamnet and Judith Sadler, as well as Margaret Reynolds, to whose son he would bequeath money to buy a memorial ring. Ordinarily, the extended closing of the theatres for most or all of Lent – this year from 5 March to 20 April – was a convenient time for Shakespeare to make the three-day ride home and see his wife, daughters and ageing mother. And since the Prince's Men had been invited to play at court during Shrovetide, he might have been able to leave earlier, counting on at least a month, perhaps a bit longer, before returning to his professional obligations (and to his own official parish, St Olave's). With the resumption of playing on 21 April (and in previous years sometimes a few weeks before Easter), it's likely that he would have still been in his home town when the recusant community began conferring, as it surely did, about the risks and importance of showing loyalty to their faith at this critical time. Shakespeare would have learned, if he hadn't known it already, that among those who would refuse to receive Communion in Holy Trinity Church was his elder daughter, Susanna.

It took a very bold twenty-two-year-old unmarried woman to assert her independence in this way. This was especially the case since none of Susanna's Stratford kin, including her mother, sister, grandmother and uncles, had chosen to defy the authorities in this way, nor were they able to talk her out of her decision. If Shakespeare tried to discourage her, he failed as well. All twenty-one who refused to receive Communion were summoned to appear on 6 May before the new vicar, John Rogers, and explain themselves. This was the so-called Bawdy Court, best known for handling such transgressions as adultery, pregnancy out of wedlock and drunkenness, the kind of human struggles that Shakespeare had long woven into plays like *Measure for Measure.* This session would be largely devoted to religious failings. Some of the recusants who appeared before the vicar that day gave various excuses, pleading poverty or family dissension, while others dutifully promised to receive the Sacrament before the next court convened. But a minority, making a bolder statement, held out longer. Hamnet and Judith Sadler simply refused to appear at their first summons. So did Susanna Shakespeare and four others, and her penalty too was postponed to the next court. A note later added under her entry – 'dismissed' – indicates that in her case, as well as all the others in town, compliance and conformity were the end result. The Sadlers seem to have held out the longest and were called before the court again seven months later, in early December, to force their capitulation. Pleading for more time to 'cleanse their conscience', they were assigned a day on which to receive Communion, and finally agreed to obey that order.

Any concerns Shakespeare might have had that this would hurt Susanna's marriage prospects were misplaced. The following year she married a thirty-two-year-old physician, John Hall, who had recently moved to Stratford-upon-Avon and established a practice there. Adding to the mystery of this story, Hall was a man of strongly Protestant leanings, who, like Susanna, must have known what he was getting into in this marriage. How Shakespeare felt about Susanna's actions – whether he was proud and supportive of his eldest daughter or furious at her unwillingness to play along or concerned about having to pay her £20 fine if it came to that – is lost to us, though it provides the rarest of glimpses into the ways in which the national concerns that infused his works touched so close to home.

12 : Unfinished Business

A surprisingly high proportion of plays in the 1590s, including Shakespeare's, were sequels. During the first half of his career Shakespeare frequently imagined his next play as a follow-up to the last one and even wrote about such plans in an epilogue to *Henry the Fourth, Part 2.* His earliest four history plays (the three parts of *Henry the Sixth* and *Richard the Third*) formed an exciting sequence, as did the four-part drama a few years later that began with *Richard the Second*, ran through the two parts of *Henry the Fourth* and culminated in *Henry the Fifth*. Some of his comedies were also linked: *Love's Labour's Won*, which doesn't survive, was apparently paired with *Love's Labour's Lost*, while the Falstaff-centred *Merry Wives of Windsor* cashed in on the popularity of the contemporary *Henry the Fourth* plays.

Julius Caesar, written in 1599, was as ripe for a sequel as any of his Elizabethan plays. In contrast to the finality of the endings

Lady Anne Clifford as Cleopatra (*c.*1610)

of his two previous tragedies – *Titus Andronicus* and *Romeo and Juliet* – its closure seems deliberately inconclusive. The three-legged stool of the Roman triumvirate in power at the end of the play remains wobbly; Antony and Octavius discuss how to get rid of Lepidus but the play ends before he is cashiered. It also ends before the struggle for pre-eminence between Octavius and Antony is settled. At the outset of the fateful battle at Philippi, in an exchange that is Shakespeare's invention, we glimpse the hostility between the two when Octavius flatly refuses to follow the battle plans of Antony, the more experienced soldier. The simmering conflict extends to the play's final lines, traditionally spoken by the most powerful character on stage. Antony gives what he (and playgoers) assume is the closing speech, eulogising the defeated Brutus as 'the noblest Roman of them all' (5.5.68). The play *wants* to end with this great speech, but Octavius will have none of it, insisting on his superior status by getting in the last, brusque and anticlimactic words: 'So call the field to rest, and let's away / To part the glories of this happy day' (5.5.80–1). Their showdown is inevitable and the ending has the feel of one of those early *Henry the Sixth* plays where Shakespeare left playgoers eager to learn what happens next.

We'll never know in what direction Shakespeare might have taken an Elizabethan sequel to *Julius Caesar*; if he contemplated writing one, contemporary events intervened, making the politics of Antony's downfall and his relationship with Cleopatra too dangerous to explore. We know this indirectly, through the experience of the author and courtier Fulke Greville. Greville grew up and lived near Stratford-upon-Avon and, like his father (who had played such a major role in hunting down the Gunpowder plotters in Warwickshire), was probably well known to Shakespeare. He wrote closet drama, works that he had no intention of staging or even of seeing in print during his lifetime. Late in Elizabeth's reign he wrote and shared with friends three politically charged plays set in distant times and places. The third of these, written around the same time as Shakespeare's *Julius Caesar*, was called *Antony and Cleopatra*. Not long after he wrote it, Greville burned his manuscript and no copies survive. We don't know how widely his play circulated or whether Shakespeare had heard of it. All we know of the play derives from Greville's account written a decade later in a long digression in his *Life of Sidney* (itself left unpublished until 1652, a quarter-century after his death). Not long after Greville wrote *Antony and Cleopatra* the Earl of Essex returned without permission from leading England's disastrous campaign to crush the rebellious Irish. On his return he burst in unannounced on Queen Elizabeth; that day was the last that Essex, who had been the queen's favourite (and by many accounts beloved by her), was allowed in her presence. Put under house arrest and stripped of his offices, in February 1601 he and a few followers rose unsuccessfully against Queen Elizabeth. Essex was executed later that month.

Had Greville written about the relationship of Antony and Cleopatra a few years earlier, any implicit political critique of Elizabeth's reign might have passed unnoticed, much as Samuel Daniel had avoided trouble in his published (though never staged) closet drama *Cleopatra* from 1594, which in any case safely began after Antony's death. But Greville recognised that in light of current events a play about the Egyptian queen's relationship with Rome's fallen soldier would be read as a barely veiled version of Elizabethan affairs, in his words, 'not poetically, but really, fashioned in the Earl of Essex then falling'. Friends to whom he showed his play, sensing danger, urged him to destroy *Antony and Cleopatra*, since much in it was 'apt enough to be construed or strained to a personating of vices in the present governors and government'. Insofar as it had now become potentially linked with Queen Elizabeth, the story of the ageing Cleopatra and her charismatic and martial lover had become too dangerous to retell, and not just for Greville. With his fellow actor-sharers still nervous about having had to defend their politicised staging of *Richard the Second*, and knowing that John Hayward was in the Tower of London for having written a history (dedicated to Essex) of the reign of Henry IV that was taken for one about Elizabeth's, any plans Shakespeare might have had to bring to a close the story he had begun in *Julius Caesar* would have to be set aside. Happily for posterity he decided to write a different tragedy, *Hamlet*.

Despite his close friendship with Essex, Greville was still trusted and rewarded by Elizabeth until the end of her life. But his influence at court waned under her successor and Greville chafed at being kept at arm's length by King James. Seven years after Elizabeth's death, when a frustrated Greville finally recounted his story of the making and unmaking of his *Antony and Cleopatra*, his play's political message had changed. With the passage of time and the growing nostalgia for good Queen Bess, the play that he had destroyed now retrospectively served to expose the excesses and blatant favouritism of the Scottish king (in contrast to King James, he writes, Elizabeth 'never chose or cherished favourite, howsoever worthy, to monopolise over all the spirits and business of her kingdom'). Greville hoped that by revisiting this past, he might turn the once scandalous story of *Antony and Cleopatra* into something noble and heroic: 'Thus have I (by the reader's patience) given that Egyptian and Roman tragedy a much more honourable sepulture than it could ever have deserved, especially in making their memory to attend upon my sovereign's hearse.' In exhuming *Antony and Cleopatra* in this way, Greville hoped to give it – and by implication Elizabeth and Essex, now seen as heroic figures of the late and greater era – what he considered a proper reburial in his *Life of Sidney*. By 1606, when Shakespeare finally returned to unfinished business, picking up where he had left off in *Julius Caesar*, any play about Antony and Cleopatra would have been seen as a reflection on the past regime as well as on the present one; it would also measure how much had altered in the political landscape during those seven years.

Shakespeare's main source for a belated sequel would have been *The Life of Antony*, the longest and arguably richest of Plutarch's fifty biographical portraits. At roughly thirty-seven thousand words it is longer than *Hamlet*, a substantial read. Of all Plutarch's biographies, it held a special attraction for Shakespeare and was a story to which he found himself returning in the early years of James's reign. Whether it was because he knew he wasn't quite done with it yet, because he was discovering in it connections to new cultural preoccupations, or because he found himself identifying with the character of Antony – or even some combination of all of these – we just don't know. While he had first read it closely when writing *Julius Caesar* in 1599, in his early forties Shakespeare was drawn back to it more deeply and ended up refashioning material from it in three of his Jacobean plays.

The first of these was the collaborative *Timon of Athens*, most likely in 1605. The character of the bitter and isolated Timon had appealed to Shakespeare a decade earlier in *Love's Labour's Lost*, where he speaks of 'critic Timon laugh[ing] at idle toys' (4.3.166). While Plutarch never wrote a full 'Life of Timon', he included a brief biographical sketch in a long digression in his *Life of Antony*. It was prompted by how Antony, at rock bottom after he was betrayed by Cleopatra and defeated by Octavius at the Battle of Actium, 'forsook the city and company of his friends, and built him a house in the sea . . . and dwelt there, as a man that banished himself from all men's company, saying that he would lead Timon's life, because he had the like wrong offered him.' When he wrote *Timon* Shakespeare mined this section of the *Life of Antony* extensively, lifting a story about how a bitter Timon invited his fellow Athenians to hang themselves from a tree he was about to cut down, and even quoting verbatim the pair of epitaphs that Timon was thought to have left behind. But as much as Shakespeare had been absorbed in *Timon* in exploring what might drive someone to withdraw from the world, he wasn't interested in retelling the same story or even in hinting at this side of Antony's character, and so in writing *Antony and Cleopatra* ignored this illuminating episode from the *Life* entirely.

When writing *Macbeth* a year or so later, Shakespeare found himself returning to *The Life of Antony*, this time almost surely from memory. He recalled how in Plutarch's account a soothsayer warns Antony to avoid Octavius Caesar: 'Thy Demon,' Antony is told, 'the good angel and spirit that keepeth thee, is afraid of his; and being courageous and high when he is alone, becometh fearful and timorous when he cometh near unto the other.' Macbeth finds much the same holds true with his one-time friend and now nemesis Banquo. 'There is none but he,' Macbeth says, 'Whose being I do fear; and, under him / My genius is rebuked, as, it is said, / Mark Antony's was by Caesar' (3.1.55–8). It was to Plutarch, rather than to his main source for *Macbeth*, Holinshed's *Chronicles*, that Shakespeare turned in trying to articulate Macbeth's fears and foreshadow his downfall. Yet it comes at a price, for the classical allusion seems strangely out of context: what is a medieval Scot doing paraphrasing Plutarch and identifying with Antony? It feels as if Shakespeare's protagonist is as deeply immersed as he himself is in the *Life of Antony* – and it's one of those times in his career when you suspect that Shakespeare, while at work on one play, was already thinking about the next one.

This isn't the only time that Shakespeare borrowed from the *Life of Antony* when writing *Macbeth*. Banquo himself draws on it earlier, though less explicitly, when, after encountering the Weird Sisters, he asks Macbeth, 'have we eaten on the insane root / That takes the reason prisoner?' (1.3.84–5). Shakespeare here recalls Plutarch's account of great famine in Antony's camp, when 'they were compelled to live off herbs and roots . . . and were enforced to taste of them that were never eaten before: among the which there was one that killed them, and made them out of their wits'. Notably, this is taken from the extended account of Antony's disastrous Parthian campaign, which amounts to roughly a fifth of the entire *Life of Antony*, yet another section of the story that Shakespeare almost entirely ignored when he returned a final time to this *Life* a few months later in *Antony and Cleopatra*. Like Antony's identification with Timon's hatred of the world, it didn't suit the story he now wanted to tell.

Such indebtedness to a single source is unusual for Shakespeare, who when tackling a new play habitually read everything on a subject that he could get his hands on. Though he had certainly read Samuel Daniel's *Cleopatra*, he doesn't take much from it, and his debt to a few other works, such as translations of Appian's *The Roman Wars* and Plutarch's *Moralia*, seems marginal at best. One reason for his near-exclusive focus on Plutarch's *Life of Antony*, other than the powerful appeal this biography clearly held for him, was the absence of anything approaching a genuinely alternative take on the lovers or the politics behind their story. The official version of events that emerged in the wake of Antony's defeat at Actium had stuck, as first-century authors writing during Octavius's long reign (and some under his patronage) turned the history of this costly civil war into a more palatable story of the defeat of a once noble Roman brought down by a foreign temptress. So, for example, for Horace in his *Odes*, Antony was subdued by a femme fatale praiseworthy only for her heroic suicide. Virgil took an equally dim view of the pair in his *Aeneid*. Much the same could be said of every classical source Shakespeare might have turned to, from Pliny's *Natural History* to Lucan's *Pharsalia*. And it was a judgement that persisted, virtually unchallenged, into medieval and early modern times. Dante consigned Cleopatra to the second level of hell along with other carnal sinners, while Boccaccio berated Antony's ambition and Cleopatra's promiscuity. Even Montaigne, whose essays Shakespeare was reading closely at this time in Florio's translation, judged Antony harshly; in his 'The History of Spurina' he argued that unlike Julius Caesar, whose ambition was never compromised by his womanising, Antony was one of those 'great persons whom pleasure hath made to forget the conduct of their own affairs'. While there were a few outliers – Chaucer called Antony a man of discretion and praised Cleopatra for sacrificing her life for love – there was no sustained model or precedent for seeing a pair of ageing, adulterous lovers as tragic, let alone transcendent.

If anything, the pendulum had swung even further against the lovers by the time Shakespeare finished *Julius Caesar*, as writers in late Elizabethan England were discovering in Octavia, Cleopatra's rival and Antony's long-suffering wife, a tragic figure to be celebrated. Samuel Brandon published a closet drama called *The Tragicomedy of the Virtuous Octavia* in late 1598; Samuel Daniel included alongside his *Tragedy of Cleopatra* a moving 'Letter from Octavia to Marcus Antonius' the following year; and Fulke Greville wrote admiringly about Octavia at this time in an unpublished *Letter to a Lady* in which he condemned the 'lascivious' and 'licentious affection of Antony toward Cleopatra'. The main source for each of these works was the *Life of Antony*, where Plutarch had written sympathetically and at length about Octavia's eight-year marriage to Antony. Her unswerving loyalty to the wayward father of her children, he writes, had unintended consequences, 'for her honest love and regard to her husband made every man hate him, when they saw he did so unkindly use so noble a lady'. The emerging interest in Octavia's tragedy complicated the longstanding triangulation of characters, replacing the political showdown between Octavius and Antony (distracted by his love for the queen of Egypt) with a domestic drama that revolved around a spurned wife, an absent husband and an adulterous paramour. It also made it harder to see Antony and Cleopatra's affair in a favourable light, though, as Daniel had shown (as had his patron Mary Sidney before him in her 1590 translation of Garnier's *The Tragedy of Antony*), Cleopatra could still independently be portrayed as a tragic figure when focusing narrowly on her choice of suicide over the humiliation of being paraded in Octavius's triumph. There is little question, though, that by the time Shakespeare returned to where he had left off in *Julius Caesar*, the vilification of Antony and Cleopatra's relationship was deeply entrenched. In addition, admiration predominated for Octavius, who defeated them at Actium and re-established one-man rule in Rome as Augustus Caesar. Any author questioning these near-universal judgements faced a steep challenge. The literary landscape, no less than the political one, had made a tragic sequel encompassing the intertwined lives of Antony and Cleopatra far more difficult to imagine.

Shakespeare's copy of Thomas North's vivid translation of Plutarch, published by his schoolmate from Stratford-upon-Avon Richard Field, was likely to have been propped open before him as he wrote *Antony and Cleopatra.* He was especially taken by those instances where Plutarch enlivens a scene or underscores a point with reported quotations. So, for example, near the end of his narrative Plutarch recounts how when one of Caesar's soldiers reproached Cleopatra's attendant Charmian, 'Is that well done, Charmian?' she answered, 'Very well . . . and meet for a princess descended from the race of so many noble kings.' Shakespeare barely altered a word when copying out this exchange: 'What work is here, Charmian? Is this well done?' – to which she replies, 'It is well done, and fitting for a princess / Descended from so many royal kings' (5.2.325–7).

Examples can easily be multiplied; in no other play does he hover so consistently close to the language of his source. Take Antony's dying words to Cleopatra. In Plutarch he tells her that

> she should not lament nor sorrow for the miserable change of his fortune at the end of his days; but rather that she should think him the more fortunate for the former triumphs and honours he had received, considering that while he lived he was the noblest and greatest prince of the world, and that now he was overcome not cowardly, but valiantly, a Roman by another Roman.

Not much tinkering was needed here either to transpose North's translation into Antony's free-flowing speech (I've italicised words and phrases that Shakespeare borrows):

> *The miserable change* now *at my end*
> *Lament nor sorrow* at, but please your thoughts
> In feeding them with those my *former fortunes*,
> *Wherein I lived, the greatest prince o'th' world*,
> *The noblest*; and do now not basely die,
> *Not cowardly* put off my helmet to
> My countryman – *a Roman by a Roman*
> *Valiantly* vanquished.
> (4.15.53–60)

Yet the extent to which he copied with such seeming deference to his source masks how strenuously Shakespeare found himself, for the first time, resisting the arc of Plutarch's narrative. When he had previously drawn on the *Lives* he had more or less accepted the broader contours of Plutarch's interpretation of politics and character and simply skipped over what didn't serve his purposes. This time around that wouldn't work. Yes, he could darken Plutarch's rosy view of Octavius, downplay his descriptions of Antony as a drunk given to pleasure, and ignore some of the nastier details in his portrait of Cleopatra (including how in seeking painless ways to die she experimented 'upon condemned men in prison'). But that wouldn't get him far enough. At some point Shakespeare recognised that he had to break with Plutarch, even as he would continue to make use of those occasions when Plutarch, almost despite himself, expresses wonder at these dazzling and larger-than-life figures. Plutarch's traducing of Antony and Cleopatra seems to have rubbed Shakespeare the wrong way and in retelling their story he would challenge his source's moralising assumptions and conclusions much as he had recently rejected the happy ending (and much else) in the old play of *King Leir*.

For Plutarch, a Greek citizen of the Roman Empire who had visited both Rome and Egypt, the story of Antony and Cleopatra was not ancient history; the Battle of Actium had been fought just seventy-seven years before he was born. His own grandfather, he tells us, was one of his sources, and shared with him a story about a friend on good terms with one of Antony's cooks who invited him to see prepared an extravagant feast in which twelve guests were served 'eight wild boars roasted whole' (a wonderful detail that finds its way into Shakespeare's play [2.2.189–90]). Whether it was from stories his grandfather told him or from the standard version of events found in a host of Roman writers (whose focus was more on Octavius's triumph than on love), for Plutarch this was a story of politics and character, one defined by excess and weakness. He goes out of his way to condemn both

Antony and Cleopatra before introducing their love affair, framing it as a story of a Roman leader possessed of a 'noble mind' in whom his Egyptian lover brought out the worst and stifled the best: she 'did waken and stir up many vices yet hidden in him and were never seen to any; and if any spark of goodness or hope of rising were left him, Cleopatra quenched it straight, and made it worse than before'.

The obstacles Shakespeare faced in turning Plutarch's account into one that portrays their love as ennobling and tragic were formidable. If Shakespeare had been the sort of playwright who invented rather than adapted stories he might have fashioned the tragedy of Antony and Cleopatra out of whole cloth, but that was not the way he wrote plays, least of all tragedies and histories. He was saddled with working from a *Life* that was relentlessly judgemental, its flashes of sympathy or wonderment few and far apart. Plutarch's Cleopatra was manipulative and duplicitous, and Antony, whose mind was turned 'effeminate' by her, became 'so carried away with the vain love of this woman as if he had been glued unto her'. The solution to this problem, for Shakespeare, was in creating a dramatic experience that structurally resembled his own belated turn against this moralising *Life*. To that end, rather than ignore Plutarch's criticism of the lovers, Shakespeare initially gives voice to it, borrowing Plutarch's own technique of describing characters through others' reactions to them. And recognising the extent to which the implicit greatness of the lovers was downplayed in his source, Shakespeare punctuates his version with evocations of past glories, lifting stories of Antony's heroism and grit from much earlier in the *Life*. These backward glances helped make nostalgic longing a defining feature of his tragedy.

Plutarch offered almost no moments of self-reflection or shared intimacy, steering clear of what the lovers might have felt. While at this stage of his career Shakespeare could easily have created an interior life for each of his lovers through sympathetic and self-revealing soliloquies, he decided not to. Soliloquies, in which he excelled, and, with the exception of *Hamlet*, never so brilliantly as in his recent *Macbeth*, had to go. Playgoers in 1606 watching *Antony and Cleopatra* must have experienced a growing sense of unease as scene after scene passed without any soliloquies or unmediated access to what the lovers think or feel. And when Shakespeare does allow a character to speak briefly in soliloquy, as Antony does in Act 2, scene 3, it reveals nothing we don't already know.

Rather than inventing intimate scenes not found in Plutarch, Shakespeare follows his source and *never* lets us see Antony and Cleopatra alone together on stage. This too must have come as something of a surprise for playgoers. We need only compare this with how memorably he had captured the private moments of earlier couples – Romeo and Juliet confessing their love for each other or the Macbeths plotting Duncan's murder – where we get a chance to glimpse what they are like together. Since what Antony and Cleopatra say and do is always witnessed by onstage audiences (then judged by them), we end up evaluating the lovers through the observers' perspectives. Antony grows so habituated to being observed that he expects this will hold true even in the afterlife, as he tells Cleopatra: 'Where souls do couch on flowers, we'll hand in hand, / And with our sprightly port make the ghosts gaze' (4.14.51–2). And since these lovers are also political figures who are always conscious that they are being observed, we are left wondering whether what they are doing or saying publicly is simply part of a performance. There's no way of knowing. The framing of scenes with onstage moralising commentators makes judging them with any confidence nearly impossible.

The play's opening scene introduces much of this innovative approach. Shakespeare chose to begin his story just a year or so after the events that bring *Julius Caesar* to a close and came upon a passage roughly a third of the way into the *Life* that served as a useful point of entry to Act I, scene I:

> Now Antonius was so ravished with the love of Cleopatra, that though his wife Fulvia had great wars, and much ado with Caesar for his affairs . . . he yielded himself to go with Cleopatra into Alexandria, where he spent and lost in childish sports (as a man might say) and idle pastimes the most precious thing a man can spend . . . and that is, time. For they made an order between them, which they called *Amimetobion* (as much to say, no life comparable and matchable with it) one feasting each other by turns, and in cost exceeding all measure and reason.

Rather than stage a version of this private compact or otherwise allow us direct access to the pair, Shakespeare begins his play instead in the midst of a heated conversation between two Roman soldiers who initially disagree over their assessment of Antony. The first to speak, Philo, has seen enough to reject his friend Demetrius's apparent sympathy for Antony, and his words confirm Plutarch's view of how far the ravished Antony has fallen:

> Nay, but this dotage of our general's
> O'erflows the measure. Those his goodly eyes,
> That o'er the files and musters of the war

Have glowed like plated Mars, now bend, now turn
The office and devotion of their view
Upon a tawny front. His captain's heart,
Which in the scuffles of great fights hath burst
The buckles on his breast, reneges all temper
And is become the bellows and the fan
To cool a gipsy's lust.
Look, where they come:
Take but good note, and you shall see in him
The triple pillar of the world transformed
Into a strumpet's fool. Behold and see.
(1.1.1–13)

Instead of suppressing Plutarch's key terms – 'measure and reason' – Shakespeare reassigns them to a stand-in, a judgemental Roman. Evaluated from such a perspective, in which all that is valued must be restrained, masculine, measured and reasonable (in juxtaposition to that Nile-like, overflowing, feminine, dark and disordered Egyptian), what conclusion are we likely to draw other than that Antony is a strumpet's fool?

Philo and Demetrius are interrupted by the spectacular entrance of Antony and Cleopatra, and the lovers exchange hyperbolic words that echo (though also, for the benefit of those observing them, perhaps mock) the Roman obsession with order and setting limits:

Cleopatra. If it be love indeed, tell me how much.

Antony. There's beggary in the love that can be reckoned.

Cleopatra. I'll set a bourn how far to be beloved.

Antony. Then must thou needs find out new heaven, new earth.
(1.1.14–17)

They soon depart, but Demetrius has seen enough to concede that Philo is right:

I am full sorry
That he approves the common liar, who
Thus speaks of him at Rome.
(1.1.61–2)

For much of the play – the first thirty-five of its forty-two scenes – this scenario will be repeated, as onstage Roman commentators (including Scarus, Canidius, Eros, an unnamed soldier, and most often Enobarbus) enter, followed by the main actors, whose actions they frame and whose words they then evaluate, encouraging us to judge the lovers through the prism of Plutarchan 'measure and reason'.

A passage that seems to have struck Shakespeare with particular force in *The Life of Antony* was Plutarch's stirring account of how Cleopatra first won Antony's love. It comes right at the beginning of his account of their relationship:

When she was sent unto by divers letters, both from Antonius himself, and also from his friends, she made so light of it and mocked Antonius so much, that she disdained to set forward otherwise, but to take her barge in the river of Cydnus, the poop whereof was of gold, the sails of purple and the oars of silver, which kept stroke in rowing after the sound of the music of flutes, hautboys, citherns, viols, and such other instruments as they played upon in the barge. And now for the person of herself: she was laid under a pavilion of cloth of gold of tissue, apparelled and attired like the goddess Venus commonly drawn in picture: and hard by her, on either hand of her, pretty fair boys apparelled as painters do set forth god Cupid, with little fans in their hands, with the which they fanned wind upon her.

Much of this vivid description couldn't be bettered, and at first glance Shakespeare doesn't even seem to try, translating Plutarch's prose into flowing blank verse with great economy (again, borrowings are italicised).

> *The barge* she sat in, like a burnished throne
> Burnt on the water. *The poop* was beaten *gold*;
> *Purple the sails*, and so perfumed that
> The winds were lovesick with them. *The oars were silver*,
> Which to the tune of *flutes kept stroke*, and made
> The water which they beat to follow faster,
> As amorous of their strokes. *For her own person*,
> It beggared all description: she did lie
> In her *pavilion – cloth-of-gold of tissue* –
> O'erpicturing that *Venus* where we see
> The fancy outwork nature. On each side her
> Stood *pretty* dimpled *boys*, like smiling *Cupids*,
> With divers-colored *fans*, whose wind did seem
> To glow the delicate cheeks which they did cool,
> And what they undid did.
> (2.2.201–15)

But the differences between Plutarch's and Shakespeare's versions are more significant than these surface resemblances. Shakespeare utterly transforms North's translation by infusing it with hyperbolic and eroticised language, turning his stirring rendering of Plutarch's report into poetry capable of registering the paradox and allure at the heart of Cleopatra's appeal. It's as if Shakespeare is saying that while Plutarch may describe this fatal encounter, he fails to capture its mystery: so where Plutarch's sails were purple, Shakespeare's are perfumed and so captivating that the winds are 'lovesick with them'. Where Plutarch describes pretty boys fanning a Cleopatra dressed like Venus, Shakespeare's queen is truly godlike and the boys attendant Cupids. And in a paradoxical image that sums up the scene (and underscores how far historians fall short of what poets are capable of imagining), their fanning her 'did seem / To glow the delicate cheeks which they did cool, / And what they undid did'.

Shakespeare must have decided early on that his play would somehow end where Plutarch began, at Cydnus. But before glancing back nostalgically to this moment when Cleopatra's powers were at their height, he had to find a suitable place for this description in his own narrative. He puts it far later than Plutarch did, midway through the play, right after Antony promises to return to Rome and marry Octavia, and he assigns it to Enobarbus. Enobarbus appears only in passing in Plutarch as one of Antony's followers, but Shakespeare seized on his name and fashions one of his finest creations out of this hint. He had to, for he needed to flesh out a Roman character, otherwise missing in his source, who could move comfortably between the worlds of Rome and Egypt and who emerges in the course of the play as the one person whose judgements we come to trust.

It helps that Enobarbus always seems to be right. After regaling his friendly rivals in Caesar's camp with the story of the famous meeting at Cydnus, Enobarbus assures them – once again, correctly – that despite what they might think of Antony's plans to wed Octavia, there is no chance that he will abandon Cleopatra for long. Here too, his account of Cleopatra is suffused with paradox and hyperbole:

> Age cannot wither her, nor custom stale
> Her infinite variety. Other women cloy
> The appetites they feed, but she makes hungry
> Where most she satisfies; for vilest things
> Become themselves in her, that the holy priests
> Bless her when she is riggish.
> (2.2.245–50)

Not even Antony can silence Enobarbus, a blunt truth-teller with a clear-headed sense throughout of the choices Antony must make in love as well as in war. When Antony's self-destructive choices seem like those of a fool in love, Enobarbus's Roman values prevail and he abandons Antony's camp for Octavius's (only to discover to his great shame that Antony, ever loyal and bountiful, has sent his thanks, and gold, after him). And it is here, through Enobarbus, that Shakespeare initiates the sharp turn three-quarters of the way through the play, at the end of Act 4, scene 6, where for the first time he introduces a self-revealing soliloquy. In it Enobarbus admits how badly he has misjudged Antony:

> I am alone the villain of the earth,
> And feel I am so most. O Antony,
> Thou mine of bounty, how wouldst thou have paid

> My better service, when my turpitude
> Thou dost so crown with gold! This blows my heart.
> (4.6.31–5)

When he dies in a ditch soon after, of a broken heart – his last words 'O Antony! O Antony!' (4.9.26) – we are left rudderless; the bias and limits of Roman judgement, the kind that informed Plutarch's *Life* and the views of those on stage commenting on the lovers, are manifest.

What is left, for Shakespeare, in the handful of scenes that follow Antony's defeat at Actium, is to provide a convincing alternative, one that encourages audiences to take a leap of faith. There will always be cynics, such as George Bernard Shaw, who dismiss this as mere sleight of hand on Shakespeare's part:

> After giving a faithful picture of the soldier broken down by debauchery, and the typical wanton in whose arms such men perish, Shakespeare finally strains all his huge command of rhetoric and stage pathos to give a theatrical sublimity to the wretched end of the business, and to persuade foolish spectators that the world was well lost by the twain.

For many playgoers, though, Shakespeare makes this sublimity seem real enough. The invitation to take that leap of faith is likely to have caught earliest audiences off guard, since the love affair until now has been so consistently described as debauched and wanton. For it to happen, the play's style must change abruptly. First, things slow down. The headlong rush of scenes until this point – thirty-five in all, where most of Shakespeare's plays until now had consisted of a dozen or twenty at most, and some fewer than that – meant that many of these scenes feel fleeting. Making it even more difficult to find our bearings, the action until this point has shifted restlessly from Rome to Egypt to Syria to Athens and back again. In the final seven scenes of the play, including the last and longest, we remain in Egypt. Moralising commentators who have framed the action disappear and brief soliloquies are at last spoken, though the time for self-revelation seems long overdue. As the play nears its end we are at last offered a rare glimpse into Antony's sense of abandonment; he is left feeling as wounded and exposed as a tree stripped of its bark:

> All come to this? The hearts
> That spanieled me at heels, to whom I gave
> Their wishes, do discandy, melt their sweets
> On blossoming Caesar; and this pine is barked,
> That overtopped them all.
> (4.12.20–4)

One of the most telling exchanges in these final scenes is between Cleopatra and the Roman Dolabella. He is sent by Octavius to ensure her safe capture following Antony's suicide. The dissonance in how they experience the world could not be greater, as Cleopatra offers a soaring vision of Antony's greatness nowhere found in Plutarch:

> His legs bestrid the ocean; his reared arm
> Crested the world; his voice was propertied
> As all the tuned spheres, and that to friends;
> But when he meant to quail and shake the orb,

He was as rattling thunder. For his bounty,
There was no winter in't; an autumn 'twas
That grew the more by reaping. His delights
Were dolphinlike; they showed his back above
The element they lived in.
(5.2.81–9)

For an exasperated Dolabella, Cleopatra's hyperbolic vision bears no relationship to his measured reality. When pressed by her – 'Think you there was, or might be, such a man / As this I dreamt of?' – he can only answer like a Roman, 'Gentle madam, no,' to which she replies:

You lie, up to the hearing of the gods.
But, if there be, or ever were one such,
It's past the size of dreaming. Nature wants stuff
To vie strange forms with fancy; yet, t'imagine
An Antony, were nature's piece 'gainst fancy,
Condemning shadows quite.
(5.2.92–9)

The choice is now ours whether to agree with Dolabella or to accept Cleopatra's passionate defence of the paradox that was her Antony, a defence of their love for each other that looks beyond their many and transparent individual failings.

After repudiating Plutarch's moralising view of their love and offering this defence of the imagination, Shakespeare goes one step further in one of the most daring passages in the canon. In it he shatters the dramatic illusion playgoers have experienced until this moment, forcing them to own up to their imaginative investment in what, in the end, is nothing more than a play, staged by a dozen or so men and three boys playing women's parts. Cleopatra has been warned of the fate that awaits her in Rome; she will be the centrepiece in Octavius's triumphant procession (and in case there was any doubt about what such a Roman procession would be like, Shakespeare went out of his way to stage a brutal and humiliating one led by Antony's lieutenant Ventidius earlier in the play). Cleopatra knows that she and Antony will be caricatured by crowd-pleasing Roman playwrights as a whore and a drunk:

> The quick comedians
> Extemporally will stage us, and present
> Our Alexandrian revels; Antony
> Shall be brought drunken forth, and I shall see
> Some squeaking Cleopatra boy my greatness
> I'th' posture of a whore.
> (5.2.216–21)

It's an almost reckless move by Shakespeare at a point in his tragedy where sympathy for the lovers stands in the balance. Even as he conjures up an image of how they will be memorialised in Rome (and indeed would continue to be remembered, if not quite so mockingly, in Plutarch), Shakespeare reminds Jacobean playgoers that they themselves are listening to some squeaking cross-dressed boy speak these lines. Only the imaginative powers that spectators bring to the playhouse allow them to accept and see past these limitations of the stage, and, by extension, see beyond Plutarchan measure and reason to a world in which the hyperbolic and paradoxical can register a deeper truth. Fittingly, in taking her own life, Cleopatra frustrates Octavius's planned triumph by enacting one of her own, as Shakespeare ends where Plutarch began: 'I am again for Cydnus,' she tells us, as she prepares to put on her crown and robes and take hold of the asp that will kill her, 'to meet Mark Antony' (5.2.228–9).

*

A remarkable Jacobean painting – the only portrait to survive from the period based on a scene from a play – also portrays Cleopatra's final, fatal act with great sympathy (see the image that introduces this chapter). We don't know who painted it and until the twentieth century scholars didn't know it existed. The portrait surfaced in 1931 at a Christie's sale; it was resold at auction in 1948 for eight guineas and then disappeared. Its whereabouts are currently unknown. Fortunately, before that last sale a photograph of it was taken by the National Portrait Gallery.

Yasmin Arshad, who has closely studied this portrait, has persuasively identified the Jacobean woman re-enacting Cleopatra's death as Lady Anne Clifford, one of the great patrons of the arts of her day and an early English diarist. Clifford, born in 1590, was married at nineteen to Richard Sackville, third Earl of Dorset. It is presumably his image, in Roman garb – her Antony – that adorns the miniature she wears around her neck. Her exotic costume closely resembles the one that Inigo Jones designed for her part as Berenice of Egypt in Ben Jonson's *The Masque of Queens*, staged shortly before her marriage in 1609, a detail that helps to pin down the date of the painting, probably executed not long after that, perhaps around 1610. Contemporaries described Lady Anne Clifford as formidable, proud of her looks, wilful and remarkably gifted – John Donne said of her that 'she knew well how to discourse of all things' – so her self-identification with Egypt's queen is not entirely surprising.

Precluding any ambiguity about what scene is being depicted, in the painting's top right corner is a folded playscript containing sixteen lines from the death scene in Samuel Daniel's *Cleopatra*. It strengthens the attribution, for Daniel had been Clifford's tutor, had even dedicated a sonnet to her in his 1607 volume that included *Cleopatra*, and they would long remain on good terms. The lines are copied from either the revised 1607 edition of Daniel's play or its 1611 reprint. This too is an important detail, since scholars have long recognised that some of the changes that Daniel made between the 1605 and 1607 editions of his play are clearly indebted to Shakespeare's language and staging (and confirm that *Antony and Cleopatra* must have been staged by late 1606). After seeing it at the Globe or perhaps at an unrecorded performance of the play at court late that year, Daniel had only a narrow timeframe to make these changes.

The painting is provocative in so many ways – and the surviving photograph of it known to so few – that even the handful of scholars who have considered it are still at a loss to decipher its mysteries. Might it be, as Arshad has proposed, a record of Clifford's private performance of Daniel's closet drama? Does the painting – and its striking choice of subject matter as well as defiant accompanying text – express, as seems highly likely, personal as well as political messages, and if so, what might they be? Arshad speculates that if the portrait was painted a few years later, the appended text might even signal a rebuke of King James, perhaps the 'proud tyrant Caesar' obliquely alluded to in the quoted lines, for having sided against Clifford in a long-running dispute over her contested inheritance, while Clifford's biographers have noted that her husband was both unfaithful and profligate. There is the further puzzle of why Clifford, who was already married, chose to appear in the portrait with exposed breasts. At the time this was a sign of one's unmarried status and explains why, for example, Queen Elizabeth, into the last decade of her life, could appear at court in outfits that were bare-breasted. Still, not even Elizabeth had her portrait painted this way.

One possible explanation for her appearance may have to do not with Clifford's marital status but with Shakespeare's depiction of Cleopatra's suicide. In all of Daniel's versions of the story, following Plutarch's account, the asp bites Cleopatra on her bare arm. But the death of Shakespeare's Cleopatra is at once more erotic and maternal; the cross-dressed teenage actor playing Egypt's queen at the Globe dies after placing the asp not on his arm but on his exposed breast, while saying, 'Dost thou not see my baby at my breast, / That sucks the nurse asleep?' (5.2.309–10). The powerful and original stage image was almost immediately imitated: before the year was out Barnabe Barnes would write a play for the King's Men, *The Devil's Charter* (performed at court the following February), in which a murderer kills two sleeping princes by putting 'to either of their breasts an aspic'. Barnes even calls these asps 'Cleopatra's birds'. That Clifford holds a sceptre in her left hand may also owe a debt to Shakespeare's portrayal of Cleopatra. While a sceptre is nowhere mentioned in either Plutarch's *Life of Antony* or Daniel's various versions of *Cleopatra*, in the scene in which she declares her resolution to take her own life, Shakespeare's Cleopatra speaks of hurling her 'sceptre at the injurious gods' (4.15.81), and it's possible that as she prepares to commit suicide and orders Charmian to fetch her 'crown and all', her royal sceptre was one of these props (5.2.232).

By the time Lady Anne Clifford had her portrait painted, Shakespeare's stage version may well have shaped the way in which a now celebrated Cleopatra was popularly imagined, so it wouldn't be surprising if the painting were indebted in complex ways to both Shakespeare and Daniel (fittingly, since they each owed something to the other's retelling of the story). While answers to so many questions raised by this striking portrait remain provisional, one thing was now clear: no longer Plutarch's treacherous flatterer and seductress, this Jacobean Cleopatra was a defiant heroine worthy of emulation, one who spoke to the here and now.

13 : Queen of Sheba

On the morning of 18 July 1606, 'multitudes' rushed down to the Thames to witness a scene that rivalled the celebrated encounter at Cydnus. A Danish fleet of eight great ships had anchored at Gravesend the previous evening. The crowd was soon rewarded with a breathtaking spectacle, as King James and his entourage made their way downriver towards the Danish ships on three dozen barges. James had hurriedly returned from hunting at Oatlands to greet his brother-in-law King Christian IV of Denmark, who welcomed him aboard his flagship, the *Tre kroner*. Unbeknownst to most onlookers lining the riverbanks that morning, James and Christian had agreed to a state visit, a highly unusual event since European rulers rarely set foot in each other's kingdoms. The last monarch to visit England had been the Holy Roman Emperor Charles V, during the reign of Henry VIII. James and Christian had met only once before, in Denmark, when the young King of Scots had sailed off to bring

Tomb of Queen Elizabeth in Westminster Abbey,
after Maximilian Colt (*c.*1620)

home his fourteen-year-old bride, Anne, in 1589. Though seventeen years had passed since then, and while James knew of the grown-up Christian's reputation for drinking and womanising, he wasn't fully prepared for the transformation of Anne's younger brother into so martial and charismatic a figure.

English writers reporting on the scene gushed at the splendour of the Danish flagship, 'gilded and covered with flags', and those aboard it. Christian himself was dressed 'in black cut out on cloth of silver' and 'about his hat he wore a band of gold, wrought in form of a crown and set with precious stones'. Few monarchs have ever identified more closely with their navy than Christian, who personally oversaw the design of his warships. The sight of his mighty flagship bristling with seventy-two brass cannon beggared description, and contemporary reports of the splendid appearance of the Danes and their fleet go on for pages.

Private greetings were exchanged between the kings aboard the flagship before they transferred to James's royal barge, which would convey them upriver to Greenwich and Queen Anne. The barge they sat in was ornately decorated; according to one eyewitness, it was 'made in fashion of a tower or little castle, all close with glass windows, and casements fairly carved, and gilt, and wrought with much art; the roof of it was made with battlements, pinnacles, pyramids and fine imagery.' The royal barge may have inspired wonder, but when moored alongside the Danish flagship, the dainty faux castle was overshadowed by the formidable three-tiered warship. And while from Cleopatra's famous 'barge / A strange invisible perfume hits the sense / Of the adjacent wharfs' (2.2.221–3), those lining the Thames were struck by the more noxious smell of gunpowder, for as the royal parties in

James's barge were towed upstream, the Danish warships fired such massive salvoes that 'the smoke dimmed the sky' and the noise of the cannonfire was 'heard a far ways off'. King James, who hated the smell of gunpowder, and of late had good reason to, was probably less enamoured of this magnificent display than were his admiring subjects.

In this contest of royal symbolism, the very name of Christian's flagship may have piqued James, who was still hoping to secure, and by peaceful means, his own union of three kingdoms. He would have known that the ship's name was both a provocation and long a source of tension between the Danes and the Swedes, who had originally claimed this as an exclusive national symbol and feared that Denmark, in appropriating it as part of its royal coat of arms and in naming a flagship 'Three Crowns' – intimating a union of Denmark and Norway that would extend to Sweden as well – was aggressively signalling its imperial aspirations. The size and splendour of the Danish ships (a pair of which, including the *Tre kroner*, had recently been built by a Scot) might have unsettled James as well, for it could have drawn attention to how, in the aftermath of his peace treaty with Spain, he had been quietly downsizing Queen Elizabeth's fabled navy. Christian's militant Protestantism was not his style. He had chosen a different path, that of the peacemaker, and saw himself as a modern-day Octavius (later to become Augustus Caesar), so much so that in his coronation medal he presented himself clad like a Roman and identified (in translation from the Latin) as 'James I, Caesar Augustus of Britain, Caesar the heir of the Caesars'. He would likely have approved of Octavius's hope in Shakespeare's play:

The time of universal peace is near.
Prove this a prosp'rous day, the three-nooked world
Shall bear the olive freely.
(4.6.5–7)

Left unmentioned by those who reported on the meeting of the two kings was James's latest assertion of British union. Onlookers would have noticed that every English and Scottish ship in the Thames was now flying a newly designed national flag, one that would come to be known as the Union Jack. Three months earlier James had issued a royal proclamation ordering all Scottish and English ships to fly the new flag in their maintop. The Scots soon let him know of their displeasure, for the design superimposed an English cross of St George upon their St Andrew's cross; they found being topped by England in this way 'derogatory to Scotland' and suggested an alternative pattern, which was ignored. Even this symbolic royal gesture ended up underscoring the profound obstacles facing James's longed-for Union.

Also overlooked by reporters was an undistinguished trio of English vessels outfitting at Blackwall docks for a long ocean voyage: the *Susan Constant*, the *Godspeed* and the pinnace *Discover.* These three small ships would leave a far greater legacy than the majestic *Tre kroner*, for they were bound for Virginia, where their passengers would found the first permanent English colony in the Americas, which they named Jamestown. King James's peace treaty with Spain had opened the door to colonisation there, and on 10 April James authorised the Virginia Company's charter. The voyage caused something of a stir and the poet and playwright Michael Drayton rushed a patriotic poem into print – 'To the Virginian Voyage' – celebrating the endeavour. The small fleet sailed on 20 December 1606 and made landfall six weeks later. Shakespeare was focused on events at home. Five years would pass before he belatedly turned his attention in *The Tempest* to the Americas and the challenges of empire there.

The visit of King Christian that summer, as rich a source in its own way as Plutarch's *Life of Antony*, brought into sharper relief much that is explored in the play to which Shakespeare was now turning – both for its author and for London playgoers for whom memories of the state visit remained fresh. The correspondences, if at times coincidental, are also uncanny, most obviously the invitation to compare the styles and personalities of two powerful leaders (one inclined to wine and women, the other self-identified with a peace-loving Octavius), the ways in which Queen Anne (caught between husband and brother) mirrored Octavia's uncomfortable position, and above all, the frustrating gap between the public and private, between what we are invited to see and what was actually taking place. The words of an awestruck writer observing the meeting of the two kings apply equally well to the experience of watching the interaction of the various rulers in *Antony and Cleopatra*: 'What love, what accomplishments, what repetitions of natural affections passed between them is not for vulgar minds to imagine, none but so great hearts know them.' That held true even for Shakespeare, who as part of James's official entourage as well as a member of a playing company that performed three times before the two kings, and who almost surely participated in their ceremonial procession through London, had a chance to observe their interactions more closely than most. Historians of James's reign have passed over this episode in relative silence, since for them little of consequence came of it. That's unfortunate, because commentary about the visit, as well as works of art influenced by it, especially *Antony and Cleopatra*, drew attention to some of the cracks that were beginning to show three years into James's reign.

The previous August, Henrik Ramel, one of King Christian's chief ministers, had arrived in England for a month-long visit, accompanied by a retinue of fifty Danes. Two years earlier King Christian had received *in absentia* the Order of the Knighthood of the Garter, and Ramel had now been sent 'to be solemnly installed in his right'. The Danish delegation was housed in Somerset House and attended by 'the king's Gentlemen Ushers, Yeomen of the Guard [and] Grooms of the Chamber'. It would have looked shabby had James not arranged for such a substantial retinue to attend upon Ramel, who had himself recently entertained the Earl of Rutland with 'bacchanal entertainments' in Elsinore. The charge would have been familiar to the King's Men; a year earlier, in their official capacity as Grooms of the Chamber, they had been summoned to Somerset House, that time to attend upon a Spanish delegation, there to sign a peace treaty. The yards of red cloth Shakespeare and his fellow shareholders had each received for their royal livery after having been chosen as the King's Men were no symbolic gesture. This was the downside of being part of James's household, especially during the profitable summer season at the Globe. While surviving records confirm that they served as court attendants for eighteen straight days in August 1604, because no record of payments is extant for their labours in 1605 Shakespeare's biographers have overlooked this return visit to Somerset House. It wouldn't have taken a month to handle the formalities surrounding the Knight of the Garter, so it's likely that the embassy was also there to work out the itinerary of the Danish state visit planned for the following spring (when England would play host to a distinguished royal party that would include in all close to four hundred Danes). If so, the King's Men may well have been among the first to learn of the planned forty-day visit and of the role they might be expected to play in the festivities as both actors and attendants.

During his stay King Christian would have to be entertained on a scale that would tax the resources and, with luck, line the pockets of England's poets, portrait painters, musicians and acting companies. Inigo Jones had recently worked at Christian's court, as had one of England's finest musicians, John Dowland, and those eager to appeal to Christian's tastes might have spoken with them or with some of the English actors who had performed in Elsinore. King James spared no expense in playing host, burning through much of the nearly half-million-pound subsidy he had recently wrested from Parliament. Cooks were kept busy, as were goldsmiths, shipwrights, armourers, dance-masters, fencers, wrestlers and vintners. Drummond of Hawthornden spoke for many when he described how during the state visit 'there is nothing to be heard at court but sounding trumpets, hautboys, music, revellings and comedies'.

According to contemporary reports, Christian had been expected to arrive as early as April. As the weeks passed with no sign of his fleet, word circulated that he was 'expected very soon', so the many artists commissioned to entertain the two kings must have begun their labours considerably earlier, by late February or early March. Edmund Tilney, the Master of the Revels, would have known by then that he was expected to vet a sizeable number of plays to be performed at court during the visit. The first week of March had at last brought an end to the extended season of Christmas festivities in which he had overseen eighteen plays at court by the King's Men, Paul's Boys, Queen Anne's Men and the Prince's Men. Tilney would now be called upon to select and oversee perhaps as many plays again. And he had to do this knowing that he must soon secure another dozen or more plays for the following Christmas season, a seemingly impossible task, for there simply were not that many new plays being staged or old ones still in repertory that the royal family hadn't already seen. His burden eventually lightened when Christian decided to cut short his stay and left two weeks early. But Tilney and the players he had lined up for additional performances during those weeks would not have known this in advance of their preparations.

Much of the festivity recalls the sort of royal entertainment Shakespeare had mocked in *A Midsummer Night's Dream*, where Theseus asks his master of the revels, 'What abridgement have you for this evening? / What masque? what music?' and is invited to choose from such dismal fare as 'The battle with the Centaurs' or 'The riot of the tipsy Bacchanals, / Tearing the Thracian singer in their rage' (5.1.39–49). James and Christian had to endure a steady diet of 'learned, delicate and significant shows and devices', including a civic entertainment at the Fleet Conduit of 'a nymph captivated by satyrs' as well as an elaborate welcome at Theobalds by three mythological figures that a mystified Dane described in his diary as 'three small and nicely dressed boys presenting some sort of device'. The script for the latter show was dashed off by Ben Jonson not long after he finished *Volpone*; he was paid over

£13 for this slight contribution (a lot of money, though less, he surely noticed, than the £23 awarded to Inigo Jones for designing the spectacle). The allegory of the nymph and satyrs was written by another leading playwright, the satirist John Marston, who flattered the kings and pleased the civic patrons who paid him without a hint of his trenchant irony or wit.

Nearly all of the commissioned writing was little more than shameless flattery; four hundred years later it is almost unreadable. The same holds true for the freelancing efforts of younger or less established writers, eager to take advantage of this golden opportunity, including the twenty-year-old John Ford (best known today for great plays like *'Tis Pity She's a Whore*, written decades later). Recently expelled from the Middle Temple, Ford was badly in need of patronage and rushed into print a pair of works on the visit, neither of which seems to have attracted much attention, including a brief and unctuous poem called 'The Monarchs Meeting'. Edmund Bolton's Latin poem about the visit, '*Tricorones*', and John Davies of Hereford's no less laboured '*Bien Venu*' were equally forgettable. The youngest author to join in this collective act of adulation was probably Henry King, the future poet and Bishop of London, who had just turned fourteen. His untitled quatrain was included with ninety-seven other poems, all in Latin, that Oxford scholars wrote in celebration of the occasion. The bound collection – *Charites Oxonienses sive Laetitia Musarum* – was probably part of extensive preparations for Christian's visit to the university town, which in the end didn't take place. Presentation copies had to be forwarded to the two kings, a vestige of what was no doubt a rich array of planned entertainments in Oxford. We don't know their original itinerary, but within a week of his arrival, Christian announced that he 'meant not to stay so long, nor to visit so many parts of the kingdom, as he purposed, when he first prepared to come for England', and James instructed the Lord Mayor of London to prepare for their elaborate welcome to the City earlier than expected. It's hard to explain what the King's Men were doing in Oxford on 31 July, ten days after Christian landed; it may well be that they were there in anticipation of the royal visit and had to rush back to Greenwich to perform there for the two kings later that week.

Records of theatrical performances during Christian's visit are sparse. Scholars have tried to fill the gaps by speculating about what plays might have best pleased the Danish guest, who didn't speak English, or his Scottish host. *Hamlet*, in retelling the story of a Prince of Denmark, might have been an obvious choice, and perhaps, too, Shakespeare's recent Scottish play, *Macbeth*. The few records and passing references in letters and diaries provide the name of only a single play that was staged before the two kings: the now lost *Abuses*, performed by the nearly defunct Paul's Boys at Greenwich on 30 July. The previous evening Tilney had arranged for the out-of-favour Children of Blackfriars to play there as well, suggesting a certain desperation on the part of the authorities. The following week there were at least four more performances, though the names of the companies that staged them are not known. Even this list feels incomplete, for it would have been a slight to James's heir, who got along famously with his uncle, if the Prince's Men weren't asked to perform too. Shakespeare's company was paid to stage three unnamed plays, one at Hampton Court on 7 August, and the other two, probably before that date, at Greenwich.

Sermons were a significant part of the royal entertainment at James's court and Jacobean preachers held to a very high standard. For Christian's visit those chosen to preach had the added challenge of doing so in Latin so that both kings would understand what they were saying. Records of three of the seven delivered during the visit – each Sunday and Tuesday – survive. The Cambridge divine Thomas Playfere gave an early one and the reviews were harsh, with Dudley Carleton reporting to a friend that Playfere had 'more than half shamed himself'. Henry Parry, a fortnight later, didn't fare much better (this time Carleton complained that in turning from divinity to philosophy Parry became 'so obscure . . . that he lost himself'). Happily for Parry, Christian liked what he heard well enough to reward him with a valuable ring.

Only Lancelot Andrewes, the greatest preacher of the age, rose to the occasion. He had been asked to deliver a sermon on 5 August commemorating the sixth anniversary of the Gowrie plot against James's life, which couldn't have been easy given Andrewes's doubts about the truthfulness of the official version of the story. His sermon, though published in Latin in 1610, remains little known, perhaps because it didn't appear in English until 1641, appended to the fourth edition of his magisterial collection, *Ninety-Six Sermons.* Like England's best playwrights, leading preachers like Andrewes had their finger on the pulse of the day, and their sermons both registered and defined the cultural moment.

Andrewes chose to preach on Psalm 144, verse 10 – 'It is He that giveth salvation unto kings, who delivereth his servant David from the perilous or malignant sword' – confident that everyone would recognise its contemporary relevance and see 'that it fits, both to this our purpose, and to the time'. Quickly dispensing with the unsavoury Gowrie story, he turned instead to the traumatic events of the previous November: 'He that six years since hath delivered him from the hurtful sword, very lately, this year, hath delivered him from the perilous Gunpowder.' The threat the previous November had been visceral. Had the plot succeeded it 'would have made it rain blood, so many baskets of heads, so many pieces of bodies cast up and down'. Andrewes – who along with most royal preachers had for the past months steered clear of Catholic-bashing – surprisingly attacks the 'monster-like' Jesuits, 'traitors to kings' who are committed to 'the overthrow of kingdoms, in what state forever they get footing'. He may well have been motivated by a desire to find common ground between the two staunchly Protestant monarchs he was addressing (and to send a message to the international audience that the published Latin version of his sermon was meant to reach). Andrewes singled out for special condemnation Jesuitical equivocation: what King David 'calls lying', he preached, 'they call equivocation', before arguing that the minds of the misguided Jesuits are 'estranged from God', an estrangement that propels them 'to whet these perilous swords, to mingle poisons, to give fire to Powder-plots'.

His sermon suggests that although nine months had passed since that plot had been exposed, the nation had not yet come to terms with this trauma: 'it almost exceeds our belief, who yet our selves have seen it. Later ages, sure enough (I think) will scarcely credit it, that ever there were in man's shape, such locusts from the nethermost hell, who should devise so hellish practices.' While Andrewes may have pleased both rulers by speaking warmly of divine right (and surely made James happy with his trinitarian nod to Union as 'three kingdoms in one, to one in three'), he was equally capable of chastising both men for their vain pursuits: James for his incessant hunting and Christian for his over-investment in his navy: 'there is no safety for kings', Andrewes warned, either 'in the strength of a horse' or 'in their naval forces': 'let kings know', he adds, that deliverance comes solely from heaven.

His sermon at Greenwich is best read as the first of a two-part sequence, for three months later Andrewes would deliver the first annual Gunpowder sermon at Whitehall. There, speaking in English and for domestic consumption, he changed course and shifted blame from the Jesuits to the devil himself: 'not man but the devil devised' the Gunpowder Plot, and 'not man but God defeated it'. He had to do so if he were to acknowledge – as he hadn't in his Gowrie sermon – that at stake here was more than deliverance; it was nothing short of a 'miracle' that truly justified a permanent national holiday. Holidays until recently had been truly holy days, until celebrations of the Accession Day of Queen Elizabeth and more recently Gowrie Day had blurred the line between the political and the theological. But for Andrewes, God's role in defeating the forces of evil on the Fifth of November made it exceptional: 'This day should not die, nor the memorial thereof perish, from ourselves, or from our seed, but be consecrated to perpetual memory, by a yearly acknowledgement to be made of it, throughout all generations.' And perhaps recalling the unholy feasting and drinking that followed his recent Gowrie Day sermon, Andrewes warned his listeners that this should not be another day in which celebrants, in behaviour displeasing to God, 'sat down to eat and drink and rose up to play'.

Dudley Carleton, who heard this Gowrie Day sermon too, thought that Andrewes had hit the mark and that 'in all men's opinions exceeded himself'. There's a better than even chance that Shakespeare's company played at Greenwich either the previous night (which had been spent in 'plays and dancing') or were part of that very evening's 'delightful sport'. Whether or not his new play, *Macbeth*, was staged one of those nights at Greenwich (or perhaps later in the week at Hampton Court) remains unknown, but if it was, its corresponding interest in equivocation, estrangement and hellish practices would have resonated with both the sermon and the national mood that Andrewes etches so sharply.

The first week of Christian's visit was spent at Greenwich, where Queen Anne was recovering from the loss of her newborn, Sophia, who had died a month earlier and was interred at Westminster Abbey. The depressing loss put a damper on the visit. James had been expecting yet another heir; Christian had hoped to congratulate his sister on the birth of a child named after their mother; and (we know from contemporary letters) courtiers had hoped to profit from the largesse typically dispensed on such occasions. Anne would not be 'churched' or resume her regular activities until 3 August. It was an unhappy turning point in royal relations; Sophia would be their last child. This first week seems to have been mostly private, with no reported plays or entertainments other than a tennis match. The kings spent day after day hunting, which Christian, though he enjoyed the sport, soon tired of.

On Thursday 24 July the royal parties made their way to Theobalds, Salisbury's fabulous estate twelve miles north of London.

'Multitudes of people as were not to be numbered' swarmed after them and for the first three or four miles the crowds were so thick that 'there was hardly way left for their royal company to pass them'. The royal parties stayed at Theobalds for four nights before an exasperated Christian headed back to Anne and Greenwich (at first, shockingly, without James). Word circulated that he was disgusted by James's obsession with hunting; according to Dudley Carleton, Christian found 'fault with it as a sport wherein were more horses killed in jest than the Low Country wars consumed in earnest'. James for his part couldn't fathom the 'small pleasure his brother of Denmark took in it'. The tension between the two probably had less to do with their competing notions of manly activities or with Christian's irritation at a dozen horses being ridden to death in a single day of hunting than with the King of Denmark's anger at James's insensitivity to Queen Anne. The French ambassador, de la Boderie, reported home soon after that Christian had 'remonstrated' with James about how he treated his sister.

Comparisons of James with his more athletic brother-in-law were inevitable – and invidious. James might have winced at the Soothsayer's warning to Antony in *Antony and Cleopatra* that 'If thou dost play with him at any game, / Thou art sure to lose' (2.3.26–7), for James was similarly shown up, most memorably when he competed with Christian at the running at rings (a defeat, it was noticed, that put James 'into no small impatiences'). James may have been angered but not surprised when shortly after Christian left for home he received an anonymous letter warning him 'to think on the good government' rather than 'running after wild animals', and urging him 'to take example from the King of Denmark, and devote himself to really king-like employments; he would otherwise lose all affection and respect on the part of his people'.

Aside from the fees for the elaborate welcome provided by Ben Jonson and Inigo Jones, there are no records of payments for other shows at Theobalds. But it would be surprising if nothing else had been planned, for Salisbury had spared no expense; a staggering amount was spent on food and alcohol. Sir John Harington, godson to Queen Elizabeth, author, wit, translator, and marginalised figure at James's court, reflected in a letter on the gluttony, promiscuity and drunkenness he witnessed this week at Theobalds, a remarkable description that deserves to be quoted at length:

> I came here a day or two before the Danish king came, and from the day he did come until this hour, I have been well nigh overwhelmed with carousal and sports of all kinds. The sports began each day in such a manner and such sort, as well nigh persuaded me of Mahomet's paradise. We had women, and indeed wine too, of such plenty, as would have astonished each sober beholder. Our feasts were magnificent; and the two royal guests did most lovingly embrace each other at table. I think the Dane hath strangely wrought on our good English nobles; for those, whom I never could get to taste good liquor, now follow the fashion, and wallow in beastly delights. The ladies abandon their sobriety, and are seen to roll about in intoxication. In good sooth, the parliament did kindly to provide his Majesty so seasonably with money; for there hath been no lack of good living; shows, sights and banquetings, from morn to eve.

Harington can't quite believe the decadence of the sodden Jacobean court, all the more surprising given King James's own abstemiousness (even the hostile seventeenth-century biographer

Anthony Weldon conceded that James drank 'rather out of custom than any delight', and 'seldom at any one time above four spoonfuls, many times not above one or two'). For Harington, though, while the heavy drinking may have started with the Danes, the carousing reflected far more poorly on their hosts: 'I do often say (but not aloud) that the Danes have again conquered the Britains, for I see no man, or woman either, that can now command himself or herself.' Only months after having been spared annihilation, James's mindless court seemed bent on self-destruction: 'The gunpowder fright is not out of all our heads, and we are going on, hereabouts, as if the devil were contriving every man should blow up himself, by wild riot, excess and devastation of the time and temperance.'

The debauchery, Harington continued, reached new levels in a masque at Theobalds performed before the two kings: 'One day, a great feast was held, and, after dinner, the representation of "Solomon his Temple and the coming of the Queen of Sheba" was made, or (as I may better say) was meant to have been made, before their majesties, by device of the Earl of Salisbury and others.' The story of Sheba's visit to Solomon's court would have been an apt one to stage before James, who identified with the wise and peace-loving King of Israel. Sheba's words upon arriving at his court would have been recalled as especially flattering to James during this state visit: 'It was a true report that I heard in mine own land of thy acts and of thy wisdom; howbeit I believed not the words, until I came, and mine eyes had seen it; and behold, the half was not told me; thy wisdom and thy prosperity exceedeth the fame which I heard' (1 Kings, 10:6–7). James himself had popularised this analogy when he wrote in his advice book to Prince Henry, *Basilikon Doron*, 'that when strangers shall visit your court, they may with the Queen of Sheba, admire your wisdom in the glory of your house and comely order among your servants'. It's an unusual coincidence that even as Shakespeare was writing of a famous encounter with one African queen, Harington's letter describes another. Sheba was known as a queen of Ethiopia and of Egypt, with a palace near the Nile, and many, including Shakespeare, associated her with political wisdom. In his late and collaborative play *Henry the Eighth*, Archbishop Cranmer prophesies that the infant Elizabeth I will be even wiser than this famous queen: 'Sheba was never / More covetous of wisdom and fair virtue / Than this pure soul shall be' (5.5.24–6).

The entertainment's promising storyline was belied by the shameful behaviour at Theobalds, as the masque of Sheba turned into a drunken orgy:

> But alas! As all earthly things do fail to poor mortals in enjoyment, so did prove our presentment hereof. The lady who did play the queen's part, did carry most precious gifts to both their majesties; but, forgetting the steps arising to the canopy, overset her caskets into his Danish majesty's lap, and fell at his feet, though I rather think it was in his face. Much was the hurry and confusion. Cloths and napkins were at hand, to make all clean. His majesty then got up and would dance with the Queen of Sheba; but he fell down and humbled himself before her, and was carried to an inner chamber and laid on a bed of state; which was not a little defiled with the presents of the queen which had been bestowed on his garments, such as wine, cream, jelly, beverage, cakes, spices and other good matters. The entertainment and show went forward, and most of the presenters went backward, or fell down; wine did so occupy their upper chambers.

In anatomising the decadence of the Jacobean court, Harington's letter seems – and probably was – too good to be true. The alleged recipient of his letter, his 'good friend' Secretary Barlowe, has never been identified. No other writer ever alluded to so infamous an event. Women didn't play these sorts of role in Jacobean masques. The conventions governing contemporary descriptions of court masques – naming the performers, describing the music, structure, design and especially the elaborate costumes – are completely ignored. And the allegory of Hope, Faith, Charity and Victory that Harington goes on to describe (in which the first two are 'sick and spewing' their guts 'in the lower hall' while Victory's offer of a 'rich sword' to King James is 'put by with his hand') seems wildly contrived, the latter gesture a not-so-subtle dig at a decidedly pacifistic James. To post a letter as borderline treasonous as this would have been near suicidal. Most likely his letter was never intended to be sent but written to be read aloud in private to trusted friends. Almost two hundred years passed before it was published.

Yet his fictional description wasn't that far from the truth. Many at court recalled the Twelfth Night celebrations two years earlier when the partying after *The Masque of Blackness* got out of hand: a banquet table was overturned and a mad scramble ensued, as 'chains, jewels, purses' and even 'the honesty' of a woman who was 'surprised at her business' were lost. The drinking and promiscuity at Theobalds may well have been prodigious. Harington's portrait was far from a parody of a drunken and lecherous King of Denmark. Christian was known to keep a diary in which he marked with a cross the days on which he was so drunk he had to be carried to bed (and added extra crosses if he had passed out).

He could handle 'thirty or forty goblets of wine' in an evening and was no doubt pleased when, in honour of his tour of London, the civic authorities ordered that 'the conduit in Cornhill . . . run with claret wine'. One of his principal ministers recorded how, after a drinking session, Christian asked him about the availability of young girls at the local inn. The Danish king sired at least twenty children with two wives and various mistresses. It's unlikely that James tried to keep pace with his alcoholic brother-in-law, not even when hosting him during the last days of the visit aboard a pair of English vessels linked with a gangway (where a pair of English noblemen got so drunk they fell into the Thames and one emerged naked from the waist down). The wild drinking scenes aboard ship in *Antony and Cleopatra* in which Pompey has to be carried off dead drunk have no source in Plutarch and may well owe a debt to reports of the heavy drinking on board during Christian's visit.

This probably isn't the only example of Harington's surviving correspondence that is not a letter in the traditional sense but rather a brilliant work of epistolary fiction, one that, like Shakespeare's *Antony and Cleopatra*, finds in an imaginative retelling access to truths about the current state of affairs otherwise impossible to register. One of the things that both writers were feeling their way towards articulating at this moment is a growing nostalgia for England's late queen. In many ways, this is the moral of the Sheba story: 'I have much marvelled at these strange pageantries,' Harington concludes, 'and they do bring to my remembrance what passed of this sort in our queen's days; of which I was sometime an humble presenter and assistant: but I never did see such lack of good order, discretion and sobriety, as I have now done.' Both Harington and Shakespeare, in the aftermath of King Christian's visit, found themselves treading much the same ground as Fulke Greville would a few years later when he spoke of his efforts to give the play he had written about Antony and Cleopatra 'a much more honourable sepulture', once the Elizabethan past was viewed afresh in light of the Jacobean present.

To compare the previous and present monarch, as both Harington and Greville recognised, could be life-threatening. And to write about Antony and Cleopatra, as first Greville and now Shakespeare understood, was necessarily political and topical – and potentially seditious. So we cannot expect Shakespeare's new play to be anywhere near as explicit as his recent British histories in touching upon contemporary events. And yet it says something even more powerful and insightful, though obliquely, about the transition from Elizabethan days to life under James. *Antony and Cleopatra* is a play intensely self-conscious about epochal change (even if that change is not fully visible to those living through it). Audiences at the Globe would have gathered as much from the casual allusion to 'Herod of Jewry' (3.3.3) midway through the play, a reminder that far greater historical forces and trajectories are at work here than the protagonists of the story are aware of, the very shift we ourselves call to mind when we speak of history in terms of BC and AD.

In its retelling of ancient history, *Antony and Cleopatra* juxtaposes the giants that once inhabited Rome – those who are already gone, including Julius Caesar, Pompey, Brutus and Cassius, and those who will soon join them, Antony and his Egyptian queen – with the play's ostensible victor: the much diminished Octavius, who is happier sending others into battle than risking combat himself, who plots and manoeuvres his way to world domination, fantasises about leading his enemies in triumph, and uses the burial of those celebrated figures he has outlived to raise his own profile. I suspect that for Shakespeare, much as for Harington, the visit of the martial King Christian and his fleet this summer crystallised what many at the time must have been feeling. The Elizabethan past, a world marked by victories over the Armada and the Irish, and similarly filled with a larger-than-life cast of characters who were now dead, executed or imprisoned – including Essex, of course, but also Sir Walter Ralegh, the queen's formidable adviser (and Salisbury's father) Lord Burleigh, the recently deceased Lord Mountjoy and Queen Elizabeth herself – had been succeeded by an era of less impressive figures, especially King James. If that hadn't been obvious when the new king was seen in isolation, the visit and hasty departure of the charismatic King Christian had made it abundantly clear. *Antony and Cleopatra* is a tragedy of nostalgia, a political work that obliquely (for there are never reductive and dangerous one-to-one correspondences between ancient and modern figures) expresses a longing for an Elizabethan past that, despite its many flaws, appeared in retrospect far greater than the present political world.

*

As her long reign neared its end, Queen Elizabeth saw no need to monumentalise herself with an expensive tomb. When she died in 1603 she was interred in Westminster Abbey in the tomb of her grandfather, Henry VII; fittingly, the first and the last of the Tudors were buried side by side. But King James had other plans for her, and for that spot. And so, in 1606, he had Elizabeth exhumed – at the cost of forty-six shillings and four pence – then reburied a few yards away on top of the bones of her half-sister Mary. He then arranged for an elaborate eight-column monument to be erected over their remains, on which a marble sculpture of Elizabeth reclined. Executed by Maximilian Colt, with detail work by the noted painter Nicholas Hilliard, the tomb was completed some time in 1606 at the considerable cost of £765. It captured, in its way, another Cydnus moment, preserving for posterity a frozen image of Elizabeth at the time of her passing, for her marble visage was based on the lifelike and life-size effigy used in her funeral (which had been fabricated by John Colt, Maximilian's brother, who almost surely relied on a death mask to render her features).

Elizabeth's reburial in 1606 was part of a complicated act of revisionist history. Even as Shakespeare was rewriting the past in light of the present, so too was his monarch (who would probably have disagreed with the prediction in Sonnet 55 that 'Not marble nor the gilded monuments / Of princes shall outlive this powerful rhyme' [1–2]). Three years into his reign and still insecure about the place of the Stuarts in the pantheon of English monarchs, James coveted the plot in which Elizabeth had been buried, a site that identified its occupant as the rightful heir to Henry VII, from whom he traced his own claim to the English throne. And when he died in 1625 that's where James was interred. The line descending from Henry VII would henceforth be seen to branch. On the north aisle in Westminster visitors would come upon the sterile, dead-end line: James's immediate predecessors, the two childless Tudor queens, Mary and Elizabeth, along with his own daughters who died young, Mary and Sophia (the latter, in a nice domestic touch, resting under a tomb depicting her in an alabaster cradle, her tiny hands visible under a velvet coverlet). The visitors could then trace in parallel in the south aisle the more fruitful line of tombs commemorating Henry VII's mother, Lady Margaret Beaufort, and then Margaret, Countess of Lenox, a crucial link between Tudors and Stuarts, since she was both granddaughter to Henry VII and mother-in-law to King James's mother, Mary, Queen of Scots, who appears next in line. To create this narrative in stone James had to have his mother dug up from where she had been buried twenty-four years earlier in Peterborough and reinterred in Westminster in 1612 in a lavish tomb that cost nearly three times what was spent on Elizabeth's. By situating his mother opposite her nemesis Elizabeth, James positioned himself as the great peacemaker, levelling victor and vanquished, even as he symbolically reconciled the religious differences between the Catholic and Protestant Tudor queens, affixing to the tomb that covered them both a Latin plaque proclaiming how Mary and Elizabeth rested there 'in the hope of one resurrection'. It's hard to decide which of the two would have resented this more.

It's unclear whether work on Elizabeth's tomb was completed in time for King Christian's tour of the abbey (he was accompanied that day by Prince Henry and various lords, though not by James; the kings had clearly wearied of each other's company). As Margaret Owens has shown, in anticipation of this visit King James had also paid to have the effigies of seven of England's greatest kings and queens 'newly beautified, amended, and adorned with royal vestures'. Funeral effigies of English royalty had been stored in the abbey since at least the time of Edward II. These were life-size mannequins, typically constructed out of wood, plaster, fabric, straw and wax. Their lifelike faces were painted, they were dressed in wigs and finery fit for kings and queens, and they were built with moveable joints so that they could be positioned to sit, stand or recline. Three years earlier Elizabeth's had cost £10 to make, and her tailor William Jones was paid to dress her in a robe of crimson satin, lined with white fustian. Great care and expense were taken in constructing what were variously called 'images' or 'representations' of the monarch; the nomenclature suggests a sense of strain when it comes to describing just what these effigies were. In the early seventeenth century, Westminster Abbey seems to have been partly a religious site, partly a mausoleum and partly a precursor to Madame Tussaud's.

The royal retinue refurbished for Christian's visit consisted of Edward III, Henry V, Henry VII and their queens, along with Elizabeth I. It's unlikely that anyone had ever tried to gather them together in this way before. Christian viewed what might strike us today as a bizarre spectacle, for King James had also ordered that a special display case or 'press' be built in order that the seven kings and queens could be seen standing together, like actors on a stage, in a tableau. There's a possibility that Shakespeare had heard of the restoration work being done at the abbey in late winter or early spring of 1606, and that it influenced his own 'show of eight kings' in Act 4 of *Macbeth*, where a royal line going back to Banquo appears silently on stage, a line that, to Macbeth, seems to 'stretch out to th' crack of doom' (4.1.117). Shakespeare's text doesn't make clear whether they stand together or enter and exit one at a time. More likely, James's and Shakespeare's 'show of kings' were fashioned independently at roughly the same time, and shared a common purpose: advertising the extent and legitimacy of James's royal lineage. The display in the abbey in which James's royal predecessors appeared must have been roughly eleven feet long and three feet deep, for the press had been built in part from a recycled thirteenth-century oak panel painting of that size, the Westminster Retable. If we can trust the report of George Vertue, who viewed Queen Elizabeth's effigy in the early eighteenth century before it was reconstructed, the queen appeared as she had at the end of her life: 'not tall, but middling, her head cut in wood. Ancient, a little wrinkly her face.' When her effigy was first seen in 1603, the Venetian ambassador reported that it was 'coloured so faithfully that she seems alive'.

We don't know what Christian made of it, but it seems to have had a powerful impact on another play staged by Shakespeare's company at the Globe not long after, Middleton's *The Revenger's Tragedy*. That play's belatedness in relation to the earlier Elizabethan revenge drama is signalled from the outset, when the actor who first starred as Hamlet, Richard Burbage – and who famously held up the skull of Yorick in the gravedigger scene – enters playing a different avenger, Vindice. Once again Burbage holds a skull, one that belonged to Vindice's 'once betrothed wife', which he has been lugging around with him for the past nine years. She had been poisoned by the Duke for refusing his advances. In a climactic scene midway through the play, Vindice takes this *memento mori* and transforms it into a sort of effigy (the stage direction explains that he enters 'with the skull of his love dressed up in tires'). After spreading poison on 'her pretty hanging lip', he tricks the lecherous Duke into kissing this 'bashful lady'. As the poisoned Duke dies in agony, Vindice reveals the identity of his killer: 'View it well, 'tis the skull / Of Gloriana.' His beloved has never been named before in the play, and the name 'Gloriana' may well have shocked Jacobean playgoers, for that is what Queen Elizabeth had so often and famously been called. It's an opaque play, and this scene especially bizarre. But it seems unmistakable that in a play that is so much about a longing for a lost and irrecoverable past, in naming Vindice's dead betrothed as he does, Middleton also partakes in that larger if still inchoate nostalgia for England's own beloved and lost Gloriana – one visible in other plays this year, including Thomas Dekker's *The Whore of Babylon*, in which Elizabeth is trotted out in her old role as 'the Fairie Queene', and which ends with a recollection of her rousing Armada speech to the English troops at Tilbury.

When Francis Bacon heard about the monument to Elizabeth that James was raising in Westminster he thought it (surely with unintended irony) 'a very just and princely retribution' and recognised its political implications: 'As statues and pictures are dumb histories, so histories are speaking pictures.' But even dumb histories can be read in multiple and often unintended ways; James, in seeking to displace Elizabeth, inescapably drew renewed attention to her. His grand design depended on the dynamic relationship between the various tombs in the abbey. But Elizabeth's iconic image was soon yanked from this context and circulated independently, frustrating James's goal. Decades later Thomas Fuller described how an engraving of the tomb that James had built for Elizabeth soon adorned parish churches across the land: 'the live draught of it' is 'pictured in every

London and in most country churches, every parish being proud of the shade of her tomb; and no wonder, when each loyal subject created a mournful monument for her in his heart'.

Even as Bacon praised James for raising a monument to Elizabeth, he couldn't help but wax nostalgic for his predecessor: 'If Plutarch were alive to write lives by parallels, it would trouble him both for virtue and fortune, to find for her a parallel amongst women.' It would be an exaggeration to say that soon after he wrote this Shakespeare did just that in his retelling of Plutarch – though the character of his Egyptian queen, and the sense of nostalgia that pervades the play, is surely inflected by the change of heart English men and women were beginning to feel towards their dead queen. Shakespeare, given his proximity to the court during the last decade of her reign, must have seen the late queen in all her moods: vain, decisive, witty, churlish, flirtatious, brave and imperious. And yet, as with Cleopatra, what mattered most was how she would be remembered. Bishop Godfrey Goodman, reflecting back on the early years of the seventeenth century, recalls that by the time of Elizabeth's death her people had grown 'very generally weary of an old woman's government'. That changed quickly enough under James, he adds, for 'When we had experience of the Scottish government, then in disparagement of the Scots, and in hate and detestation of them, the queen did seem to revive; then was her memory much magnified, such ringing of bells, such public joy and sermons in commemoration of her.' Goodman also recognised the role played by 'the picture of her tomb painted in many churches', which produced 'in effect more solemnity and joy in memory of her coronation than was for the coming in of King James'. Like King James,

Shakespeare's Octavius is keenly aware that his legacy is tied to those he inters, even as a Jacobean Cleopatra, in calling for her robes and orchestrating her final moments, understands that her final image will define her legacy. At the end of Shakespeare's play, after Cleopatra has frustrated Octavius's plans to lead her in triumph to Rome, Octavius changes course and makes the best of this setback. He comes up with a solution that, while securing the reputation of the dead lovers, also enhances his own, joining them in death and memorialising them not as one-time rivals to him in power, but rather as celebrated lovers:

> She shall be buried by her Antony.
> No grave upon the earth shall clip in it
> A pair so famous.
> (5.2.358–60)

14 : Plague

In late July 1606, in the midst of a thrilling theatrical season that included what may well be the finest group of new plays ever staged, the King's Men lowered their flag at the Globe and locked their playhouse doors. Plague had returned to London. Its sudden resurgence caught Londoners off guard, given how promisingly the year had begun. A weekly bill of plague deaths, listed parish by parish, was printed every Thursday morning by the civic authorities and closely scrutinised. It had averaged in the single digits from January to mid-March and except for a brief spike in late April remained under twenty a week through late June. Two years earlier, after the outbreak in which over thirty thousand Londoners had died, the Privy Council decreed that public playing should cease if weekly plague deaths rose 'above the number of thirty'; performances could only resume once it dipped below that figure. A casual observation in Thomas Middleton's *Your Five Gallants* (1607) confirms that London's actors were keenly

'Lord Have Mercy on Us', from Thomas Dekker,
A Rod for Run-awayes (1625)

aware of that official cutoff: 'If the bill rise to above thirty, here's no place for players.'

In practice though, as with theatre closures for the duration of Lent, there seems to have been some leeway, with players intent on earning a living occasionally bending the rules, resuming performances when plague deaths dipped under forty or so. Since the number of parishes in the city and its suburbs that were counted in London's plague bills in the late sixteenth and early seventeenth centuries had gradually increased from roughly 100 to 121 in 1606, the cutoff that mandated the closing of the theatres would likely have risen as well. Privy Council records for this period were lost in a fire in 1619 so we will never know exactly what number triggered any specific closure. But flexibility is hinted at in Lording Barry's play *Ram Alley* (1608), where a character says, 'I dwindle as a new player does at a plague bill certified forty.' In any case, by late July 1606, with the number of plague deaths well over that figure and rising week by week, public playing was finished, for the summer at least. Nobody had dared mention it in published accounts, but it was probably the reason why for all but two days of his curtailed visit, the King of Denmark was kept outside the contagious city (as early as the first week of July, James himself acknowledged the rise in plague deaths and was 'grieved with the growing sickness in London'). London's playing companies, when they weren't summoned to perform before the two kings, took to provincial touring. Their expectation was that cooler autumnal weather would, as in the past, bring plague deaths in the city down to an acceptable level, perhaps not much later than the start of Michaelmas term in late September.

Despite the prevalence of plague in London during the first seven years of James's reign, when it struck every year, sometimes more violently, sometimes less so, before mysteriously disappearing until a major outbreak in 1622, the first-hand experience of these terrible visitations and their effects on families and neighbourhoods went largely unrecorded. Most of what we know, then, comes from official documents, medical texts, plague pamphlets, sermons and a few letters, including those of the Spaniard Luisa de Carvajal y Mendoza, who relayed the news in London to her friends abroad, writing in early March 1606 that there 'is nothing new to report, except that the plague spread dramatically last week', and in mid-July sardonically capturing the heightened anxiety in London's streets: the 'fear is that the ever-present plague is going to spread. Yet another lovely feature of this place!'

We learn from surviving records that those caught escaping from a quarantined house who didn't have the marks of plague on them could be whipped and those with visible plague sores were guilty of a felony and subject to execution. To reduce the size of crowds, funeral attendance was limited to six, including the pallbearers and minister, though these and other rules were often ignored. It was forbidden to move bedding from house to house. Those who tended to the infected had to carry a three-foot-long red rod or wand, so that passers-by in London's crowded streets could give them a wide berth. Yet as informative as such details are, the paucity of evidence leaves unanswered crucial questions about what it was like to live through the plague.

During plague time London certainly sounded different. Each funeral resulted in the ringing of a knell – sometimes for an hour or longer – at one of the 114 churches in London's twenty-six wards.

It was a cacophony. When a character in *Volpone* mocks Lady Would-be's loud voice, this tolling comes to mind: 'The bells in time of pestilence ne'er made / Like noise' (3.110). For some, it was clearly maddening; the 'perpetuity of ringing' in plague time so torments Morose in Jonson's *Epicene, or The Silent Woman* (1609) that he yearns for 'a room with double walls and treble ceilings, the windows close shut and caulked' (3.399). Surely among Shakespeare's greatest gifts, living directly across from St Olave's on Silver Street, must have been his ability to shut out this melancholy clamour as he wrote – if indeed he sought to do so.

At the same time, other street sounds were now strangely absent, including barking. Dogs that ran free in London were massacred and those ordered to kill them paid a penny a carcass. John Fletcher offers a rare protest against this practice in his 1609 play, *The Scornful Lady*: 'I would 'twere lawful in the next great sickness to have the dogs spared, those harmless creatures.' But what else were civic authorities, charged with protecting the populace, to do, since they were unsure what caused plague? Was it interplanetary alignment? Divine anger? Miasma? Shakespeare's Timon hedges his bets and seems to opt for elements of all three when he speaks of plague's mysterious source: 'Be as a planetary plague, when Jove / Will o'er some high-viced city hang his poison / In the sick air' (4.3.111–13). Others were more sure of its source; a preacher named T. White, addressing Londoners from Paul's Cross in 1577, blamed the theatre: since 'the cause of plagues is sin' and 'the cause of sin are plays', it follows that 'the cause of plagues are plays'.

Centuries would pass before scientists discovered that this plague was caused by *Yersinia pestis*, a strain of a bacterium passed on either through the bite of an infected flea (invading the lymph nodes and producing painful swelling or buboes) or by an infected person's cough or breath, a mode of transmission that rapidly led to lung failure. The fleas were carried by rodents, especially rats, who found London's many thatched timbered houses far more hospitable than the few made of brick or stone. Fleas thrived in humid weather of about twenty to twenty-five degrees Celsius, so if summer temperatures persisted into a rainy autumn, they could survive for quite a while.

The symptoms that followed a bite by an infected flea were horrible: fever, a racing pulse and breathlessness, followed by pain in the back and legs, thirstiness and stumbling. As a contemporary put it, worsening symptoms also included 'great dolour of head with heaviness, solicitude and sadness in mind'. That depression is not surprising, given what victims knew was to follow. The skin soon felt hot and dry and lesions formed, dark discolorations known as 'God's tokens'. Buboes – hard swellings of a lymph gland called botches or plague sores in Shakespeare's day – would form in the groin, armpit or neck, then rupture, causing pain so agonising that some victims would leap from windows or throw themselves into streams. Finally, speech would become difficult, and victims would rave or suffer delirium before succumbing to heart failure. It was an awful way to die – and an awful thing to witness. Cruelly, those aged between ten and thirty-five proved especially vulnerable.

The theatre, which provides such insight into almost every other aspect of daily life, disappoints when it comes to plague. Dramatists of the day delved into almost every troubling or taboo subject; playgoers saw rape victims stagger on stage and flinched as throats were slit and eyes gouged out. But one thing they never saw depicted was a plague victim or their symptoms. Even a passing mention of plague is rare. Was this because it was bad for business to remind playgoers packed into the theatres of the risks of transmitting disease or because a traumatised culture simply couldn't deal with it? Glancing allusions to plague's devastation in Shakespeare's works, when they do appear, are that much more striking. The most haunting is surely the dense one in *Macbeth* that alludes to the ringing of church bells for the dead and dying, so incessant that people no longer ask for whom the bells toll. The seemingly healthy turn out to be dead men walking. Though less than four lines long, there's probably not a better description of the terror and malaise plague carried with it:

> The dead man's knell
> Is there scarce asked for who, and good men's lives
> Expire before the flowers in their caps,
> Dying or ere they sicken.
> (4.3.171–4)

Four centuries later, we have lost much of the shock audiences must have felt when hearing a furious Lear call Goneril a 'plague sore, an embossed carbuncle in my / Corrupted blood' (7.381–2) or when in *Antony and Cleopatra* a soldier, asked which side is winning, replies that the situation is hopeless, 'like the tokened pestilence, / Where death is sure' (3.10.9–10). For playgoers in 1606, all too familiar with plague sores and God's tokens, these terrifying images were more than metaphorical and more terrifying than they can ever be for us.

The approach of autumn seemed at first to bring relief, as the number of plague victims receded from a peak of 116 a week at the end of August to a still disturbingly high eighty-seven by the end of September. King James, worried that Parliament would not be able to meet and approve his plans for Union before Christmas, pressured the Privy Council to do more to combat the outbreak. They in turn demanded greater vigilance on the part of local authorities. The Lord Mayor wrote back rejecting their accusation that he had not taken 'meet care in repressing the contagion of the plague within this city' and assuring them that he and his underlings had done their utmost. The councillors had complained that too many Londoners were washing off the red crosses painted over the doors of infected households; the Lord Mayor promised that steps would be taken to use oil-based rather than water-based paint to prevent that. And he begged them to press authorities in the suburbs to enact precautions as strict as those in the city – 'otherwise it will be very dangerous for this city, they having their daily recourse hither for buying and providing of their necessaries'; with suburbanites resorting to London to shop, controlling the spread of the contagion was becoming more difficult. That same week King James, still safely in the countryside hunting, pressed again for more action, demanding weekly reports from the Lord Mayor and urging that tougher measures, such as those employed in his native Scotland, be used in London as well. With numbers remaining too high for him to return to the city, James issued a proclamation on 23 September; fearing the spread of plague due to the 'great resort of people' coming to London to press 'their suits and causes' during Michaelmas term, he ordered the delay of the start of this legal season.

The royal order was well advised, since in early October weekly plague numbers unexpectedly soared to 141. Contemporary letters register the consternation this produced; John Chamberlain no doubt spoke for many when he wrote that 'this last week's increase makes us all startle'. Nearly six hundred Londoners died in October as the outbreak took on new life. Flight was more tempting than ever. The Venetian ambassador wrote home this month that 'the plague is on the increase; all the ambassadors are leaving. I will move presently.' The Lord Mayor promised to respond with harsher measures, expelling beggars from the city, posting watchmen outside every infected house 'and suffering no persons to go more out of the said house'. But everyone knew that these were not promises he could easily keep: with well over a thousand Londoners now infected, the authorities lacked both the resources and the manpower to ensure the quarantine of so many homes.

On 1 November King James, who had now returned to the capital, issued another proclamation, forbidding 'all Londoners and other inhabitants of places infected to resort to the court'. The following day Richard Stock preached at Paul's Cross, praying 'that God would remove his plagues from us, and renew them no more; but alas, who seeth not the contrary?' In a bit of gallows humour, he half-joked about a recommended cure – fleeing from the infected city. For those in the crowd, Stock's sermon must have offered scant reassurance: 'This is the dealing of God when he cometh to visit; where he findeth sin generally spread over all, then will he bring a general judgement upon all.' The best 'preservative' he could offer was: 'Cease to do evil; learn to do well.' Those who were infected and were desperate to know whether they would live or die from their plague sores may have turned to some of the medical recipes circulating in manuscript, such as Mrs Corlyon's, written this year:

> Take a gum called galbanum, and dissolve it with the juice of field daisies, then spread it upon the flesh side of glover's leather, but let the plaister be no broader than the sore is discolored, then lay it upon the sore and hold it on with your hand, the space of a quarter of an hour; if then it do cleave, the party will live without doubt, if not he will die.

Her recipes were hardly more reassuring than Stock's bromides.

Almost no first-hand stories survive of what it was like to be locked into a house with plague victims, or to lose one's loved ones, or what it felt like to catch the plague. One of the very few that does can be found in the notebooks of Simon Forman, astrologer and physician, and it reveals a great deal about the hostility and suspicion that were a by-product of an outbreak. Among those who perished this October was a twelve-year-old servant boy in Forman's household in Lambeth. Years earlier Forman had himself been stricken. He records having plague sores 'as broad as a half-pence' but managed to survive by lancing his boils and drinking a special concoction. It took him over five months to recover and he probably developed immunity from subsequent outbreaks. Forman went on to write at length about the plague's source and treatment in his unpublished notebooks, and, unlike many other physicians, remained in town to minister to those who had contracted the disease. In his writings Forman would return repeatedly and angrily to the plague-related episode that took place on 27 October 1606, a date he remembered well because that very day his young wife, Jean, gave birth at home to their first son, Clement. Despite the death a week earlier of their servant boy, the house had apparently not been quarantined, though neighbours must surely have been suspicious when the boy's corpse was removed for burial and his death recorded.

Another one of Forman's servants, a maid named Cissely, had been at nearby Lambeth Marsh that day, perhaps assisting with the treatment of one of his patients. She fell ill there and was brought back home by Forman's neighbours. It would not have been unusual for them to have suspected Forman of sending her from the house knowing that she was plague-stricken, a common enough occurrence, since some masters preferred that their servants die abandoned in London's streets rather than infecting the rest of their household. His neighbours were wrong to think that Forman was this sort of master. Yet their fears that he was putting their own lives at risk, especially after his servant boy had died of plague a week earlier, are understandable. Having escorted the sick Cissely back home, they began to beat upon Forman's door, then 'railed on him and on his wife, being but two hours before delivered'. Taking matters into their own hands, they then decided to barricade Forman and his family and servants inside the house, telling him, Forman writes, that 'it was better that I and my household should starve and die than any of them should be put in danger'. Forman, his wife, their infant son and their servants found their doors 'shut up', leaving them, in Forman's words, 'destitute' and 'abused'.

Imprisoning a family within a house for a month or longer and posting guards outside may have slowed the spread of plague but it was a terrible thing for those locked in to endure; if the plague didn't kill them, starvation or madness might. In less anxious times, a 'searcher' from the quarantined house was typically allowed out to forage for food and supplies, red wand in hand. Not now. Forman and his family were trapped, dependent on what stores they had at home. Forman fulminated – calling his neighbours 'stiff-necked Jews' and worse – but he had little recourse.

Forman was convinced that only melancholy types, those who were subject to 'fear, thought and grief', could be infected, and Cissely didn't fit that profile. It was some small satisfaction to Forman that he was proven right, for he records that Cissely was 'lodged in the same chamber and bed and in the same bedclothes within seven days after the boy died' and no harm came to her. She even cleaned that chamber and aired the bedclothes and remained there 'till she was well, yet [she] had not the said plague'. As far as Forman was concerned, 'The great injury the Lambithians did to me and my wife shall rest in record until the day of doom.' What especially galled him was that among those who had abused him and his family in this way were some whom he had treated: 'I did not then shut up my compassion from any nor my doors as they have done to me.' If this clash between neighbours was in any way representative, the pestilence was even more destructive than we can tabulate from plague bills, not only carrying off so many Londoners, especially the young, but also creating the kind of distrust and enmity that wasn't easy to forget or forgive. If London's playwrights couldn't or wouldn't directly address plague, their problem comedies and dark tragedies could certainly engage, obliquely, the corrosive distrust and enmity that were its side effects.

When plague spread through much of London in July, Shakespeare's parish was spared. St Olave's was a tiny parish, and in the decade before 1606 its church bells had only tolled for the dead an average of twice a month (with the exception of the plague year of 1603, when 125 parishioners died). Even as dozens were dying every week of plague elsewhere in London in the summer of 1606, not a single burial had been recorded in the backwater of St Olave's since April, and only two others died in the parish before the end of August.

John Flint, a Cambridge-educated vicar, kept St Olave's parish register. When he recorded deaths he listed only the date and the deceased's name and occupation (and, if a servant, wife or child, his or her relation to a householder). While Flint occasionally included a stray detail, his entries were brief; he didn't, as other ministers sometimes did, record the cause of death. And the parish's weekly tabulations of the number who died (and how many of these died of pestilence) that had to be submitted to those compiling the plague bills no longer survive. Any effort then to trace the impact of plague in Shakespeare's parish must be reconstructed by other means.

The parish's good fortune continued into September. Only one person died and was buried that month in St Olave's: Frauncis Franklin, servant to a Mr Bredwell. At Sunday prayers in the old church, so decayed that it had to be torn down and rebuilt in 1609, parishioners must have felt the protective hand of Providence at work. Shakespeare, born shortly before an outbreak of plague that ravaged Stratford-upon-Avon, and miraculously spared then and ever since, may well have thought so too. He may simply have been exceedingly lucky or at some point along the way, perhaps as an infant, developed a degree of immunity.

In early October, St Olave's luck ran out. It seems likely that Frauncis Franklin died of plague, for on 4 October another one of Bredwell's servants also died, followed less than a week later by a sojourner, Thomas Lowth, who was lodging in Bredwell's house. Bredwell and members of his immediate family, including a son and daughter, were spared, perhaps because they lived in an uninfected part of the house. Soon, a nearby household was visited: Henry Milande's servant John Cooke died on 5 October and his fellow servant Margaret died three weeks later. How plague passed from one house to the next in St Olave's is unknown, but its spread seemed both localised and inexorable; 'Whole households and whole streets are stricken,' as Thomas Dekker put it in his *News from Gravesend*. 'The sick do die, the sound do sicken.' Yet another household that suffered multiple losses near Shakespeare's lodgings was that of William Tailer, an embroiderer. Tailer's servant Anthony Shepherd was the first to die, on 7 November. Tailer himself died next, on 6 December, followed within a week by another servant, Timothy Lande, then by two of Tailer's sons, George and William. Tailer's infant daughter was spared. Her name was Cordelia, and she had been christened in November 1605, while Shakespeare was writing *King Lear*.

Alan Nelson was the first to discover this remarkable coincidence, and Charles Nicholl, who has written brilliantly of Shakespeare's years in St Olave's and drew on Nelson's archival findings, wondered whether William Tailer had done some work for his neighbours, Marie Mountjoy and her husband, who could have used the help of an embroiderer in their work fabricating elaborate headwear. If so, he may have come into contact with

Shakespeare, their lodger. It's otherwise a mystery why Tailer would have chosen for his daughter this highly unusual name, while so conventional in naming his sons. Anglicising the Welsh Cordula or Cordella (as it had appeared in the old *Leir* play) wasn't Shakespeare's invention, but the name Cordelia was nearly unknown at this time in London (I've found a Cordelia Gibson and a Cordelia Clarke, both baptised in St Giles, Cripplegate in the 1590s, and parish records turn up a few older Cordelias as well, but that's about it). The tantalising detail only underscores how much is lost of the fabric of Shakespeare's daily life.

If we take multiple deaths under one roof in a short span of time as an indication of plague, by the end of December 1606 the outbreak in St Olave's had claimed at least a dozen lives. All but two of these were young, either servants or children. Not all of those who died in these households were necessarily felled by plague, and not all of the other dozen deaths recorded by Flint this autumn necessarily died of other causes; it is notable that ten of those twelve were likewise servants or children. There's a pretty strong likelihood, then, that plague, which struck the young disproportionately, was responsible for some and perhaps most of their deaths. That leaves two other deaths unaccounted for. One was that of the almsman or beggar William Howson, age unknown, who might have died from any number of causes at the end of December. The other was Shakespeare's landlady, Marie Mountjoy; she had probably not yet turned forty when she was buried in St Olave's churchyard, at the height of the infestation, across the street from where she had lived, on 30 October.

Jacobean London in 1606, though its population had swollen to two hundred thousand, could be a surprisingly small world.

As fate would have it, Mrs Mountjoy also knew Simon Forman and had sought his astrological services in 1597 when she had lost a valuable purse. She visited his house in Lambeth a year or so later, this time to see him as a physician and learn whether she was pregnant (Forman thought that she was, but believed she would miscarry). Her feared pregnancy may well have been the result of an affair with another one of Forman's clients, a mercer named Henry Wood. From what little we know of Mr Mountjoy, who appears to have been an unpleasant and stingy man, he too seems to have engaged in extramarital affairs, and was censured by the religious authorities for them.

One of the odd facts about the surviving shards of Shakespeare's life is that we know more about what words passed between the playwright and Mrs Mountjoy than we do about any conversations he had with his own wife. In 1604 Shakespeare was asked to help resolve a domestic crisis in the Mountjoy household. The Mountjoys, who had lost a child a decade earlier, had only one surviving heir, a daughter named Mary. They also had a skilled worker living under their roof, Stephen Belott, an eligible young man who the Mountjoys hoped would marry Mary and to whom they 'willingly offered' her. We know this, along with details of Shakespeare's subsequent involvement and testimony, from a dispute over the promised dowry that ended up in the courts eight years later, records of which were discovered in 1910. Shakespeare told the court in his deposition, in his words, that Mrs Mountjoy 'did solicit and entreat' him to 'move and persuade' Belott 'to effect the said marriage', and that he 'accordingly' complied with her wishes.

Shakespeare's testimony is confirmed by another friend of the family, Daniel Nicholas, who told the court that the young couple 'were made sure by Mr Shakespeare by giving their consent, and agreed to marry'. He also said (though this testimony was crossed out, presumably because it was considered hearsay and therefore inadmissible) that, after persuading the reluctant bachelor, Shakespeare even joined the young lovers in a handfast – 'giving each other's hand to the hand' – precisely what takes place in *As You Like It*, when Rosalind and Orlando are joined by Celia, a symbolic act of marital union legally binding at this time. The playwright who had staged such scenes in the theatre now found himself performing in one in real life. The handfast probably occurred the first week of November 1604; the church wedding took place a few weeks later at St Olave's.

The court testimony provides us with almost the only record we have of Shakespeare's spoken words, and his language here is fascinating, especially his description of how Mrs Mountjoy did 'solicit and entreat' him, terms that suggest urgency on her part and an unusual degree of intimacy between the worldly landlady and her no less worldly lodger. 'Entreat' is a strong verb, one that Shakespeare used surprisingly often in his plays and poems, 159 times in all, almost always in the same and now mostly obsolete way: 'to intercede or supplicate'. 'Solicit', too, is one of those words whose shades of meaning once connoted a good deal more: 'to urge, importune; to ask earnestly or persistently'. The deposition suggests that Mrs Mountjoy didn't ask Shakespeare to intervene only once, nor did she do so casually. To urge him to persuade Belott to marry Mary was not something a landlady might lightly ask of a tenant or stranger. Clearly, she was on more intimate terms with Shakespeare than her husband was, for there doesn't seem to have been (as one might expect in this sort of case in such a patriarchal society) a man-to-man conversation. Shakespeare's testimony before those gathered in the court, including her husband, makes her request sound more formal than it probably was. She needed help, knew Shakespeare well enough to reach out to him, must have sensed his ambivalence about becoming involved, and did her best to persuade him, most likely speaking with him about it on more than one occasion. All this, too, feels like something lifted from one of his plays.

The young married couple soon moved out; there seems to have been only one set of rooms in the house for a lodger or sojourner, and at this time that was Shakespeare's, who evidently had not been asked to find other lodgings. Mary could no longer live in family quarters or Stephen with servants or apprentices. And if the subsequent court dispute over the dowry is any indication, friction may already have arisen between Belott and his tight-fisted father-in-law, hastening their departure. Their new lodgings introduce another connection to Shakespeare, for they moved into a house owned by George Wilkins, who would be Shakespeare's collaborator a few years later on *Pericles*. In early 1606 Wilkins first wrote a solo-authored play for Shakespeare's company, *The Miseries of Enforced Marriage*. Wilkins's day job was as a 'victualler', which meant that he ran a tavern with rooms to let (and, if his many appearances in court are any indication, most likely also ran a bawdy house). Either Shakespeare put them in touch with Wilkins or perhaps met his future co-author through the newlyweds he had helped bring together.

Shakespeare had moved to Silver Street around 1602; he returned to Southwark and is recorded as living there in 1609. He seems to have left St Olave's shortly after the death of Mrs

Mountjoy, for Stephen and Mary Belott soon moved back in. Perhaps they did so because Shakespeare's lodgings were now available, perhaps also to assist Mr Mountjoy, who briefly took on Stephen as his partner. The vicar didn't record what Mrs Mountjoy died of and the court proceedings of 1612 make no mention of it. With the prevalence of plague in St Olave's at this time, there is a good chance that she was one of its victims. If so, plague must have struck closer to home for Shakespeare than we realise, especially if local authorities ordered the quarantining of infected houses in what was one of the last pockets of the disease during this outbreak.

By the time that Marie Mountjoy was buried in late October, Shakespeare's latest play, *Antony and Cleopatra*, was finished, or nearly so. We can only wonder whether he felt any connection between the untimely death of that play's heroine and Marie Mountjoy's. What Shakespeare thought of the woman who had entreated and solicited him, and why he abandoned Silver Street so soon after her death, must remain, like so much else about his emotional life, a mystery. The episode reminds us how few are the surviving traces of his existence, especially those that reveal anything about his relationships. But it is also confirmation that there are records out there, if we can piece them together, that can tell us more about what his life was like. The remarkable discovery a century ago of the legal dispute over the dowry, in conjunction with the survival of plague records for St Olave's, allows us the briefest of glimpses into what may have been one of the happier times of Shakespeare's life and, soon after, one of the more troubling and frightening. He may not have been alone in thinking that he had been twice spared of late, first from the Gunpowder explosion and flames, then from an outbreak of plague that had reached his doorstep.

It took until mid-November, and what must have been significantly chillier weather, for deaths from plague to plummet. The number of victims dropped rapidly from sixty-eight on 6 November to forty-one on the 13th, and to the more reassuring level of twenty-eight and twenty-two in the third and fourth weeks of that month. While the visitation was largely spent, its devastation was still felt by those, now fewer in number, who continued to die every week, those quarantined, those struggling for weeks or months to recover their health, and those who had buried and now mourned for lost children, parents, spouses and friends.

With the number of weekly plague victims safely below the official cutoff of thirty, the public theatres could at last reopen after a four-month hiatus. Despite these figures, there is an unquestioned if unwarranted consensus among Shakespeare scholars that the public theatres nonetheless remained shut through the rest of 1606 and would stay closed for twenty-one months in all, except for a brief reopening in April 1607. This consensus is based largely on the arguments and tables presented in Leeds Barroll's groundbreaking study, *Politics, Plague, and Shakespeare's Theater*, which takes the closure number of thirty as hard and fixed. This is all the more surprising, because the number of scripts that playwrights were writing certainly did not drop off during this period, nor did any of the adult playing companies sell off their plays at this time, as they had during other extended closures for plague when they were desperate for cash. It matters for those interested in when Shakespeare's plays were first performed, for if the theatres remained closed there would have been no opportunity for the King's Men to stage *Antony and Cleopatra* before mid-1607, making it hard to understand how other dramatists whose plays from early 1607 are clearly indebted to the staged version of Shakespeare's tragedy could possibly have seen it. The only other explanation is that the play had its debut at court, something unprecedented at this time, for the Master of the Revels only authorised court performances for plays that had first been staged in the public theatres. It's worth noting that Tilney, in billing the court for his work vetting the upcoming holiday season of sixteen plays and a masque, dated the beginning of his labours to 31 October 1606.

The adult touring companies all seem to have returned to London by early November, for there are no records of subsequent payments for their provincial performances this year. The Prince's Men, who had been paid to play in Ipswich in mid-October, had returned in advance of their performance before Prince Henry on 1 December. The King's Men ended months of touring, mostly in the southeast in towns along the Kent coast but also in Oxford and Cambridge, and were apparently back by mid-November. The third leading adult company, Queen Anne's Men, who had appeared in Ludlow, Beverley and Coventry earlier this autumn, were back as well and playing this winter at the Boar's Head Theatre. We know this from the testimony of their leading actor, Thomas Green, who spoke in defence of one of their gatekeepers, Mary Phillips, who had been called a whore for working at the theatre. 'In the winter time last,' he told the court in June 1607, 'at such time as plays were used to be played and acted at the Boar's Head', a man named Ellis Phillips had told him that Richard Christopher or his wife had slanderously said 'that there were no women that kept playhouse doors but were whores'. We also know that the Children of the Queen's Revels resumed playing indoors at Blackfriars in mid-November from a lawsuit in which a mother of one of their boy players testified that for half a year, beginning on 14 November 1606, her son Abell Cook had honoured the terms of apprenticeship 'and played at Blackfriars as often as he was required'. Fortunately for London's actors and playwrights, although the number of plague deaths spiked to forty-five the first week of December, it remained safely below forty during the Christmas holidays and remained at that level through to the following Easter. The theatres had reopened.

The outbreak of plague that persisted into November proved more cruel to the young than to the old and more punishing to the boy companies than to their adult rivals, who helped make ends meet through provincial touring. Just a few years earlier, when the primacy of the adult companies was seriously challenged by the boy players, Shakespeare had written in *Hamlet* of those 'children' who 'are now the fashion' and 'berattle the common stages' with their satiric plays (2.2.339–42). The extended plague of 1606 seems to have killed off the most celebrated of the boy companies, Paul's Boys, who never recovered from the closure that year. They marked their last recorded performance in July 1606 and not long after that their recent plays began appearing in London's bookstalls, the sell-off a telling sign of a theatre company in its death throes. Other plays from their repertory found their way into the hands of the last surviving boy company, the Children of the Queen's Revels.

The Children of the Queen's Revels performed at London's

most attractive indoor theatre, Blackfriars, enabling them to charge more and attract a more upscale and discriminating audience. And they now no longer had to compete with the boys of St Paul's for the talented crop of satirical freelance playwrights – including Thomas Middleton, Francis Beaumont, John Fletcher, John Marston, John Day and, more often than not, Ben Jonson – who much preferred to write for boy players than for even the best of the adult companies. The adult players, more fearful that their livelihood might come to an end, were far less keen on performing satires that bordered on the libellous, if not seditious, plays that the boys seemed to get away with staging. One result was a split, not only between children and adult players, but also between theatre companies in which playwrights held greater sway and those in which actor-shareholders dominated. A short-lived attempt in late 1606 to establish another playwright-centred company, performing indoors at Whitefriars, quickly fizzled out. If not for plague the Jacobean theatre might have taken a markedly different turn.

When plague struck in July 1606, the company formerly known as the Children of the Queen's Revels, while not as vulnerable as Paul's Boys, were already hurting, though their wounds were largely self-inflicted: the political missteps of Samuel Daniel's *Philotas* in 1604 had been exacerbated the following year when their scandalous *Eastward Ho* landed Jonson and Chapman in prison. Their offensive *Isle of Gulls*, staged in February 1606, was nearly the last straw, costing them royal patronage and protection. When the following month Anne issued a warrant to Queen Anne's Men, her other and now favored adult company, to perform under her protection both in London and in the provinces, it was surely taken as a signal of her displeasure with her former boy company, who now had to trim their name to the Children of the Revels. Another and now nearly fatal blow to their fortunes came in November 1606, when they were ordered to stop recruiting boy players from among the ranks of child choristers, since 'it was not fit or decent that such as should sing the praises of God Almighty should be trained up or employed in such lascivious or profane exercises'. Until now, they had operated very much like a naval press gang and believed that the company's choirmaster had 'authority sufficient so to take any nobleman's son in this land'. No longer. With 'the boys daily wearing out', the change effectively sealed off the pipeline of talent on which the company had long depended.

Back in 1604, after the last major outbreak of plague, their weary and financially strapped manager, Henry Evans, had opened negotiations with Richard Burbage about cancelling their twenty-one-year lease at Blackfriars, once he saw that the 'great visitation of sickness' meant that there would be little 'hoped for and expected' profit. These discussions were protracted, 'continuing still for a good space of time in speech and communication', and the agreement restoring the Blackfriars Theatre to the King's Men was not signed until 1608. But by 1606 it was increasingly clear to the King's Men that it was more a question of when, not if, they would repossess a space originally designed for them back in 1597. To regain this indoor theatre would also mean acquiring the Blackfriars consort, some of the best professional musicians in the land, along, perhaps, with a few of the rising adolescent stars of the company who could replenish their ageing ranks. A decade earlier Shakespeare had first contemplated the kinds of plays he could write for that candlelit and intimate space and more sophisticated audience; by 1606 he could begin thinking of just such plays again.

Those young and daring playwrights who had preferred writing for boy actors could see which way the winds were blowing; 1606 marks the moment when they turned to the King's Men as the leading adult company best suited to showcasing their talents – though their bite was not quite so sharp. The infusion of satiric new work into the company's repertory meant that Shakespeare's own offerings would be seen in their light. At the outset of his career Thomas Middleton had written a series of hits for the children's companies. In 1605 he was still working for them though flirting with the King's Men, for whom he seems to have written *A Yorkshire Tragedy* and collaborated on *Timon of Athens*. In late 1606 he offered the King's Men his greatest play yet, *The Revenger's Tragedy*. Ben Jonson, having been burned by *Eastward Ho*, sold his masterpiece *Volpone* to the King's Men this year as well. Other up-and-coming dramatists who had so far defined their careers as writers for the children's companies, most notably Beaumont and Fletcher, would soon shift their allegiance to Shakespeare's company. The pair's first collaboration in early 1606, *The Woman Hater*, was one of the last of the boys' plays at St Paul's; by the time the King's Men moved into Blackfriars they seem to have acquired the services of both writers, and Fletcher would later become the company's principal playwright.

The impact of all this on Shakespeare was considerable. Biographers like to attribute the turns in Shakespeare's career to his psychological state (so he must have been in and out of love when writing comedies and sonnets, depressed when he wrote tragedies and in mourning when he wrote *Hamlet*). Surely what he was feeling must have deeply informed what he wrote; the problem is that we have no idea what he was feeling at any point during the quarter-century that he was writing – other than by, in circular fashion, extrapolating this from his works. We know a great deal more about how a rodent-borne visitation in 1606 altered the contours of Shakespeare's professional life, transformed and reinvigorated his playing company, hurt the competition, changed the composition of the audiences for whom he would write (and in turn the kinds of play he could write) and enabled him to collaborate with talented musicians and playwrights – an outbreak of plague that may also have come close to killing him.

*

'Now that the plague has ceased,' the Venetian ambassador reported in early November, 'everybody here is occupied with the meeting of Parliament.' He may have been overly optimistic about the cessation of plague, but he was right about how all eyes were now on Parliament. James had asked it to reconvene on 18 November and to resolve at last the long-delayed question of Union, confirming by law what 'is already in his person made by the singular providence of God'. With no other major business before them, the question of Union could not be postponed, as the legislators had managed to do repeatedly over the course of a year in which they had chosen instead to debate anti-Catholic measures, grudgingly authorised a subsidy for James, and tried to strip the crown of its right to raise money through the often corrupt practice of purveyance, when goods or services for the king's household were requisitioned at unfair prices by royal officials.

James took the unusual step of pleading his case in person before Parliament. Resplendent in his imperial robes and crown, he spoke for ninety minutes in what was judged a 'very long' and 'eloquent' speech. After so many parliamentary checks and delays, he knew that this was probably his last chance to secure even a watered-down version of what he had long sought. The king began by reminding them of their close call a year earlier, 'that treason which was most terribly intended against us all'. Yet that shared deliverance had not resulted in finding common ground. He singled out for blame parliamentary hotheads, chastising those 'tribunes of the people whose mouths could not be stopped' and who had lost sight of the greater good of the commonwealth. So sharp a royal attack was surely unhelpful (though James's resonant and dismissive phrase – 'tribunes of the people' – would, within a year or so, find its way into the fraught political struggle of *Coriolanus* [2.2.152]).

A ruler who relished debate, James on that November day was at the top of his game. He showed an exceptional command of the issues, dismissing possible objections to the Union, clarifying his own motives and reminding everyone of the potential benefits to both kingdoms. He warned the members of Parliament how bad it would look abroad if they refused him now: 'If it failed, it would be imputed either to his folly to propose it, or to the obstinacy of his people, not to approve it.' Surely they wouldn't want to embarrass themselves, or dare embarrass their king, in the eyes of the world. James wasn't demanding much from Parliament; at this point he was willing to meet the legislators at least halfway, asking only that they resolve the four points addressed in the

Instrument of Union which had been negotiated by Scottish and English commissioners back in 1604 and was now before them: eliminating hostile laws between the two nations, abolishing the separate legal status of the Borders, negotiating a commercial union and resolving questions of naturalisation (the knottiest of the issues to resolve, since it touched on both national and legal identity).

Despite these modest goals, James would be rebuffed, humiliatingly so. As Conrad Russell has put it in his trenchant account of this parliamentary session, the 'Commons were good enough at delaying business when they did not try, but when they did, they were formidable'. By early December it had become clear to close observers like the Venetian ambassador that the 'longer they deal with it the less clear becomes the road to a solution. Indeed the negotiations are more likely to divide than to unite the minds of these two peoples; both are hostile and also tenacious of their own; seeking to gain rather than to give.' It was no longer just about Union. The social and political fabric began to fray as sharp differences about law, national identity and the rights of kings emerged. In such a climate a speech in defence of a bill calling King James the 'Emperor of Great Britain' first 'moved laughter in the House', followed by a no less disturbing half-hour of stony silence.

As both houses of Parliament hotly argued over these issues for the next four weeks, nationalist sentiment, nastier than anyone expected, couldn't easily be contained. Dudley Carleton, who witnessed these exchanges, recounted to his friend John Chamberlain some of the more outrageous anti-Scottish jibes. One member of the House of Commons gave 'a long declamation' against the 'Britons, that they were first an idolatrous nation and worshippers of the devil', while another spoke out bitterly against England's neighbours, 'calling them beggarly Scots'. The previous November, Guy Fawkes had mocked the Scots, threatening to blow them back to where they came from; members of Parliament were now indulging in similar taunts. On 18 December, with Christmas almost upon them, recognising that pressure had only made things worse, King James called the deliberations to a halt and sent the members of Parliament home for the holidays.

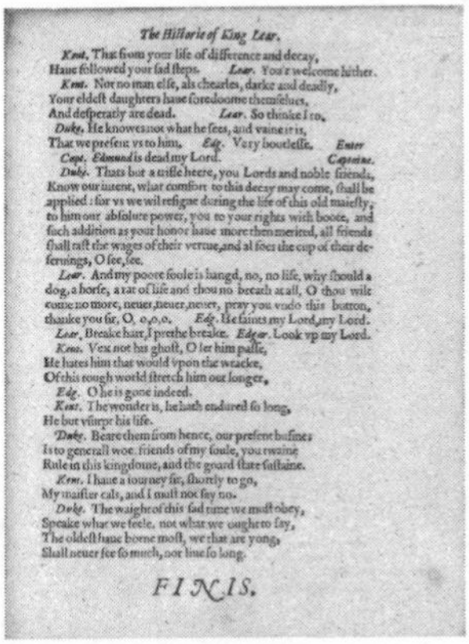

The Hiſtorie of King Lear.

Kent. That from your life of difference and decay,
Haue followed your ſad ſteps. *Lear.* You'r welcome hither.
Kent. Nor no man elſe, als chearles, darke and deadly,
Your eldeſt daughters haue foredoome themſelues,
And deſperatly are dead. *Lear.* So thinke I to.
Duke. He knowes not what he ſees, and vaine it is,
That we preſent vs to him. *Edg.* Very bootleſſe. *Enter*
Capt. *Edmund* is dead my Lord. *Captaine.*
Duke. Thats but a trifle heere, you Lords and noble friends,
Know our intent, what comfort to this decay may come, ſhall be
applied : for vs we wil reſigne during the life of this old maieſty,
to him our abſolute power, you to your rights with boote, and
ſuch addition as your honor haue more then merited, all friends
ſhall taſt the wages of their vertue, and al foes the cup of their de-
ſeruings, O ſee, ſee.
Lear. And my poore foole is hangd, no, no life, why ſhould a
dog, a horſe, a rat of life and thou no breath at all, O thou wilt
come no more, neuer, neuer, neuer, pray you vndo this button,
thanke you ſir, O, o, o, o. *Edg.* He faints my Lord, my Lord.
Lear. Breake hart, I prethe breake. *Edgar.* Look vp my Lord.
Kent. Vex not his ghoſt, O let him paſſe,
He hates him that would vpon the wracke,
Of this tough world ſtretch him out longer.
Edg. O he is gone indeed.
Kent. The wonder is, he hath endured ſo long,
He but vſurpt his life.
Duke. Beare them from hence, our preſent buſines
Is to generall woe, friends of my ſoule, you twaine
Rule in this kingdome, and the goard ſtate ſuſtaine.
Kent. I haue a iourney ſir, ſhortly to go,
My maiſter cals, and I muſt not ſay no.
Duke. The waight of this ſad time we muſt obey,
Speake what we feele, not what we ought to ſay,
The oldeſt haue borne moſt, we that are yong,
Shall neuer ſee ſo much, nor liue ſo long.

FINIS.

Epilogue: 26 December 1606

On Christmas Day 1606, Lancelot Andrewes returned to Whitehall Palace to deliver the annual Nativity sermon. He had preached there the previous Christmas and his sermon that day, delivered only seven weeks after the Gunpowder Plot had been exposed, had been surprisingly hopeful. Andrewes spoke about what they had all been through, recalling how if the plot had succeeded, 'the powder there laid had even blown us all up', but God had delivered them 'from the dangers that daily compass us about; even from the last, so great, and so fearful, as the like was never imagined before'. Andrewes saw a silver lining in the thwarted attack, the possibility of collective purpose and greater self-understanding. His upbeat sermon gave no hint of the dark clouds that were in the offing. On that day celebrating new beginnings it seemed possible that recent events might help bring an anxious nation together.

When Andrewes returned to preach before the king and court on Christmas Day in 1606 the mood had darkened considerably.

Final Page of the Quarto of *King Lear* (1608)

Andrewes chose as his text Isaiah 9:6 – 'For unto us a child is born, and unto us a Son is given, and the government upon his shoulder.' Like Isaiah, he found himself delivering a message in dark times. Why, Andrewes asked, did Isaiah come to prophesy? His answer: 'The times grew very much overcast . . . The chiefest prophecies of Christ came ever in such times.' And not only Isaiah and Christ: the apostle Peter had likened 'the word of prophecy' to a candle 'in a dark room'. The application was clear; like these predecessors Andrewes had come to deliver words of warning and consolation: 'Ever in dark times, who therefore needed most the light of comfort.'

The aftershocks of the Gunpowder Plot were still being felt across the land. Lord Harington wrote during this holiday season to his cousin John Harington, expressing concern that the threat wasn't really over: he knew of some 'evil-minded Catholics in the west, whom the prince of darkness hath in alliance', and he urged his cousin to 'watch in your neighbourhood and give such intelligence as may furnish inquiry'. Lord Harington's letter goes on to give a sense of the trauma some were still experiencing over a year after that fateful November day. He wrote that he himself had 'not yet recovered from the fever occasioned by these disturbances', and described with sadness how Princess Elizabeth, who was in his safekeeping, having heard of the traitors' plan to place her on the throne after her family was murdered, 'doth often say, "What a queen should I have been by these means? I had rather have been with my royal father in the Parliament House, than wear his crown on such condition."' The young princess, he added, still hadn't 'recovered [from] the surprise, and is very ill and troubled'.

She was not alone in this respect. In his sermon Andrewes recognised that a troubled nation had not fully recovered either. His sermon pivoted to the political realm, and he spoke of Christ as a prince ruling over a principality in which 'neither the popular confusion of many, nor the factious ambition of a few, bear all the sway, but where one is sovereign. Such is the government of heaven; such is Christ's government.' But not James's. Like everyone else at Whitehall, Andrewes was aware of continued fears and suspicions in the land as well as of the corrosive parliamentary debate over Union that had abruptly ended a week earlier. In a message directed at the king, Andrewes preached that in easy times rulers might 'bear their people only in their arms, by love; and in their breasts, by care. Yet if need be they must follow Christ's example and patience, here.' But these were not easy times. King James found himself facing factional ambition and would need to show a Christ-like patience. Intelligence was not enough; his shoulders would have to bear a heavier load, for at such times governments 'need not only a good head, but good shoulders, that sustain them'.

The day after Lancelot Andrewes spoke at Whitehall, Shakespeare's company arrived there to perform the darkest of plays about a divided kingdom, *King Lear.* Their performance at court on St Stephen's Day 1606 must have struck contemporaries as worthy of commemorating, for its date, venue and royal audience were all recorded when the play was entered in the Stationers' Register and were then advertised on the title page of the 1608 quarto. This had never happened before with one of Shakespeare's plays nor would it again. This Christmas season at court *Lear* was given pride of place. It was the first of fifteen plays to be staged by London's theatre companies and the first of nine performed by the King's Men. *Lear* was staged in Whitehall's Great Chamber, which workers had prepared earlier that month for the holiday performances. Its name was misleading, for the Great Chamber was among the smallest and most intimate venues in which the King's Men performed, smaller than the alternatives at Whitehall, the Banqueting House and the Great Hall. It was an attractive playing space, sixty feet long by thirty feet wide with a twenty-foot-high ceiling; with a wooden floor and woven tapestries covering its walls in winter the acoustics would have been good too. Once a scaffold was installed for the actors, the Great Chamber could accommodate only three hundred or so spectators, so that only the most privileged at court would have been able to see *King Lear* that evening, far fewer than those invited to see *Hymenaei*.

By the time the play was staged at court, the world in which Shakespeare had begun writing it had changed. Back then, some form of Union seemed all but assured and his exploration of the 'division of the kingdoms' timely if unthreatening. Given where things now stood, a play about the fracturing of a unified Britain may well have caused a shudder or two at Whitehall. The Gunpowder Plot had rekindled old fears about divided loyalties within the kingdom, and the increasingly divisive Union question had focused fresh attention on the boundaries of political authority. In such a climate, issues that may not have seemed so problematic when Shakespeare had written the play now took on a sharper edge. Are those who join Cordelia's invading army treasonously siding with a foreign power against British rule? Is Regan right in calling Gloucester a 'filthy traitor' (14.29)? Shakespeare could not have known when he wrote his play's opening scene that many in England would soon face a different kind of loyalty test in which refusing to say and do what was expected would invite punishment. It's no small irony that Shakespeare's own daughter Susanna was among those who, Cordelia-like, refused to bend so easily to the will of the authorities.

The 1608 quarto of *King Lear* is not the only text of the play to survive. Fifteen years later another version was published in the 1623 folio. Scholars have identified over a thousand differences between these two texts, mostly inconsequential, though a few dozen are substantial. All told, the folio includes a hundred lines that don't appear in the quarto while the quarto includes three hundred lines missing from the folio. Since Alexander Pope in 1723, editors have dealt with this problem by conflating the two versions, essentially picking and choosing from each the bits they like best. No two editions since Pope's have been identical. In the 1980s a new generation of editors recoiled at this practice, proposed that the folio version was Shakespeare's later and wholesale revision of the quarto, and urged that the two texts be published separately. A quarter of a century later a more nuanced view is emerging, one that is more sceptical about the argument for systematic authorial revision yet accepts that both the quarto and the folio are flawed texts which have different histories and tell different stories.

It's clear that all sorts of errors were introduced into the quarto in Nicholas Okes's printing house. This was, unfortunately, the first time Okes had ever printed a play. The compositors he employed to typeset Shakespeare's messy manuscript were also inexperienced and struggled to decipher the handwriting.

Working backwards from obvious errors and confusion in the quarto, scholars have deduced that Shakespeare didn't bother using capital letters at the start of every line of blank verse and also added material in the margins, so that all too often the compositors set verse as prose or simply misread and mangled things. Okes also ran short of paper, forcing the compositors to cram the long text into too few pages.

The folio text brings with it an even more daunting set of editorial challenges. It was apparently derived from a scribal copy of Shakespeare's draft in 1606 that served as the basis of the company's promptbook. Over the course of the next decade and a half, as the play was revived, this promptbook was altered by actors, prompters, censors and dramatists (no doubt including Shakespeare himself), and later by the editors and compositors who saw it into print. The folio text of *Lear* reflects a good deal of shrewd theatrical intervention. It's impossible, though, to know who was responsible for the various changes to what Shakespeare had first written, or even when, over this extended stretch of time, the many alterations were made. Given such complicated trajectories, it's hardly surprising that the two versions diverge as much as they do, though it is also clear that back in late 1606, Shakespeare's original draft and the scribal copy that became the basis of the promptbook had not yet grown that far apart.

These textual issues matter hugely because the endings of the two versions of the play diverge sharply in their handling of how Lear dies and in who speaks the final words. If any part of *King Lear* was overhauled by Shakespeare himself it is likely to have been its ending, for the bold changes made to the play's conclusion can't easily be attributed to the incompetence of compositors or to those in the playhouse trying to freshen up an old play. For what was likely to have been staged in December 1606, we are left with the sometimes muddled testimony of the quarto, derived from Shakespeare's handwritten copy, and we find in that text the most painful and apocalyptic ending imaginable.

Lear enters with the strangled Cordelia in his arms. She has been murdered on Edmund's orders. Lear then dies agonisingly aware that she is lost forever, dead and gone:

> And my poor fool is hanged. No, no life.
> Why should a dog, a horse, a rat have life,
> And thou no breath at all? O, thou wilt come no more.
> Never, never, never. Pray you, undo
> This button. Thank you, sir. O, O, O, O!
> (24.300–4)

Those closing four 'O' sounds are Shakespeare's shorthand for Richard Burbage to groan his last, followed a moment later by his dying words, in which a distraught Lear wills his own death: 'Break, heart, I prithee break' (24.306). For those at the court performance familiar with earlier versions of the story in which the king is restored to the throne and reconciled with his youngest daughter, this outcome must have been shocking, the image and horror of the collapse of the state and the obliteration of the royal family akin to the violent fantasy of the Gunpowder plotters a year earlier.

The closing speech of the play, a few lines later, is spoken in the quarto by the character whom playgoers would have expected to deliver it, the Duke of Albany. He is the highest-ranking nobleman left alive and possessor of half the kingdom. Having outlived his brother-in-law Cornwall and all of Lear's daughters, upon Lear's death he is left, however reluctantly, in charge:

> The weight of this sad time we must obey,
> Speak what we feel, not what we ought to say.
> The oldest have borne most. We that are young
> Shall never see so much, nor live so long.
> (24.318–21)

While it may have pleased King James to hear a Scot take command (for that was Albany's original kingdom, and James himself had held this title), the widowed and childless Albany offers little prospect for the renewal of the kingdom. The quarto even lacks the almost obligatory closing stage direction indicating that the survivors march off. The play ends instead with the frozen tableau of the dead king holding his murdered daughter – a mockery of the pieties expressed moments earlier, when Albany had declared that 'All friends shall taste / The wages of their virtue, and all foes / The cup of their deservings' (24.297–9). While it may have suited its own dark times, the court performance of this version of *Lear* on St Stephen's Day in 1606, so bleak and hopeless, represents a nadir in the play's long stage history.

The play's conclusion proved to be *too* dark, *too* unbearable. Whoever was responsible for the folio version flinched and pulled the ending back from the abyss. Two substantive changes were made. One reassigned the play's final speech to Edgar. It's an unexpected switch, insofar as the higher-ranking Albany is still alive. Its effect is to allow for the possibility of a less grim future, as a younger generation is empowered. Other changes made in the folio version reinforce this narrative, so that what Edgar has endured seems purposeful in retrospect and directed to this end. A closing stage direction that was added reinforces this new trajectory: the survivors in the folio solemnly head off together, 'Exeunt, with a dead march' (5.3.332 stage direction). Loss is given meaning in that it has contributed to the education of the next ruler. In many ways this makes for a more conventionally satisfying narrative.

The revised text also backs away from the agony of watching a broken Lear confront the utter finality of his beloved daughter's death. In the folio, those 'O' groans are gone, as is Lear's final cry asking for his heart to break; that line is reassigned to Kent. In its place is a Lear who dies believing in his last moments that Cordelia's lips move, that she yet breathes. Though the others on stage know, as do we, that Lear is engaged in wishful thinking and that the strangled Cordelia can't possibly be alive, the folio version nonetheless offers playgoers the consolation of a Lear who has suffered enough and is allowed to die deluded:

> And my poor fool is hanged! No, no, no life?
> Why should a dog, a horse, a rat have life,
> And thou no breath at all? Thou'lt come no more,
> Never, never, never, never, never!
> Pray you undo this button. Thank you sir.
> Do you see this? Look on her, look, her lips,
> Look there, look there!
>
> *He dies.*

It's still a brutal ending. In the eighteenth century Samuel Johnson spoke for many when he recalled how he was 'so shocked by Cordelia's death, that I know not whether I ever endured to read again the last scenes of the play till I undertook to revise them as an editor'.

The folio revisions marked the first step in a much longer retreat from what playgoers found unbearable. By 1681, little more than a half-century after that text was published, the repudiation in the playhouse of both the quarto and folio endings was near total. In that year Nahum Tate published *The History of King Lear*, a revival of Shakespeare's *Lear* that not only restored *Leir*'s happy ending but took it even further: Lear lives and Cordelia and Edgar will marry and inherit his kingdom. 'Truth and justice', Edgar reassures us, 'shall at last succeed.' It's easy to smile at this now, but for the following century and a half actors and playgoers found it more satisfying than either the quarto or the folio ending: Tate's version of the play ruled the stage from 1681 to 1838.

From the moment of its creation until the present day the meaning of *King Lear* continues to be subject to the form and pressure of the time. Whether we look at the history of the play in the late twentieth century (when in a nuclear and post-Holocaust world its exploration of the apocalyptic seemed so central) or in the early twenty-first century (when productions have focused more on Lear as father than as king and in which the spectre of dementia looms increasingly large), *King Lear* has managed to find fresh ways to speak to the moment. Shakespeare understood this process, and in the course of 1606 witnessed it himself, as rapidly unfolding events that year shaped how audiences responded to what he had so recently written and even altered what the actors could say (so that, for example, Edmund could no longer swear by God's foot ('Fut'), nor the Fool joke about great men hungering after monopolies [2.122; 4.146]).

The next three years were relatively quiet ones for Shakespeare, in which he wrote *Pericles* (with George Wilkins), *Coriolanus* and *All's Well that Ends Well.* After that he had two great creative bursts. During the first of these, in 1610–11, he wrote three romances: *Cymbeline*, *The Winter's Tale* and *The Tempest.* The rhythm of a fallow period followed by intense productivity would be realised once more, this time collaboratively, when he teamed up with John Fletcher in another trio of plays in 1613–14: *Henry the Eighth*, *The Two Noble Kinsmen* and the lost *Cardenio.* Two years later he died in Stratford-upon-Avon at the age of fifty-two.

For the Jacobean Shakespeare, who had struggled to find his footing in the early years of the reign, no year's output would be more extraordinary than that of 1606. The three tragedies he finished this year – *King Lear*, *Macbeth* and *Antony and Cleopatra* – form a trilogy of sorts that collectively reflect their fraught cultural moment. Their indelible lines have left their mark on our language and on our imaginations, rendering worlds in a handful of words that have acquired the force of aphorisms: 'I am a man more sinned against than sinning' (*Lear*, 9.60). 'Age cannot wither her, nor custom stale her infinite variety' (*Antony*, 2.2.245–6). 'How sharper than a serpent's tooth it is to have a thankless child' (*Lear*, 4.279–80). 'Life's but a walking shadow, a poor player that struts and frets his hour upon the stage and then is heard no more' (*Macbeth*, 5.5.24–6). And 'I am bound upon a wheel of fire, that mine own tears do scald like molten lead' (*Lear*, 21.44–6). In his tribute to Shakespeare prefacing the 1623 folio, Ben Jonson came as close as anyone to describing the personal cost of hammering out such resonant lines:

> Who casts to write a living line must sweat
> (Such as thine are) and strike the second heat
> Upon the Muses' anvil; turn the same,
> (And himself with it).
> (5.641)

In a famous and much copied portrait, King James wears 'The Mirror of Great Britain', a fabulous piece of jewellery whose large diamonds collectively symbolised the Union he so desperately sought. It was perhaps the richest ornament ever to adorn a British monarch. One part of it came from pillaging Queen Elizabeth's jewellery collection, another from his mother's finest jewel, the 'great Harry', and a third was purchased from France, the Sancy diamond brought from India in the late fifteenth century. King James declared that it would be 'inseparably' and 'forever . . . annexed to the kingdom of this realm'. But before his death in 1625, that fabulous object was broken up, its diamonds pawned. Styles had changed, the Union was not going to happen in his lifetime, and the king needed money. By then James had buried Queen Anne as well as Prince Henry, who had died in 1612 at the age of eighteen, a devastating loss for the royal family and for the nation. James married off his surviving daughter, Elizabeth, but her rule as Queen of Bohemia would be short-lived and she would spend much of her life in exile. Prince Charles, who succeeded his father to the throne, also inherited many unresolved fiscal, religious and political problems and would soon face insurrection and then revolution. He was deposed, then publicly executed on a scaffold in front of a rebuilt Banqueting House in 1649.

Two years before 'The Mirror of Great Britain' was sold off, *Macbeth* and *Antony and Cleopatra* were published for the first time, along with sixteen other plays by Shakespeare never before printed. *King Lear* was included in that 1623 volume too, as were seventeen other histories, comedies and tragedies that had already been published in quarto. It is known today simply as the First Folio, and its author has a better claim to be celebrated as the true 'Mirror of Great Britain', his multifaceted plays brilliantly reflecting the fears and aspirations of his times.

A Note on Dating the Plays

Scholars are in broad agreement that *King Lear*, *Macbeth* and *Antony and Cleopatra* were composed in that order (and stylistic tests confirm this). *Lear* was performed at court on 26 December 1606, a date specified in the 1607 Stationers' Register entry as well as on the title page of the 1608 quarto. How much earlier could Shakespeare have written it? Scholars have demonstrated that Shakespeare's debt to his major source – the old Queen's Men's play *King Leir* – was so extensive that he must have worked closely from a printed text rather than being familiar with it from having seen it or acted in it. The first printed edition of *King Leir* was entered in the Stationers' Register in May 1605. Typically, plays were published two months or so after they were registered, so it is likely that the very earliest that Shakespeare began working closely from his main source was late in the summer of 1605. Had he finished *King Lear* by December 1605, when the playhouses reopened (having been closed since October), there would have been enough time for the King's Men to have the play vetted by the Master of the Revels for selection as one of the ten they were asked to perform before King James between late December 1605 and early March 1606. Since *King Lear* was not performed at court until December 1606 the evidence suggests that, while it was begun by the autumn of 1605, *King Lear* was not finished and staged at the Globe until the early months of 1606.

No version of *Macbeth* was published before the 1623 folio, so arguments for dating it are more circumstantial than for *King Lear*. Its allusion to King James (in the 'show of kings' scene) confirms that it was written after 1603. The first recorded notice of a performance was made by Simon Forman, who saw it at the Globe in April 1610. There are no records of court performances of *Macbeth*, despite claims that it must have been staged in the summer of 1606 before King James and King Christian of Denmark, during the latter's state visit. But based on its striking topicality, especially the Porter scene (with its explicit allusions to Jesuitical equivocation), scholars from Edmond Malone in the late eighteenth century until the present day are in near-universal agreement that it was written in 1606, in the aftermath of the trials and executions of the Gunpowder plotters.

Antony and Cleopatra seems to have been on Shakespeare's mind while he was writing *Macbeth*; Macbeth even compares himself and Banquo to Antony and Octavius Caesar: 'There is none but he / Whose being I do fear; and under him / My genius is rebuked, as it is said / Mark Antony's was by Caesar.' On 20 May 1608 the publisher Edward Blount entered two works in the Stationers' Register: *Pericles* and 'A book called *Antony and Cleopatra*'. While *Pericles* was published in quarto in 1609, *Antony and Cleopatra* remained unpublished until 1623. Allusions in contemporary plays help pinpoint an earlier date. Shakespeare's company staged Barnabe Barnes's *The Devil's Charter* at court on 2 February 1607. The printed quarto of that play includes a scene in which a villain hopes to poison others with a box of 'aspics' and calls the snakes 'Cleopatra's birds' as he applies them to the breasts of victims – a detail invented by Shakespeare that departs from the Plutarchan tradition of having the asp bite its victim's arm. The scene clearly alludes to Shakespeare's earlier depiction of Cleopatra's death. Barnes was not alone in being influenced by Shakespeare's version of this story before the end of 1606. Back in 1594, Samuel Daniel had written a closet drama, *The Tragedy of Cleopatra*; in 1607, after thirteen years and five editions (the last in 1605), he republished it in an altered version, lifting minor characters from Shakespeare's play and rewriting Antony's death scene in a way that suggests that he was drawing on what he had seen staged. Both writers had probably seen Shakespeare's play by late 1606 – by which time the play was completed and staged – either at a Christmas court performance (much more likely for Daniel) or at the Globe in late November or early December, after the theatres reopened following their closure since early July for plague.

For similar conclusions and additional detail (including stylistic evidence for dating the plays), see Stanley Wells and Gary Taylor, eds, *William Shakespeare: A Textual Companion* (Oxford, 1987), 128–30, as well as the authoritative individual Arden, Cambridge and Oxford editions of the three plays.

Bibliographical Essay

What follows is intended to serve the needs of those searching for a particular source as well as those interested in a broader guide to the material covered in this book. Before turning to specific citations in individual chapters, readers may find it helpful to look at the principal sources of Shakespeare's life and work, Jacobean theatre and early seventeenth-century British history that have guided my assumptions and conclusions throughout these pages.

PRINCIPAL SOURCES

Shakespeare's Life

The bare facts of Shakespeare's life have been collected in a few key sources: E. K. Chambers, *William Shakespeare: A Study of Facts and Problems*, 2 vols (Oxford, 1930) and S. Schoenbaum, *William Shakespeare: A Documentary Life* (Oxford, 1975). J. O. Halliwell-Phillipps, *Outlines of the Life of Shakespeare* (11th impression; London, 1907) is still useful. More recent discoveries can be found in David Thomas, ed., *Shakespeare in the Public Records* (London, 1985) and Robert Bearman, ed., *Shakespeare in the Stratford Records* (Stroud, Gloucestershire, 1994). Relevant documents about Stratford-upon-Avon in Shakespeare's day can be located through James O. Halliwell, *A Descriptive Calendar of the Ancient Manuscripts and Records in the Possession of the Corporation of Stratford-upon-Avon* (London, 1863). See too the six published volumes of the *Minutes and Accounts of the Corporation of Stratford-upon-Avon and Other Records*, vols 1–4 (Hertford, 1921–30), ed. Richard Savage and E. I. Fripp; vol. 5 (Hertford, 1990), ed. Levi Fox, and the one most relevant for the year 1606, vol. 6: *Minutes and Accounts of the Stratford-upon-Avon Corporation, 1599–1609*, ed. Robert Bearman (Bristol, 2011). For Shakespeare in Stratford-upon-Avon and its environs, see: Edgar I. Fripp's several volumes: *Master Richard Quyny, Bailiff of Stratford-upon-Avon and Friend of William Shakespeare* (Oxford, 1924); *Shakespeare's Stratford* (Oxford, 1928); *Shakespeare's Haunts Near Stratford* (Oxford, 1929); and *Shakespeare: Man and Artist*, 2 vols (Oxford, 1938); Charlotte Carmichael Stopes, *Shakespeare's Warwickshire Contemporaries* (rev. edn, Stratford-upon-Avon, 1907); as well as Mark Eccles's outstanding *Shakespeare in Warwickshire* (Madison, 1961). Two other valuable studies are Robert Bearman, ed., *The History of an English Borough: Stratford-upon-Avon 1196–1996* (Stroud, Gloucestershire, 1997) and Jeanne Jones, *Family Life in Shakespeare's England: Stratford-upon-Avon 1570–1630* (Stroud, Gloucestershire, 1996).

I have consulted a number of modern biographies: Peter Thompson, *Shakespeare's Professional Career* (Cambridge, 1992); Park Honan, *Shakespeare: A Life* (Oxford, 1998); Jonathan Bate, *The Genius of Shakespeare* (New York, 1998); Anthony Holden, *William Shakespeare: His Life and Work* (London, 1999); Katherine Duncan-Jones, *Ungentle Shakespeare* (London, 2001); Michael Wood, *In Search of Shakespeare* (London, 2003); Stanley Wells, *Shakespeare for All Time* (Oxford, 2003); Stephen Greenblatt, *Will in the World* (New York, 2004); René Weis, *Shakespeare Revealed: A Biography* (London, 2007); and Lois Potter, *The Life of William Shakespeare: A Critical Biography* (Malden, Mass., 2012). I also draw on the research that found its way into my own study, *1599: A Year in the Life of William Shakespeare* (London, 2005).

All too little of Shakespeare's London remains. In recreating its topography, I have relied on John Stow, *The Survey of London* (London, 1598; 1603); the later edition is also available in a modern edition, C. L. Kings-ford, ed. (Oxford, 1908; rpt 1971). Lena Cowen Orlin, ed., *Material London, ca. 1600* (Philadelphia, 2000) has also proved useful. I have been greatly aided by a pair of London Topographical Society publications: Adrian Prockter and Robert Taylor, eds, *The A to Z of Elizabethan London* (London, 1979) and Ann Saunders and John Schofield, eds, *Tudor London: A Map and a View* (London, 2001). See too Ida Darlington and James Howgego, *Printed Maps of London, circa 1553–1850* (London, 1964; rev. edn, 1979). E. H. Sugden, *A Topographical Dictionary to the Works of Shakespeare and His Fellow Dramatists* (Manchester, 1925) remains indispensable. For the calendar of holidays and times of sunrise and sunset I've relied on Edward Ponde, *A New Almanacke and Prognostication* (London, 1606).

Shakespeare's Plays and Poems

Any study of Shakespeare's work begins with editions. The starting point – once past the original quartos, octavos and folios – is H. H. Furness's multi-volume Victorian *Variorum Shakespeare*, supplemented by a superb trio of series: *The Arden Shakespeare* (both Arden 2 and Arden 3), *The Oxford Shakespeare* and *The New Cambridge Shakespeare*. For the three plays Shakespeare was writing in 1606, see for *King Lear*: *A New Variorum Edition of Shakespeare: King Lear*, ed. Horace Howard Furness (Philadelphia, 1908). See too: *King Lear*, ed. R. A. Foakes (London, 2006); *The Tragedy of King Lear*, ed. Jay L. Halio (Cambridge, 1992); and *The History of King Lear*, ed. Stanley Wells, on the basis of a text prepared by Gary Taylor (Oxford, 2000). In comparing the 1608 and 1623 versions of the play I have made use of *King Lear: A Parallel Text Edition*, ed. René Weis, 2nd edn (Harlow, 2010), as well as *The Complete King Lear, 1608–1623, William Shakespeare; Texts and Parallel Texts in Photographic Facsimile*, ed. Michael Warren (Berkeley, 1989). For *Macbeth*: *A New Variorum Edition of Shakespeare: Macbeth*, ed. Horace Howard Furness, 3rd edn (Philadelphia, 1903); *Macbeth*, ed. Kenneth Muir (London, 1972); *Macbeth*, ed. A. R. Braunmuller (Cambridge, 2008); and *The Tragedy of Macbeth*, ed. Nicholas Brooke (Oxford, 1990). For *Antony and Cleopatra*: *A New Variorum Edition of Shakespeare: Antony and Cleopatra*, ed. Marvin Spevack (New York, 1977); *Antony and Cleopatra*, ed. M. R. Ridley (London, 1984); *Antony and Cleopatra*, ed. John Wilders (London, 1995); *Antony and Cleopatra*, ed. David Bevington (Cambridge, 1990); and *The Tragedy of Anthony and Cleopatra*, ed. Michael Neill (Oxford, 1994). For the sources of Shakespeare's plays, see: Geoffrey Bullough, *Narrative and Dramatic Sources of Shakespeare*, 8 vols (London, 1957–75), as well as Kenneth Muir, *The Sources of Shakespeare's Plays* (London, 1977). And for a concordance to Shakespeare's works, see Marvin Spevack, ed., *The Harvard Concordance to Shakespeare* (Cambridge, Mass., 1973). Quotations from Ben Jonson's works, which figure largely in this book, are quoted (by volume and page number) from *The Cambridge Edition of The Works of Ben Jonson*, ed. David Bevington, Martin Butler and Ian Donaldson, 7 vols (Cambridge, 2012).

Shakespeare on Stage and in Print

Still unsurpassed are E. K. Chambers, *The Elizabethan Stage*, 4 vols (Oxford, 1923) and G. E. Bentley, *The Jacobean and Caroline Stage*, 7 vols (Oxford, 1941–68). I am also indebted to R. A. Foakes and R. T. Rickert, eds, *Henslowe's Diary* (Cambridge, 1961) for information about the culture of playwriting. Other major sources include: *Annals of English Drama, 975–1700*, ed. Alfred Harbage, S. Schoenbaum and Sylvia Stoler Wagonheim (3rd edn, New York, 1989); R. A. Foakes, *Illustrations of the English Stage, 1580–1642* (Stanford, 1985); and Herbert Berry, *Shakespeare's Playhouses* (New York, 1987). Relevant documents can also be found in *English Professional Theatre, 1530–1660*, ed. Glynne Wickham, Herbert Berry and William Ingram (Cambridge, 2000). Two new resources – the Henslowe–Alleyn Digitisation Project and the Database of Early English Playbooks – are welcome additions to the field.

I have also consulted Andrew Gurr's influential books: *The Shakespearean Stage 1574–1642* (Cambridge, 1970; 3rd edn, 1992); *Playgoing in Shakespeare's London* (Cambridge, 1987; 2nd edn, 1996); *The Shakespearian Playing Companies* (Oxford, 1996); *The Shakespeare Company, 1594–1642* (Cambridge, 2004); and *Shakespeare's Opposites: The Admiral's Company, 1594–1625* (Cambridge, 2009). No less helpful are Bernard Beckerman, *Shakespeare at the Globe 1599–1609* (New York, 1962); Roslyn Lander Knutson, *The Repertory of Shakespeare's Company, 1594–1613* (Fayetteville, 1991), and her *Playing Companies and Commerce in Shakespeare's Time* (Cambridge, 2001); John H. Astington's invaluable *English Court Theatre 1558–1642* (Cambridge, 1999); Stanley Wells, *Shakespeare and Co.: Christopher Marlowe, Thomas Dekker, Ben Jonson, Thomas Middleton, John Fletcher and the Other Players in His Story* (London, 2006); Eva Griffith, *A Jacobean Company and Its Playhouse: The Queen's Servants at the Red Bull Theatre* (Cambridge, 2013); James P. Bednarz, *Shakespeare and the Poets' War* (New York, 2001); the many helpful essays collected in John D. Cox and David Scott Kastan, eds, *A New History of Early English Drama* (New York, 1997); and Richard Dutton, ed., *The Oxford Handbook of Early Modern Theatre* (Oxford, 2009). For information on boy companies I've drawn on H. N. Hillebrand, *The Child Actors: A Chapter in Elizabethan Stage History* (Urbana, 1926); Michael Shapiro, *Children of the Revels: The Boy Companies of Shakespeare's Time and Their Plays* (New York, 1977); Reavley Gair, *The Children of Paul's: The Story of a Theatre Company, 1553–1608* (Cambridge, 1982); and Lucy Munro, *The Children of the Queen's Revels: A Jacobean Theatre Repertory* (Cambridge, 2005). For Jacobean tournaments, see Alan Young, *Tudor and Jacobean Tournaments* (London, 1987). And for information about actors, see Edwin Nungezer, *A Dictionary of Actors* (New Haven, 1929), supplemented by Mark Eccles's four essays on 'Elizabethan Actors' in *Notes and Queries*, vols 236–8 (1991–3). See too: John H. Astington, *Actors and Acting in Shakespeare's Time: The Art of Stage Playing* (Cambridge, 2010). For an accessible study that straddles theatre history and archaeology, see Julian Bowsher, *Shakespeare's London Theatreland: Archaeology, History and Drama* (London, 2012). And for censorship of the stage, see Janet Clare, *Art Made Tongue-tied by Authority: Elizabethan and Jacobean Dramatic Censorship*, 2nd edn (Manchester, 1999), and Richard Dutton, *Mastering the Revels: the Regulation and Censorship of English Renaissance Drama* (Iowa City, 1991).

Any discussion of Shakespeare in print begins with A. W. Pollard and G. R. Redgrave, eds, *A Short-Title Catalogue of Books Printed in England, Scotland, & Ireland and of English Books Printed Abroad, 1475–1640*, 2 vols (2nd edn, rev. London, 1976); Edward Arber, ed., *A Transcript of the Registers of the Company of Stationers of London 1554–1640*, 5 vols (London, 1875–7); W. W. Greg, *A Companion to Arber. Being a Calendar of Documents in Edward Arber's 'Transcript of the Registers of the Company of Stationers of London'* (Oxford, 1967); and Greg's *A Bibliography of the English Printed Drama to the Restoration*, 4 vols (London, 1939–59). For more recent studies, see Douglas A. Brooks, *From Playhouse to Printing House: Drama and Authorship in Early Modern England* (Cambridge, 2000); David Scott Kastan, *Shakespeare and the Book* (Cambridge, 2001); Andrew Murphy, *Shakespeare in Print: A History and Chronology of Shakespeare Publishing* (Cambridge, 2003); and Lukas Erne, *Shakespeare as Literary Dramatist* (Cambridge, 2003), as well as his *Shakespeare and the Book Trade* (Cambridge, 2013).

Jacobean Letters, Journals, Sermons and State Papers

I have tried throughout to let Jacobean men and women speak for themselves. Two sources that I rely on at many points are *The Letters of John Chamberlain*, ed. Norman E. McClure, 2 vols (Philadelphia, 1939) and *Dudley Carleton to John Chamberlain, 1603–1624: Jacobean Letters*, ed. Maurice Lee, Jr. (New Brunswick, 1972). I've also had frequent occasion to quote from Sir John Harington's letters, collected in *Nugae Antiquae*, ed. T. Park, 2 vols (London, 1804) and *The Letters and Epigrams of Sir*

John Harington, ed. Norman E. McClure (Philadelphia, 1930). See too Thomas Birch, *The Court and Times of James the First*, 2 vols (London, 1848); Arthur Collins, ed., *Letters and Memorials of State* (London, 1746); and Edmund Sawyer, ed., *Memorials of Affairs of State in the Reigns of Q. Elizabeth and K. James I. Collected (Chiefly) from the Original Papers of the Right Honourable Sir Ralph Winwood*, 3 vols (London, 1725). And for a valuable collection of contemporary materials, see John Nichols, ed., *The Progresses, Processions, and Magnificent Festivities of King James the First*, 4 vols (London, 1828).

Tourists and ambassadors are a major source of information; see William B. Rye, ed., *England as Seen by Foreigners in the Days of Elizabeth and James the First* (London, 1865). See too, in addition to the reports of the Venetian ambassadors Nicolo Molino and Zorzi Giustinian (who overlapped briefly in January 1606 before Giustinian succeeded Molino) preserved in the state papers, the letters of the French ambassador to the Jacobean court published in *Ambassades de Monsieur de la Boderie, en Angleterre* (n.p., 1750), as well as the vivid letters of a Spanish woman visiting England at this time, in Glyn Redworth, ed., *The Letters of Luisa de Carvajal y Mendoza*, 2 vols (London, 2012). Sermons, as much as poems, plays and paintings, help illuminate the cultural moment. While I refer to specific sermons by various preachers in individual chapters, no collection is more valuable than that of Lancelot Andrewes, who delivered sermons this year before the king on Easter Sunday, Whitsunday, Gowrie Day, the second Hampton Court Conference, the first anniversary of the Gunpowder Plot and Christmas Day. His collected sermons can be found in *XCVI Sermons by the Right Honourable and Reverend Father in God, Lancelot Andrewes* (London, 1629).

No history of this year would be possible without the calendars of state papers. I draw on them freely, especially the *Calendar of State Papers Domestic: James I, 1603–1610,* ed. Mary Anne Everett Green (London, 1857); *Calendar of State Papers Relating to English Affairs in the Archives of*

Venice, vol. 10: 1603–1607, ed. Horatio F. Brown (London, 1900); *Calendar of State Papers Relating to Ireland, of the Reign of James I*, vol. 1, ed. C. W. Russell and John P. Prendergast (London, 1872); and *Calendar of State Papers, Colonial: East Indies 1513–1616*, ed. W. Noel Sainsbury (London, 1862). See too the *Calendar of the Cecil Papers in Hatfield House*, part 18 (1606), ed. Montague Spencer Giuseppi (London, 1940). For Scottish affairs, see *Register of the Privy Council of Scotland*, vol. 7 (1604–7), ed. David Masson (Edinburgh, 1885). Unfortunately, English Privy Council records for this year were destroyed in a fire at Whitehall in 1619. For the lives and careers of the many individuals discussed in these pages I have frequently turned to the invaluable *Oxford Dictionary of National Biography* (henceforth ODNB).

King James and Jacobean History

For studies of King James's early reign in England, see, first and foremost, his own collected writings in *The Works of the Most High and Mighty Prince James* (London, 1616). See too Johann P. Sommerville, ed., *King James VI and I: Political Writings* (Cambridge, 1994); Neil Rhodes, Jennifer Richards and Joseph Marshall, eds, *King James VI and I: Selected Writings* (Burlington, 2003); G. P. V. Akrigg, ed., *Letters of King James VI and I* (Berkeley, 1984); and Daniel Fischlin, Mark Fortier and Kevin Sharp, eds, *Royal Subjects: The Writings of James VI and I* (Detroit, 2002). For royal proclamations, see James F. Larkin and Paul L. Hughes, eds, *Stuart Royal Proclamations*, vol. 1 (Oxford, 1973). For contemporary chronicles, see John Stow, *The Abridgement or Summarie of the English Chronicle, First Collected by Master John Stow*, by E[dmund] H[owes] (London, 1607); John Stow, *The Annales, or a Generall Chronicle of England Begun First by Maister John Stow, and After Him by Edmund Howes* (London, 1615); and Robert Johnston, *Historia Rerum Britannicarum, 1572–1628* (Amsterdam, 1655).

For biographies of James and analysis of his reign, see: Anthony Weldon, *The Court and Character of King James* (London, 1650); Arthur Wilson, *The History of Great Britain, being the Life and Reign of King James the First* (London, 1653); David Harris Willson, *King James VI & I* (New York, 1956); Robert Ashton, *James I by His Contemporaries* (London, 1969); Graham Parry, *The Golden Age Restor'd: The Culture of the Stuart Court, 1603–42* (Manchester, 1981); Maurice Lee, Jr., *Great Britain's Solomon: James VI and I and His Three Kingdoms* (Urbana, 1990); Linda Levy Peck, ed., *The Mental World of the Jacobean Court* (Cambridge, 1991); David M. Bergeron, *Royal Family, Royal Lovers: King James of England and Scotland* (London, 1991); W. P. Patterson, *King James VI and I and the Reunion of Christendom* (Cambridge, 1997); Roger Lockyer, *James VI and I* (London, 1998); Leeds Barroll, *Anna of Denmark, Queen of England: A Cultural Biography* (Philadelphia, 2001); Pauline Croft, *King James* (Houndmills, Basingstoke, 2003); Alan Stewart, *The Cradle King: A Life of James VI and I* (London, 2003); Diana Newton, *The Making of the Jacobean Regime: James VI and I and the Government of England 1603–1605* (Woodbridge, 2005); and Tim Harris, *Rebellion: Britain's First Stuart Kings, 1567–1642* (Oxford, 2014). See too the crucial revisionist work of Jenny Wormald, in her pair of influential essays 'James VI and I: Two Kings or One', *History* 68 (1983), 187–209, and 'Gunpowder, Treasons and Scots', *Journal of British Studies* 24 (1985), 141–68, as well as her ODNB entry on King James; Richard Dutton, '*King Lear*, *The Triumphs of Reunited Britannia*, and "The Matter of Britain"', *Literature and History* 12 (1986), 139–51; and Christopher Wortham, 'Shakespeare, James I and the Matter of Britain', *English* 45 (1996), 97–122. I am deeply indebted to Kevin Sharpe, *Image Wars: Promoting Kings and Commonwealths in England, 1603–1660* (New Haven, 2010). I have also profited from two excellent collections: *James VI and I: Ideas, Authority, and Government*, ed. Ralph Houlbrooke (Aldershot, Hampshire, 2006) and *The Accession of James I: Historical and Cultural Consequences*, ed. Glenn Burgess, Rowland Wymer and Jason Lawrence

(Basingstoke, Hampshire, 2006). I am also indebted at many points in this book to two studies: Henry N. Paul, *The Royal Play of Macbeth* (New York, 1950), despite its unpersuasive insistence that *Macbeth* was intended to flatter King James and was staged before him and King Christian on 7 August at Hampton Court; and Leeds Barroll's groundbreaking *Politics, Plague, and Shakespeare's Theater: The Stuart Years* (Ithaca, 1991), the best exploration of the dating of the plays of 1606 as well as the impact of plague that year on Shakespeare's writing.

PROLOGUE

For performances at court, see John Astington, *English Court Theatre.* For Whitehall Palace and the old Banqueting House see Simon Thurley, *Whitehall Palace: An Architectural History of the Royal Apartments, 1240–1698* (New Haven, 1999) and his *The Royal Palaces of Tudor England* (New Haven, 1993); G. S. Dugdale, *Whitehall through the Centuries* (London, 1950); and *The London County Council Survey of London, The Parish of St Margaret, Westminster*, part II, vol. 1, Neighbourhood of Whitehall (London, 1930). See too Martin Butler, *The Stuart Court Masque and Political Culture* (Cambridge, 2008); Stow, *The Survey of London*; and for an eyewitness description of this masque, William S. Powell, *John Pory, 1572–1636: The Life and Letters of a Man of Many Parts* (Chapel Hill, 1977). For more on this masque, see below, chapter 8. Other than calculating from the size of the venue (when empty, roughly 5,500 square feet), it is difficult to determine how many spectators could cram into the old Banqueting House for a masque – especially when space had to be saved for Inigo Jones's complex staging (including a globe large enough to hide eight courtiers), the elaborate dancing and the king's central seating. So the capacity suggested here of six hundred or so for the old Banqueting House is far more conservative than the estimate of a thousand or more offered in otherwise authoritative sources (such as Astington, *Eng-*

lish Court Theatre, 170–1, who, given the elaborate dress required for such courtly entertainment, nonetheless assumes an unrealistic eighteen inches of width per person, and relies heavily on the testimony of the Venetian Orazio Busino – the only such approximation we have from the period – who counted six hundred ladies alone when he saw Ben Jonson's *Pleasure Reconciled* at an uncomfortably packed Banqueting House in 1618).

For the dating and order of Shakespeare's early Jacobean plays – about which there is currently no scholarly consensus – I have largely followed *The Oxford Shakespeare: The Complete Works*, ed. Stanley Wells and Gary Taylor with John Jowett and William Montgomery (Oxford, 2005). While some scholars believe that *Timon of Athens* was written after *King Lear*, perhaps in 1607, I don't find that plausible, nor is there compelling evidence for that view. But I do agree with revisionist scholars who believe that *All's Well that Ends Well* was probably written between 1607 and 1609. See in this regard Laurie Maguire and Emma Smith, 'Many Hands – A New Shakespeare Collaboration?' in the *Times Literary Supplement*, 19 April 2012, and the several responses to it; see too Lois Potter, *The Life of William Shakespeare*, and Gordon McMullan, 'What Is a Late Play?' in *The Cambridge Companion to Shakespeare's Last Plays*, ed. Catherine M. S. Alexander (Cambridge, 2009), 5–28.

For the lives of Shakespeare and his family, see E. K. Chambers, *William Shakespeare: A Study of Facts and Problems*. For the original of Poulett's letter, see British Library Add. MS 11757, ff. 105–106b. For a full account of it, see Hilton Kelliher, 'A Shakespeare Allusion of 1605 and Its Author', *The British Library Journal* 3 (1977), 7–12. For Shakespeare in London's bookstalls, see Andrew Murphy, *Shakespeare in Print* and Lukas Erne, *Shakespeare and the Book Trade*. For the 1607 'fee list' of actors that omits Shakespeare's name, see Peter R. Roberts, 'The Business of Playing and the Patronage of Players at the Jacobean Court', in *James VI and I: Ideas, Authority, and Government*, ed. Ralph Houlbrooke, 88. Among recent biographers who have made too much of Shakespeare's supposed dalliance in 1606 with Jennet (or Jane) Davenant, mother of the future playwright William Davenant, who was the source of the rumour slandering her (so that he would be taken for Shakespeare's son, albeit an illegitimate one), see Park Honan, *Shakespeare: A Life* and René Weis, *Shakespeare Revealed.* The first recorded version of the story can be traced back to John Aubrey, writing three-quarters of a century after the alleged assignation (see E. K. Chambers, *Facts and Problems*). The recent discovery that Shakespeare carved his name on the panelling of the Tabard Inn was first reported by Martha Carlin in the 26 September 2014 issue of the *Times Literary Supplement*, 15; the anonymous description can be found in the Edinburgh University Library (MS La. II 422/211).

1. THE KING'S MAN

For the streets in Shakespeare's neighbourhood, see Adrian Prockter and Robert Taylor, eds, *The A to Z of Elizabethan London*. On the Queen's Men, see Scott McMillin and Sally-Beth MacLean, *The Queen's Men and Their Plays* (Cambridge, 1998) and Brian Walsh, *Shakespeare, the Queen's Men, and the Elizabethan Performance of History* (Cambridge, 2009). For payments for *King Leir*, see R. A. Foakes and R. T. Rickert, eds, *Henslowe's Diary*. For Fiennes's and Clayton's stories, see Peter R. Roberts, 'The Business of Playing and the Patronage of Players at the Jacobean Court', 95–104. For more on Laurence Fletcher, see, along with Roberts, 'The Business of Playing', Sir James Fergusson, *The Man Behind Macbeth and Other Studies* (London, 1969), 13–21. For the plague of 1603, see: Paul Slack, *The Impact of Plague in Tudor and Stuart England* (London, 1985); J. F. D. Shrewsbury, *A History of Bubonic Plague in the British Isles* (Cambridge, 1970); F. P. Wilson, *The Plague in Shakespeare's London* (Oxford, 1927, rpt 1963); and Charles Creighton, *A History of Epidemics in Britain* (Cambridge, 1891). See too Thomas Dekker, *The Wonderfull Yeare. Wherein Is Shewed the Picture of London Lying Sicke of the Plague* (London, 1603) and

F. P. Wilson, ed., *The Plague Pamphlets of Thomas Dekker* (Oxford, 1925).

For records of touring, see E. K. Chambers, *Facts and Problems*, and the many individual volumes in the *Records of Early English Drama*, as well as the helpful overview in Peter Greenfield, 'Touring', in Dutton, ed., *The Oxford Handbook of Early Modern Theatre*, 292–306. And for information on Shakespeare and the King's Men at court, see Astington, *English Court Theatre*. For the Revels Account of 1604/1605, see W. R. Streitberger, ed., 'Jacobean and Caroline Revels Accounts, 1603–1642', *Malone Society Collections* 13 (Oxford, 1986). Cope's letter of 11 January 1605 can be found in *HMC Report on the Calendar of the MSS of the Marquess of Salisbury* (London, 1933), 16:415. Richard Flecknoe's recollection of Burbage can be found in his *Euterpe Restored* (London, 1672). For other actors in Shakespeare's company, see the individual biographies in Nungezer's *Dictionary of Actors*, Eccles's essays on 'Elizabethan Actors' in *Notes and Queries*, Astington's *Actors and Acting in Shakespeare's Time*, and individual entries for the more prominent figures in the ODNB. On 'stuttering Heminges', see: E. K. Chambers, *Elizabethan Stage*, 2:421. For more on Kemp and Armin, see David Wiles, *Shakespeare's Clown: Actor and Text in the Elizabethan Playhouse* (Cambridge, 1987); and for the possibility that Kemp survived until 1610 or so, see K. Duncan-Jones, 'Shakespeare's Dancing Fool', *Times Literary Supplement*, 13 August 2010, as well as Martin Butler's ODNB entry. Scholars have paid surprisingly little attention to the age at which Elizabethan and Jacobean actors retired from the stage, but from the available records it seems that the number of those who continued into their fifties or beyond could be counted on the fingers of one hand (and would have included John Lowin, Joseph Taylor, Robert Leigh and possibly Kemp). Based on surviving evidence, after 1603 Shakespeare was one of the oldest players still performing. And for John Dryden's recollections of Ben Jonson on *Macbeth*, see his 'Defence of the Epilogue' in George Watson, ed., *John Dryden. Of Dramatic Poesy and Other Critical Essays*, 2 vols (London, 1962), 1:173.

2. DIVISION OF THE KINGDOMS

For the most authoritative account of the Union question, see Bruce Galloway, *The Union of England and Scotland 1603–1608* (Edinburgh, 1986). For Union tracts, see Bruce R. Galloway and Brian P. Levack, eds, *The Jacobean Union: Six Tracts of 1604* (Edinburgh, 1985). See too Roger A. Mason, ed., *Scots and Britons: Scottish Political Thought and the Union of 1603* (Cambridge, 1994); Brian P. Levack, *The Formation of the British State: England, Scotland and the Union, 1603–1707* (Oxford, 1987); *Shakespeare and Scotland*, ed. Willy Maley and Andrew Murphy (Manchester, 2004); David M. Bergeron, 'King James's Civic Pageant and Parliamentary Speech in March 1604', *Albion* 34 (2002), 213–31; as well as a pair of essays by Jenny Wormald: 'The Creation of Britain: Multiple Kingdoms or Core and Colonies?', *Transactions of the Royal Historical Society*, 6th Series, vol. 2 (1992), 175–94, and 'The Union of 1603' in Mason, ed., *Scots and Britons*, 17–40. For contemporary texts, see: *The King's Majesty's Speech . . . in Parliament, 19 March 1603* (i.e., 1604); John Thornborough, *The Joyful and Blessed Reuniting the Two Mighty and Famous Kingdoms* (Oxford, 1605) and Ben Jonson, 'Panegyre, On the Happy Entrance of James Our Sovereign to His First High Session of Parliament in This His Kingdom, the 19th of March, 1604', in *The Cambridge Edition of the Works of Ben Jonson*, 2:473–82. For a modern edition of Antony Munday, *The Triumphs of Re-united Britannia*, see *Renaissance Drama: An Anthology of Plays and Entertainments*, ed. Arthur F. Kinney, 2nd edn (Malden, 2005).

For parliamentary discussion of the Union question, see William Cobbett, ed., *The Parliamentary History of England*, vol. 1 (London, 1806); *Journal of the House of Commons*, vol. 1 (London, 1802); *The Parliamentary Diary of Robert Bowyer*, ed. D. H. Willson (Minneapolis, 1931); 'Certain Articles or Considerations Touching the Union of the Kingdoms of England and Scotland', in *The Works of Francis Bacon*, ed. James Spedding, Robert Leslie Ellis and Douglas Denon Heath, 14 vols (London, 1857–74), 10:218–34; and

'The Journal of Sir Roger Wilbraham ... for the years 1593–1616', ed. Harold Spencer Scott, in *Camden Miscellany* 10 (London, 1902). See too Andrew Thrush, *The House of Commons, 1604–1629* (Cambridge, 2011), vol. 1. For an incisive discussion of these debates, see Conrad Russell, *King James VI and I and His English Parliaments: The Trevelyan Lectures*, ed. Richard Cust and Andrew Thrush (Oxford, 2011). See too Wallace Notestein, *The House of Commons 1604–1610* (New Haven, 1971). For other helpful discussions, see David L. Smith, *The Stuart Parliaments, 1603–1689* (New York, 1999); Megan Mondi, 'The Speeches and Self-Fashioning of King James VI and I to the English Parliament, 1604–1624', *Constructing the Past* 8 (2007); Annabel Patterson, *Censorship and Interpretation: The Conditions of Writing and Reading in Early Modern England* (Madison, 1984), 58–72; John Draper, 'The Occasion of *King Lear*', *Studies in Philology* 34 (1937), 176–85; Philip Schwyzer, 'The Jacobean Union Controversy and *King Lear*' in *The Accession of James I*, ed. Glenn Burgess, Rowland Wymer and Jason Lawrence, 34–47; Jenny Wormald, 'Gunpowder, Treason and Scots'; and Alex Garganigo, '*Coriolanus*, the Union Controversy, and Access to the Royal Person', *Studies in English Literature* 42 (2002), 335–59. For Sir Edward Hoby's letter of 7 March 1606 to Sir Thomas Edmondes about the discussion in Parliament of *The Isle of Gulls*, see Thomas Birch, *The Court and Times of James the First*, 1:60–1. See too Tristan Marshall, *Theatre and Empire: Great Britain on the London Stages under James VI and I* (Manchester, 2000). My analysis in this chapter, as well as in my discussions of the historical and political contexts of *King Lear* and *Macbeth*, is indebted to John Kerrigan's outstanding *Archipelagic English: Literature, History, and Politics 1603–1707* (Oxford, 2008).

3. FROM LEIR TO LEAR

Quotations from *King Leir* are from Tiffany Stern, ed., *King Leir* (London, 2002). For another modern edition of *King Leir*, see Donald M.

Michie, ed., *A Critical Edition of The True Chronicle History of King Leir and His Three Daughters, Gonorill, Ragan, and Cordella* (New York, 1991). For John Wright, see: R. B. McKerrow, *A Dictionary of Printers and Booksellers in England, Scotland and Ireland, and of Foreign Printers of English Books 1557–1640* (London, 1910), 197–8, and Lemuel Matthews Griffiths, *Evenings with Shakspere* (Bristol, 1889), 299–300. For the relationship of the two plays, see, in addition to the introductions to the Cambridge, Oxford and Arden editions of *King Lear* cited above: Wilfred Perrett, *The Story of King Lear from Geoffrey of Monmouth to Shakespeare*, in *Palaestra* 35 (Berlin, 1904); Richard Knowles, 'How Shakespeare Knew *King Leir*', *Shakespeare Survey* 55 (2002), 12–35; Martin Mueller, From *Leir* to *Lear*', *Philological Quarterly* 73 (1994), 195–217; Meredith Skura, 'What Shakespeare Did with the Queen's Men's *King Leir* and When', *Shakespeare Survey* 63 (2010), 316–25; Roger Adger Law, '*King Leir* and *King Lear*: An Examination of the Two Plays' in Don Cameron Allen, ed., *Studies in Honor of T. W. Baldwin* (Urbana, 1958), 112–24; and Scott McMillin and Sally-Beth MacLean, *The Queen's Men and Their Plays*, 160–6. Of the many studies of the language of *King Lear*, see especially: Frank Kermode, *Shakespeare's Language* (London, 2000) and Leslie Thomson, '"Pray you, undo this button": Implications of "un-" in *King Lear*', *Shakespeare Survey* 45 (1993), 79–88. For the possibility of Shakespeare's hand in the revision of Kyd's *Spanish Tragedy*, see Douglas Bruster, 'Shakespearean Spellings and Handwriting in the Additional Passages Printed in the 1602 *Spanish Tragedy*', *Notes and Queries* (2013). And for Samuel Johnson on the ending of *King Lear*, see Arthur Sherbo, ed., *Johnson on Shakespeare*, in *The Yale Edition of the Works of Samuel Johnson*, vol. 8 (New Haven, 1968), 659–705.

4. POSSESSION

For the report of the Florentine ambassador (on plague and the killing of London's dogs) see John Orrell, 'The London State in the Florentine Correspondence, 1604–1618', *Theatre Research International* 3 (1978), 157–76. For an account of King James's visit to Oxford in 1605, see Antony Nixon, *Oxfords Triumph: in the Royall Entertainement of His Moste Excellent Majestie, the Queene, and the Prince: the 27 of August Last, 1605* (London, 1605). For the translation of Matthew Gwinne's Latin, see Bullough, *Narrative and Dramatic Sources of Shakespeare*, 7:470–2. For Anne Gunter and quotations from her story, see James Sharpe's brilliant study, *The Bewitching of Anne Gunter: A Horrible and True Story of Football, Witchcraft, Murder and the King of England* (London, 1999); I have also quoted Sharpe's translation from Robert Johnston's *Historia Rerum Britannicarum*. For the theatricality of possession in the period, see Richard Raiswell, 'Faking It: A Case of Counterfeit Possession in the Reign of James I', *Renaissance and Reformation* 23 (1999), 29–48.

The literature on the subject of witchcraft and possession in Early Modern England and Scotland is vast. I have found the following studies most useful: James Sharpe, *Instruments of Darkness: Witchcraft in England 1550–1750* (London, 1996); Keith Thomas, *Religion and the Decline of Magic: Studies in Popular Beliefs in Sixteenth- and Seventeenth-Century England*, rev. edn. (London, 1973); D. P. Walker, *Unclean Spirits: Possession and Exorcism in France and England in the Late Sixteenth and Early Seventeenth Centuries* (London, 1981); Nancy Caciola, *Discerning Spirits: Divine and Demonic Possession in the Middle Ages* (Ithaca, 2003); Hilaire Kallendorf, *Exorcism and Its Texts* (Toronto, 2003); Moshe Sluhovsky, *Believe Not Every Spirit: Possession, Mysticism, and Discernment in Early Modern Catholicism* (Chicago, 2007); *Witchcraft and Hysteria in Elizabethan London: Edward Jorden and the Mary Glover Case*, ed. Michael MacDonald (London, 1991); and *Witchcraft and the Act of 1604*, ed. John Newton and Jo Bath (Leiden, 2008). For Harsnett, Darrell and *King Lear* see: Kenneth Muir, 'Samuel Harsnett and *King Lear*', *Review of English Studies* 2 (1951), 11–21 (as well as his Arden edition of *King Lear*); Stephen Greenblatt, 'Shakespeare and the Exorcists', *Shakespearean Negotiations* (Berkeley,

1988), 94–128; and especially F. W. Brownlow, *Shakespeare, Harsnett, and the Devils of Denham* (Newark, 1993), from which Harsnett's *A Declaration of Egregious Popish Impostures* is quoted. See too: Amy Wolf, 'Shakespeare and Harsnett: "Pregnant to Good Pity"?', *Studies in English Literature* 38 (1998), 251–64; Marion Gibson, *Possession, Puritanism and Print: Darrell, Harsnett, Shakespeare and the Elizabethan Exorcism Controversy* (London, 2006); John L. Murphy, *Darkness and Devils: Exorcism and 'King Lear'* (Athens, Ohio, 1983); Nina Taunton and Valerie Hart, 'King Lear, King James and the Gunpowder Treason of 1605', *Renaissance Studies* 17 (2003), 695–715; and Thomas Freeman, 'Demons, Deviance and Defiance: John Darrell and the Politics of Exorcism in Late Elizabethan England' in Peter Lake and Michael C. Questier, eds, *Conformity and Orthodoxy in the English Church, c.1560–1660* (Woodbridge, 2000). On canon law outlawing exorcism without special permission, see: *Constitutions and Canons Ecclesiastical Treated upon by the Bishop of London* (London, 1604), chapter lxxii. And for Poor Tom's language, see S. Musgrove, 'Thieves' Cant in *King Lear*', *English Studies* 62 (1981), 5–13. For John Harington's conversation with King James about witches, see his *Nugae Antiquae*, 1:366–71.

5. THE LETTER

Much of what we now know about the Gunpowder Plot survives in materials in the Public Records Office at Kew, first collected and preserved by the Jacobean government and known since the mid-nineteenth century as the 'Gunpowder Book'. My account, like all others by modern historians, relies heavily on this cache of documents. Modern studies of the plot that I have usefully consulted – the literature here too is vast – are: Mark Nicholls's authoritative *Investigating Gunpowder Plot* (Manchester, 1991), as well as his incisive contributions to the ODNB on the subject and on individual conspirators; James Travers, *Gunpowder: The Players Behind the Plot* (Kew, Richmond, 2005), which is perhaps the best introduction to the topic; Antonia Fraser, *The Gunpowder Plot: Terror and Faith in 1605* (London, 1996), and her exercise in counterfactual history, 'The Gunpowder Plot Succeeds' in *What Might Have Been* (London, 2004); George Blacker Morgan's privately printed *The Great English Treason for Religion*, 2 vols (London, 1931–2); Henry Hawkes Spink, *The Gunpowder Plot and Lord Monteagle's Letter* (London, 1902); Paul Durst, *Intended Treason* (London, 1970); Francis Edwards, *The Enigma of Gunpowder Plot, 1605: The Third Solution* (Dublin, 2008); Alan Haynes, *The Gunpowder Plot: Faith in Rebellion* (Dover, New Hampshire, 1994); Jenny Wormald, 'Gunpowder, Treason and Scots'; and David Cressy, *Bonfires and Bells: National Memory and the Protestant Calendar in Elizabethan and Stuart England* (Berkeley, 1989). See too Paul Wake, 'Plotting as Subversion: Narrative and the Gunpowder Plot', *Journal of Narrative Theory* 38 (2008), 295–316.

For contemporary writings about the Gunpowder Plot, see: William Barlow, *The Sermon Preached at Paules Crosse, the Tenth Day of November Being the Next Sunday after the Discoverie of This Late Horrible Treason* (London, 1606); *His Majesty's Speech in the Last Session of Parliament as Near His Very Words as could be Gathered at the Instant. Together with a Discourse of the Maner of the Discovery of This Late Intended Treason, Joyned with the Examination of Some of the Prisoners* (London, 1605); Thomas Morton, *An Exact Discoverie of the Romish Doctrine in the Case of Conspiracie and Rebellion* (London, 1605); *A True and Perfect Relation of the Whole Proceedings against the Late Most Barbarous Traitors* (London, 1606); Thomas Campion, *De Pulverea Conjuratione*, ed. David Lindley, with transl. by Robin Sowerby (Leeds, 1987); Francis Edwards, trans. and ed., *The Gunpowder Plot: The Narrative of Oswald Tesimond alias Greenway* (London, 1973); and Samuel Garey, *Great Brittans Little Calendar: or Triple Diarie, in Remembrance of Three Days* (London, 1618). For Lord Harington's letter to his cousin, see John Harington, *Nugae Antiquae*, 1:371–5. For Edmondes's correspondence, see Winwood, *Memorials*. Digby's account of Percy declaring the succession at Charing Cross appears in 'Several Papers or Letters of Sir Everard Digby, Chiefly Relating to the Gunpowder-Plot', first published as an appendix to *The Gunpowder Treason: With a Discourse of the Manner of Discovery* (London, 1679). For Lewkenor's account of the crush at the trial, see Willson, ed., *The Parliamentary Diary of Robert Bowyer*, 10; and for the suggestion that Tresham was behind the Monteagle letter, see Oliver Ormerod, *The Picture of a Papist . . . Together with a Discourse of the Late Treason, and of the Execution of Some of the Traitors* (London, 1606), 124. Ormerod also supplies the wonderful epithet about Fawkes as the 'Machiavellian with a match'. For more on Ben Jonson and the Gunpowder Plot, see Ian Donaldson, *Ben Jonson: A Life* (London, 2011); Richard Dutton, *Ben Jonson, Volpone and the Gunpowder Plot* (Cambridge, 2008); and the documents, searched as 'Gunpowder Plot', to be found in *The Cambridge Edition of the Works of Ben Jonson Online*.

6. MASSING RELICS

For Shakespeare's Midlands and the plot, see: Robert Bearman, ed., *Minutes and Accounts of the Stratford-upon-Avon Corporation, 1599–1609*; Michael Hodgetts, 'Coughton and the Gunpowder Plot' in *Catholic Gentry in English Society: The Throckmortons of Coughton from Reformation to Emancipation*, ed. Peter Marshall and Geoffrey Scott (Farnham, Surrey, 2009), 93–121, as well as his 'The Plot in Warwickshire and Worcestershire', *Midland Catholic History* 12 (2006), 16–34; Edgar I. Fripp, *Shakespeare Studies, Biographical and Literary* (Oxford, 1930), as well as his *Shakespeare: Man and Artist*, *Shakespeare's Stratford*, and *Shakespeare's Haunts near Stratford*; Richard Wilson, *Secret Shakespeare: Studies in Theatre, Religion and Resistance* (Manchester, 2004); and W. Salt Brassington, *Shakespeare's Homeland* (London, 1903). For Shakespeare's personal connections to the plotters, see Leslie Hotson, *I, William Shakespeare*

(London, 1937); John W. Hales, 'At Stratford-on-Avon', *Fraser's Magazine* (April 1878), 413–27; and Francis Edwards, trans. and ed., *The Gunpowder Plot: The Narrative of Oswald Tesimond.* On Catholic goods that were seized at Clopton House, see Stratford's Shakespeare Centre Library and Archive, ER 1/1/56; Richard Savage, *Catalogue of the Books, Manuscripts, Works of Art, Antiquities, and Relics at Present Exhibited in Shakespeare's Birthplace* (Stratford-upon-Avon, 1910); and the 'List of such as were apprehended for the Gunpowder Plot. The names of such as were taken in Warwick and Worcestershire and brought to London', British Library Add. MS 5847, ff. 322–323; For the sale of vestments in Stratford in the early 1570s, see J. R. Mulryne, ed., *The Guild and Guild Buildings of Shakespeare's Stratford: Society, Religion, School and Stage* (Farnham, Surrey, 2012), 167.

7. REMEMBER, REMEMBER

This chapter relies on many of the same sources detailed in chapters 5 and 6, especially Mark Nicholls, *Investigating Gunpowder Plot*; James Travers, *Gunpowder*; Antonia Fraser, *The Gunpowder Plot*; Paul Durst, *Intended Treason*; Francis Edwards, *The Enigma of Gunpowder Plot*; Alan Haynes, *The Gunpowder Plot: Faith in Rebellion*; *A True and Perfect Relation of the Whole Proceedings against the Late Most Barbarous Traitors*; Michael Hodgetts, 'Coughton and the Gunpowder Plot' and his 'The Plot in Warwickshire and Worcestershire', along with various state papers. See too Mary Whitmore Jones, *The Gunpowder Plot and the Life of Robert Catesby* (London, 1909). For Sir Thomas Edmondes's letter, see Winwood, *Memorials*, 2:183–4. For a full account of the trial of the plotters, see *A Complete Collection of State Trials, and Proceedings for High-Treason*, ed. Francis Hargrave, 4th edn (London, 1776). For more on the poetry inspired by the Gunpowder Plot, see Edward Hawes, *Trayterous Percyes & Catesbyes Prosopopeia* (London, 1606); Richard F. Hardin, 'The Early

Poetry of the Gunpowder Plot: Myth in the Making', *English Literary Renaissance* 22 (1992), 62–79; Robert Appelbaum, 'Milton, the Gunpowder Plot, and the Mythography of Terror', *Modern Language Quarterly* 68 (2007), 461–91; and David Quint, 'Milton, Fletcher, and the Gunpowder Plot', *Journal of the Warburg and Courtauld Institutes* 54 (1991), 261–8. For '*In Quintum Novembris*' and Milton's other poems about the Fifth of November, as well as translations, see John Milton, *Complete Poems and Major Prose*, ed. Merritt Y. Hughes (1957; Indianapolis, 2003). Sir Arthur Gorges's letter can be found in the Cecil papers. For the smell of gunpowder in *Macbeth*, see Jonathan Gil Harris, 'The Smell of *Macbeth*', *Shakespeare Quarterly* 58 (2007), 465–86. For Ben Jonson's literary response to the Gunpowder Plot, see, in addition to Ian Donaldson's biography, *Ben Jonson: A Life*, Frances Teague, 'Jonson and the Gunpowder Plot', *Ben Jonson Journal* 5 (1998), 249–52, and Richard Dutton, *Ben Jonson, Volpone and the Gunpowder Plot*. The best book on the cultural legacy of the Fifth of November is James Sharpe, *Remember, Remember the Fifth of November: Guy Fawkes and the Gunpowder Plot* (London, 2005). See too: A. W. R. E. Okines, 'Why Was There So Little Reaction to Gunpowder Plot?', *Journal of Ecclesiastical History* 55 (2004), 275–92.

8. *HYMENAEI*

For texts of the masque, see Ben Jonson, *Hymenaei: or The Solemnities of Masque, and Barriers Magnificently Performed on the Eleventh, and Twelfth Nights, from Christmas; at Court* (London: 1606); *The Workes of Benjamin Jonson* (London, 1616); David Lindley, ed., *Hymenaei*, in *The Cambridge Ben Jonson,* 2:657–712; and Stephen Orgel, ed., *Ben Jonson: The Complete Masques* (Yale, 1969). The masque has been well served by critics; see: D. J. Gordon, '*Hymenaei*: Ben Jonson's Masque of Union', *Journal of the Warburg and Courtauld Institute* 8 (1945), 107–45; Stephen Orgel, *The Illusion of Power: Political Theater in the English Renaissance* (Berkeley, 1975);

Stephen Orgel and Roy Strong, *Inigo Jones and the Theatre of the Stuart Court*, 2 vols (Berkeley, 1973); David Lindley, 'Embarrassing Ben: The Masques for Frances Howard', *English Literary Renaissance* 16 (1986), 343–59, as well as his *The Trials of Frances Howard: Fact and Fiction at the Court of King James* (Routledge, 1993); Alastair Bellany, *The Politics of Court Scandal: News Culture and the Overbury Affair, 1603–1660* (Cambridge, 2002); and Martin Butler, *The Stuart Court Masque and Political Culture*. See too: Marie H. Loughlin, '"Love's Friend and Stranger to Virginitie": The Politics of the Virginal Body in Ben Jonson's *Hymenaei* and Thomas Campion's the *Lord Hay's Masque*', *English Literary History* 63 (1996), 833–49; Barbara Ravelhofer, *The Early Stuart Masque: Dance, Costume, and Music* (Oxford, 2006); Lesley Mickel, 'Glorious Spangs and Rich Embroidery: Costume in the *Masque of Blackness* and *Hymenaei*', *Studies in the Literary Imagination* 36 (2003), 41–59; and Kevin Curran, *Marriage, Performance, and Politics at the Jacobean Court* (Burlington, Vermont, 2009). For the costs of performing *Hymenaei*, see *HMC Rutland*, 4:457–8, and W. R. Streitberger, ed., 'Jacobean and Caroline Revels Accounts, 1603–1642', 18. On Queen Elizabeth's wardrobe, see Janet Arnold, *Queen Elizabeth's Wardrobe Unlock'd* (Leeds, 1988). Pory's description of *Hymenaei* can be found in William S. Powell, *John Pory, 1572–1636*. On the barriers, see Alan Young, *Tudor and Jacobean Tournaments*. For *The Tempest* and *Hymenaei*, see Stephen Orgel's discussion of the masque in his edition of *The Tempest* (Oxford, 1982); David Lindley, 'Music, Masque, and Meaning in *The Tempest*' in Lindley, ed. *The Court Masque* (Manchester, 1984), 47–59; Catherine Shaw, '*The Tempest* and *Hymenaei*', *Cahiers Elisabéthains* 26 (1984), 29–39; and Andrew Gurr, '*The Tempest*'s Top', *Notes and Queries* 59 (2012), 550–2. For Tilney and Shakespeare, see, in addition to Richard Dutton, *Mastering the Revels*, Dutton's 'The Court, the Master of the Revels, and the Players' in Dutton, ed., *The Oxford Handbook of Early Modern Theatre*, 362–79; and for Thomas Heywood on the Revels office, see his *Apology for Actors* (London, 1612), E1v.

The courtiers in the masque were Lord Willoughby, Lord Walden, Sir James Hay, the Earl of Montgomery, Sir Thomas Howard, Sir Thomas Somerset, the Earl of Arundel and Sir John Ashley. The young gentlewomen who performed were: Susan Herbert, Countess of Montgomery; Cecily Sackville, daughter of the second Earl of Dorset; Lady Dorothy Hastings, the Earl of Huntingdon's second daughter, married to a Scot, Sir James Stuart; Lucy Russell, Countess of Bedford, elder daughter of Sir John Harington of Exton, and a patron of the arts; Elizabeth Howard, sister of the bride, who had so recently been married off to the ageing Sir William Knollys; Lady Berkeley, daughter of Shakespeare's former patron Sir George Carey, at twenty-nine the oldest of them; Lady Blanche Somerset, sixth daughter of the Earl of Worcester; and Elizabeth Manners, Countess of Rutland, only child of Sir Philip Sidney and Frances Walsingham, stepdaughter to the executed second Earl of Essex, and wife of the fifth Earl of Rutland, a follower of Essex.

9. EQUIVOCATION

I have drawn extensively in this chapter on Mark Nicholls, *Investigating Gunpowder Plot*; James Travers, *Gunpowder*; Antonia Fraser, *The Gunpowder Plot*; Paul Durst, *Intended Treason*; Francis Edwards, *The Enigma of Gunpowder Plot*; Alan Haynes, *The Gunpowder Plot: Faith in Rebellion*; and Michael Hodgetts, 'Coughton and the Gunpowder Plot', as well as Calendars of State Papers Domestic and Venetian, and the exceptionally useful entries in the ODNB. For more detailed studies, see, for Southwell: Pierre Janelle, *Robert Southwell the Writer* (London, 1935); Christopher Devlin, *The Life of Robert Southwell: Poet and Martyr* (London, 1956); R. Simpson, 'Father Southwell and His Capture', *The Rambler*: *A Catholic Journal and Review* n.s. 7 (1857), 98–118; Thomas M. McCoog, *The Society of Jesus in Ireland, Scotland, and England, 1589–1597* (Farnham, Surrey, 2012); Henry Foley, SJ, *Records of the English Province of the Society of Jesus*

(London, 1877), vol. 1, which reprints *A Brefe Discourse of the Condemnation and Execution of Mr. Robert Southwell* (Stonyhurst College, MS Anglia A. III, 1–11); and Nancy Pollard Brown, 'Robert Southwell: The Mission of the Written Word' in *The Reckoned Expense: Edmund Campion and the Early Jesuits* (Woodbridge, Suffolk, 1996), 196–7. For Southwell's late writings, see Robert Southwell, *Two Letters and Short Rules of a Good Life*, ed. Nancy Pollard Brown (Charlottesville, 1973). For an excellent discussion of Anne Bellamy, see Anne Swärdh, *Rape and Religion in English Renaissance Literature* (Uppsala, 2003). For additional information on Bellamy's story, see William Done Bushell, 'The Bellamies of Uxendon. Lecture Delivered before the Harrow Church Reading Union. Feb. 19th, 1914', *Harrow Octocentenary Tracts* 14 (Cambridge, 1914), 1–55; and M. A. Tierney, ed., Charles Dodd [i.e., Henry Tootell], *Church History of England*, vol. 3 (London, 1840), Appendix 37, cxcvii–cxcviii. For Henry Garnet, see: Samuel R. Gardiner and Henry Garnett, 'Two Declarations of Garnet Relating to the Gunpowder Plot', *English Historical Review* 3 (1888), 510–19; Philip Caraman, *Henry Garnet 1555–1606 and the Gunpowder Plot* (London, 1964) and his *A Study in Friendship: Saint Robert Southwell and Henry Garnet* (St Louis, 1995); John Gerard, *The Autobiography of an Elizabethan*, trans. Philip Caraman and intro. Michael Hodgetts (Oxford, 2006); and Edwards, *The Enigma of Gunpowder Plot*. For Garnet's capture, see C. Don Gilbert, 'Thomas Habington's Account of the 1606 Search at Hindlip', *Recusant History* 25 (2001), 415–22. For the fullest contemporary account of Garnet's trial, see *A True and Perfect Relation of the Proceedings at the Severall Arraignments of the Late Most Barbarous Traitors* (London, 1606). See too H. L. Rogers, 'An English Tailor and Father Garnet's Straw', *Review of English Studies* 16 (1965), 44–9.

Garnet's treatise on equivocation, in his hand, can be consulted in Oxford: Bodleian Library, MSS Laud Misc. 655. A second manuscript copy can be found in Rome: Venerable English College, MS. Z. 53 (*Collectanea* F, ff. 8r–39v). It has twice been edited and reprinted, first in David

Jardine, ed., *A Treatise of Equivocation* (London, 1851), and more recently in Henry Garnet, '"Treatise of Equivocation", ca. early 1598' in Ginevra Corsignani, Thomas M. McCoog and Michael Questier, with the assistance of Peter Holmes, eds, *Recusancy and Conformity in Early Modern England: Manuscript and Printed Sources in Translation*, *Monumenta Historica Societatis Iesu*, n.s. 7 (Rome, 2010), 298–343. See too: Archibald E. Malloch and Frank L. Huntley, 'Some Notes on Equivocation', *PMLA* 81 (1966), 145–6; and A. E. Malloch, 'Father Henry Garnet's Treatise of Equivocation', *Recusant History* 15 (1981), 387–95. For early modern equivocation, see, for the seminal tract the English Jesuits drew on heavily: Martin Azpicueta (Doctor Navarrus), *Commentarius in cap. Humanae Aures XXII q. V: de veritate responsi partim verbo, partim mente concepti; et de arte bona et mala simulandi* (Rome, 1584). See too Caraman's translation of John Gerard, *The Autobiography of an Elizabethan*, Appendix E, on 'Southwell's Defense of Equivocation', 279–80, and Appendix F, 'Report of Fr Gerard's Examination concerning Equivocation', 281; Johann P. Sommerville, 'The New Art of Lying: Equivocation, Mental Reservation, and Casuistry' in *Conscience and Casuistry in Early Modern Europe*, ed. Edmund Leites (Cambridge, 1988), 159–84; Stefania Tutino, 'Nothing But the Truth? Hermeneutics and Morality in the Doctrines of Equivocation and Mental Reservation in Early Modern Europe', *Renaissance Quarterly* 64 (2011), 115–55, and her *Law and Conscience: Catholicism in Early Modern England, 1570–1625* (Aldershot, Hampshire, 2007); A. E. Malloch, 'Equivocation: A Circuit of Reasons' in Patricia Bruckmann, ed., *Familiar Colloquy: Essays Presented to Arthur Barker* (Ottawa, 1978), 132–43; Janet E. Halley, 'Equivocation and the Legal Conflict over Religious Identity in Early Modern England', *Yale Journal of Law & the Humanities* 3 (1991), 33–52; Paula McQuade, 'Truth and Consequences: Equivocation, Inwardness, and the Secret Catholic Subject in Early Modern England', *Ben Jonson Journal* (2001), 277–90; Arthur Marotti, *Religious Ideology and Cultural Fantasy: Catholic and Anti-Catholic Discourses in Early Modern England* (Notre Dame,

2005); Michael Carrafiello, 'Robert Parsons and Equivocation, 1606–1610', *Catholic Historical Review* 79 (1993), 671–80; and Todd Butler, 'Equivocation, Cognition, and Political Authority in Early Modern England,' *Texas Studies in Literature and Language* 54 (2012), 132–54. For contemporary treatises that engage equivocation, see Thomas Morton, *An Exact Discovery of Romish Doctrine in the Case of Conspiracie and Rebellion* (London, 1605); Thomas Morton, *Full Satisfaction Concerning a Double Romish Inquiry, Rebellion, and Equivocation* (London, 1606); Robert Parsons, *A Treatise Tending to Mitigation* (London, 1607); and the Earl of Salisbury's *An Answer to Certain Scandalous Papers* (London, 1606). Bill Cain's wonderful play on this subject, *Equivocation* (2009), published in 2014 by the Dramatist's Play Service, is highly recommended.

For *Henry the Sixth, Part 2* and witchcraft, see: Nina S. Levine, 'The Case of Eleanor Cobham: Authorizing History in *2 Henry VI*', *Shakespeare Studies* 22 (1994), 104–21, and Ronald Knowles, ed., *King Henry VI, Part 2* (London, 1999). For Puttenham and his influence on Shakespeare, see: George Puttenham, *The Art of English Poesy*, ed. Frank Wigham and Wayne A. Rebhorn (Ithaca, 2007); and William Lowes Rushton, *Shakespeare and 'The Arte of English Poesie'* (Liverpool, 1909). For Coke (including his use of Shakespeare), see: Robert Pricket, *The Lord Coke His Speech and Charge* (London, 1607), which recounts Coke's 4 August 1606 address at the Norwich Assizes; and Marc L. Schwarz, 'Sir Edward Coke and "This Scept'red Isle": A Case of Borrowing', *Notes & Queries* 233 (1988), 54–6. See too Allen D. Boyer, *Sir Edward Coke and the Elizabethan Age* (Stanford, 2003), and F. A. Inderwick, *A Calendar of the Inner Temple Records* (London, 1898), vol. 2.

10. ANOTHER HELL ABOVE THE GROUND

For Francis Bacon's letter to Tobie Matthew, see James Spedding, ed., *Letters and Life of Francis Bacon*, 7 vols (London, 1861–74), 4:10. For a discussion of the print of 'The Powder Treason', see Michael Hunter, ed., *Printed Images in Early Modern England: Essays in Interpretation* (Farnham, Surrey, 2010), and Jonathan Bate and Dora Thornton, eds, *Shakespeare: Staging the World* (New York, 2012). The undated broadsides from which its language draws, *Princeps Proditorum: The Popes Darling: Or, a Guide to his Twelve Apostles*, date most likely from 1606 or 1607; only the first of these is extant and can be found in the British Museum. For Coleridge and De Quincey on the knocking in *Macbeth*, see Samuel Taylor Coleridge, *Lectures 1808–1819 on Literature II*, in *The Collected Works*, vol. 5, ed. R. A. Foakes (Princeton, 1987), 149; Thomas De Quincey, 'On the Knocking at the Gate in Macbeth', first published in the *London Magazine* (October, 1823) and reprinted in *The Collected Writings of Thomas De Quincey*, ed. David Masson, vol. 10 (1890), 389–94. For Garnet as 'Mister Farmer', see Glyn Redworth, ed., *The Letters of Luisa de Carvajal y Mendoza*, 1:118. For equivocation and *Macbeth*, see, in addition to discussions in the introductions to the major editions of the play, Frank L. Huntley, 'Macbeth and the Background of Jesuitical Equivocation', *PMLA* 79 (1964), 390–400; and H. L. Rogers, *'Double Profit' in Macbeth* (Melbourne, 1964). See too, more generally: Henry N. Paul, *The Royal Play of Macbeth*; Stephen Greenblatt, 'Shakespeare Bewitched' in *New Historical Literary Study: Essays on Reproducing Texts, Representing History* (Princeton, 1993), 108–35; and Arthur F. Kinney, *Lies Like Truth: Shakespeare, Macbeth, and the Cultural Moment* (Detroit, 2001). And for the vision of the knives and halter in Harsnett, see Brownlow, *Shakespeare, Harsnett, and the Devils of Denham.* For John Deacon and John Walker's book on Darrell, see: *A Summarie Answere to Al the Material Points in Any of Master Darel His Bookes* (London, 1601). For Lancelot Andrewes's Gunpowder sermons, see his *XCVI Sermons*, where they are arranged chronologically. For sermons and tracts from 1606 that touch on equivocation, see: John Dove, 'A Sermon Preached at St Paul's Cross the First of June 1606', Folger MS V.a.151; and Lancelot Andrewes, 'A Sermon Preached before Two Kings, on the Fifth of August, 1606', appended to *XCVI Sermons* (London, 1641). And for Oliver Ormerod, see his *The Picture of a Papist* (London, 1606). For Forman's widely reprinted account of a performance of *Macbeth*, see Nicholas Brooke's Oxford edition, 234–6.

I am deeply grateful to Nathalie Cohen at the National Trust as well as James Wright at the Museum of London Archaeology and to their colleagues for sharing with me and discussing their fascinating research about the apotropaic symbols at Knole. I am also grateful to the National Trust for allowing me to draw here on a commissioned report, 'Knole House: Under-floor Survey', which will soon appear in article form, the substance of which was reported to the press in November 2014 and can be found in articles published in a number of British newspapers at that time, including, for example, the *Guardian* (http://www.theguardian.com/culture/2014/nov/05/witch-marks-king-james-i-knole-sevenoaks-national-trust).

For Thomas Middleton and *Macbeth*, in addition to the introductions to the Oxford, Cambridge and Arden editions, see Gary Taylor and John Lavagnino, eds, *Thomas Middleton: The Collected Works* (Oxford, 2007), as well as their companion volume, *Thomas Middleton and Early Modern Textual Culture* (Oxford, 2007). On the myth of the curse of *Macbeth*, see Laurie Maguire and Emma Smith, *30 Great Myths about Shakespeare* (Chichester, West Sussex, 2013); see too Stanley Wells, 'Shakespeare in Max Beerbohm's Theatre Criticism', *Shakespeare Survey* 29 (1976), 133–45. On Jonson's *Volpone*, see Richard Dutton's introduction to the play in David Bevington, Martin Butler and Ian Donaldson, eds, *The Cambridge Edition of the Works of Ben Jonson*, vol. 3, as well as Dutton's *Ben Jonson, Volpone and the Gunpowder Plot*. See too James P. Bednarz, 'Was *Volpone* Acted at Cambridge in 1606?', *Ben Jonson Journal* 17 (2010), 183–96; Martin Butler, 'Ben Jonson's Catholicism', *Ben Jonson Journal* 19 (2012), 190–216; and James Tulip, 'Comedy as Equivocation: An Approach to the Reference of *Volpone*', *Southern Review* 5 (1972), 91–100, and his 'The

Contexts of *Volpone*' in *Imperfect Apprehensions: Essays in English Literature in Honour of G. A. Wilkes* (Sydney, 1996), 74–87. For what we know of the *Isle of Gulls* scandal, see Sir Edward Hoby's letter to Sir Thomas Edmondes on 7 March 1606, in Thomas Birch, *The Court and Times of James the First*, 1:60–1; and Lucy Munro, *Children of the Queen's Revels*, 29.

11. THE KING'S EVIL

For accounts of the rumour that King James had been assassinated, see: *Calendar of State Papers Venetian*, 1603–1607, 332–3; Chamberlain's letter is reprinted in Winwood's *Memorials*; Arthur Wilson, *History of Great Britain*, 32–3; John Stow, *The Abridgement or Summarie of the English Chronicle* (1607); Stow, *Annales* (1614); David Harris Willson, *The Parliamentary Diary of Robert Bowyer*, 88–91; and Edmund Lodge, ed., *Illustrations of British History, Biography, and Manners* (London, 1791), 3:305–6. On Gowrie, see: *The Earle of Gowries Conspiracy against the Kings Majestie. At Saint Johnstown upon Tuesday the Fifth Day of August* (London, 1603); Samuel Garey, *Great Brittans Little Calendar*; Andrew Lang, *James VI and the Gowrie Mystery* (London, 1902); and Edward Cardwell, *Documentary Annals of the Reformed Church of England*, 2nd edn, 2 vols (Oxford, 1844), 2:59. See too the ODNB entries on John and Alexander Ruthven. On Lancelot Andrewes's doubts about the veracity of the Gowrie story, see John Hacket, *A Century of Sermons* (London, 1675). On Gowrie and witchcraft, see Roy Booth, '*Macbeth*, King James and Witchcraft' in Lawrence Normand and Gareth Roberts, eds, *Witchcraft in Early Modern Scotland* (Exeter, 2000), 47–68.

On the Evil: see William Clowes, *Right Fruitful and Approved Treatise, for the Artificial Cure of That Malady Called in Latin Struma, and in English, the Evil* (London, 1602); Raymond Crawfurd, *The King's Evil* (Oxford, 1911); Marc Bloch, *The Royal Touch: Monarchy and Miracles in France and England*, trans. J. E. Anderson (1961; New York, 1989); Keith

Thomas, *Religion and the Decline of Magic*, 192–8; Deborah Willis, 'The Monarch and the Sacred: Shakespeare and the Ceremony for the Healing of the King's Evil' in Linda Woodbridge and Edward Berry, eds, *True Rites and Maimed Rites: Ritual and Anti-Ritual in Shakespeare and His Age* (Chicago, 1992), 147–68; and Daniel Fusch, 'The Discourse of the Unmiraculous Miracle: Touching for the King's Evil in Stuart England', *Appositions: Studies in Renaissance / Early Modern Literature & Culture* 1 (2008). See too Richard C. McCoy, '"The Grace of Grace" and Double-Talk in *Macbeth*', *Shakespeare Survey* 57 (2004), 27–37; and Frank Barlow, 'The King's Evil', *English Historical Review* 95 (1980), 3–27. For James touching for the evil in 1606, see *Calendar of State Papers Venetian*, 10:44. On the possibility that the scene about the Evil was partly censored, see Nevill Coghill, 'Have We Lost Some Part of the Scene at the Court of King Edward the Confessor?' in *The Triple Bond*, ed. Joseph G. Price (London, 1975), 230–4.

On the second Hampton Court Conference, see James Melvill, *The Autobiography and Diary of Mr. James Melvill*, ed. Robert Pitcairn (Edinburgh, 1842), 653–7. For the four sermons, see: William Barlow, *One of the Four Sermons Preached before the Kings Majestie at Hampton Court* (London, 1606); John Buckeridge, *A Sermon Preached at Hampton Court before the Kings Majestie* (London, 1606); Lancelot Andrewes, *A Sermon Preached before the Kings Majestie, at Hampton Court* (London, 1606); and John King, *The Fourth Sermon Preached at Hampton Court* (Oxford, 1606). See too: Peter E. McCullough, *Sermons at Court* (Cambridge, 1998); David Calderwood, *The History of the Kirk of Scotland*, ed. T. Thomson and D. Laing (Edinburgh, 1842–9), 6:477–81, 568–83; the ODNB entry on Andrew Melville; and Lori Anne Ferrell's illuminating *Government by Polemic: James I, the King's Preachers, and the Rhetorics of Conformity, 1603–1625* (Stanford, 1998). See Redworth, *The Letters of Luisa de Carvajal y Mendoza*, 1:118, for the gossip about the 'treasonous' ministers. On the 'Act To Restrain Many Abuses of Players', see: Sir Edward Hoby's letter to Sir

Thomas Edmondes on 7 March 1606, in Thomas Birch, *The Court and Times of James the First,* 1:60–1; and Hugh Gazzard, 'An Act to Restrain Abuses of Players (1606)', *Review of English Studies* 61 (2010), 495–528. Surprisingly, scholars have not linked Hoby's letter to the parliamentary action against the players. See too, Dutton, *Mastering the Revels*; and Gary Taylor and John Jowett, *Shakespeare Reshaped, 1606–1623* (Oxford, 1993). On the magical mirror in *Macbeth*, see: the 'Diary of the Journey of Philip Julius, Duke of Stettin-Pomerania, through England in the Year 1602', ed. Gottfried von Bülow and Wilfred Powell, *Transactions of the Royal Historical Society*, n. s. 6 (1892), 57; and Margaret Downs-Gamble, '"To the Crack of Doom": Sovereign Imagination as Anamorphosis in Shakespeare's "Show of Kings"' in Willy Maley and Rory Loughnane, eds, *Celtic Shakespeare: The Bard and the Borderers* (Farnham, Surrey, 2013), 157–68.

On the Oath of Allegiance, see Bernard Bourdin, *The Theological-Political Origins of the Modern State: The Controversy between James I of England & Cardinal Bellarmine*, trans. Susan Pickford (Washington, DC, 2010); Michael Questier, 'Loyalty, Religion and State Power in Early Modern England: English Romanism and the Jacobean Oath of Allegiance', *Historical Journal* 40 (1997), 311–29; Michael Questier, 'Catholic Loyalism in Early Stuart England', *English Historical Review* 123 (2008), 1132–65; and Stefania Tutino, *Law and Conscience*. For parliamentary actions, see *The Parliamentary Diary of Robert Bowyer.* The information about Susanna Shakespeare was discovered in 1964: see Hugh A. Hanley, 'Shakespeare Family in Stratford Records', *Times Literary Supplement*, 21 May 1964, 441. For more on Susanna Shakespeare and recusants in Stratford-upon-Avon, see: E. R. C. Brinkworth, *Shakespeare and the Bawdy Court of Stratford* (London, 1972); Schoenbaum, *William Shakespeare: A Documentary Life*; and Park Honan, *Shakespeare: A Life*. And for Luisa de Carvajal y Mendoza's account of the experience of English Catholics at this time, see Redworth, ed., *The Letters of Luisa De Carvajal y Mendoza.*

12. UNFINISHED BUSINESS

On the possibility of an Elizabethan sequel to *Julius Caesar*, see Geoffrey Bullough, *Narrative and Dramatic Sources of Shakespeare*, 5: 215–19. For Fulke Greville and the destruction of his play, see: Ronald A. Rebholz, *The Life of Fulke Greville, First Lord Brooke* (Oxford, 1971); Joan Rees, *Fulke Greville, Lord Brooke, 1554–1628: A Critical Biography* (Berkeley, 1971); and the ODNB entry for Fulke Greville. For a modern edition of Greville's *Life of Sidney* and his *A Letter to an Honourable Lady*, see Mark Caldwell, ed., *The Prose of Fulke Greville, Lord Brooke* (New York, 1987). For more on the Essex circle, see Paul E. J. Hammer, *The Polarisation of Elizabethan Politics. The Political Career of Robert Devereux, 2nd Earl of Essex, 1585–1597* (Cambridge, 1999), as well as Hammer's ODNB entry on Essex. And for earlier Cleopatra plays, see: Karen Raber, *Dramatic Difference: Gender, Class, and Genre in the Early Modern Closet Drama* (Cranbury, New Jersey, 2001), and Paulina Kewes, '"A fit memoriall for the times to come . . .": Admonition and Topical Application in Mary Sidney's *Antonius* and Samuel Daniel's *Cleopatra*', *Review of English Studies* 63 (2012), 243–64.

For Shakespeare's use of Plutarch in *Antony and Cleopatra*, see C. B. R. Pelling, ed., Plutarch, *Life of Antony* (Cambridge, 1988), esp. 37–45; M. W. MacCallum, *Shakespeare's Roman Plays and Their Background* (London, 1910); and Gordon Braden, 'Shakespeare' in Mark Beck, ed., *A Companion to Plutarch* (Chichester, 2014), 577–91. See too *Cleopatra: A Sphinx Revisited*, ed. Margaret M. Miles (Berkeley, 2011), and the excellent discussions in the introductions to the Arden, Oxford and Cambridge editions of the play, as well as Marvin Spevack's extensive discussion in his Variorum edition. On source traditions, in addition to Bullough, *Narrative and Dramatic Sources*, and Muir, *The Sources of Shakespeare's Plays*, see Marilyn L. Williamson, *Infinite Variety: Antony and Cleopatra in Renaissance Drama and Earlier Tradition* (Mystic, Conn., 1974). I have quoted Montaigne's 'The History of Spurina' from the Everyman edition of John

Florio's translation: Montaigne, *Essays*, 3 vols (New York, 1980), 2:462. For G. B. Shaw on the play, see his Preface to *Three Plays for Puritans* (London, 1900). For my discussion of the style and structure of *Antony and Cleopatra* I am profoundly indebted to Janet Adelman's wonderful book, which remains the best on the play: *The Common Liar: An Essay on Antony and Cleopatra* (New Haven, 1973). For more on Enobarbus, see Elkin Calhoun Wilson, 'Shakespeare's Enobarbus' in James G. McManaway et al., eds, *Joseph Quincy Adams Memorial Studies* (Washington, DC, 1948), 291–408. And for a pair of reflections on the cultural contexts of *Antony and Cleopatra*, quite different from my own, see Paul Yachnin, '"Courtiers of Beauteous Freedom": *Antony and Cleopatra* in Its Time', *Renaissance and Reformation* 26 (1991), 1–20, as well as his 'Shakespeare's Politics of Loyalty: Sovereignty and Subjectivity in *Antony and Cleopatra*', *Studies in English Literature* 33 (1993), 343–63. On the remarkable portrait of what is persuasively argued to be Lady Anne Clifford in the guise of Cleopatra, see Yasmin Arshad, 'The Enigma of a Portrait: Lady Anne Clifford and Daniel's *Cleopatra*', *The British Art Journal* 11 (2011), 22–3. On Samuel Daniel's revisions to his *Cleopatra* and his debt to Shakespeare: see M. Lederer, *Daniel's The Tragedie of Cleopatra nach em Drucke von 1611* (Louvain, 1911); Joan Rees, 'An Elizabethan Eyewitness of *Antony and Cleopatra*', *Shakespeare Survey* 6 (1953), 91–3; and Arthur M. Z. Norman, 'Daniel's *The Tragedy of Cleopatra* and the Date of *Antony and Cleopatra*', *Modern Language Review* 54 (1959), 1–9.

13. QUEEN OF SHEBA

On the visit of King Christian to England in 1606, see John Chamberlain's *Letters*; Howes's continuation of Stow's *Annales*; letters in Winwood's *Memorials*; the French and Italian ambassadors' accounts; and the following contemporary sources: Anon., *The King of Denmarkes Welcome* (London, 1606); and Henry Robarts, *The Most Royall and Honourable*

Entertainement of the Famous and Renowmed King Christiern [*sic*] (London, 1606) and his *England's Farewell to Christian the Fourth* (London, 1606). On Christian's fleet and his flagship, the *Tre kroner*, see Martin J. Bellamy, *Christian IV and His Navy: A Political and Administrative History of the Danish Navy, 1596–1648* (Boston, 2006). For Christian's criticism of James's treatment of his sister, see de la Boderie, *Ambassades*, 1:311. For the cultural significance of Christian's visit and its links to *Antony and Cleopatra*, see the path-breaking work of H. Neville Davies, especially 'Jacobean *Antony and Cleopatra*', *Shakespeare Studies* 17 (1985), 123–58. See too his 'The Limitations of Festival: Christian IV's State Visit to England in 1606' in J. R. Mulryne and Margaret Shewring, eds, *Italian Renaissance Festivals and Their European Influence* (Lewiston, New York, 1992), and, in collaboration with J. W. Binns, 'Christian IV and *The Dutch Courtesan*', *Theatre Notebook* 44 (1990), 118–22. On the ambassadorial visit of Henrik Ramel in August 1605, see John Nichols, *Progresses . . . of King James*, 1:577; on Shakespeare's role as a Groom of the Chamber, see Ernest Law, *Shakespeare as a Groom of the Chamber* (London, 1910). For James's self-representation as Caesar, see Kevin Sharpe, *Image Wars*, 80–1, and Edward Hawkins, Augustus Franks and Herbert Grueber, *Medallic Illustrations of the History of Great Britain and Ireland*, 2 vols (London, 1885), 1:187, 191. For the newly created Union flag, in addition to the royal proclamation of 12 April 1606 'declaring what flags South and North Britaines shall bear at sea' in Larkin and Hughes, *Stuart Royal Proclamations*, 135–6, see Nick Groom, *The Union Jack: The Story of the British Flag* (London, 2006). For a letter from Scottish shipmasters (dated 1 August 1606) complaining about the design, see the *Register of the Privy Council of Scotland*, 7:498. On the responses of English writers to the visit, see John Marston, 'The Argument of the Spectacle Presented to the Sacred Majesties of Great Britain and Denmark as They Passed through London' in *The Poems of John Marston*, ed. Arnold Davenport (Liverpool, 1961), 185–8; for John Ford, see the excellent introduction to 'Honor Triumphant' and

'The Monarches Meeting', as well as an excellent chronology of King Christian's visit, in *The Collected Works of John Ford*, ed. Gilles Monsarrat, Brian Vickers and R. J. C. Watt, vol. 1 (Oxford, 2012); John Davies of Hereford, *Bien Venu: Great Britaines Welcome to Her Great Friends, and Deare Brethren, the Danes* (London, 1606); Edmund Bolton, *Tricorones* (London, 1607); and *Charites Oxonienses sive Laetitia Musarum*, British Library Royal MS 12 A. LXIV.

For the Jamestown expedition, see: Philip L. Barbour, *The Jamestown Voyages under the First Charter, 1606–1609*, 2 vols (London, 1969); Karen Ordahl Kupperman, *The Jamestown Project* (Cambridge, Mass., 2007); and Peter C. Mancall, *Hakluyt's Promise: An Elizabethan Obsession for an English America* (New Haven, 2007). And for the unsuccessful 'Northern Virginia' expedition that sailed for the coast of Maine in August 1606, not discussed here, see Henry S. Burrage, *The Beginnings of Colonial Maine, 1602–1658* (Portland, Maine, 1914). For the poem celebrating the enterprise, see Michael Drayton, 'To the Virginian Voyage. Ode 11', *Poemes Lyrick and Pastorall* (London, 1606). The poem was entered in the Stationers' Register on 19 April 1606, a week after Hakluyt signed on as a grantee of the Charter. Andrewes's Gowrie Day sermon was first published in Latin in 1610, though not in English until added to his collected *Ninety-Six Sermons* in 1641. For an excellent discussion of this sermon, see Lori Anne Ferrell, *Government by Polemic*, 88–95. For the extravagant expense of food and drink at Theobalds – as well as the fees paid to Ben Jonson and Inigo Jones – see Hatfield House, Cecil Papers, 111, f. 162, which can be accessed through the *Cambridge Edition of the Works of Ben Jonson Online*. On Christian's drinking and womanising, see Michael Srigley, '"Heavy-headed revel east and west": Hamlet and Christian IV of Denmark' in *Shakespeare and Scandinavia* (Newark, 2002), 168–92. For Harington's letter, see *Nugae Antiquae*, 1:348–54. For analysis of it, see Martin Butler, *Stuart Court Masque*; William Tate, 'King James I and the Queen of Sheba', *English Literary Renaissance* 26 (1996), 561–85; Clare

McManus, 'When is a Woman Not a Woman?', *Modern Philology* 105 (2008), 437–74; and J. Scott-Warren, *Sir John Harington and the Book as Gift* (Oxford, 2001), 185–8. On King James as Solomon, see Maurice Lee, Jr., *Great Britain's Solomon*. And for the anonymous letter warning James, see Friedrich Ludwig von Raumer, *History of the Sixteenth and Seventeenth Centuries*, 2 vols (London, 1835), 2:217.

On nostalgia for Queen Elizabeth, links between her and Cleopatra, and her monument, see: Helen Morris, 'Queen Elizabeth I "Shadowed" in Cleopatra', *Huntington Library Quarterly* 32 (1969), 271–8; Keith Rinehart, 'Shakespeare's Cleopatra and England's Elizabeth', *Shakespeare Quarterly* 23 (1972), 81–6; Hannah Betts, 'The Image of this Queene so Quaynt: The Pornographic Blazon, 1588–1603', in *Dissing Elizabeth: Negative Representations of Gloriana*, ed. Julia M. Walker (London, 1998), 153–84; Anne Barton, 'Harking Back to Elizabeth: Ben Jonson and Caroline Nostalgia', *English Literary History* 48 (1981), 706–31; Peter Hyland, 'Re-membering Gloriana: *The Revenger's Tragedy*' in Elizabeth H. Hageman and Katherine Conway, eds, *Resurrecting Elizabeth I in Seventeenth-Century England* (Madison, New Jersey, 2007), 82–94; Catherine Loomis, *The Death of Elizabeth: Remembering and Reconstructing the Virgin Queen* (New York, 2010), 119–56; Julia Walker, *The Elizabethan Icon, 1603–2003* (New York, 2004); Nigel Llewellyn, 'The Royal Body: Monuments to the Dead for the Living' in *Renaissance Bodies: The Human Figure in English Culture*, ed. Lucy Gent and Nigel Llewellyn (1990), 218–40; and David Howarth, *Images of Rule: Art and Politics in the English Renaissance, 1485–1649* (London, 1997). On the funeral effigies in Westminster, see Margaret Owens, 'Afterlives of the Royal Funeral Effigies', *Paper Presented at the Annual Meeting of the RSA, Grand Hyatt, Washington, D.C.*, 21 March 2012; see too her 'Effigy and Ruin: *The Revenger's Tragedy* as *Trauerspiel*' (forthcoming in *Studies in English Literature*, 2015), and her book in progress, tentatively entitled *Afterlives of the Royal Funeral Effigies.* For details about their construction, see W. H. St John Hope, 'On the Funeral Effigies of the Kings and Queens of England', with a 'Note on the Westminster Tradition of Identification' by Joseph Armitage Robinson, *Archaeologia* 60 (1907), 517–70; and R. P. Howgrave-Graham, 'Royal Portraits in Effigy: Some New Discoveries in Westminster Abbey', *Journal of the Royal Society of the Arts* 101 (1953), 465–74; Anthony Harvey and Richard Mortimer, eds, *The Funeral Effigies of Westminster Abbey*, rev. edn (Woodbridge, 2003); and A. P. Stanley, *Historical Memorials of Westminster Abbey*, 5th edn, (London, 1882). See too Jennifer Woodward, 'Images of a Dead Queen', *History Today* 47 (1997), 18–23; and her *The Theatre of Death: The Ritual Management of Royal Funerals in Renaissance England, 1570–1625* (Woodbridge, Suffolk, 1997). For Bishop Godfrey Goodman's nostalgia for Elizabeth, see *The Court of King James the First*, 2 vols (London, 1839), 1:98. For Bacon's letter about Elizabeth's tomb, see Spedding, ed., *Letters and Life of Francis Bacon*, 3:249–50.

14. PLAGUE

For the history of plague in early modern England, see Paul Slack, *The Impact of Plague in Tudor and Stuart England*; J. F. D. Shrewsbury, *A History of Bubonic Plague in the British Isles*; F. P. Wilson, *The Plague in Shakespeare's London*; and Charles Creighton, *A History of Epidemics in Britain*. See especially Leeds Barroll's *Politics, Plague, and Shakespeare's Theater*, and his earlier 'The Chronology of Shakespeare's Jacobean Plays and the Dating of *Antony and Cleopatra*' in *Essays on Shakespeare*, ed. Gordon Ross Smith (University Park, 1965), 115–62. See too Rebecca Totaro and Ernest P. Gilman, eds, *Representing the Plague in Early Modern England* (New York, 2011); Ernest P. Gilman, *Plague Writing in Early Modern England* (Chicago, 2009); and Rebecca Totaro, *The Plague in Print: Essential Elizabethan Sources, 1558–1603* (Pittsburgh, 2010). We owe the survival of plague records, otherwise destroyed in the Great Fire of 1666, to John Bell, *London's Remembrancer: Or a True Accompt of Every Particular Week's*

Christenings and Mortality in All the Years of Pestilence (London, 1665). See John Graunt's *Natural and Political Observations* (London, 1662) for annual plague figures from 1605 to 1610. For Dekker's extensive writings on the plague, see F. P. Wilson, ed., *The Plague Pamphlets of Thomas Dekker*, and E. D. Pendry, ed., *Thomas Dekker*, The Stratford-upon-Avon Library 4 (Cambridge, Mass., 1968). For other sources and letters on the plague, see John Chamberlain's *Letters*, as well as *The Letters of Luisa de Carvajal y Mendoza*. For the contemporary recipe for treating plague, see Mrs Corlyon, *A Booke of Such Medicines as have been Approved by the Speciall Practize* (*c.*1606), Folger MS Add 334. For the regulation of the plague see, in addition to Wilson, Slack, Barroll and various State Papers, foreign and domestic, the *Analytic Index to the Series of Records Known as the Remembrancia. Preserved among the Archives of the City of London. A.D. 1579–1664* (London, 1878). For Stock's sermon, see Richard Stock, *A Sermon Preached at Paules Crosse, the Second of November 1606* (London, 1609). For Simon Forman's unpublished manuscripts, housed in the Bodleian Library, Oxford, see especially Ashmole MS 1436, f. 72. I am deeply grateful to Elizabeth Williamson for transcribing the relevant materials for 1606 from this archive. For more on Forman, see: Barbara Traister, *The Notorious Astrological Physician of London* (Chicago, 2001), as well as her '"A plague on both your houses": Sites of Comfort and Terror in Early Modern Drama' in *Representing the Plague in Early Modern England*, 169–82; and Lauren Kassell, *Medicine and Magic in Elizabethan London: Simon Forman, Astrologer, Alchemist, and Physician* (Oxford, 2005). For Shakespeare and the Mountjoys, see Charles Nicholl's illuminating *The Lodger: Shakespeare on Silver Street* (London, 2007), which includes a transcription of Shakespeare's testimony, and Alan H. Nelson, 'Calling All (Shakespeare) Biographers! Or, a Plea for Documentary Discipline' in Takashi Kozuka and J. R. Mulryne, eds, *Shakespeare, Marlowe, Jonson: New Directions in Biography* (Aldershot, Hampshire, 2006), 55–67. I am indebted to Alan Nelson for his path-breaking work transcribing the parish records of St Olave's. For this and other London parishes, consult Ancestry.com.

For sources confirming that the theatres were reopening in the late autumn and early winter of 1606, see, for the Queen's Men, Mark Eccles, 'Elizabethan Actors II: E–J', *Notes & Queries* 236 (1991), 456, and Eva Griffith, *A Jacobean Company and Its Playhouse*; for the Children of the Queen's Revels: Lucy Munro, *Children of the Queen's Revels* and H. N. Hillebrand, *The Child Actors*, 197–8. If further confirmation were needed that the playhouses had reopened, we have it at the other end of the season: on 12 April 1607, a week after Easter, when the number of weekly plague deaths was at twenty-three, the Lord Mayor, still anxious about recurrent plague now that spring and warmer weather had arrived, wrote to the Lord Chamberlain requesting his help 'in restraining such common stage plays as are daily shown and exercised and do occasion the great assemblies of all sorts of people in the suburbs and parts adjoining to this city'. He also asks that, in an effort to keep plague numbers down, the privy councillors give orders 'that there may be a better care had of Whitechapel, Shoreditch, Clerkenwell' – that is to say, where the actors in the northern suburbs were then playing at the Boar's Head, Curtain and Red Bull theatres (as quoted in Tanya Pollard, ed., *Shakespeare's Theater: A Sourcebook* [Oxford, 2004], 328–9). See, on Tilney's billing for court activities this year, W. R. Streitberger, ed., 'Jacobean and Caroline Revels Accounts, 1603–1642', 15–25. See too, on the flexibility of plague closures, Andrew Gurr, *The Shakespearian Playing Companies*, 87–92. For more on the theatrical scene in 1606 that I draw upon, see Chambers, *The Elizabethan Stage*; Andrew Gurr, *The Shakespeare Company* and *Shakespeare's Opposites*; Reavley Gair, *The Children of St Paul's*; Frederick G. Fleay, *A Chronicle History of the London Stage 1559–1642* (London, 1890); H. N. Hillebrand, 'The Children of the King's Revels at Whitefriars', *Journal of English and Germanic Philology* 21 (1922), 318–4; Albert H. Tricomi, *Anticourt Drama in England, 1603–1642* (Charlottesville, 1989); William

Ingram, 'The Playhouse as an Investment, 1607–1614: Thomas Woodford and Whitefriars', *Medieval and Renaissance Drama in England* 2 (1985), 209–30; Julian Bowsher, *Shakespeare's London Theatreland*; Eva Griffith, 'Martin Slater and the Red Bull Playhouse', *Huntington Library Quarterly* 74 (2011), 553–74; David Kathman, 'How Old Were Shakespeare's Boy Actors?', *Shakespeare Survey* 58 (2005), 220–46; R. V. Holdsworth, '*The Revenger's Tragedy* on the Stage' in R. V. Holdsworth, ed., *Three Jacobean Revenge Tragedies: A Casebook* (London, 1990), 105, 118–19; Roslyn L. Knutson, 'Falconer to the Little Eyases: A New Date and Commercial Agenda for the "Little Eyases" Passage in *Hamlet*', *Shakespeare Quarterly* 46 (1995), 1–31; and for Thomas Middleton's career at this time, see Gary Taylor, ed., *The Collected Works of Thomas Middleton* and *Thomas Middleton and Early Modern Textual Culture: A Companion to The Collected Works*. For the 'Mirror of Great Britain,' see Roy Strong, 'Three Royal Jewels: the Three Brothers, the Mirror of Great Britain and the Feather', *Burlington Magazine* 108 (1966), 350–2.

EPILOGUE

For more on Lancelot Andrewes, see Peter McCullough, ed., *Lancelot Andrewes: Selected Sermons and Lectures* (Oxford, 2005), as well as his *Sermons at Court*. For the Nativity sermons, see Andrewes's *XCVI Sermons*. For Whitehall Palace, see Simon Thurley, *Whitehall Palace* and his *The Royal Palaces of Tudor England*. For the fact that Whitehall's Great Chamber was prepared for plays this December, see W. R. Streitberger, ed., 'Jacobean and Caroline Revels Accounts, 1603-1642', 13. Lord Harington's letter to his cousin can be found in Harington, *Nugae Antiquae*, 1:371–5.

On the vexed textual issues raised by *King Lear*, see Richard Knowles, 'The Evolution of the Texts of *Lear*' in Jeffrey Kahan, ed., *King Lear: New Critical Essays* (New York, 2008), 124–55; Madeleine Doran, *The Text of King Lear* (Stanford, 1931) and her 'Elements in the Composition of *King Lear*', *Studies in Philology* 30 (1933), 34–58; Steven Urkowitz, *Shakespeare's Revision of King Lear* (Princeton, 1980); Gary Taylor and Michael Warren, eds, *The Division of the Kingdoms: Shakespeare's Two Versions of King Lear* (Oxford, 1983); and Peter W. M. Blayney, *The Texts of King Lear and Their Origins* (Cambridge, 1982). For the cultural shifts marked by the production history of *King Lear*, see R. A. Foakes, *Hamlet versus Lear: Cultural Politics and Shakespeare's Art* (Cambridge, 1993). See too Alexander Pope, *The Works of Shakespear*, 6 vols (London, 1723–5); Nahum Tate, *The History of King Lear* (London, 1681); and for Samuel Johnson on the ending of the play, see Arthur Sherbo, ed., *Johnson on Shakespeare*, 659–705. For the suggestion that Shakespeare wrote *Cymbeline*, *The Winter's Tale* and *The Tempest* in close proximity to each other, see John Pitcher's excellent introduction to his Arden edition of *The Winter's Tale* (London, 2010).

Acknowledgements

I'm deeply indebted to the friends and scholars – James Bednarz, Stanley Wells, Richard McCoy, Mary Cregan, Alvin Snider, Robert Griffin, Andrew Hadfield and David Kastan – who patiently read early drafts and challenged me to write a better book. Others provided crucial assistance along the way. In a singular act of generosity, Mairi Macdonald, formerly head of local collections at the Shakespeare Birthplace Trust, gave me her extensive cache of records relating to Warwickshire and the Gunpowder Plot. Robert Bearman, retired head of archives at the Shakespeare Birthplace Trust, was also helpful on this subject. Lori Anne Ferrell steered me to a crucial Lancelot Andrewes sermon of which I was unaware; John Pitcher shared his great knowledge of Samuel Daniel; Margaret Owens generously shared her forthcoming work on the effigies at Westminster Abbey; H. Neville Davies, the leading authority on King Christian's visit to England, answered repeated inquiries; an evening spent with Charles Nicholl deepened my understanding of Shakespeare's relationship with Marie Mountjoy; Michael Boyd was especially helpful on the Porter scene in *Macbeth*; Arnold Hunt shared his suspicions about the fictionality of some of John Harington's letters; Alan Nelson helped with London parish records; Mark Nicholls, whose knowledge of the Gunpowder Plot is unrivalled, graciously answered my questions about the army organised to suppress the feared Midlands rising; Elizabeth Williamson did a superb job of transcribing Simon Forman's manuscripts; and, over the years, Alan Stewart and H. Aram Veeser have patiently heard out many of the arguments in these pages. The long bibliographical essay gives some sense of how much I owe to generations of scholars.

My understanding of Jacobean culture was enriched in the course of making a three-hour BBC documentary that aired in 2012: *The King and the Playwright: A Jacobean History* (subsequently released as *Shakespeare: The King's Man*), made in collaboration with Phil George and Steven Clarke; I am grateful to them both and to our wonderful crew. Many outstanding stage productions of *King Lear*, *Macbeth* and *Antony and Cleopatra* in recent decades have shaped my understanding of these plays. I am especially indebted to the directors and actors with whom I have had the opportunity of speaking and working. A generation of talented Columbia students, including those I have taught in graduate and undergraduate seminars on 1606, have sharpened my understanding of Shakespeare and his times.

I have spent much of the past decade in the archives and it is there that the story in these pages took shape. I am beholden to the expert librarians at the Folger Shakespeare Library, the British Library, the New York Public Library, the British Museum, the Public Records Office, the Bodleian Library, the Columbia University Libraries, the Union Theological Seminary Library and the Shakespeare Birthplace Trust.

I am blessed in my literary agent and friend Anne Edelstein, and I have had the privilege of working again with two of the finest editors in the publishing world: Bob Bender and Julian Loose. I'm also grateful to Rachel Calder as well as Johanna Li, Kate Murray-Browne and Kate Ward. I've dedicated the book to Mary Cregan and our son, Luke; without their great patience, insight and support it could not have been written.

TEXT ILLUSTRATION PERMISSIONS

1 Photo by Rischgitz/Getty Images
17 © The British Library Board, C.34.k.18, title page
39 Timewatch Images / Alamy
55 STC 22292, Houghton Library, Harvard University
75 The National Library of Scotland (public domain)

103 National Archives
121 © The British Library Board, Maps.145.c.9 18
137 Culture Club / Contributor / Getty Images
155 Private Collection / Bridgeman Images
178 The Bodleian Library, University of Oxford, MS. Laud Misc. 655, fol. 3
208 © The Trustees of the British Museum
233 Bibliotheque Nationale, Paris, France / Bridgeman Images
261 © National Portrait Gallery, London (NPG Z3915)
289 Private Collection / Bridgeman Images
318 © The British Library Board, Ashley 617
347 STC 22292, Houghton Library, Harvard University

PLATE SECTION PERMISSIONS

1 Scottish National Portrait Gallery, Edinburgh, Scotland / Bridgeman Images
2 © Museum of London
3 Fine Art Images/Heritage Images/Getty Images
4 © National Portrait Gallery, London (NPG 6918)
5 © National Portrait Gallery, London (NPG D20306)
6 © The British Library Board, G.6103, after 32. plate 2
7 © The Trustees of the British Museum
8 © National Portrait Gallery, London (NPG 1)
9 © National Portrait Gallery, London (NPG 2752)
10 The Bodleian Library, University of Oxford, Lane Poole 84
11 © Dulwich Picture Gallery, London, UK / Bridgeman Images
12 © National Portrait Gallery, London (NPG 107)
13 © National Portrait Gallery, London (NPG 3121)
14 National Library of Scotland
15 Woburn Abbey, Bedfordshire, UK / Bridgeman Images
16 Copyright: Dean and Chapter of Westminster

Index

Numbers in *italics* show pages with illustrations.